The Path of Desire

The Path of Desire

LIVING TANTRA
IN NORTHEAST INDIA

Hugh B. Urban

THE UNIVERSITY OF CHICAGO PRESS
CHICAGO AND LONDON

The University of Chicago Press, Chicago 60637
The University of Chicago Press, Ltd., London

Published 2024

33 32 31 30 29 28 27 26 25 24   1 2 3 4 5

ISBN-13: 978-0-226-83110-7 (cloth)
ISBN-13: 978-0-226-83112-1 (paper)
ISBN-13: 978-0-226-83111-4 (e-book)
DOI: https://doi.org/10.7208/chicago/9780226831114.001.0001

Library of Congress Cataloging-in-Publication Data

Names: Urban, Hugh B., author.
Title: The path of desire : living Tantra in northeast India / Hugh B. Urban.
Other titles: Living Tantra in northeast India
Description: Chicago ; London : The University of Chicago Press, 2024. | Includes bibliographical references and index.
Identifiers: LCCN 2023021461 | ISBN 9780226831107 (cloth) | ISBN 9780226831121 (paperback) | ISBN 9780226831114 (ebook)
Subjects: LCSH: Tantrism—India—Assam. | Folk religion—India—Assam. | Desire—Religious aspects—Hinduism.
Classification: LCC BL1283.84 .U726 2024 | DDC 294.5/5140954162—dc23/eng/20230816
LC record available at https://lccn.loc.gov/2023021461

Contents

List of Figures and Tables vii

INTRODUCTION

The Path of Desire

Living Tantra, Vernacular Religion, and the Study of Secrets · 1

CHAPTER ONE

The Left-Hand Path

Secrecy, Transgression, and the Kaula Tradition in Assam · 29

CHAPTER TWO

"The Land of Black Magic"

Healing, Enchantment, and Witchcraft · 59

CHAPTER THREE

The Politics of Sacrifice

Blood Offerings and the Struggle over Local and National Identity in Modern India · 87

CHAPTER FOUR

Dancing for the Snake

Possession, Performance, and Gender in Manasā Pūjā · 113

CHAPTER FIVE

"The Cradle of Tantra"

Modern Transformations of a Tantric Center from Nationalist Symbol to Tourist Destination · 135

CHAPTER SIX
"Sinister *Tāntriks*"
Tantra in Popular Culture, Fiction, and Film · *161*

CONCLUSIONS
The Path of Desire in an Age of Capital
Living Tantra in the Context of Globalization and Neoliberalism · *183*

Acknowledgments and Entanglements *195*
Notes *197*
Selected Bibliography *253*
Index *267*

Figures and Tables

FIGURES

0.1 Kāmākhyā Temple 2
0.2 Goddess Kāmākhyā from Kāmākhyā temple complex 2
0.3 Holy woman from Bengal at Ambuvācī Melā 3
0.4 Billboard for Ambuvācī Melā 4
0.5 Figure outside of Siddheśvara Temple (probably Kāmeśvarī) 10
0.6 Ardhanārīśvara, Tokreśvara Temple 15
1.1 Bhairava, rock-face image behind Bhairavī Temple 34
1.2 Cāmuṇḍā, outside Kedareśvara Temple 35
1.3 Aghorīs at the Bhūtnāth cremation ground 52
1.4 Aghorī performing corpse ritual at the Bhūtnāth cremation ground 54
2.1 Phaṇidhar Nāth 60
2.2 "Welcome to Mystic Mayong" sign, Mayong Museum 61
2.3 Cover image of *Ādi o āsal Kāmarūp Kāmākṣā Tantramantra Sār* 66
2.4 Birubālā Rābhā 70
2.5 Tilak Hāzarikā 78
2.6 Phaṇīdhar Nāth with handwritten notebook of *mantras* 80
2.7 Prabīn Śaikīyā 82
2.8 Diagram illustrating *tantra-mantra* 85
3.1 "Corāsī Devatā Ovālī Gāy" 93
3.2 *Bali-kaṭā* sacrificing goat, Kāmākhyā Temple 100
3.3 Sacrificial post for buffaloes, Kāmākhyā Temple 101
3.4 Buffalo waiting to be sacrificed 102
3.5 Mahiṣāsuramardinī, Assam State Museum 103
4.1 Manasā, Assam State Museum 114
4.2 Manasā, Mayong, Assam 115
4.3 Male *deodhāi,* Manasā Pūjā 121
4.4 Male *deodhāi,* Manasā Pūjā 122
4.5 Female *deodhanī* dancers 130

5.1 Billboard, Kāmākhyā Temple 136
5.2 Billboard, Guwahati, Assam 137
5.3 Lajjā Gaurī, Kāmākhyā Temple 140
5.4 Vendor from Bengal selling various goods 144
5.5 New images of Śiva and Kāmākhyā behind glass and metal bars 153
5.6 Lajjā Gaurī covered 155
6.1 Billboard for *Śaitān Tāntrik* 162
6.2 Advertisement for *Tārānāth Tāntrik* web series 175
6.3 Pitch deck for *Tāśrī* 177
7.1 Diagram illustrating the place of Tantra today 186

TABLES

4.1 Deities possessing dancers, Manasā Pūjā 124
4.2 Gender dynamics in the male *deodhāi* dance 127
4.3 Comparative gender dynamics in the male *deodhāi* and female *deodhanī* dances 132

[INTRODUCTION]

The Path of Desire

Living Tantra, Vernacular Religion, and the Study of Secrets

> Engaged in desire, established in the midst of desire, enveloped by the god of desire, the desirous one should desire with desire and join desire in desire.
>
> *Kālikā Purāṇa* (tenth or eleventh century)[1]

> Rather than placing desire and liberation in opposition to each other, and rather than denying the one to benefit the other, the [Tantric] theory holds, quite to the contrary, that desire is the hallmark of each and every individual's initiation into the path of salvation. It is the seal of the divine in man, so long as he is schooled in the proper techniques for its transformation.
>
> Madeleine Biardeau, *Hinduism: The Anthropology of a Civilization* (1981)[2]

> Desire causes the current to flow, itself flows in turn, and breaks the flows.
>
> Gilles Deleuze and Félix Guattari, *Anti-Oedipus* (1983)[3]

Each summer in late June, thousands of pilgrims travel from all over South Asia to converge on the temple of the mother goddess Kāmākhyā in the state of Assam, northeast India, for the celebration of Ambuvācī Melā. Known in Sanskrit literature as Kāmarūpa (the "place" or "form of desire"), Assam has long been identified as one of the oldest and most important "seats of power" (*śākta pīṭhas*) or sites of the goddess's divine energy. Since at least the eighth century, Kāmarūpa has been recognized as the site of the goddess's *yoni* (womb and/or sexual organ) and thus as one of the most powerful seats of goddess worship in South Asia.[4] Still, today, it remains one of the liveliest centers of Tantric practice in contemporary India, as a key node where esoteric Tantric lineages flourish alongside popular devotional movements, practitioners of folk magic, and a wide range of vendors of both spiritual and secular wares.

Coinciding roughly with the arrival of the monsoon, the Ambuvācī festival celebrates the coming of the goddess's annual menstruation, which, like life-giving waters (*ambu*), brings fertility to the earth and blessings to

FIGURE 0.1. Kāmākhyā Temple, Guwahati, Assam, 2017. Photo by the author.

FIGURE 0.2. Goddess Kāmākhyā from Kāmākhyā temple complex, Guwahati, Assam, 2022. Photo by the author.

FIGURE 0.3. Holy woman from Bengal at Ambuvācī Melā, 2017. Photo by the author.

her devotees.[5] As such, it is at once a huge public festival that draws hundreds of thousands of pilgrims *and* a Tantric festival rooted in a deep belief in the power of sexual fluids that also attracts hundreds of black-clad Aghorīs, naked Nāga ascetics, wandering minstrels such as the Bāuls, and an array of others engaged in the more esoteric side of Tantric practice. For example, in the dead of night during the 2018 festival, even as thousands of devotees were gathered around the main temple complex, a highly esoteric ritual with human skulls, alcohol, sexual fluids, and other transgressive

FIGURE 0.4. Billboard for Ambuvācī Melā, 2017. Photo by the author.

offerings was taking place among the Aghorīs and other *tāntriks* (Tantric practitioners) gathered in the Bhūtnāth cremation ground just down the hill.[6] Like much of living Tantra in modern India, Ambuvācī is a striking mixture of the exoteric and the esoteric, of mass public worship and transgressive secret ritual. As a path of desire, it is a tradition in which the goal of spiritual liberation coexists with very practical desires for health, prosperity, and material well-being, as well as with desires for magic and occult power.

While rooted in traditions dating back at least 1,200 years, the Tantric traditions of northeast India have also undergone a series of profound transformations in the contemporary period, in the wake of colonialism, nationalism, and a rapidly changing Indian economy. In the last five or six years, for example, Ambuvācī Melā has grown from a fairly obscure Tantric festival into a massive tourist spectacle that is now aggressively promoted by state and local governments. Today, visitors to the festival are greeted by giant billboards inviting them to come "Be with the Goddess" in "Awesome Assam." As we will see in chapter 5, Ambuvācī has been absorbed into a much larger initiative led by conservative Hindu politicians (including Prime Minister Narendra Modi himself) to use Kāmākhyā Temple as part of an ambitious plan for economic development in the northeast region as a new site of "religious and spiritual tourism."[7]

All of this is deeply ironic given that the practices at Kāmākhyā involve highly transgressive Tantric rituals that are filled with sexual symbolism and bloodshed. While Ambuvācī itself centers on the annual menstruation of the goddess, the festival also involves large amounts of animal sacrifice—a practice adamantly condemned by Modi's Bharatiya Janata Party (BJP) and most conservative Hindu political groups.[8]

The popular marketing of Tantra is something that is all too familiar to most readers in the United States, England, and Europe, where popular literature on Tantra (usually identified as "spiritual sex") has been widely available since the 1960s. One need only browse the shelves of Barnes and Noble or surf Amazon.com to find a vast array of books and videos such as *The Complete Idiot's Guide to Tantric Sex*, or *Sex Magic, Tantra, and Tarot*, or—my personal favorite—*Urban Tantra: Sacred Sex for the Twenty-First Century*.[9] Yet this was one of the first times I had seen Tantra being advertised in a *positive* way to an Indian audience. Tantra has long been a trope in Bollywood film, popular Indian literature, and comic books, though usually associated with the frightening power of black magic and sorcery; it is still fairly rare to see Tantra being rebranded and marketed in a positive way to an Indian audience of spiritual consumers.

These recent changes in the celebration of Ambuvācī Melā are emblematic of the modern transformations of Tantra as a living tradition, deeply entwined with the shifting dynamics of contemporary Indian politics, global capitalism, current religious debates, and popular culture. As a path of desire (*kāma*) in all its many forms, Tantra has always been entwined with the shifting dynamics of South Asian history, culture, politics, and economics.[10] Thus it is perhaps not surprising that, in the twenty-first century, it should also become entangled with the new dynamics of economic development, tourism, nationalist politics, and mass media—though all the while retaining many of its oldest and most esoteric roots.

Living Tantra in Contemporary India

Despite their historical and contemporary importance, the Tantric traditions of Assam have received surprisingly little scholarly attention. Apart from my own work, Loriliai Biernacki's *Renowned Goddess of Desire*, some recent dissertations, and a few books by Indian scholars, there is still little serious research on this key region.[11] More broadly, there is still very little research on Tantra as a living tradition in contemporary India. There is, of course, a large body of outstanding scholarship on Tantra as a historical and textual tradition, ranging from the many volumes on Tantric philosophical schools such as Kashmir Śaivism to the work of Alexis Sanderson, David Gordon White, Ronald Davidson, Geoffrey Samuel, and others. Yet with a very few exceptions, such as the recent work of June McDaniel, Mani Rao, and Sukanya Sarbadhikary,[12] there is still surprisingly little scholarship on Tantra as a *lived practice* in the twenty-first century.

The Path of Desire is thus one of the first detailed studies of living Tantra in contemporary India and the first extensive study of living practice in the Tantric heartland of Assam. As an embodied and lived religion in areas such as northeast India today, Tantra is not simply an elite textual tradition but also very much a popular folk practice, as much tied to magic, healing, and spirit possession as it is to philosophical speculation or priestly ritual.

The primary focus of this book is the key Tantric concept of *kāma*, or desire. As scholars such as Madeleine Biardeau and André Padoux suggest, Tantra in general is perhaps best defined as "the path of desire." Rather than viewing desire and spiritual liberation in opposition, Tantric traditions instead aim, in Biardeau's words, at "harnessing *kāma*—desire (in every sense of the word)—to the service of deliverance."[13] Desire in this sense, however, has little to do with the Americanized popular forms of "Tantric sex" currently sold on most bookstore shelves. Rather, in its living forms in regions such as Assam, *kāma* is often tied to far more *mundane and worldly* sorts of desires, such as healing, childbearing, material well-being, and personal power.

This book follows the trajectory of my work on Tantra in northeast India over the last twenty years. In my earlier work, I have explored the development of Tantra in Bengal and Assam, with special focus on the British colonial era and the complex transformations of Tantra in response to imperialism, Christian missionaries, and modern capitalism.[14] At the same time, I have also examined both European/American and modern Indian discourses surrounding Tantra, critically analyzing the ways in which this category has been imagined, represented, and misrepresented over the last two hundred years. *The Path of Desire* is a logical sequel to my previous work, examining Tantra as a living tradition in contemporary Assam and using the tools of both historiography and ethnography to explore one of the few surviving Tantric centers in modern India. The book relies on archival and field research conducted during numerous trips to Assam and other parts of northeast India between 2000 and 2022, with generous assistance from many practitioners and local scholars.

The Tangled Threads of Tantra: Tracing the Paths of Desire

The term *tantra* has long been and remains one of the most confused, contested, and conflicted categories in the history of South Asian religions. This confusion is present not only in American popular discourse but in modern scholarship and in Indian popular culture as well. Derived from the Sanskrit root *tan*, "to extend, spread, spin out, weave, or stretch," the term *tantra* has been used since Vedic times in a wide variety of ways, signifying everything from a model, type, system, or framework to a remedy or drug. Following the etymology of "weaving" or "stretching," one of the earliest uses of *tantra* is as meaning "loom," or more specifically the "warp" on a loom. Most commonly, however, *tantra* refers to a particular kind of text—in the sense of a discourse woven with the threads of words and thought—though one that may or may not contain the sorts of things that we normally associate with "Tantra" today.[15]

Historically, as a religious movement, Tantra refers to a bewilderingly diverse array of texts, traditions, and ritual practices that spread through the Hindu, Buddhist, and Jain communities of South, East, Southeast, and Central Asia from roughly the sixth century onward.[16] Along the way, it developed into a wide range of sects and schools, including the Kāpālika, Kaula, Krama, Nātha Siddha, Pāñcarātra, Pāśupata, Sahajiyā, Śākta, Śrīvidyā, Trika, Vajrayāna, and many others. As André Padoux persuasively argues, the abstract category of "Tantrism"—as a singular, unified "ism"—is a relatively recent invention, in large part the creation of Orientalist scholars and Hindu reformers writing in the nineteenth century: "Tantrism is a protean phenomenon, so complex and elusive that is practically impossible to define it. . . . Tantrism is, to a large extent, a 'category of discourse in the West' and not, strictly speaking, an Indian one. . . . The term Tantrism was coined by Western Indologists of the latter part of the nineteenth century whose knowledge of India was limited."[17]

In the course of my own research throughout South Asia, I have interviewed a wide range of both *tāntrik* and non-*tāntrik* practitioners and have heard a vast number of conflicting definitions of the term *tantra*. Even at a single location, such as the Kāmākhyā temple complex in Assam, I encountered an array of divergent opinions. Many priests I asked simply equated *tantra* with *mantra* or the use of sacred sounds, texts, and chanting in worship. Likewise, in popular discourse throughout South Asia, the terms *tantra-mantra* are often used together and/or interchangeably.[18] Others, however, defined *tantra* more specifically in terms of the physical body and the use of the senses in ritual practice (creatively adapting it from the Sanskrit term *tanu*, one meaning of which is "the body"). As one priest named Heman Sarma put it, "We pray *tāntrika*. *Tān* means body in Sanskrit. [I] pray in my body also . . . that is the *tāntrika*!"[19] Still others, however, define Tantra primarily in terms of *yoga* and *bhoga*, that is, as the practice that uses pleasure or enjoyment (*bhoga*) as the means or steppingstone to spiritual discipline (*yoga*). According to one initiate in the Kulācāra Tantra Mārga at Kāmākhyā, "Tantra is the practice of enjoyment; having fulfilled enjoyment, the supreme means of worship lies in *yoga*."[20]

For most Indians today, however, the term *tantra* has deeply ambivalent if not profoundly negative connotations, typically associated with black magic and the darker side of power. These negative associations with black magic, sorcery, and evil have been greatly amplified through the power of the Bollywood movie industry, where the character of the "sinister *tāntrik*" is a stock villain in countless films such as *Gahrāī* (Depth), *Saṅgharṣ* (Struggle), *Śaitān Tāntrik* (Satanic *Tāntrik*), and myriad others.[21]

Even groups that are usually labeled "Tantric" by modern scholars are often extremely critical of the term. For example, while at Ambuvācī Melā in 2017, I ran into a Bāul singer from Bishnupur, Bengal, named Śrī Gopāl Dās Bāul. A loose group of itinerant musicians, the Bāuls (holy "madmen") are often classified as Tantric because of their practice of highly transgressive rituals (such as the consumption of bodily fluids and a form of ritual sexual union).[22] When I asked Gopāl Dās if his practice was a form of "Tantric" *sādhanā* (spiritual discipline), he immediately said, "No, no! Bāul practice is completely different from *tantra*. *Tantra* is not a good thing [*bhālo jiniś noy*]. It is impure [*aśuddho*]; it is a very bad practice!"[23]

Perhaps the most infamous and extreme of India's various *sādhus* (holy men) are the Aghorīs—"those without fear"—who are known for dwelling in charnel grounds, carrying skulls for their begging bowls, and consuming all manner of polluting substances. Often identified as the quintessential *tāntriks*, the Aghorīs are commonly found around the Bhūtnāth cremation ground near Kāmākhyā and gather there in large numbers for secret rituals during Ambuvācī Melā. Yet even the Aghorīs have a complex view of the term "Tantra," with its sinister yet powerful connotations. When I asked one Aghorī from Kolkata whether his practice was *tāntrik sādhanā*, he answered immediately: "Certainly it's *tāntrik sādhanā*; we worship in cremation grounds! [*abaśya-i tāntrik sādhanā ache; āmrā śmaśāne pūjā kori*]."[24] However, when I asked another Aghorī from Punjab, he firmly said, "No, no, the *tāntrik* path roams around [*ghumne ghumne*], while the Aghorī path is a straight [*sīdhā*] road to liberation."[25] In short, as Ronald Barrett explains, Aghorīs will at different times embrace and reject the category of Tantra, depending on the particular audience that happens to be at hand: "Aghoris are more explicit about their ambivalence to Tantra. They are acutely aware of Tantra's popular associations with sexuality and sorcery and distorted representations in the Indian and Western media. . . . Nevertheless the Aghori have been pragmatic in adapting the term to suit particular circumstances. One senior renunciate eschewed the term when discussing Aghor with visitors from central India but reversed his position when speaking with Bengalis from Calcutta, where Tantra has more positive cultural connotations."[26]

While there are many, perhaps innumerable, ways of defining Tantra,[27] I find it most useful for the purposes of this book to define Tantra in terms of the key concept of *kāma*, or desire. As Madeleine Biardeau elegantly put it in her study of Hinduism, most South Asian traditions view desire as the primary obstacle on the path to spiritual liberation, the source of our bondage to and entanglement in the material world. Yet the Tantric path aims precisely to utilize desire as a means toward liberation, to alchemically transmute sensual pleasure into the most rapid but potentially dangerous path to self-realization; indeed, "desire is the hallmark of each and every individual's initiation into the path of salvation."[28] This concept of transforming desire is present even in early Tantric texts, such as the Buddhist *Guhyasamāja Tantra* (eighth century), where the adept is not asked to engage in extreme austerities but rather to indulge in all desires at will: "Giving yourself up to the enjoyment of all desire [*sarvakāmopabhogaiś*] at pleasure, by this practice you will soon attain the Buddha-nature. Giving yourself up to the enjoyment of all desires at pleasure, united with your own deity, worship the self and others. Success is not gained by following ascetic vows and extreme practices, but by the enjoyment of all desires it is soon attained [*sarvakāmopabhogais tu sevayaṃś caśu sidhyati*]."[29]

The concept of *kāma*, however, is subtle and complex, with a vast, rich, and varied semantic range. While most American and European readers associate *kāma* with sexual desire (usually imagined in the form of the exotic sexual poses of the *Kāma Sūtra*), the Sanskrit term really embraces the full breadth of desire in all its many forms. Indeed, its vast range of meanings includes "wish, desire, longing, love, affection, object of love or pleasure, enjoyment, sexual love or sensuality, Love or Desire personified, the god of love, semen virile," and so on.[30] As André Padoux observes, the meanings of desire here include but ultimately far exceed the narrow level of sexual desire as understood in contemporary discourse: "*Kāma*, which is central to Tantra, is not mere sex or desire but passion, a joyful, receptive opening to and enjoying of the beauty, fullness and infinite diversity of the world.... Sex is just a part of it."[31]

In Tantric metaphysics, the highest level of *kāma* refers to the divine desire or creative energy that creates and sustains the entire universe. This idea of the cosmogonic power of desire is present even in the earliest stratum of Hindu sacred literature, the *Ṛg Veda*, where desire represents the first movement from the primordial darkness of the Void toward the creation of the world: "Darkness was hidden by darkness in the beginning; with no distinguishing sign, all this was water. The life force that was covered

FIGURE 0.5. Figure outside of Siddheśvara Temple (probably Kāmeśvarī), Guwahati, Assam, 2022. Photo by the author.

with emptiness, that one arose through the power of heat. Desire [*kāma*] came upon that one in the beginning; that was the first seed of mind."[32]

Later Tantric literature takes this metaphysical idea of desire much further. According to the thirteenth-century Sanskrit text the *Kāmakalā Vilāsa*, desire is the power that brings the universe itself into being through the love-play of the divine male and female principles. It is the primary inspiration for the supreme Lord Śiva—as Kāmeśvara or the "Lord of Desire"—to manifest in a form outside of himself, as if projecting a reflection into a mirror. In turn, the reflected image is his female consort and creative power, Śakti—who thus appears as Kāmeśvarī, the "Lady of Desire." Her manifestation is then described as "the movements of the beautiful woman Kāma-kalā, which ever attract the desire of the amorous Para-Śiva."[33] As John Woodroffe explains in his introduction to the text: "At the beginning of creation, God, the ever changeless Being, desired to be an ever-changing seeming. The absolute being took on the role of relative becoming. This desire and its fruition brought on the entire universe of name and form. . . . This initial impulse responsible for the creation of the world is given the name Kāma. The desireful supreme entity is known as Kāmeśvara, and his attractive desire as Kāmeśvarī. The entire universe is the outcome of the union of these primary parents."[34]

One of the most important early works from Assam is the *Kālikā Purāṇa*, a Tantric-influenced Śākta text composed around the tenth or eleventh century. As we see in the passage quoted above in the epigraph to this introduction, desire is at once the *object* of worship (the goddess herself), the *subject* of worship (the desirous one who seeks to honor the goddess) and the *means* of worship (devotional love): "Engaged in desire [*kāmasthaṃ*], established in the midst of desire [*kāmamadhyasthaṃ*], enveloped by the god of desire [*kāmadevapuṭīkṛtam*], the desirous one should desire with desire and join desire in desire [*kāmena kāmayet kāmo kāmaṃ kāme niyojayet*]."[35] This emphasis on the divine power of desire is echoed in the *Kāmākhyā Tantra*, a text that probably dates to eighteenth-century Assam, which describes the goddess as she who "bears the arrow of Madana [the god of love]; she is a desirous woman [*kāminī*] and grants desires [*kāmadātrī*]. She is pleasure for all beings, the goddess Bhavānī, who can assume any form at will. She is the destroyer of all the impurities of the Kali Yuga. She is the form of the *yoni*."[36] *Kāma* is thus the pervasive energy that flows through all things, emanating from the generative power of the goddess and returning to her through the love of her human devotees.

This understanding of Tantra as closely tied to the power of desire is often articulated by both initiated *tāntriks* and ordinary devotees alike. While visiting the Dhūmāvatī temple below the main Kāmākhyā temple one afternoon, I was invited by a *tāntrik* from Bengal to sit for a while and smoke a chillum with him. As we were discussing the various meanings of *tantra*, we were joined by another Bengali—an employee of a local NGO—who offered his own definition of the term in mixed Bangla and Hindi: "Tantra is basically power [*śakti*]. In the language of physics, it is the energy that makes up everything. But it can be used for good or bad, for spiritual things or for black magic. It's a matter of the user's intention." To this, the *tāntrik* added (in Hindi), "It is also desire [*kām*]. That's why the goddess is called Kāmākhyā. This is the *yoni pīṭh* [seat of the *yoni*]. The *yoni* is source of creation [*sṛṣṭi*]. From desire comes the power of creation [*kām se śṛṣṭi kī śakti hai*]."[37]

In addition to this lofty, abstract, and metaphysical dimension, however, *kāma* also signifies desire on many other levels, including the most worldly, sensual, and material. Outside the confines of esoteric Tantric practice, desire often refers to the more mundane needs of ordinary people making their way through the hardships of daily life—the desire for healing, the desire for material well-being, the desire for success in business, the desire for children, the desire for domestic tranquility, the desire for good crops, the desire for protection, and so on. This understanding is desire neither as sexual energy nor as the divine power coursing through all of creation, but rather as simply the "wish to survive," the need to get by, and perhaps even the hope to prosper in a complex world pervaded by both natural and supernatural dangers. As we see in Assamese villages such as Mayong—infamous today as the "heartland of magic"—most ordinary men and women seek out a local practitioner of *tantra-mantra* called a *bej* or *ojhā* (folk healer) for quite pragmatic sorts of desires. Typically, these have less to do with spiritual liberation than with desires for healing, protection, or countering the effects of witchcraft.

Accordingly, some scholars such as Ariel Glucklich make a useful distinction between two basic understandings of Tantra in South Asian history. The first he calls Tantra in the strict sense, that is, the tradition rooted in Tantric texts and developed in philosophical lineages such as the Trika of Kashmir, the Śrīvidyā of South India, or the Śākta traditions of Bengal and Assam, and so on. Practitioners of this form of Tantra "study medieval Tantric texts and follow Tantric practices, which can be antinomian and often include polluted or forbidden substances such as wine or meat and, in rare (and carefully concealed) instances, sexuality and necromancy."[38] The second and today far more pervasive side of Tantra in places such as Varanasi (where Glucklich conducted his research) or Bengal and Assam (where I have lived for long periods of time) is the popular, everyday sense of *tantra-mantra* as basically "practical magic for mundane ends."

It is worth noting, however, that this popular/magical/non-elite side of Tantra is by no means simply a contemporary phenomenon or a by-product of modernity and postcolonial India. On the contrary, it is evident even in the very earliest references to texts called *tantras* in South Asian literature. One of the first mentions of the term *tantra* to refer to a kind of manuscript appears in Bāṇabhaṭṭa's seventh-century novel, *Kādambarī*. Here, the author satirically describes a creepy old ascetic and devotee of the goddess Caṇḍikā, who carries around his *tantras* and uses them mainly to perform magic and woo women: "He had collected manuscripts containing information about jugglery, mystical formulas and spells [*tantras* and *mantras*]. . . . He had the madness of belief in alchemy. He was obsessed with a yearning to enter the world of demons. . . . Though he had taken a vow of celibacy he threw powder that was thought to make women sexually active on the old female ascetics who had come from foreign lands."[39]

This early reference to *tantra* is a clear example of the intertwining of the Sanskritic and the folk or vernacular traditions. While appearing in a classical Sanskrit text, the Tantric practitioner here is closely associated with the realm of magic, material gain, and the most physical aspects of desire. This intertwining of the Sanskritic and the "folk" characterizes living Tantra to this day.

Subjects of Desire: Tantra in Critical Dialogue with Modern Theory

In its broader theoretical framework, this book also attempts to place Tantra and South Asian concepts such as *kāma* into complex dialogue with contemporary European and American critical theory. My reason for doing so is not simply to impose the latest hip Western theory onto South Asian religions or to show the ways in which another culture can be easily run through the cookie-cutter theory mill. Rather, my hope is to engage in a more complex critical exchange that would also allow South Asian ideas to "talk back," as it were, to our own contemporary theoretical concerns, often challenging us to revise and rethink own biases and preconceptions.[40]

Here, I borrow insights from authors such as Gilles Deleuze, Michel Foucault, and Judith Butler, who have examined the role of desire in relation to various constructions of identity, gender, and power.[41] In many ways, perhaps the closest analogue to the Tantric notion of *kāma* in contemporary theory is Deleuze's provocative view of "desire as flow" and desire as a kind of productive plenitude or excess. Much of modern discourse, and particularly psychoanalytic discourse, Deleuze argues, has tended to "reduce sexuality to sex";[42] that is, it has limited the complex diversity of desire to the singular act of genital sex. In contrast to a Freudian model, Deleuze sees desire not as simply a lack or longing for some lost object, and not simply as a matter of genital sexuality; rather, desire is fundamentally generative, a source of power and potentiality that far exceeds the confines of genital orgasm. Whereas psychoanalysis had "shut up sexuality in a bizarre sort of box painted with bourgeois motifs," as if it were some sort of "dirty little family secret," Deleuze wants to recast desire along entirely different lines, as something more like a "fantastic factory of Nature and Production."[43] As such, "Deleuze's desire is quite different from that of other thinkers. . . . [D]esire is usually understood as something abnormal, avaricious and excessive, the opposite of rationality, to be controlled and suppressed. . . . Deleuze's desire is much wider, referring not only to man, but also to animals, objects and social institutions. In Deleuze's view, desire is not a psychic existence, not lack, but an active and positive reality, an affirmative vital force."[44] Desire in this sense has less in common with Freud's *libido* than it does with Nietzsche's "will to power."[45]

This concept of desire as a vital force that is productive, affirmative, and powerful does indeed have quite a lot of theoretical overlap with the Tantric understanding of *kāma* as the driving energy that flows through the cosmos and the human body. At the same time, however, there are also aspects of Deleuze's work that are lacking and might well benefit from some "talking back" from non-Western theoretical perspectives. Perhaps most importantly, as many feminist critics have pointed out, Deleuze in general is quite male-centric in his perspective and for the most part "does not have much to say explicitly about feminism" or woman's issues more broadly.[46] The French feminist theorist Luce Irigaray was even more critical in her assessment of Deleuze's understanding of desire in particular, which she saw as "an erasure of the feminine and of the specificity of women's bodies and their desires into a neutral desire, which, as with most things positioned as neutral is actually masculine."[47]

It is true that Deleuze and Guattari do suggest the intriguing yet controversial idea of "becoming woman." To become woman is to embrace processes of change, transformation, dissolution, and hybridity in place of the patriarchal and hierarchal structures of the dominant systems of power: "Becoming-woman is a becoming minor. . . . To become minor is to jostle the reins of the majority identity in order to investigate new possibilities, new ways of becoming that are no longer found to the dominant molar lines. . . . It is to break with identity, which is always the identity of the majority, in favor of difference as yet unactualized."[48] Yet this idea of becoming woman has been intensely controversial among many feminist theorists, who argue that it is largely uninformed by women's actual experiences or historical struggles and even reinforces a stereotyped notion of women as defined by change, dissolution, becoming, and lack of identity.[49]

In this respect, I do think that a perspective derived from a tradition such as South Asian Tantra could be a useful way of "talking back" to contemporary theory and of offering new ways to conceptualize desire. In contrast to Deleuze's rather gender-blind approach, the Tantric traditions of northeast India generally make questions of gender, femininity, and different expressions of male and female sexuality quite central and explicit. In its masculine form, *kāma* is closely identified with male figures such as Kāmadeva (the Indian counterpart to Cupid) and Śiva as Kāmeśvara (the Lord of Desire, the masculine generative energy, identified with the *liṅgam*, or phallus). In its feminine forms, *kāma* is then closely tied to *yoginīs* (divine female beings) and to goddesses such as Kāmākhyā, who is fundamentally identified with the *yoni*.[50] As we will see in the chapters that follow, complex relations between male and female bodies, the power of male and female sexual fluids, and the creative potential of male-female union are all central to Tantric practice. Every male body is believed to contain the female energy of the goddess in the form of Kuṇḍalinī, the serpent power, who lies coiled at the base of the spine; likewise, every female body contains the presence of Śiva, the divine masculine principle, at the top of the head; and the ultimate state

FIGURE 0.6. Ardhanārīśvara, Tokreśvara Temple, Guwahati, Assam, 2017. Photo by the author.

of spiritual perfection is described as the union of male and female energies, Śiva and Śakti, within the body, which is in turn the ultimate transformation of desire and its sublimation into spiritual bliss.[51] This union of male and female energies is often portrayed in the androgynous form of Ardhanārīśvara, the "lord who is half woman," and in the abstract form of the conjoined *liṅgam* and *yoni*.[52] Moreover, in states of spirit possession—as we will see in chapter 4—one can actually "become woman" in an experiential way, as male practitioners become possessed by a variety of female divinities, even as female practitioners become possessed and empowered to act in characteristically "masculine" ways.[53] Through Tantric practice, then, one "becomes woman" not simply in an abstract or theoretical sense; rather, one often becomes woman through *actual practice*, in which one awakens and/or invokes divine feminine power within one's own body.

In sum, the Tantric traditions of Assam not only theorize desire in complex ways, they also conceptualize desire quite explicitly in terms of gender and femininity. At the same time, they connect this notion of desire to a variety of different gender formations that are often highly fluid and capable of complex exchanges between male and female bodies.

The Womb of Tantra: Assam as Historical, Textual, and Imaginal Homeland of Tantra

While the world of Asian Tantra is vast, diverse, and complex, this book focuses primarily on the living traditions of Assam. My reasons for focusing on this particular region are twofold: first, Assam has historically been identified as one of the oldest and most important centers of Tantric practice in South Asia. Called Kāmaru in early Hindu and Buddhist sources[54] and Prāgjyotiṣa (the land of eastern lights) in the Sanskrit epic, the *Mahābhārata*,[55] Assam has long been identified as a realm of yoga, magic, and supernatural power. In medieval literature, the region became known as Kāmarūpa—a Sanskritization of Kāmaru and possibly of other indigenous terms[56]—and was widely revered as one of the most powerful seats of the goddess.

The sacred landscape of South Asia is dotted with a series of "seats of power" (*śākta pīṭhas*), or holy sites where the pieces of the goddess's body are believed to lie. Kāmarūpa is cited as one of the oldest *pīṭhas* in texts such as the *Tantrasadbhāva Tantra* (eighth century?) and *Hevajra Tantra* (eighth to tenth centuries), and, as the seat of the goddess's *yoni* (womb or sexual organ), it has also long been revered as one of the most important and powerful of the *pīṭhas*.[57] As we will see in chapter 1, Kāmarūpa is also often cited as the place where the great Tantric master Matsyendranātha first learned the secrets of Tantra from the many female *yoginīs* dwelling there.[58] As the Austrian-born scholar and Tantric initiate Agehananda Bharati (Leopold Fischer) described Assam and its role in the formation of Tantra,

> On the easternmost slopes of the Himalaya, lies the luxurious land of Assam, only partly Indian in ethnic and linguistic constitution, tropical, wild, moist, and always very warm. Assam has been the home of magic and the home of *tantric* practice from times immemorial. It is not impossible that the *tantric* tradition . . . might have had its origin here. Assam's tutelary deity is the Goddess, the Magna Mater. . . . Assam has remained one of the centres of esoteric initiation up to this day. . . . The tantric initiates of India meet here in Assam during the season when the Goddess menstruates. They learn supreme self-control, not through giving a wide berth to woman, but through her company. The tantric learns control through the senses, not against them.[59]

In addition to this revered history as an early site of Tantra and goddess worship, however, Assam also has a darker reputation as a place of black magic, witchcraft, sorcery, and human sacrifice. According to a Tibetan author of the seventeenth century, "There are so many witches (*ḍākinīs*) and various kinds of demons . . . that even a person who has fully mastered the Tantras can hardly stay there."[60] This negative reputation was only intensified and exaggerated by British colonial administrators and Christian missionaries writing in the nineteenth and early twentieth centuries. According to the missionary Paul Olaf Bodding, much of the dangerous aura of the region can be blamed on its women, who are said to possess sinister powers of seduction and transformation: "The traditional Kamru country is a country of strange people with strange powers; the inhabitants can at will turn a man into a dog or any other animal. . . . All in all, Kamru country is a land full of magic and witchcraft; but the stories told seem to imply that it is the women who are so dangerous and powerful."[61] British and European Orientalist scholars were generally no more favorable in the description of Assam, which they typically denounced as a region of gross superstition, tribal magic, sexual licentiousness, and grisly sacrifice. As Sir Charles Eliot put it in his text *Hinduism and Buddhism* in 1921, "Anyone who visits . . . Kamakhya in Assam . . . must be struck with the total absence in the shrines of anything that can be called beautiful, solemn or even terrible. The general impression is of something diseased, unclean and undignified. The figure of the Great Goddess of life and death might have fired the invention of artists but as a matter of fact her worship has paralyzed their hands and brains."[62]

This dark reputation surrounding Assam has survived well into the twenty-first century. The town of Mayong in Morigaon district, for example, is widely known as "India's black magic capital" and has been featured in numerous documentary films.[63] Indeed, the town has recently even tried to use the reputation for magic to promote itself as a sort of tourist destination through numerous websites and a large poster advertisement featuring skulls, bones, and candles that welcomes the visitor to "Mystic Mayong." However, Assam's reputation for black magic often takes a more sinister turn, and the state remains infamous for the stunning number of witchcraft accusations and killings that continue to take place each year. In the last two decades, hundreds of individuals (mostly women) have been murdered following accusations of witchcraft, while many others were beaten, ostracized, and driven from their homes because of suspected black magic.[64] While this popular image of witchcraft and black magic may not have much to do with Tantra in its classical formulations in Sanskrit texts, it is very much what most ordinary Indians think of when they hear the word *tantra* today.[65]

The Tantric Tongue(s): Vernacular Tantra in South Asia

The methodology underlying this book is a combination of history, ethnography, and comparative analysis, with special attention to forms of practice that Robert Orsi calls "lived religion" and what others such as Leonard Primiano, Marion Bowman, and Ülo Valk call "vernacular religion."[66] Rather than focus solely on the Sanskritic, priestly forms of Tantra practiced in major temples such as Kāmākhyā, this book also examines the more *everyday* varieties of Tantra expressed through Assamese, Bangla, Hindi, and other vernacular languages. This sort of lived, vernacular practice disrupts our usual boundaries between "official" and "folk" religion, revealing the complex interplay between these two domains; it highlights, for example, contested relations between *brāhmaṇs* (priests) reciting Sanskrit *mantras* and local *deodhāis* (lower-class temple dancers) who undergo ecstatic spirit possession—at the same temple, during the same festival—or the tense dynamics between the priestly tradition at major temples and the many local *ojhās*, or practitioners of folk magic, throughout the villages of Assam.

As Primiano argues, however, vernacular religion is not simply a category set in opposition to "high" or "elite" religion, nor is it simply a new term to describe what used to be called "folk" or "popular" religion. Rather, it problematizes the very idea of an "official religion" and emphasizes instead the need to study "religion as it is lived: as human beings encounter, understand, interpret and practice it."[67] In other words, it is intended to shift our gaze away from the realm of abstract belief and instead to examine the creative ways in which ordinary practitioners interpret and reinterpret their religious worlds:

> What makes the concept of vernacular religion conceptually valuable . . . is that it highlights the power of the individual and communities of individuals to create and re-create their own religion. . . . Vernacular religion is not the dichotomous or dialectical partner of "institutional" religious forms. Vernacular religion . . . shifts the way one studies religion with the people being the focus of study and not "religion" or "belief" as abstractions. Religious traditions, and the institutions which can be related to them, therefore, have vernacular religion as their foundation. . . .
>
> Vernacular religious theory understands religion as the art of individual interpretation and negotiation of any number of religious sources.[68]

In his study of spirit possession in South Asia, Frederick M. Smith suggests a similar approach to the vernacular side of religious practices. By no means homogeneous or monolithic, the Sanskritic tradition was never universal but was always deeply intertwined with a variety of vernacular practices: "What we find in India is that certain cultures, highly refined (*saṃskṛta*) yet at the same time comfortably 'vernacularized,' share certain features that allow considerable spontaneity and emotion, positioning them more or less against the grain of 'Sanskritic culture.'"[69] Or, to use Wendy Doniger's terms, the living practices of South Asia reflect not just a process of "Sanskritization"—that is, the transformation of local cultures by the elite, Sanskritic tradition—but also a kind of "*deśī-fication*"—that is, the transformation of the elite Sanskritic traditions by a variety of local (*deśī*), indigenous, and non-*brāhmaṇic* practices.[70]

In the study of Tantra, a vernacular approach would ask us to look not only at classical Sanskrit sources and the highly philosophical schools such as Kashmir Śaivism; it would also challenge us to look at the common, mundane, and often nonexotic forms of Tantra that we see expressed in vernacular languages such as Assamese, Bangla, Hindi, and Oriya, not to mention in a variety of indigenous languages such as Bodo, Khasi, and others. But as Primiano rightly reminds us, this approach is not a matter of simply reinforcing the binary of the elite/Sanskritic/*brāhmaṇic* versus the folk/vernacular/tribal; rather, it is a matter of refocusing our attention on the living forms of Tantric practices that are at once *intimately intertwined with* the Sanskritic priestly tradition and *also creatively rework* that tradition in relation to the needs of ordinary practitioners.

The Kāmākhyā temple complex contains a variety of living, vernacular traditions that intersect in complex ways with the Sanskritic, priestly tradition. As Patricia Dold has shown, one of the more important vernacular traditions is that of the women's songs or *Nām*, which are passed down orally outside of priestly institutions; yet they play a key role in the ritual life of the temple, particularly at festivals such as Manasā Pūjā, the celebration of the snake goddess: "As an oral tradition, these women's hymns would have remained invisible to historical research. Here in Kāmākhyā's oral tradition of Nām performance, there is no official lineage for the hymns as one typically finds in textualized Hindu *bhakti* song poems. There is no formal institution controlling performances of the songs. . . . Here, there simply is a repertoire of hymns performed only by women."[71]

Thus, a closer attention to the vernacular, non-elite dimensions of Tantra also sheds new light on deeper gender and class dynamics, revealing the roles of female and lower-class practitioners that might otherwise be overshadowed by the male, Sanskritic tradition.

Studying Secrets: The Ethical-Epistemological Double Bind of Esoteric Religion

The study of living Tantric traditions—and really, the study of any esoteric tradition—poses a number of profound methodological challenges. Perhaps foremost among these is the problem of secrecy: namely, how can one—or indeed *should* one—study traditions that are largely esoteric and closed to noninitiates? There is now a good deal of excellent sociological, anthropological, and historical scholarship on the role of secrecy in specific religious traditions, ranging from studies of African and Australian indigenous religions to ancient Greek and Roman mystery religions, from Jewish mysticism to Hindu and Buddhist Tantra, from modern European fraternal orders to modern magic.[72] But in this book I want to focus specifically on the complex methodological question of *how* one goes about (or *should* one go about) studying esoteric traditions. Elsewhere, I have called this problem the "ethical and epistemological double bind" of secrecy, which involves two deeply entangled issues: First, how can one ever know with certainty the content of a tradition that is supposed to be secret? And second, should one really even attempt to do so at all? Is the very attempt to penetrate the esoteric knowledge of another culture itself an act of violence or cultural theft or indeed a kind of neocolonialism?[73]

This problem is only compounded by the fact that I am a white, male, tenured professor from an American university who is studying traditions in a part of the world that has suffered a history of colonialism, imperialism, and economic exploitation. One may legitimately ask whether I wield a very real kind of symbolic power (and potential symbolic violence) that is in many ways as problematic as that of my colonial and Orientalist predecessors.[74]

This ethical-epistemological double bind is particularly acute in the study of Tantra, which is an inherently esoteric tradition and contains many aspects that require initiation (*dīkṣā*) and/or oral instruction at the feet of a guru. "Tantric traditions are secret," Padoux notes, "a point that is constantly underlined."[75] Tantric texts repeatedly describe this knowledge as not merely private but as "the most secret" (*guhyatama*) and "more secret than any secret" (*guptād guptataraṃ*),[76] comparing it to the need to conceal one's wealth, one's most intimate body parts, or the act of sexual intercourse. According to the *Kāmākhyā Tantra*, these teachings must be kept "extremely secret [*gopanīyaṃ gopanīyaṃ*] with great effort. Just like the secrecy of sexual intercourse or the region of the breast, just like the secrecy of the *yoni*, so too, this supreme initiation [must be kept secret]. Just as a man conceals his wealth under the ground, so too, what I have revealed to you must be kept secret."[77]

To make matters still more complicated, Tantric lineages are multiple and extremely diverse, such that interpretations of basic concepts or rituals vary dramatically from one to the next. Even within a single lineage, interpretations may vary widely from one teacher to another and from one historical period to the next. An obvious example of this "conflict of interpretations"[78] is the role of sexual practice in Tantric ritual—the practice that is most often associated with Tantra in the minds of most American and European readers.[79] Is sex here understood purely metaphorically, as the symbolic union of masculine and feminine energies inside the individual practitioner? Or is it practiced literally, as a physical union between male and female initiates? And even in the latter interpretation, there is a wide range of conflicting opinions. Should the semen be ejaculated into the female partner, then mixed with her fluids, collected, and consumed as a sacramental meal?[80] Or should the semen be retained, sublimated, and transformed in a kind of internalized sexual union?[81] If there is a female partner involved, what is her role? Should she be menstruating or not?[82] Does she share equally in the benefits of the ritual, or is she more of a tool to be used by the male adept?[83] The problem of secrecy in the study of Tantra is not so much a "conflict" but more like a "maelstrom of interpretations"; the problem is not that there is "no" secret but rather that there are *too many secrets*.[84]

This proliferation of secrets and interpretations is particularly clear in the case of the living Tantric traditions of Assam. What we find at temple complexes such as Kāmākhyā and neighboring sites is not so much a singular esoteric system but rather a complex fabric of secrecy made up of many different threads. The most purely "Tantric" tradition centered at the Kāmākhyā temple complex is the Kulācāra Tantra Mārga, which traces its lineage through a chain of gurus and disciples back to the prehistorical past of Kāmarūpa.[85] As Rajib Sarma, a local priest, archivist, historian, conservationist, and initiate of the Mārga explains,

> The teachings, rituals, techniques, Guru-Shishya Parampara of the Kulacara Tantra Marga are the most closely guarded secrets of the Kamakhya Temples' Complex and at any cost or circumstances the same will not be exposed to outsiders and at the same time no information whatsoever will be disclosed to outsiders and the Sadhakas / Sadhikas would prefer to die than revealing anything to any outsiders. The elements of the Kulacara Tantra Marga have been passed down orally to the initiates by the Guru strictly to maintain its secrecy within the members (initiates) of the Kula (family) and to protect it from any invasion. The secrets are even not shared with family members.[86]

Apart from the Kulācāra lineage, however, the Kāmākhyā temple complex houses a variety of other bodies of esoteric knowledge, each with its own secret channels of transmission. For example, the *mantras* used in Kāmākhyā's morning worship when offering the daily sacrifice (*bali-dān*) are carefully guarded and passed on by one particular priestly lineage. As such, even initiated adepts in the Kulācāra lineage may be excluded from these teachings. As Sarma puts it,

> The mantras recited during offering the sacrifice are secret and except the priests (from hereditary Sebait family), even the Balikatas and other initiated Sebaits (hereditary servitors) of the Kamakhya Temples' Complex do not have access to these mantras. Moreover, most of the mantras (including the mantras related to sacrifice) are orally preserved, practiced and passed on to the next generation of eligible priests. . . . Although I am a senior initiated Sadhaka (Purnabhiseka) of the Tantra Marga of the Kamakhya Temples' Complex . . . I also do not have access to the very secretive ritualistic texts related to the Puja, Rituals, Festivals, etc. performed in the temples.[87]

To make matters still *more* complicated, there are also numerous other Tantric groups scattered around the region that may or may not be accepted as legitimate by the dominant Kulācāra lineage centered at Kāmākhyā. There are, for example, many Aghorīs who regularly make pilgrimage to

Assam and congregate around the Bhūtnāth cremation ground; there are Nāth Siddhas who frequent the region with their own esoteric practices; there are Bāuls, wandering minstrels from Bengal, who have their own unique style of Tantric sexual practices; there are local *bejs* and *ojhās* (folk healers), who have their own vernacular version of *tantra-mantra and* their own bodies of secrets, such as knowledge of medicinal plants.[88] And there are also various Tantric teachers around the northeast region, such as Śrī Bicitrānanda Bāba, a man from Bengal who resides in a small hut on the western footpath leading to the main Kāmākhyā temple and prominently advertises himself as a Tantric guru (displaying a large, full-color banner over his dwelling). While Bicitrānanda is not recognized as authentic by the more formal Kulācāra Tantra Mārga and is dismissed as a mere poser by many, he and other similar *tāntriks* have their own bodies of secret knowledge, initiations, rituals, and lines of transmission.

To use the metaphor of *tantra* as a "loom" that "stretches" and "weaves" multiple "threads" (*tanu*), the Kāmākhyā complex and Śākta Tantra more broadly may be understood as a complex *fabric* of secrecy, consisting of multiple threads drawn from many different lineages and traditions. There is by no means a singular esoteric tradition, but instead a dense tangle or complex web of claims to esoteric knowledge.

The study of secrecy is therefore not a simple matter of becoming initiated and then penetrating "the" secret. For example, I was encouraged by members of the community on multiple occasions to become initiated, which I declined on ethical grounds since I am simply a scholar, not a believer or practitioner.[89] Yet even initiation into this lineage would not resolve the epistemological question of all the *other* secrets and esoteric currents circulating around this complex tradition. Again, the problem is not that there is one secret to be uncovered, but rather that there are many secrets—a proliferation of esoteric bodies of knowledge, lines of transmission, and layers of concealment. This proliferation might be better described as a kind of complex network of exchange or an "economy of secrets,"[90] in which many different actors possess and circulate different forms of knowledge, which are always partial and incomplete.

Within this economy of secrets, the scholar is also inevitably a participant to one degree or another. In my case, for example, I forged complex relationships of friendship, exchange, and collaboration with several Tantric practitioners, such as Rajib Sarma—the local priest, archivist, and conservationist quoted above—and Prem Saran—a retired senior official of the Indian Administrative Service who was initiated in Assam and has written extensively about South Asian Tantra (I should add that I also befriended several male and female practitioners who asked to remain anonymous in this book).[91] While scholars may be excluded from many kinds of esoteric knowledge that a priest or guru might possess, they are often given access to some sources of information precisely *because* of their outsider status. For example, scholars may have access to a variety of textual and historical sources that are unknown even to advanced *tāntriks* due to the complex history of colonialism and globalization. In my case, I have been able to obtain and copy numerous manuscripts in collections in the UK, Nepal, Germany, and parts of India that were not accessible to my Tantric friends such as Rajib and Prem, and, in turn, they were willing to share a good deal of information with me that they would probably not have without that relationship of trust and reciprocity. At the same time, however, they were still reluctant to share certain levels of sensitive knowledge with a noninitiate such as myself, and, even if I were an initiate, there would always remain further layers of secrecy as well as layers and channels of esoteric information to which they themselves would not have access. And to make matters still *more* complicated, Rajib and Prem are initiates from two different branches of the same lineage, and they have rather different opinions about key aspects of Tantric practice, such as sexual rituals.

The study of secrecy is thus infinitely more complex than a simple binary of insider versus outsider or initiated practitioner versus uninitiated scholar; rather, it is a complex web of relations and exchanges that is always partial and incomplete, within which the scholar is also enmeshed in complicated ways. In my own case, I have tried to approach this tradition neither as a colonizing imperial scholar probing for valued hidden gems nor as a spiritual seeker asking for initiation into esoteric traditions; rather, I approach it more like authors such as Karen McCarthy Brown in her classic study of Vodou, *Mama Lola*.[92] While not a believing Vodou practitioner herself, Brown formed close relationships with the community in Brooklyn, befriending a Vodou priestess and becoming entwined with this complex religious world. This sort of relationship of friendship and reciprocity is similar to the one I experienced while working on this project.

Here I would also borrow some metaphors from the anthropologist Anna Tsing, who uses the language of *entanglement* to describe the work of ethnography and the relationship between the scholar and those whom she studies. The study of secrecy is perhaps less a matter of penetrating to some imagined inner core of knowledge than of allowing oneself to become entangled in the many threads of concealment. It is a matter of building up networks of relations that spread in ever more complex threads between a scholar and the communities they study, while remaining humble about one's level of understanding and acknowledging that there are many (perhaps infinite) other layers of concealment to which no one has complete access.

This entanglement, moreover, need not be purely parasitic or a one-way process of information extraction that solely benefits the CV of an American professor such as myself. Rather, it can also be a collaborative project, in which scholar and practitioner work together in various ways, even if with different agendas and toward different goals. "Collaborative projects," Tsing suggests, ". . . draw groups into common projects at the same time that they allow them to maintain separate agendas."[93] My work with Sarma, Saran, and others has often been collaborative in this sense, as I have tried to help them build archival collections, gather texts, and date archeological materials,[94] even as they have in turn given me access to many key sources of information. This relationship is, to be sure, imperfect, filled with all sorts of evasions, miscommunications, and occasional benign dissimulations, but so too is every ethnographic relationship—indeed, perhaps every human relationship, whether scholarly or not.

In this sense, the double bind of secrecy remains irresolvable, but it can also be strangely productive in many unexpected ways. While we can never escape the ethical and epistemological problems inherent in the work of a white male American scholar studying the esoteric traditions of India, we can perhaps mitigate them to some degree by developing a relationship with the community based on mutual respect and trust. And we can strive to do so in a *self-reflexive and self-critical* way; that is, rather, than simply imposing Western theoretical categories onto the Indian example, we can instead allow South Asian categories to "talk back" to modern scholarship, forcing us to critically rethink some of our own assumptions and presuppositions.

Outline of the Book: Genealogies of Desire

The six chapters that follow move progressively from the most "esoteric" or secret dimensions of Tantra to its most "exoteric" or public dimensions. Thus, the first two chapters focus primarily on the more esoteric Tantric lineages, transgressive rituals, and the practice of magic, while the later chapters shift toward large-scale public rituals, major annual celebrations, and finally the popular representation of Tantra in comic books, film, and television. The trajectory of the book moves from the inner to the outer, from the secret to the public, from the esoteric to the increasing "exotericization" of Tantra in the twenty-first century.

In chapter 1, "The Left-Hand Path," I delve directly into the most esoteric side of Tantric practice, exploring the living Tantric lineages of Kāmākhyā and related areas in the northeast. Today, Kāmākhyā is often claimed to be the seat of one of the last remaining lineages of the "left-hand path" (*vāma-mārga*) and the more radically transgressive form of Tantra, also known as the Kula Mārga (the "family practice"). Among other Tantric rites, the chapter examines the infamous "five Ms" (*pañcamakāra*) or the use of five forbidden substances or practices that begin with *ma-* in Sanskrit, including the most controversial "fifth M" of sexual union (*maithuna*). While most American readers today associate Tantra with spiritual sex, the fifth M of *maithuna* is today perhaps the most sensitive and ambivalent even for the most explicitly "left-hand" Tantric practitioners in Tantric heartlands such as Assam; as such, it highlights the profoundly ambivalent place of Tantra and transgressive Tantric ritual in contemporary India.

In chapter 2, "The Land of Black Magic," I then explore the close association between living Tantric practice and various forms of magical healing, enchantment, and witchcraft. For most Indians today, Tantra is much less associated with sexuality than with magic (*indrajāl* or *jādu*); indeed, the phrase *tantra-mantra* is more or less synonymous with black magic in popular discourse. While there is a long tradition of magic—including malevolent magic or sorcery (*abhicāra*)—in South Asian Tantra, the region of Assam is often identified as the "land of black magic" par excellence, infamous for its witches and sorcerers. Ironically, some towns such as Mayong have even begun to exploit their reputation as a site of black magic in order to promote tourism and economic development in the region. Yet on the darker side, Assam has also witnessed the highest incidence of witchcraft accusations in India, with hundreds of people (mostly women) being accused of—and in some cases killed for—black magic each year. The chapter focuses on three well-known practitioners of *tantra-mantra* in Mayong (called *bejs* or *ojhās*), examining the ways in which they have navigated these competing forces of tourism, economic development, and associations with witchcraft in the twenty-first century.

Chapter 3, "The Politics of Sacrifice," examines the central role of animal sacrifice (*yajña* or *bali-dān*) in Tantric practice and its increasingly controversial status in modern India. While blood offerings have been a basic part of Tantric worship from its inception—with roots in the oldest Vedic and Purāṇic traditions—they have become intensely contested in the late twentieth and twenty-first centuries. Above all, in the face of a newly empowered Hindu nationalist movement, animal sacrifice has been targeted as a dangerous and deviant practice (not least because of its association with Islam and with indigenous or tribal religions). Now banned in many Indian states, animal sacrifice has become a particular issue of controversy in Assam, where it has long and deep roots in both Tantric and indigenous practices. As such, the politics of sacrifice raise profound questions not only about the nature of Tantra but of the boundaries and definitions of the nation-state in an age of religious nationalism.

In chapter 4, "Dancing for the Snake," I examine one of the two major summer festivals that take place at Kāmākhyā Temple, Manasā Pūjā, or the worship of the snake goddess, Manasā. According to her own mythology, Manasā was originally a non-Hindu goddess who was only grudgingly accepted into the Hindu pantheon, and her worship clearly reflects a complex negotiation between indigenous and Hindu practices. Surely the most spectacular aspect of Manasā Pūjā at Kāmākhyā is the dance of the *deodhāis*, a group of special male performers who become possessed by a number of powerful gods and goddesses and engage in a variety of ecstatic acts, such as drinking blood from severed goats' heads and dancing on the blades of sacrificial swords. While possession (*āveśa*) by deities has historically been an important part of Tantric practice, the dance of the *deodhāis* also involves a significant element of indigenous practices from the many tribal communities of the northeast.

Chapter 5, "The Cradle of Tantra," then examines the most important summer festival that takes place at Kāmākhyā, Ambuvācī Melā or the celebration of the goddess's annual menstruation. While Kāmākhyā has long been revered as the site of the goddess's *yoni* and its life-giving blood, the temple and this festival have undergone a profound series of transformations that began in the nineteenth century and continue to the present day. First, with the rise of Hindu nationalism, Kāmākhya and other *śākta pīṭhas* were mobilized as part of an attempt to imagine a unified sacred landscape of "Mother India," a divine body linked together by this network of the goddess's body parts. Second, the temple and its festival have been massively promoted as a form of spiritual tourism and as part of a broader attempt by the Indian government to develop the Northeast region as a new economic powerhouse in the twenty-first century. All these changes have also revealed a series of deep tensions and conflicts. These include tensions between the conservative ideals of Hindu nationalism and the transgressive rites of Śākta Tantra, as well as growing conflicts within the Kāmākhyā community itself, between those who want to promote economic development and those who lament the gross touristification of this Tantric tradition.

In chapter 6, "Sinister *Tāntriks*," I explore the popular representation of Tantra in contemporary India through the media of novels, comic books, television, and films. While Tantra in the American popular imagination is almost universally equated with sexual and sensual desire, Tantra in the South Asian popular imagination is generally associated with magic and desire for power, as we see in innumerable films such as *Gahrāī*, *Saṅgharṣ*, and *Ammoru*, as well as a growing number of graphic novels and web series such as *Tārānāth Tāntrik*. Using Julia Kristeva's concept of "abjection," I argue that the figure of the sinister *tāntrik* is consistently used to represent the darkness, death, and impurity that must be cast out of the modern Indian nation—much as Tantra represents the corrupt form of practice that must be cast out of the conservative ideal of Hindutva. In the chapter, I also discuss my own personal experience working as a consultant for an Indian web series based on the Hindi novel *Tāśrī*. Centered on a powerful female character with supernatural powers, the series combines elements of Tantra with themes borrowed from *Harry Potter* and *The Matrix*. This discussion also leads me back to the initial discussion of the ethical and methodological challenges that are inevitably involved in this sort of research, as I myself became entangled in the modern representation of Tantra for a global audience.[95]

Finally, the conclusion discusses the larger implications of this focus on vernacular practice for our broader understanding of both Tantra and religion more generally. While there is now a small but growing body of work on living forms of Tantra, I argue that we also need to examine Tantra in relation to the inexorable forces of globalization, tourism, and neoliberal capitalism.[96] By no means simply practiced in isolated corners of village India, Tantra is now very much part of a global economy, film industry, and tourist network. More ambitiously, I argue that a serious encounter with living practice in Assam not only forces us to rethink "Tantra" as a category of South Asian religion; ultimately, it helps us to rethink the category of "religion" itself as a complex assemblage that is richly interwoven between scholars and practitioners, between "elite" and "vernacular" voices, between priestly and indigenous actors, between "high culture" and the most common works of film, fiction, and comics. In Primiano's terms, it problematizes the very idea of an "official religion" and asks us to approach religion "as human beings encounter, understand, interpret and practice it."[97] To return to our central metaphor of *tantra* as a loom or spinning device, religion might turn out to be not simply a richly woven text, but a snarled and messy patchwork, in which the fine threads of elite discourse are inextricably meshed with the coarser lines of everyday vernacular language. Like Tantra, religion is always entwined with the mundane realm of politics, popular culture, and ordinary human needs—always entangled, in short, with worldly desires and the manifold powers of desire.

[CHAPTER ONE]

The Left-Hand Path

Secrecy, Transgression, and the Kaula Tradition in Assam

> For the sake of eating meat, drinking wine, and enjoying sexual union with women at pleasure, I assume the form of great Bhairava [Śiva in his terrible form]. One should always worship [Bhairava] in the left-hand form using meat, wine, and so forth.
>
> *Kālikā Purāṇa* (tenth or eleventh century)[1]

> [The sacred] realm is essentially divided into two parts, the left and the right, or in other words, the pure and the impure, or even unlucky and lucky. On the whole, that which is left entails repulsion and that which is right entails attraction.
>
> Georges Bataille, "Attraction and Repulsion" (1938)[2]

Both historically and in contemporary practice, the region of Assam is often identified as the center of one the most important currents of Tantric practice: the Kaula tradition, or *kulācāra*. Derived from the term *kula*, meaning "family" or "clan," the Kaula tradition is one of the most influential but also most extreme and transgressive of the many different lineages, sects, texts, and ritual currents that are collectively lumped under the general category of "Tantra."[3] According to texts such as the *Kaulajñāna Nirṇaya* (tenth century), the seat of Kāmākhyā in Assam is identified as the original source of the Kaula tradition. In this narrative, the great sage and Tantric adept Matsyendranātha (ca. 900 CE) first learned the Kaula teaching from the many female *yoginīs* who are said to dwell in every home in Kāmarūpa.[4]

In contrast to more conservative forms of Tantra, the Kaula tradition is known for its practice of antinomian rites that involve a systematic use of impurity as a source of both spiritual liberation and worldly empowerment.[5] As such, the Kaula path is often identified with so-called left-hand (*vāmācāra*) forms of Tantra and set in contrast to the more conservative "right-hand" (*dakṣiṇācāra*) forms of practice. While the right-hand practice is based on the Vedas and orthodox rules of purity, the left-hand path engages in explicitly transgressive rites and the consumption of impure substances such as meat, wine, and (in some cases) sexual fluids as key elements in Tantric practice.[6] The point of this deliberate use of impure substances, however, is not a matter of mere hedonism or self-indulgence; rather, it is a means of harnessing and transforming the power of desire itself. Indeed, it might be considered a kind of *alchemy of desire*—that is, a means of transmuting sensual desire from a source of bondage to the material world into a source of empowerment and spiritual freedom.[7] Or to use Deleuze's terms, Tantric practice aims to "deterritorialize" the flow of desire and redirect it toward the goals of both worldly empowerment and spiritual liberation.[8] This practice is also a primary reason for the aura of danger and secrecy that surrounds Kaula practice.

Today, Assam maintains its reputation as a heartland of Tantric practice and as one of the few surviving centers of living Kulācāra Tantra. Centered on the Kāmākhyā temple complex, the current Kulācāra Tantra Mārga is a complex blend of various streams of South Asian Tantra with likely influence from the many indigenous traditions of the northeast region. While the majority of members of the Kulācāra Mārga are *brāhmaṇs* associated with the Kāmākhyā temple complex, the lineage also includes initiates of many different castes and even some foreigners.[9]

However, if the current Kulācāra tradition at Kāmākhyā identifies with the more transgressive, left-hand form of Tantra, it is also in many ways a highly orthodox, "respectable," and perhaps modified left-hand practice today. Since the nineteenth century—particularly in the wake of British colonialism, Orientalist scholarship, Christian missionary critiques, and neo-Hindu movements—many Tantric lineages underwent a profound sort of reform or "deodorization."[10] In the process, the more extreme and transgressive aspects of left-hand Tantra were often either jettisoned altogether or else cleansed of their most offensive elements. Many of the Tantric texts that emerged during the colonial era—most famously, the *Mahānirvāṇa Tantra* (late eighteenth century)—clearly reflect a kind of sanitized version of Tantra, in which the sexual elements are strongly downplayed and interpreted through the lens of respectable monogamy.[11]

The modern Kulācāra lineage in Assam, I will argue, reflects a similar tension surrounding the most extreme left-hand practices and, above all, sexual rites. Whereas the consumption of meat and alcohol remains a central part of Tantric practice in the region, the role of sexual rites is far more ambivalent and is generally either surrounded with even more secrecy or else interpreted in a more metaphorical right-hand fashion.[12]

Finally, I will briefly contrast this lineage with another band of practitioners who visit Kāmākhyā each summer: a group of Aghorīs from South India.

While some Aghorī lineages have also undergone a kind of "domestication" and reform in the modern era,[13] this particular South Indian group engages in some radically transgressive and extremely left-hand practices, such as corpse rituals and consumption of sexual fluids. Their presence is marginal, and their rites are performed not at the main Kāmākhyā temple but rather in secrecy and darkness in the Bhūtnāth cremation ground at the bottom of the hill.[14]

As such, the left-hand path in contemporary Assam is emblematic of a larger set of tensions surrounding Tantra as a "path of desire" in the twenty-first century. Foremost among these is the deep tension between *power* and *respectability*—that is, between a claim to *tantricity* as a special site of Tantric practice, on the one hand, and the desire to retain a kind of *purity* and reputation of orthodoxy, on the other.[15] This tension is particularly acute in a modern Indian context, where the more transgressive aspects of the path of desire (especially sexual aspects) have become increasingly suspect.

The Family Practice: The Kaula Tradition and Assam

The Tantric traditions of Asia are vast, diverse, and heterogeneous, encompassing a tremendous number of lineages, texts, ritual practices, and philosophical systems that spread throughout the Hindu, Buddhist, and Jain communities over a very long period of time. However, most scholars agree that the Kaula is one of the most important and also most explicitly transgressive Tantric traditions. As White explains, Kaula practices are typically "ritual acts addressed to a multiplicity of goddesses, which often involve human sexuality and sexual interactions between male practitioners and their female counterparts."[16] Kaula rituals are typically secret gatherings of male and female initiates—indeed, they are said to be "more secret than secret" (*rahasyātirahasya* or *guhyāt guhyataraṃ*)[17]—and usually involve animal sacrifice; offerings of meat, alcohol, and sexual fluids; and possession of practitioners by divine beings:

> Kaula rites are generally private and, ideally, performed in secluded places such as lonely forests, mountains, deserts, cremation grounds or sacred centres where adepts, male and female (*siddhas* and *yoginīs*), traditionally assemble. The deity worshiped is often . . . fearsome and adored with offerings of meat (including at times beef and human flesh) and wine as well as the male and female sexual fluids (*kuṇḍagolaka*) produced during ritual intercourse. The deity may be invoked to take possession of the worshippers so that he can gain its awesome power through which he perceives the deity's pervasive presence (*vyāpti*) in all things.[18]

Kaula rites also typically aim to arouse the divine energy that lies within the human body, known as *kuṇḍalī* or *kuṇḍalinī*. Literally meaning the "coiled one," *kuṇḍalinī* is the presence of Śakti or the divine energy of the goddess within each one of us, imagined in the form of a coiled serpent. Through Kaula rites, this energy is awakened and made to rise up through the centers (*cakras*) of the subtle body, until it merges with Lord Śiva, who dwells at the crown of the head. As Mark Dyczkowski explains, the transgressive rites of the Kaula circle are not simply an excuse for hedonistic excess but are rather the external means to a kind of internal bliss, precisely by harnessing and transforming the power of physical desire: "When Kuṇḍalinī awakens, it rises in the form of the Upward Moving Breath (*udānaprāna*), penetrating, as it does so, through successive levels of the cosmic order homologized to the microcosm of the adept's body. Finally, it merges . . . into the universal breath (*prāṇana*) and divine resonance of consciousness in the highest state of bliss. . . . In this way the delight of the senses become a means to liberation: one who is on the Kaula path drinks wine, eats meat, and performs ritual intercourse in order to make the innate bliss of his own nature manifest."[19]

The Kaula tradition produced a large body of texts, which were eventually systematized into a series of "transmissions" (*āmnāyas*), associated with the four directions and with specific goddesses. These include (1) the *pūrvāmnāya*, the prior or eastern transmission, identified with the triad of goddesses called Parā, Aparā, and Parāparā; (2) the *uttarāmnāya*, the higher or northern transmission, identified with the goddess Kālī; (3) the *paścimāmnāya*, the final or western transmission, identified with Kubjikā; and (4) the *dakṣiṇāmnāya* or southern transmission, identified with Tripurāsundarī. Later texts such as the *Kulārṇava Tantra* claimed to represent a fifth tradition, the *ūrdhvāmnāya* or upper transmission, and still others added a sixth transmission, flowing from the mouth of the *yoginī*, a reference to the *yoni* or sexual organ.[20]

A key figure in the early Kaula tradition was the sage Matsyendranātha, one of the most important masters (*siddhas*) in the development of both Hindu and Buddhist Tantra in South Asia. According to the narrative of the *Kaulajñāna Nirṇaya*, Matsyendranātha was taught this secret practice by the many powerful *yoginīs* who dwelled throughout the realm of Kāmarūpa, the place of desire, which is in turn the seat of the goddess Kāmākhyā: "In Kāmarūpa, this teaching of the *yoginīs* is found in every home [*kāmarūpe imaṃ śāstraṃ yoginīnāṃ gṛhe gṛhe*]."[21] Moreover, "it is said that holy women, adept at yoga, dwell at Kāmākhyā *pīṭha*. If one joins with one there, that is the same as attaining *yoginī siddhi* [the supernatural power of the *yoginīs*]."[22]

Here we should also note that the term *yoginī* can refer either to a human female practitioner of yoga or to a divine female being endowed with tremendous power and worshipped in many Tantric traditions, particularly in the famous sixty-four *yoginī* temples at sites such as Hirapur or Bheraghat.[23] Moreover, this identification of Matsyendranātha with Assam and its *yoginīs* is found throughout later Tantric traditions, including the highly philosophical Kashmir Śaivite traditions. As the great Kashmiri philosopher Abhinavagupta (ca. 1000 CE) put it in his massive synthesis of Tantric thought, the *Tantrāloka*, it was here in Kāmarūpa that Matsyendra learned the secret practice of Kaula yoga, which the goddess Bhairavī had heard from Bhairava: "Beloved, Bhairavī first obtained [the teachings concerning the practice of] Yoga from Bhairava and so pervaded [the entire universe]. Then, fair-faced one, it was obtained from their presence by the Siddha named Mīna, that is, by the great soul Macchanda [Matsyendra] in the great seat of Kāmarūpa."[24]

Today, many priests at Kāmākhyā Temple identify their lineage with the Matsyendra and his secret instruction from the *yoginīs*.[25] Although this claim is impossible to verify, it remains an important part of the contemporary mythology at the site and its broader claim to tantricity.

Other early texts also closely associate the region of Kāmarūpa with Tantra in its left-hand form. According to the mythic narrative of the *Kālikā Purāṇa* (tenth or eleventh century), the transgressive left-hand practice was first born in this region due to a curse. Once upon a time, the land of Kāmarūpa was so holy that all the people of the region were free from mortality and from the clutches of Lord Yama, the god of death. This state of affairs made Yama so upset that he beseeched the other gods to restore the balance of the universe. Lord Śiva granted his request and sent the ferocious goddess Ugratārā (Tārā in her terrible form) to the region to drive all human beings from the realm. In the process, however, she also tried to drive off the great and proud sage, Vasiṣṭha. Known for his foul temper and his terrible retribution for even the slightest insults, Vasiṣṭha cursed not only Śiva and Ugratārā but the whole region of Assam; henceforth, they would all be worshipped by *mlecchas* (barbarians and tribals) in the left-hand method.[26]

In contrast to the more orthodox right-hand practice—which involves the the observance of Vedic rituals and traditional social norms—the left-hand path involves rites in honor of fierce deities, such as the frightening goddesses Ugratārā, Caṇḍī, and Cāmuṇḍā, and the god Śiva in his wrathful form as Bhairava. In these transgressive left-hand rites, the practitioner first invokes and then identifies himself with Bhairava in order to engage in the forbidden use of wine, meat, and sexual intercourse: "For the sake of eating meat, drinking wine, and enjoying sexual union with women at pleasure, I assume the form of great Bhairava. One should always worship [Bhairava] in the left-hand form using meat, wine and so forth."[27]

FIGURE 1.1. Bhairava, rock-face image behind Bhairavī Temple, Guwahati, Assam, 2017. Photo by the author.

Despite its associations with fearsome deities and barbarians, the left-hand method is also said to be an extremely powerful sort of practice. Whereas the right-hand practices will serve to remove one's debts and bring rewards in the afterlife, the transgressive left-hand rites promise more immediate, *this*-worldly rewards, including the fufillment of all desires and tremendous material power: "He gains a body radiant like Kāma's," the *Kālikā Purāṇa* proclaims, "He subdues kings together with kingdoms. He enchants women, who are filled with desire. He can control lions, tigers, hyenas, spirits, and ghosts and travel with the speed of the wind."[28] For the follower of the left-hand path, worldly power is by no means at odds with

FIGURE 1.2. Cāmuṇḍā, outside Kedareśvara Temple, Guwahati, Assam, 2012. Photo by the author.

the goal of spiritual liberation but is its natural counterpart: "By immersion in the forbidden, the Tāntrika transcends his limits, gains all powers as well as salvation—a salvation in this world."[29]

The Murky Historical Roots of the Tantric Lineages in Assam

While early texts such as the *Kālikā Purāṇa* and *Kaulajñāna Nirṇaya* identify Assam with the mythic origins of Tantric practice, it is much more difficult to trace this lineage historically. This task is made all the more complicated by the fissured history of Assam's politics, which shifted frequently between periods of stable imperial rule and periods of violent fractures and division. Texts such as the *Kālikā Purāṇa* were likely composed during the Assamese Pāla dynasty (the counterpart to the Pāla Empire that ruled Bihar and Bengal), which held sway from the tenth to twelfth centuries. The most sophisticated sculptural works that can still be found at Kāmākhyā and in the Assam State Museum also date from this time period, so one could assume that the Pāla era was an important time for the development of Śākta Tantra in this region.[30]

Today, many priests of Kāmākhyā claim that they were brought to Assam from the famous region of Kannauj (in modern Uttar Pradesh), which is the legendary home of many great scholars and *brāhmaṇs*, including the famous grammarian Patañjali and priestly lineages that spread throughout the Rāṣṭrakūṭa, Gurjara-Pratihāra, and Pāla dynasties of western, southern, and eastern India. Many priests of modern Assam claim that their lineage was brought from Kannauj and their descendants were offered free land in the region to serve the goddess Kāmākhyā during the reign of the Assamese king Dharmapāla in the eleventh century.[31] (As a quick side note to the reader, I should add that there is some archeological evidence from Assam that may indicate a connection with Kannauj during this time period.[32])

A more proximate source for the Kāmākhyā priesthood, however, can be traced to the eighteenth century with roots in the Śākta heartland of Bengal. According to this narrative, the Ahom king Rudra Siṅgha (1696–1714) was increasingly drawn to Śākta forms of Hinduism in his later years and brought the renowned priest Kṛṣṇarāma Bhaṭṭācārya from Bengal to Assam. Rudra's son, Śiva Siṅgha (1714–1744), then took initiation from Kṛṣṇarāma and gave him management of the temple along with large areas of land.[33] As we will see below, the main family of gurus in the Kula lineage trace their descent to Kṛṣṇarāma.

The Kulācāra Mārga at Kāmākhyā Today

In the twenty-first century, the Kulācāra Tantric tradition remains a vital though largely esoteric current embedded within the social and religious landscape of the Kāmākhyā temple complex. Kāmākhyā and the many related temples on Nīlācala Hill host a diverse array of ritual specialists, roughly divided into *brāhmaṇs* (priests; *bardeurī* in Assamese) and non-*brāhmaṇs*. The *brāhmaṇs* or *bardeurīs* themselves are divided into a number of subcategories, including the *pūjārīs*, or main priests of Kāmākhyā, who are responsible for daily and annual rituals; *bidhipāṭhaks*, who are responsible for reciting *mantras* from manuscrupts (*bidhis*) during rituals; *hotas*, who are responsible for performing the fire rituals (*homa*) associated with daily and annual rites; *caṇḍīpāṭhaks*, who are responsible for performing the worship of the *Śrī Śrī Caṇḍī* text in honor of the goddess; *sūpakāras*, who prepare the daily *bhoga* (cooked offerings); and the *nānān-bardeurīs*, or priests of the many other temples on Nīlācala Hill apart from Kāmākhyā itself.[34]

The non-*brāhmaṇs*, in turn, include a wide range of other attendants of the temple complex, including *bhāṇḍār kāyasthas*, who are in charge of the warehouse and store of the temple; *bharālīs*, the store operators and distributors; *gāyan-bayāns*, singers and musicians; *bali-kaṭās*, or those responsible for performing the daily animal sacrifice; *āṭhpariās*, or those responsible for daily bathing of Kāmākhyā and the other *pīṭhas* on the hill; *dūarīs*, or gate-keepers of the temple; and many, many others. As a whole, then, Nīlācala Hill is an intricate network of ritual specialists and related actors, interconnected through complex webs of knowledge, training, and practice, both esoteric and exoteric.[35]

Only a few of these many different actors participate in the left-hand form of Tantric practice. According to Rajib Sarma's estimate, about 15 percent of the larger Kāmākhyā temple community (roughly forty-five couples) are practicing members of the Kulācāra Mārga, which is only accessible through a series of initiations (*dīkṣā*) at the hands of a guru. The precise relationship of the Kāmākhyā Kulācāra to the other historical *kula āmnāyas* mentioned above is unclear; however, it seems probable that it is most closely tied to the *ūrdhvāmnāya* and to the Tantric revival of northeast India represented by texts such as the *Kulārṇava Tantra*.[36]

The Kula tradition at Kāmākhyā in turn encompasses two main lineages known as the Śrīkula and the Kālīkula, which each have their own gurus and slightly different forms of worship. The former is centered on the worship of the benign, maternal goddesses Tripurā and Lalitā, while the latter centers on the fierce goddesses Kālī and Tārā.[37] Members of the Śrīkula are initiated by the main family of gurus at Kāmākhyā, who trace their descent from the Bengali priest mentioned above, Kṛṣṇarāma Bhaṭṭācārya, who is said to have been brought to Assam in the eighteenth century.[38] These gurus are known as *rājgurus* because of their traditional association with the Ahom king (*rāja*). Members of the Kālīkula, meanwhile, are initiated by another guru family that lives outside of Kāmākhyā in an adjacent district.[39]

As the Assamese practitioner and scholar Muktināth Śarmā explains, there are five main stages of initiation in this lineage. The first is *śāktābhiṣeka* (the consecration in *śākta* practice), in which the adept is purified of sins and begins the basic path of *sādhanā*. The second is the *pūrṇābhiṣeka*, or "full consecration." The third and fourth are the *krama dīkṣā* and *samrājya dīkṣā*, or the "gradual" and "sovereign" initiations. And finally, there is *sannyāsa dīkṣā* or *avadhūta dīkṣā*. Literally meaning what is "removed" or "shaken away," the *avadhūta* is the fully realized adept who has left behind all worldly distinctions in union with the ultimate reality: "At this time he achieves the knowledge of the *jīvātman* [individual self] and *paramātman* [Supreme Self]. This is the ultimate practice for the adept, or *Brahmanirvāṇa* [extinction in the ultimate reality]. . . . The adept's final state would be yoga, or the union of *jīvātman* and *paramātman*."[40] Here we should also note that Muktināth's account of the degrees of initiation closely resembles that of Arthur Avalon (a.k.a. Sir John Woodroffe), who describes very similar stages of *abhiṣeka* in his widely read introduction to the *Tantra of the Great Liberation*.[41]

Entry into the Tantric path is not a step to be taken lightly. Indeed, it is often said to be a dangerous undertaking that could lead the initiate down the road of vice, addiction, and physical or psychological harm. Not only is there the danger of abuse—particularly the abuse of alcohol—but Tantric practice is believed to arouse powerful energies within the body and psyche that could overwhelm those who are unprepared or undertake the rites with the wrong intentions. As Himangshu Sarma explains, the Tantric path is a kind of shortcut—a "powerful and speedy path towards divinity"[42]—but also one that is subject to potential misunderstanding or misuse. Another initiate, Heman Sarma, recalled that his own mother vehemently tried to stop him from taking this path, warning him against the dangers of Tantra and its use of impurity: "It was the time to get *tāntrika* initiation. At the beginning my mother obstructed me: 'Do not go for *tāntrika pūjā*, because it's very tough, you must take wine, fish, meat.' [At first] my mother did not allow me."[43]

These warnings surrounding the Tantric path were echoed by more or less all the individuals with whom I have spoken over the last two decades.

Tantra represents potential power, but it also contains real dangers; it can bring great benefits, both spiritual and material, but it can also bring ruin for those who are arrogant, greedy, or unqualified. Many stories circulate about *tāntriks* who go mad with power or are destroyed by arrogance, greed, and desire for material gain.[44]

However, it is important to note that the Kula lineage at Kāmākhyā does not understand itself to be in any way contrary to the orthodox, Vedic, and *brāhmaṇic* tradition; rather, it is seen as an esoteric practice that is founded upon and yet *transcends* the orthodox tradition: "They place themselves *above* the latter and claim superiority because of the effectiveness (and danger) of the tantric practices. The latter happen behind closed doors, in secret, at night. In the daylight, the *tāntrika* observes orthodox rules."[45] In this sense, the Kāmākhyā lineage is similar to other, more orthodox Tantric traditions such as the Śrīvidyā in South India. As Douglas Brooks notes, the Śrīvidyā tradition does not undermine *brāhmaṇic* authority but in fact *reinforces* it, by asserting the status of *brāhmaṇs* as ritual experts with the unique ability to transgress conventional laws of purity and to harness such dangerous power.[46] This point is an important one to keep in mind as we examine the tensions between transgression and respectability in this tradition and its distinction from more radically antinomian and non-Vedic groups such as the Aghorīs.

What about the Women? Gender Dynamics and Women in the Left-Hand Path

One of the most complex and contested questions in the study of South Asian Tantra is the role of women in these traditions.[47] Many Tantric texts proclaim the power of women, who are said to embody the divine power or energy (*śakti*) of the goddess, which is the source of all life and creation. In the words of the *Yoni Tantra* (from sixteenth-century Cooch Behar), "women are gods, women are life, women, indeed, are jewels," for all things ultimately come from the creative matrix of the *yoni*, the female sexual organ: "Hari, Hara, and all the gods, the agents of the creation, maintenance, and destruction of the universe, are all born from the *yoni*."[48] Yet at the same time, most Sanskrit Tantric texts were written by men, and women's actual roles in Tantric practice are highly variable depending on particular lineages and geographic regions.[49]

The role of women is no less complicated in the case of the Assamese traditions. Texts from Assam such as the *Kāmākhyā Tantra* typically praise the *śakti*, or female partner, as the foundation of all ritual and even of all life itself: "Practice is based on the *śakti*. Prayer is based on the *śakti*. Movement is based on the *śakti*. Life is based on *śakti*. Both this world and the afterlife are based on the *śakti*. . . . What one offers to the *śakti*, O Goddess, is offered to the gods."[50] In many Tantric lineages—particularly Śākta lineages of the northeast—this reverence for women does seem to carry over at least to some degree into actual practice, as women are also seen as key agents in the performance of Tantric rituals. As Rajib Sarma explains, "The women are an inseparable part of the Kulacara Tantra Marga and hold higher position than their male counterparts and are respected as the form of Shakti (Devi). The women play the most significant part and take leading role in the rituals performed according to the teaching and techniques of Kulacara Tantra Marga."[51]

Rajib's view is largely confirmed by other initiated members of the lineage at Kāmākhyā. As Heman Sarma similarly explains, women are the powerful ones, who have an innate *śakti*, while men can only attain *śakti* through them. The wife of the male practitioner is in many ways his own personal guru, sitting at his right hand and pouring his wine for him in rituals: "My wife took *tāntrika* initiation along with me. In the *tāntrika* initiation she is the main guru. . . . [T]hough normally she sits at my left hand, in the *tāntrika* she sits at my right hand. They [women] are the powerful ones. They pour wine for us, they control us; we cannot take wine ourselves, according to our wish. She helps me, she maintains me, she controls the amount of wine I drink."[52]

Yet at the same time, the Kāmākhyā lineage—like virtually all Tantric lineages—is by no means either feminist or radically egalitarian. While some Tantric texts do discuss roles for women as gurus,[53] the primary initiating gurus and leaders here are male (as are all the formal heads of the more exoteric institutions of the Kāmākhyā temple complex).[54] Moreover, as Sundari Johansen Hurwitt notes based on her own experience as an initiate of the tradition, all women at Kāmākhyā—including Kaula initiates—are expected to follow strict rules concerning their bodies and social interactions: "These include maintaining the highly important menstrual taboo, not associating with men who are not immediate relatives without a husband, father, brother, or adult son present, and once married, not leaving their husband's home without a close male relative as a chaperone until after their first child is born."[55] While women do engage in Tantric rituals, they do so primarily in the private sphere and keep their identity as initiates extremely secret. Any publicly perceived connection to the realm of Tantra—particularly to the consumption of alcohol and the suggestion of any sort of sexual impropriety—would be deeply embarrassing for most women: "As a rule, women practice only privately, and never perform *cakra anuṣṭhāna* [circle worship, or gathering of the *kula*] in public or semi-public spaces. . . . The primary reason . . . is fear of gossip and loss of reputation. Women participating in a Tantric ritual in a temple or other place in view of any non-initiates, particularly outsiders, may be subject to gossip over consumption of alcohol and rumors of sexual impropriety. Serious local female practitioners are also *highly* secretive about their participation."[56]

In sum, the position of women in this tradition (as in all Tantric lineages) is deeply complicated and often ambivalent. While some modern scholars have tried to read this tradition through a feminist lens—as an empowerment of women and a celebration of the female body[57]—others have read it in quite opposite terms—as a highly essentialist view of femininity and a serious limitation of women's agency.[58] It seems perhaps most accurate to say that it does not fit tidily into any modern theoretical framework and should be understood as far more complicated and multivalent than a simple matter of either "empowerment" or "exploitation."[59]

"The Five Ms" (*Pañcamakāra*): Impurity and Transgression in the Left-Hand Path

Perhaps the most distinctive feature of left-hand Kaula Tantric practice is the use of the "five Ms" (*pañcamakāra*). Consisting of five substances or practices beginning with the syllable *ma-* in Sanskrit, the *pañcamakāra* are generally identified as *madya* (alcohol), *māṃsa* (meat), *matsya* (fish), *mudrā* (parched grain),[60] and *maithuna* ([sexual] union). As Padoux notes, early Tantric texts speak only of three Ms, namely, alcohol, meat, and sexual union; however, the list of five with *matsya* and *mudrā* would eventually become standard in Tantric literature, including texts from Assam such as the *Yoginī Tantra* and many others.[61]

One of the most detailed explanations of the *pañcamakāras* in the Assamese tradition comes from Muktināth Śarmā. As Śarmā explains, the *makāras* (forbidden substances) each have a gross or physical dimension and a subtle or symbolic dimension. The former serves as the base or support for the latter—the physical springboard, as it were, for rising to the higher spiritual dimension. Thus, in the case of *madya*, the alcohol actually becomes the means to awaken the *kuṇḍalinī śakti*, the divine energy within the subtle body. As we saw above, *kuṇḍalinī* is typically imagined as a coiled serpent at the base of the spine and represents the power of the goddess that resides within each human body. Once aroused through the use of alcohol, the *kuṇḍalinī* energy rises through the subtle body, piercing each of the energy centers, or *cakras*, that are believed to lie along the axis of the spinal column, ultimately reaching the *sahasrāra cakra* at the crown of the head. Imagined in the form of a thousand-petaled lotus, the *sahasrāra* is also the repository of the divine elixir, *soma*, which then flows down through the subtle body as the true "wine" and source of spiritual intoxication. At this point, once the interior discipline of *kuṇḍalinī yoga* has begun, the use of physical substances such as alcohol is no longer necessary:

> When using alcohol for practice, one should use a vessel measuring three to five *tolas* [one *tola* = 11.663 oz]. There are special rites for it at the time of drinking. Through these procedures, the wine itself becomes the means of awakening the *kuṇḍalinī śakti* by transforming the state of drunkenness. When the *kuṇḍalinī śakti* is awakened, and when the *soma* nectar flows from the *sahasrāra* [*cakra*], the disciple no longer feels the need for drinking physical alcohol. . . . By drinking purified wine in the amount prescribed in the sacred texts, the mind becomes focused, and it is an aid to awakening the *kuṇḍalinī*. This is the basic mark of all practice. In Tantra, just as there is the arrangement for the use of gross elements (alcohol), so too there is also the use of subtle elements. Even though the gross elements are taken as an aid in the first stage, once the *kuṇḍalinī* is awakened and the *soma* nectar flows from the *sahasrāra*, then there is no need for gross elements.[62]

Ultimately, through Tantric *sādhanā*, the alcohol is said to be transformed into an interior spiritual state in which the normal effects of drunkenness are no longer felt by the practitioner. The guru Tāriṇī Prasād Śarmā, for example, is believed to embody this ideal of self-control even while consuming large quantities of alcohol: "He is said to be able to carry out the most intricate rituals with terrific accuracy, notwithstanding the large quantity of alcohol he is required to drink during . . . the performance."[63] Similarly, Rajib Sarma told me that he will sometimes drink more than a liter of whiskey[64] during a *pūjā* and yet experience no signs of physical intoxication: "Afterwards, I can drive home with no problem; the police don't stop me."[65] As Prem Saran explained, the ritual setting combined with chanting and the guidance of a guru serves to transform *madya* from an ordinary intoxicant into a source of profound spiritual experience: "I found that *madya* could indeed conduce to the mystical experience. I once partook in a 5Ms session with my guru and his sannyasi friend in his house in Kāmākhyā. . . . [W]e quaffed the raw liquor; then on the eleventh round, I entered an open-eyed samadhi state."[66]

At the same time, however, *madya* is also surrounded with stern warnings about its potential for abuse. If the material support of alcohol is consumed as an end in itself rather than as an instrument in the "alchemy of desire," it is said to be extremely destructive and even "a cause of death," both physically and spiritually.[67]

Muktināth Śarmā gives a similar explanation for the next three *makāras*: *māṃsa*, *matsya*, and *mudrā*. These are described as the material supports for and means of achieving internal spiritual states, helping to arouse the *kuṇḍalinī* energy and direct it toward union within the Supreme Self. The meat, for example, is literal meat (and, according to Rajib Sarma, it can be any kind of meat cooked by anyone, regardless of caste or religion[68]), but it serves as the material basis for an inner experience. So also with fish and parched grains: these material substances serve as the external means to trigger an internal spiritual experience. Here, Muktināth's interpretation closely follows Assamese texts such as the *Yoginī Tantra*, which states that eating meat is really symbolic of slaying "the beast of sin and merit" with the sword of knowledge, consuming fish is symbolic of controlling the senses and joining them with the Self, and so on.[69] Ultimately, Muktināth suggests, the practitioner will transcend the need for external substances altogether. The lower support of physical meat and fish will be left behind in the higher enjoyment, which is union of the divine male and female energies within oneself. In the final state of this alchemy of desire, "there is no need for the gross *pañcamakāras*."[70]

"The Fifth M Is Different": Tantric Sex in Modern India

While there is some minor disagreement about the specifics of the first four *makāras*, there is far more debate surrounding the fifth M of *maithuna*. The many various schools of Tantra differ widely on the precise interpretation of the rite, and today modern scholars also disagree intensely about the significance of *maithuna* in Tantric practice. While some authors such as David Gordon White see sexual union and the consumption of sexual fluids as the primary hallmarks of "hardcore" Tantra, others such as Christian Wedemeyer regard them as primarily textual and semiotic in nature.[71] As Shaman Hatley notes, there is in fact a wide variety of different forms of sexual practice in the vast body of Tantric literature; these forms range from various kinds of love magic, to ritualized coitus in which the sexual fluids are consumed, to highly regulated forms of coitus in secret gatherings, to sexual union as a means of esoteric gnosis, to yogic techniques designed to avoid the loss of semen and/or to internalize the sexual energies.[72]

Iconographically, *maithuna* can also be represented in various ways, from the abstract *liṅgam* and *yoni* in union, to the image of Śiva and Śakti joined in the form of Ardhanārīśvara, to the interpenetrating upward and downward triangles of the Śrī Yantra diagram.

Today, many Tantric sects of northeast India do engage in some form of sexual practice. This is particularly true in Bengal and Bangladesh, where groups such as the Sahajiyās and Bāuls still flourish. Both the Sahajiyās and Bāuls, however, usually practice a form of sexual ritual that involves non-ejaculation and retention of the semen. As Sukanya Sarbadhikary explains based on her fieldwork, the Sahajiyās regard ejaculation as a form of self-seeking pleasure driven by lust and gratification of the ego, in contrast to the egoless love of non-ejaculatory practices: "They say that a body in lust (*kama*) ejaculates but a body in love (*prem*) retains Vrindavan (body-fluids) inside."[73] In the Sahajiyā system, the semen contains the divine male principle, Lord Kṛṣṇa, while the female sexual fluids contain the divine female, his consort Rādhā. By refraining from ejaculation, the practitioner is believed to draw these principles back into himself in order to achieve an internalized divine union, enjoying the love-play of Kṛṣṇa and Rādhā within himself: "The male principle, Krishna, is embodied in semen, and Radha, in menstrual blood and/or female sexual fluid. Thus sahajiyas conceptualize these fluids' unification in the body, through . . . retaining or pulling them through yogic practices, as the union of Radha-Krishna and thus the preservation of Vrindavan's pleasures within the body."[74]

The Bāuls engage in similar kinds of sexual rites, though with somewhat different metaphysical interpretations. In the Bāul system, the Supreme Self—called the "Man of the Heart" (*maner mānuṣ*) or "Natural Man" (*sahaj mānuṣ*)—is believed to reside in the *sahasrāra cakra* at the top of the head. In the woman's body, however, he descends from this seat each month during her menstrual period and is embodied in her blood. This time is the best one in which to perform *maithuna*, since the Man of the Heart can be captured and then drawn into the male body through the practice of semen retention. The Bāuls also tend to use a variety of colorful metaphors in their songs to describe this practice, such as "catching the thief" or "catching the uncatchable." They say: "On the third day of a woman's menstrual period, the *sahaj mānuṣ* descends from the woman's *sahasrār*. . . . Through coitus the *sahaj mānuṣ* is separated out of the blood, attracted into the male's penis, and brought back to the *sahasrār*. The resulting feeling of bliss . . . is called 'catching the uncatchable' . . . or 'being dead while alive.'"[75]

Some practitioners from Assam also describe sexual union as a key if not *the* key defining feature of Tantra. Prem Saran, for example, has long been involved in Tantric practice and has conducted extensive fieldwork in northeast India and Nepal. In his view, "erotic yoga" or "ritualized sexual intercourse" is the defining feature of Tantra, and he documents numerous *tāntriks* from Nepal who discussed the details of sexual practice.[76] Thus he quotes a Newar *brāhmaṇ*, living in Bhaktapur, who describes physical intercourse as a mirror of the divine union of Śiva and his consort. It is, as such, "a kind of creation," this *brāhmaṇ* says: "Given this dimension of the sexual act as a creative act, it must be performed in the proper spirit, otherwise society would suffer. . . . [B]oth men and women should get pleasure from sexual activity. Thus, he referred to the fact that both the great (Hindu) god Shiva and his spouse Parvati indulge in sexual intercourse."[77]

In addition to Saran's fieldwork, one of the few modern accounts of Tantric sexual practices—and one of the few articulated from a woman's perspective—comes from Sravana Borkataky-Varma. A Bengali and Assamese scholar, she conducted her fieldwork in northeast India with a primary focus on women and sexuality. In one of her more fascinating interviews, she spoke with a pair of half sisters whom she first met in Bengal and then later re-encountered at Kāmākhyā Temple. At the latter site, the sisters actually performed a physical demonstration of the female partner's role in sexual rites, using a plastic bottle in place of a penis to explain in graphic detail the successive postures used in actual Tantric *maithuna*:

> In the confines of the shed, Sundari Ma provided the commentary while Kamala Ma performed the exercise. There were no male partners and instead of holding onto the penis Kamala Ma used a small plastic bottle. . . . Kamala Ma began by praying to Kālī and seeking forgiveness in advance for any errors she might make while demonstrating this secret (*gupta*) training. . . . Kamala Ma used her vagina to grab onto the small plastic bottle, took an enormous deep breath and carefully yet swiftly performed the *mūlabandha*, then moved to the *uḍḍiyāna-bandha*, and finally completed the exercise with *jālaṁdhara-bandha*. With all three *bandhas* intact, Kamala Ma stayed in that position, eyes open, not blinking, not breathing for a long time.[78]

In sum, there is ample evidence that some form of literal sexual union has long been and continues to be part of Tantric practice among many lineages in northeast India to this day.

All that being said, however . . . When I talk to Tantric practitioners at Kāmākhyā today, virtually all of them reject any kind of literal interpretation of *maithuna*—even in the sense of the Sahajiyās' and Bāuls' practice of seminal retention. One of the recurring phrases I have heard from multiple initiates is that "the fifth M is different." Many are quite happy to talk openly about the consumption of meat and alcohol (which are also quite transgressive substances), yet when asked about *maithuna*, they will typically either demur or articulate a kind of right-hand interpretation of the fifth M—that is, one explaining *maithuna* as a symbolic, internalized, spiritual union.[79] As Muktināth Śarmā explains, *maithuna* is simply the process of awakening the *kuṇḍalinī* energy and raising it up through the body where it joins with the Śiva in the highest *cakra*. Rather than an external union, it is the inner, spiritual pleasure of the divine male and female joining within oneself: "The awakening of the *kuṇḍalinī śakti* and union with the *sahasrāra* is called the union of Śiva and Śakti or *maithuna*. It is the sexual union [*ramaṇ*] of the Self."[80]

This notion that the highest form of *maithuna* is the union of Śiva and Śakti within the individual is not, of course, unique to modern practitioners. This is an old idea in Tantric literature and is repeated in Assamese texts such as the *Yoginī Tantra* (seventeenth or eighteenth century), which also states that "the union of the Self with the Supreme Śakti is considered [the true sexual union], not the union with semen."[81] However, what *is* unique in Muktināth's interpretation is that the other four Ms all have a literal material counterpart (actual alcohol, meat, fish, etc.) as a foundation, while *maithuna* does not. When I asked Rajib Sarma about this and whether *maithuna* also has a physical component, as *madya* does in the form of actual alcohol, he repeated the phrase that "the fifth M is different" and that there is no literal sexual union involved. "In twelve years of practice, I have never seen anyone do *maithuna* [in the literal sense] at Kāmākhyā. We are respectable people! We have jobs, families. *Maithuna* is an inner experience of raising [*kuṇḍalinī*] from the *mūlādhāra* [root *cakra*] to the *sahasrāra*."[82] As we will see below, this emphasis on "respectability" is key to understanding this complex tradition today.

Meanwhile, some other practitioners from the region explained *maithuna* in even more practical terms, as not so much an inner mystical state but as simply a union in the sense of an "encounter" or "exchange." According to Heman Sarma, it is simply a private "meeting" that involves the exchange of knowledge in the course of a conversation: "In the *tāntrika* five things are necessary. *Madya, māṁgsu, māca, mudrā, maithuna*. It is called *pañcamakāra*. . . . *Maithuna* is of two types. If we discuss something, like now, it's called *maithuna*, and from the discussion some result comes out. I'm giving something to you, you're getting something from me. But *maithuna* also means the sexual relation between man and woman, but this process is not practiced here."[83]

Secrecy, Sanitization, and Reform: Making Sense of the Fifth M

So what do we make of these statements that "the fifth M is different" and this reluctance to speak of *maithuna*—despite a general willingness to talk about other transgressive acts such as consuming wine and meat? Here I would suggest at least a few possible interpretations. One possibility, of course, is that sexual union really *is* practiced here but is so secret that members of the community simply refuse to discuss it with any noninitiates. It is also possible that it is practiced only by the most advanced initiates and that lower-level members of the community have not yet been granted access to such rites. This interpretation was suggested to me by Prem Saran, who is a *tāntrik* practitioner, though initiated in a different branch of the Kāmākhyā lineage than others such as Rajib Sarma. As he explained, it is likely that any practitioner involved in left-hand rites would dissemble to some degree when speaking to a noninitiate: "It seems to me that—since the *vamacarin* may perhaps not be excessively forthcoming except to an insider whom he or she knows well—people may dissemble, again in view of those 'double norms.' That would apply to the Kathmandu Valley as well as to Kamakhya: after all, one is ultimately on a highly involving spiritual trip."[84] All this disagreement is, of course, a central part of the profound epistemological problem of secrecy that we discussed in the introduction.

A second possible interpretation, however, is that this tradition—like many Tantric traditions in modern India—has undergone a certain amount of reform, particularly around sexual practices. In her study of the priests of Kāmākhyā, Majo Garigliano suggests that the current understanding of *maithuna* may well reflect a sort of sanitization of Tantric practice in the modern context. In many Tantric traditions, the use of the *pañcamakāra* takes place in the ritual called the *cakrapūjā* (circle worship) or *cakrānuṣṭhāna* (practice of the circle), the secret gathering of male and female initiates for worship with meat, alcohol, and sexual rites, along the lines of the Kaula practices described above.[85] Today, however, the *cakrānuṣṭhāna* is primarily a "gathering" (*maithuna* in the sense of "meeting") of male initiates around the guru for instruction and consumption of alcohol. Women are excluded from these gatherings: "The *cakrānuṣṭhāna* is most probably a sanitized version of the rituals which, in other contexts, entail[ed] sexual intercourse; the double meaning ascribed by Hemen Sarma to *maithuna* supports this assumption. . . . Hemen Sarma denies that sexual intercourse takes places in the secret rites for initiates, but nevertheless acknowledges the role of women who alone have *śakti*. Their role is restricted to the *dīkṣā* which they take with their husbands; neither they nor other women take part in the *cakrānuṣṭhāna*."[86]

Indeed, the main transgression that seems to take place here has little to do with sex but is mostly about the alcohol shared by male initiates gathered around the master of the circle or *cakreśa*: "In the *cakrānuṣṭhāna* the initiates talk about different religious matters . . . In the *cakrānuṣṭhāna* consumption of alcohol is mandatory."[87]

This "sanitized" attitude toward *maithuna* seems to reflect a broader reform of Tantra—and above all, of Tantric sexual practices—that took place throughout South Asia in the modern period. These reforms began internally due to intense critiques from other Hindu movements (most notably, Vaiṣṇava *bhakti*), and they accelerated rapidly with the impact of Christian missionary activity, British colonialism, Orientalist scholarship, and a new wave of Hindu reform movements.[88] Particularly in its left-handed Kaula forms, Tantra was long viewed with suspicion by non-*tāntriks* in South Asia, but it became a special target of attack from the sixteenth century onward. In northeast India, much of this reform was the result of the popular revival of devotion to Kṛṣṇa, which was led by Caitanya (1486–1534) in Bengal and Śaṅkaradeva (1449–1568) in Assam. Particularly in Assam, it is difficult to overestimate the impact of Śaṅkaradeva's teachings, which changed not only the understanding of religion but also the basic social structure in the region.[89] While emphasizing a pure, devotional relationship with God in his playful form of Kṛṣṇa, Śaṅkaradeva launched fierce criticisms at the bloody and sensual practices of Śākta Tantra: "Engaged in worship with wine, women, and meat [*strī madya māṅgsa sevā*], alas, they perish! Alas, they perish! Their lives are futile. They don't understand the deeper meaning of the Vedas."[90] It was largely because of the rapid success of Śaṅkaradeva's devotional movement that Śākta Tantra declined as the dominant religious and political force in the region from the sixteenth century onward.[91]

In his detailed study of the Kāmākhyā temple complex, Mishra suggests that the more right-handed form of worship that we see today reflects a reformist attitude, one that may well date as far back as Śaṅkaradeva's time. He notes that the text for the daily worship (*nityapūjā*) indicates the presence of a woman working together with the priest, yet today, the female presence is simply represented by a red flower. As Mishra speculates, this shift may reflect a broader reform of the tradition from an older *vāmācāra* system to a more right-handed practice, possibly due to Śaṅkaradeva's tremendous influence in the region:

> In the *Nityapūjā vidhi* there is a provision of a woman companion to co-operate with the priest. This age-old practice gives us occasion to

> speculate that there must have been a period during which *vāmācāra* system of worship was in vogue in the temple. But now, this system is dispensed with. And the priest performs the *pūjā* being accompanied by symbolic presence of a woman companion in the form of a red flower to his left side. . . . The reformative attitude is evident in Tantric literatures like the *Śaktisaṅgama Tantra*. . . . [T]his reformative period in the Tantras coincides with the time of Shankaradev.[92]

An even more intense period of critique and reform of Tantra, however, took place a few centuries later during the British colonial period. As we have seen above, colonial authorities, Christian missionaries, and Orientalist scholars frequently singled out the *tantras* as the worst and most degenerate corruption of Hinduism in modern times, and they usually identified the left-hand use of alcohol, meat, and sexual rites as the clearest evidence of this perverse mixture of religion and sensuality. According to the Sanskritist Sir Monier-Williams, Tantra is nothing less than "Hinduism arrived at its last and worst stage of medieval development," while others such as D. L. Barnett described Tantric ritual as a kind of "devil's mass purveyed in various forms."[93]

The Orientalists' critique of Tantra was echoed by many Hindu reformers, who hoped to present a more sanitized and rational form of Hinduism to a global audience. This was particularly true of reformist authors in Bengal, such as Rāmmohun Roy (1772–1833) and Swāmī Vivekānanda (1863–1902), who both singled out *vāmācāra* Tantra as a kind of degenerate disease that had crippled this once-pure religion. Heavily influenced by Orientalist views, Roy described the *tantras* as "offensive to the ears of the most abandoned of either sex." Containing rites of "human sacrifice, the use of wine, criminal intercourse and licentious songs," the *tantras* in Roy's view focus on worship of horrible goddesses such as Kālī, for whom "debauchery . . . forms the principal worship of her followers."[94] Also writing in the context of British colonial rule and Orientalist scholarship, Vivekānanda was particularly critical of Tantra in its left-hand interpretations. He warned that it was precisely this "disease" of *vāmācāra* that had weakened India and undermined its national character. The degenerate *vāmācāra* practice, he lamented, had infected the marrow of the Indian body politic, emasculating and effeminizing this once powerful nation, and allowing it to be dominated, first by the Mughals and later by the British Empire. "Just look to your own province and see how this Vamachara (immoral practices) of the Tantras has entered into our very marrow. . . . We must stem the tide of this Vamachara, which is contrary to the spirit of the Vedas,"[95] he exhorted. "Give up this filthy Vamachara that is killing your country."[96]

Even some of the most important Tantric literature from this period reflects the reformist trend. Perhaps the most famous Tantra from the modern period is the *Mahānirvāṇa Tantra* (*Tantra of the Great Liberation*), which was probably composed in Bengal in the late eighteenth century.[97] In his careful historical study of the text, J. Duncan M. Derrett makes a persuasive case that it clearly reflects changing laws surrounding marriage and inheritance in India under British rule and so can likely be dated to the period between 1773 and 1782.[98] In addition to its extensive commentary on eighteenth-century issues of caste, marriage, and inheritance, the text also contains a highly conservative interpretation of the five Ms, particularly *maithuna*. Even when such acts are mentioned, moreover, it is only "with great euphemisms."[99] The *pañcamakāras* are mentioned in just one chapter of the text, and the fifth *makāra* is given just a single line.[100] Unlike many other Tantric texts from northeast India, which recommend sexual union with low-class partners, untouchables, and menstruating women,[101] this text is exceptional in proclaiming that, in this decadent modern age, *maithuna* should be performed only with one's own wife: "When the weakness of the Kali Age becomes great, one's own wife alone should be known as the fifth tattva."[102] As various authors have observed, the text reflects a strong "reformist" tendency, endorsing rituals that would not be threatening to a Western outlook. As such, it is generally said to be less respected among more left-hand practitioners due to its "unnecessary timidity" and is even dismissed by some as a kind of "woman's Tantra."[103]

Similar patterns of reform and sanitization of Tantra have been documented in many other traditions during the modern period, particularly in northeast India. As Rachel McDermott has shown in her work on the worship of Kālī in Bengal, the goddess underwent a clear process of "sweetening" during the late eighteenth, nineteenth and early twentieth centuries.[104] The once terrifying and hideous Tantric goddess became progressively transformed into a more beautiful and attractive devotional goddess who would be more appealing to Calcutta's growing popular urban audience. In my own work, I have traced a similar pattern of reform and "sweetening" in Bengali sects such as the Kartābhajās (worshippers of the master). Originally rooted in Tantric Sahajiyā practices, the Kartābhajās became intensely ambivalent regarding sexual rituals during the early nineteenth century as they responded to British Orientalist and Christian missionary critiques and gradually morphed into a more popular devotional movement.[105]

It seems probable that the Kulācāra lineage at Kāmākhyā reflects a similar pattern of reform, particularly around the question of sexual practices. We might therefore describe it as a sort of "right-handed left-hand" path, in which the first four *makāras* are understood literally and discussed fairly openly, while the fifth *makāra* of sexual union is surrounded with intense ambivalence. In fact, John Woodroffe long ago noted a sort of right-handed variant of the left-hand path, which is characterized by a more conservative view of the fifth M of sexual union: "We may distinguish not only between Dakṣiṇācāra and Vāmācāra in which the full rites with wine and Śakti are performed, but also between a Vāma and Dakṣiṇa division of the latter. It is on the former side that there is worship with a woman (Parakīya Śakti) other than the Sādhaka's own wife."[106] It seems likely that this "*dakṣiṇa*-leaning" strand of the *vāmācāra* became increasingly widespread during the nineteenth and twentieth centuries, as Tantric sexual practices became the target of increasingly hostile attacks from missionaries, Orientalists, and Hindu reformers, and a sort of "sweetened" form of Tantra spread across northeast India.

Aghorīs, Corpses, and Cremation Grounds: Transgression and Ritual Inversion on the Margins of Kāmākhyā

If many Tantric practitioners at Kāmākhyā Temple express deep ambivalence regarding the fifth M of *maithuna*, this is not always the case with many other Tantric groups who visit the site. Because of its long reputation as the homeland of Tantra and as a quintessential land of black magic, Assam is a major destination for all variety of practitioners from across South Asia, including the most extreme and unconventional *sādhus*. Among others, Kāmākhyā is a favored site for many of the black-clad Aghorīs—those "without fear."

Aghorīs have long been infamous across India (and now the world, thanks to CNN programs and YouTube videos[107]) for their extreme acts of transgression, such as smearing their bodies with ashes from cremation grounds and consuming liquor from human skulls. Yet even the Aghorīs have experienced internal debates and divisions around the role of transgressive Tantric practices. As Jonathan Parry and Ronald Barrett have shown, the Aghorī tradition in its homeland of Varanasi has undergone a profound transformation in the contemporary period. In the last several decades it too has become an "increasingly 'domesticated' and respectable institution which has lost much of the sinister awe with which it was regarded." In part, this domestication appears to be an attempt by the current head (baba) in Varanasi to appeal to a more respectable middle-class audience: "It has . . . become progressively 'Vaishnavised'—a trend which has no doubt been encouraged by the baba's rapidly expanding middle class following."[108]

Other Aghorī communities, however, have not only continued to engage in more extreme left-hand practices but often carried them to even more transgressive extremes. One of the most interesting of these is a group of

FIGURE 1.3. Aghorīs at the Bhūtnāth cremation ground, Guwahati, Assam, 2018. Photo by Prema Goet.

about thirty Aghorīs from Tamil Nadu who make an annual trip by train to Kāmākhyā each summer during the time of Ambuvācī Melā. As we will see in more detail in chapter 6, Ambuvācī Melā is the largest festival held at Kāmākhyā and celebrates the goddess's annual menstruation, which is believed to bring life to the earth and grace to her devotees. For this South Indian Aghorī group, however, Ambuvācī is also an important occasion for the performance of some of the most extreme left-hand sorts of practices.

The scholar and photographer Prema Goet has done some remarkable research among this Aghorī group, traveling with them and filming many of their rites. While not initiated into the tradition, Goet has befriended the group and been given access to many of their otherwise quite secret practices. In 2018, he photographed their rites held at the Bhūtnāth cremation ground, which lies just to the east of the Kāmākhyā temple complex on the Brahmaputra River and is a favorite hangout for Aghorīs and various other *sādhus*.[109]

The leader of the group is Maṇikaṇdan Aghorī, also known simply as "Gurujī." During the nighttime rituals, Gurujī wears a heavy garland made of eleven human skulls, his body smeared with the *pañcamakāra* mixture. Almost all the members of his community come from Tamil Nadu, with the significant exception of one Englishman named Richard from Newcastle. Richard had served as a paramedic working in war zones such as Syria and then traveled to South India, where he encountered this group of Aghorīs.

Perhaps the Aghorīs' direct and frank acceptance of death was a meaningful and even therapeutic experience for Richard.

Another unusual feature of this Aghorī group is that it includes a number of *kinnaras* (also known as *hijṛās*)—that is, individuals who were born biologically male but live and dress as females.[110] As Goet explains, the reason for the inclusion of *kinnaras* is that the lineage had originally included women who provided the female fluids used in rituals, but at some point in history they lost access to female partners and so began to use *kinnaras* as sources of female seed: "The women are all transgender; they are all biologically male. The reason for this is that this specific group of group of Aghorīs, they can extract *dravya* from a woman, the seminal fluid from a woman, but because they have lost their lineage of whoever they can have sex with and extract the fluids form, they somehow at some point in history joined forces with the *kinnara-kāra*, and the *kinnara-kāra* has taken the role of the female *śakti*, and even though having biologically male bodies, they do produce female seminal fluid and they use it for creating the *pañcamakāra*."[111]

While the main Kāmākhyā temple was closed for the goddess's menstruation, the Aghorīs created their own temporary *yoni pīṭha* at Bhūtnāth for the duration of the Melā. This practice is indeed significant, insofar as the main temple is meant to be closed to all visitors during the goddess's menstrual impurity, whereas the Aghorīs have chosen to make this same period of impurity the most important time for their rituals. This focus on the menstrual period as an impure yet powerful and "auspicious" time has resonance throughout South Asian mythology and ritual. For example, the mythical founder of Assam was the demon king Naraka, who was said to have been conceived by Lord Viṣṇu and the goddess Earth during her menstrual period.[112] Some Tantric texts such as the *Yoni Tantra* also recommend sexual union with a female partner during her menstruation—an act that is normally considered highly impure but is regarded as the most potent time for ritual union in some traditions.[113] And other Tantric-related sects, such as the Bāuls, also see the woman's menstrual period as the optimal time for sexual rituals. The Aghorīs' decision to honor the *yoni* during her annual menstruation is clearly in continuity with these other Tantric traditions that highlight the dangerous power of menstruation.

The central focus of the Aghorī ritual is a triangular fire altar comprised of three concentric layers. The first, outer layer represents Viṣṇu; the second, middle layer represents Brahmā; and finally, the third layer represents Kālī/Kāmākhyā as the *yoni* or vulva. The rituals performed over the course of the four nights involved corpse worship (*śava sādhanā*),[114] spirit possession, numerous animal sacrifices, and consumption of the Aghorīs' own unique version of the *pañcamakāra*.

FIGURE 1.4. Aghorī performing corpse ritual at the Bhūtnāth cremation ground, Guwahati, Assam. 2018. Photo by Prema Goet.

While the primary Tantric lineage centered at Kāmākhyā sees itself in continuity with Vedic traditions, the Aghorīs make a far more radical point of inverting Vedic practices and most other social and religious norms. One of the more striking examples is an Aghorī performing an *añjali*—normally an act of supplication, obeisance, and reverence toward a deity or an honored person, with the hands held together and head bowed—in this case sitting on his head and using his feet instead of his hands.[115] Given the low symbolic significance of feet in South Asian culture, presenting them to a deity is doubly or perhaps triply transgressive.

The Aghorīs' unique mixture of the *pañcamakāra* also involves a complex series of social, religious, and ritual transgressions. In addition to the usual Tantric substances of meat, fish, grain, and alcohol (whiskey in this case), the Aghorī recipe also includes ashes from the dead and is held in a human skull. But perhaps most significantly, the Aghorī *pañcamakāra* contains a special kind of fifth M (*maithuna*), which is an unusual blend of sexual fluids. The guru in this case provides the male half of the fluids, the semen, but because this Aghorī lineage lost its source of female sexual fluids at some point, it has been using the "female seed" provided by his transgender partner, Lakṣmī Nārāyaṇa, who is the head of the *kinnaras*.[116] This practice, of course, adds a whole other level of social, sexual, and religious transgression that no doubt only amplifies the power and danger associated with this community and its Tantric rites.

In short, if the main Tantric lineage at Kāmākhyā represents a sort of "right-handed left-hand" tradition, the Aghorīs embody a distinctly "left-handed left-hand" form of Tantra. By no means grounded in the Vedas and *brāhmaṇic* practice, the Aghorī ritual is a deliberate inversion of conventional laws of social and religious purity. From using corpses and human ashes to consuming the sexual fluids of transgender individuals, the Aghorīs appear to be striving for what Georges Bataille calls a kind of "unlimited transgression," in which all boundaries between high and low, pure and impure, and finally even divine and human have been radically overcome: "In the region where the autonomy of the subject breaks away from all restraints, the categories of good and evil, pleasure and pain, are infinitely surpassed. . . . On this scale, the chain releases of atomic energy are nothing."[117]

In sum, while the more orthodox Tantric lineages remain deeply ambivalent regarding the nature of left-hand transgressions, these South Indian Aghorīs seem more interested in this sort of explosive and "unlimited" sort of transgression as the quickest path to radical non-dual awareness and a direct encounter with the oneness of reality.

Conclusions: The Path of Desire and the Politics of Respectability

To conclude, I would like to reflect on these different interpretations of the left-hand path and different Tantric understandings of desire. What are the cultural and historical reasons for this deep ambivalence toward *sexual* desire in particular, and why have some lineages rejected transgressive forms of Tantric sexuality while others have embraced them wholeheartedly? Or, to return to Deleuze's metaphor, why have some traditions restricted or "territorialized" the flow of desire while others have "deterritorialized" it in even more radical ways?

Much of the answer to this question, as I argued in this chapter, lies in a series of historical developments that took place within India and later as a result of European colonial influences from the sixteenth century onward. We see this trend beginning already with Hindu *bhakti* reformers such as Śaṅkaradeva, who attacked the bloody and sensual rites of the *tāntriks* in Bengal and Assam. These attacks were amplified by Christian missionaries, Orientalist scholars, and Hindu reformers of the nineteenth and twentieth centuries. Agehananda Bharati aptly described this reformist attitude as the "influence of Christianity, Gandhism, and the puritanism of an inceptive industrial India," which profoundly skewed modern understandings of Tantra, particularly its sexual aspects.[118] And then more recently, there is also the influence of "Neo-Tantra"—or what I have called "Tantra American Style"—which equates Tantra with sexual freedom and sensual pleasure. In sum, the concept of sexuality in Tantra has been burdened with multiple historical layers of negative, sensationalist, and often wildly distorted representations.[119]

What we find in the Kulācāra tradition at Kāmākhyā today, I think, is a deep tension that has emerged from these modern developments—namely, a tension between the desire to assert the status of Kāmākhyā as a powerful Tantric center and the need to preserve its reputation of *brāhmaṇic* purity and "respectability." As Sundari Johansen Hurwitt nicely put it, there is a simultaneous desire to advertise the site's "tantricity" while at the same time maintaining its orthodoxy by de-emphasizing the antinomian practices associated with Kaula traditions: "The community at Kāmākhyā has positioned itself very publicly as a timeless authoritative center of Tantric power and magic that nevertheless maintains orthodox sensibilities."[120] In the twenty-first century, this claim to respectability seems to center increasingly on questions of sexuality. While consumption of meat and alcohol is now common in modern India and a good deal less "transgressive" than it was several decades ago, sexuality appears to be in some ways even more fraught and surrounded with ambivalence, reservation, and silence. As Foucault famously put it, sex in modern societies tends to be seen as "*the* secret," and this phenomenon seems to be as true in contemporary India as in modern European society, although in different ways.[121]

Conversely, more radically antinomian groups such as the Aghorīs are not bound by such concerns about orthodoxy and respectability. On the contrary, they seize upon precisely the dangerous power of the left-hand path and sexuality, even exaggerating the transgressive, un-Vedic nature of their practice and deliberately inverting *brāhmaṇic* ideas of purity. And yet, such practices must be pushed to the margins of religious life, performed not in institutional spaces such as Kāmākhyā Temple but instead limited to cremation grounds in the dead of night.

As we will see in the remainder of this book, this tension between power and respectability—between the claim to tantricity and the assertion of orthodoxy—is one of the most persistent themes through the many forms of living Tantra today.

[CHAPTER TWO]

"The Land of Black Magic"

Healing, Enchantment, and Witchcraft

> *Tantra-mantra* and magic are completely different. I have seen a lot of black magic, but I would never practice it. I prefer not to speak about it.
>
> Phaṇīdhar Nāth (2017)[1]

> Real-time Hogwarts of India—Mayong Village!
>
> Vaibhavi Tiwari, *Indian Express* (2020)[2]

One humid afternoon in June 2017, I found myself sitting in the small home of Phaṇīdhar Nāth, one of the best-known healers (*bej*) of the village of Mayong. Earlier that morning, I had hired a young man with a motorcycle to drive me over muddy roads and crumbling bridges to meet some of the region's most famous practitioners of Tantric magic. A peaceful little town seated on the banks of the Brahmaputra River, next to a wildlife reserve and rolling tea gardens, Mayong today has a widespread reputation as the quintessential "land of magic."[3] There is a rich folklore surrounding Mayong that includes tales of sorcerers not only controlling all manner of spirits but also transforming themselves into animals such as tigers, pigs, goats, and others.[4]

The many manuscripts on *tantra-mantra* and magic found throughout the region and collected at the Mayong Museum do suggest that this area was historically important for magical practice.[5] Today, however, Mayong's reputation has been greatly amplified throughout the popular media as a place of mystery, magic, and supernatural power.[6] Indeed, there have been intense efforts to advertise the magical power of the village as part of a broader push to develop tourism at the nearby Pobitora Wildlife Sanctuary and adjacent hotels. When I visited in 2017, the museum even featured a large poster that depicted an altar laden with human skulls and silhouetted against a full moon, bearing the slogan "Welcome to Mystic Mayong." In the words of former state tourism minister Rockybul Hussain, "Preservation and promotion of sorcery practices is a part of our tourism promotion plan for Mayong. We plan to showcase the magical heritage of the village to attract tourists."[7] The many local healers are now widely sought after for their various areas of expertise, such as "snakebites, love magic, or exorcism."[8]

On the day that I first visited Phaṇīdhar Nāth, he was not in a very good mood. As it happened, two other visitors from Kerala were also there that day, and Phaṇīdhar had been asked to perform some of his healing for them shortly before I arrived. One of the visitors, Dr. Anup Ānandayogi, described himself as a Tantric initiate and a parapsychologist who was then traveling around India in search of paranormal phenomena. Dr. Ānandayogi had asked Phaṇīdhar to perform one of the most famous rituals of Mayong—the use of a special copper plate infused with *mantras* and applied to a person's back in order to heal back pain. Apparently, the technique had not worked, the patient felt no results, and Dr. Ānandayogi was loudly voicing the opinion that there was no real magic at work here. Phaṇīdhar, in turn, argued that his practice is definitely *not* magic (*jādu*) but rather *tantra-mantra*—a spiritual discipline that requires real knowledge, not mere trickery or sleight of hand. This same point is made by more or less every *bej* and *ojhā* in Mayong today.[9]

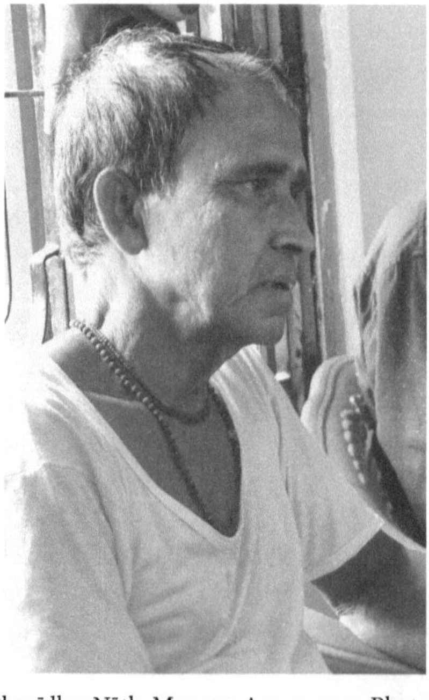

FIGURE 2.1. Phaṇīdhar Nāth, Mayong, Assam, 2017. Photo by the author.

WELCOME
TO
Mystic Mayong

FIGURE 2.2. "Welcome to Mystic Mayong" sign, Mayong Museum, Mayong, Assam, 2017. Photo by the author.

This skepticism toward Phaṇīdhar's healing and the debate over magic highlights a key tension in the contemporary role of Tantra in Assam (and in India more broadly). As a "path of desire," Tantra is concerned not simply with lofty philosophical ideas and the metaphysical dimensions of *kāma*; rather, it is also a matter of more practical desires for health, material well-being, success in business, and the ability to just get through the ordeals of everyday life. For most Indians today, as Glucklich observes, the term *tantra* is used "to connote mastery over complex ritual secrets that are intrinsically powerful, ancient, and dangerous in the wrong hands. . . . The ritual practitioner applies his skill not only . . . for the sake of spiritual liberation but for mundane reasons such as desire for wealth, financial success, and even the destruction of enemies."[10]

Yet for this same reason, Tantra is often dismissed by its many critics as either dangerous occultism or folk superstition—at best, as simple tricks to dupe the ignorant, or, at worst, as dabbling in the dark side of power. Ironically, even as Tantra has come to be almost completely identified with sexuality, optimal orgasm, and "nooky *nirvāṇa*" in the American popular imagination, it has become largely identified with *black magic* in the Indian popular imagination.[11]

This chapter explores the worldly side of desire by examining a range of popular texts and practices dealing with magic, healing, and enchantment. I begin with some historical texts from the region, such as the *Kāmaratna*

Tantra (The jewel of desire), which contains a vast array of rituals that range from practical healing to the infamous six acts (*ṣaṭ-karman*) of malevolent magic.[12] Today, this popular form of *tantra-mantra* is ubiquitous throughout cheap paperback texts sold in Bangla and Assam, which focus almost exclusively on the six acts of magic and the use of *mantras* for the fulfillment of worldly desires.[13]

At the same time, this sort of folk Tantra is also entwined in complex and sometimes violent ways with the darker side of magic—namely witchcraft. As we saw in the introduction, Assam has long been infamous as a realm of witches (*ḍāinī*) and black magic, and this reputation has continued well into the twenty-first century. Each year, dozens of people—mostly women—are attacked and killed in Assam for suspicion of witchcraft, and the local *ojhās* and *bejs* are often centrally involved in the accusations.[14] Much of this darker side of magic is, again, bound up with the power of desire—though in this case usually the desire for money, land, and/or revenge against individuals who are perceived to be rivals in particular social or economic disputes.

Finally, I explore the contemporary role of magic in villages such as Mayong, where the practice of *tantra-mantra* is widespread among local healers. Based on my time spent with practitioners such as Phaṇīdhar Nāth, Tilak Hāzarikā, and Prabīn Śaikīyā, I suggest that popular *tantra-mantra* has little to do with the elite philosophical traditions of classical Tantra. Rather, it is primarily a matter of physical and psychological healing, generally combined with traditional knowledge of local plants, trees, and animals used for medicinal purposes.[15] But recently, this folk practice has also been intensely advertised as part of a broader effort to promote Mayong and other parts of Assam as new sites of tourist development—what I will call "eco-magico-tourism"—in northeast India. Through an ironic sort of "auto-Orientalism,"[16] the mystical magic of Mayong has become a key selling in point in efforts to develop the region economically.

To conclude, I discuss the ways in which these *ojhās* struggle to navigate the multiple competing forces of magical authority, accusations of witchcraft, scholarly interest, media sensationalism, economic development, and tourism in the twenty-first century.

The Jewel of Desire: Magic—Benign and Malevolent—in Tantric History

The practice of magic remains one of the most pervasive and yet largely understudied aspects of Tantra, both as a historical tradition and as a living practice. While most of the popular literature on Tantra focuses on its sexual side, much of the contemporary scholarship has focused on the more elite philosophical aspects of Tantra; meanwhile, the widespread presence of magic throughout Tantric literature and popular practice has received relatively little attention.[17]

As Padoux observes, there is no single word that exactly corresponds to the English term "magic" in Sanskrit; moreover, the boundary between so-called magic and religion is not at all clear in Tantra (or in South Asia more broadly), since religious practice typically involves all manner of ritual acts aimed at influencing the spiritual and material realms: "The category of magic is chiefly a Western one, and . . . there is no word for 'magic' in Sanskrit. The word *abhicāra* may correspond to 'black magic' or 'sorcery,' but other 'magical' . . . deeds are a variety of ritual actions that are not different in essence from other rites. . . . The dividing line between religion and magic is far from precise."[18]

In a religious system where the entire universe is believed to be the effect of *māyā* (divine magic or illusion), "magical actions cannot but play an important role—a role particularly emphasized in Tantra."[19] As such, references to both malevolent and auspicious forms of magic can be found in early Buddhist Tantras such as the *Guhyasamāja*, throughout Hindu Purāṇic and Tantric texts such as the *Agni Purāṇa* and *Bṛhat Tantrasāra*, and above all in later compendia such as the *Indrajālavidyasaṅgraha*.[20] As Aaron Ullrey has shown, a large body of magical texts emerged during the medieval period, and similar works continue to be composed in modern times.[21]

Most of the later magical texts focus on a set of rites known as the *ṣaṭkarman* or "six acts," which first appear as a set in the circa twelfth-century text the *Śāradātilaka*. Here they are listed as *śānti* (pacification), *vaśya* (control), *stambhana* (immobilization), *vidveṣa* (creating enmity), *uccāṭana* (eradication), and *māraṇa* (death).[22] This list from the *Śāradātilaka* is repeated more or less verbatim in much of the later magical literature, including most pop-Tantra books one finds on street corners in Kolkata and Guwahati today.[23] However, some texts name the six acts a bit differently, including the rites of *ākarṣaṇa* (attraction), *mohanam* (delusion), and *puṣṭi* (acquisition).[24] As Gudrun Bühnemann explains, only one of the magical acts in these lists—*śānti*, or pacification—is generally classified as a form of benevolent magic. All the others are forms of *abhicāra*, that is, malevolent magic or sorcery: "Appeasement is defined as the curing of diseases; it is an auspicious, benevolent rite, whereas the others are destructive in nature."[25]

One of the more important Tantric texts found in Assam, which seems to be a key historical source for much of the popular magic that we see today in the region, is the *Kāmaratna Tantra*, or "jewel of desire." An Assamese version of the text was written on strips of *sāñci* bark and "kept in great secrecy" by a branch the Nā-Gosāin family of North Guwahati, which had historically served as the gurus of Assam's kings. Estimated to be at least three hundred years old, the text appears to be an Assamese translation of an earlier Sanskrit work attributed to Nāga Bhaṭṭa.[26]

A large portion of the *Kāmaratna Tantra* deals with the *ṣaṭ-karman*, although it lists them a bit differently than the *Śāradātilaka* quoted above. As we read in the opening lines of the text: "Now a discourse between Śiva and Parvatī. One day, Parvatī asked Śiva, 'O Lord, reveal to me the *Kāmaratna Tantra.*' Śiva said, 'Parvatī, I will tell you the times and methods for accomplishing the acts of subjugation [*vaśa*], attraction [*ākarṣaṇa*], causing dissension [*vidveṣaṇa*], immobilization [*stambhana*], killing [*māraṇa*], and pacification [*śāntipuṣṭi*].'"[27] The powers claimed for these magical acts are impressive indeed. As the *Kāmaratna* declares, everyone and everything, from rulers and lovers to animals and insects, can be controlled by the power of *mantra*: "The king [*nṛpati*], the son, relatives, beasts, and birds of the mountains or elsewhere, are brought under subjugation."[28]

Yet despite these grand claims, most of the techniques described in the *Kāmaratna* are far more mundane and practical in nature, having less to do with subduing kings than dealing with daily household nuisances. These include rites for preventing fire (*agni stambhana*), killing lice (*keśat okṇī nivāraṇa*), removing house pests (*gṛha kleśa nivāraṇa*), and protecting crops (*kṣetrā bandhana*).[29] In many respects, the text reads less like a manifesto for controlling the world than a practical manual for dealing with the various mundane annoyances of everyday life.

The rituals in the *Kāmaratna* are a fascinating mixture of practical advice, a specific knowledge of herbology, and a loose form of sympathetic magic. In some places, the recommendations are based on an idea of hidden connections, which is common to many systems of magic and esoteric traditions more broadly. As Antoine Faivre suggests in his work on esotericism, the idea of "correspondences"—the belief in deep symbolic connections between multiple levels of the material and spiritual realms—is central to almost all European esoteric traditions.[30] This idea is also present in South Asian traditions from the time of the Vedas onwards, and it becomes central to later Tantric texts such as the *Kāmaratna*. For example, in order to cause impotency, one is advised to bury a black hairy caterpillar in the place where the man urinates; conversely, "the removal of the caterpillar from that place restores his potency again."[31] Similarly, in order to cause quarrels, one should keep the seeds of the *saurā* and *bogori* plums together in one's house, or in order to become invisible, one should grind the liver of a black cat in oil, make it into a paste with leaves of the China rose, and apply it to the eyes.[32]

As we can see from these various examples, much of the "magic" in the *Kāmaratna* deals with a detailed knowledge of plants, animals, minerals, and other aspects of the natural world. Indeed, the text names hundreds of different plants, trees, roots, herbs, and animals used for magical purposes, along with very specific details on the proper places, times, and techniques for harvesting them.[33] Magic here is as much a kind of indigenous medicine based on botanical knowledge as it is a technique of interaction with supernatural forces.

The text does spend a great deal of time on what we can generally call "sexual matters," but these have little to do with the ideals of optimal orgasm discussed in American popular literature. Instead, the text focuses primarily on more mundane sorts of sexual problems, such as causing conception in a barren woman (*janmabandhyār garbhadhāraṇa*), preventing miscarriage (*garbhaśrava nivāraṇa*), increasing the size of the male organ (*liṅga sthūlīkaraṇa*), and so on. The techniques are usually basic home remedies combined with *mantras* and the use of local plants and animals. Thus, in order to "cause menstruation" (*ṛtukaraṇa*), one should consume the excreta of a house pigeon mixed with honey; in order to "stop menstrual flow" (*raktanivāraṇa*), conversely, one should plaster the vagina with a paste made of ground husked rice and the bulb of a water lily; in order to induce abortion (*garbhaśrava*), one should apply sesame oil and salt into the vagina; for "removing vaginal hair" (*rom utpāṭana*), one should plaster the excreta of a new born buffalo-calf over the vagina at night; and for enlarging the male organ (*liṅga sthūlīkaraṇa*), one should apply a paste made of long pepper, salt, milk, and sugar.[34] In sum, the sorts of sexual matters that are of most concern in the *Kāmaratna Tanta* have little in common with *The Complete Idiot's Guide to Tantric Sex*. Rather than addressing desire in the sense of sexual pleasure, the text is far more concerned with the desire for reproductive health, genital hygiene, and either aiding or impeding pregnancy.

While the *Kāmaratna Tantra* may be one of the best-known magical texts from Assam, it is hardly the only one. Throughout the region, there are countless manuscripts on paper and *sāṅci* bark on the topics of *mantra*, *tantra*, and magic. Dozens of these are housed in the Mayong Museum, with titles such as *Mohinī*, *Mantra*, and *Mantra Puthi*,[35] and contain a variety of spells for healing, protection, love magic, and combatting enemies. Most of the manuscripts were collected by Utpal Nāth, a local folklorist, who estimates that there are hundreds of similar magical texts scattered throughout homes and temples across the region.[36]

However, if large numbers of popular Tantric texts were produced in the pre-modern era, this genre has exploded with the development of modern print technologies. In the last fifty years, there has been a massive

FIGURE 2.3. Cover image of *Ādi o āsal Kāmarūp Kāmākṣā Tantramantra Sār*, edited by Śrīvasiṣṭha (Calcutta: Sajal Pustakālay, n.d.).

proliferation of booklets and pamphlets on the topics of *tantra-mantra*, magic, and sorcery. In general, these modern pop-Tantra texts are in continuity with the medieval magical texts or "grimoires" discussed by Ullrey,[37] usually recycling earlier works on the *ṣaṭ-karman* and translating them into vernacular Bangla, Hindi, and Assamese. However, in their modern print form, they almost always feature lurid covers with sinister *tāntriks* performing corpse rituals and other nefarious rites in cremation grounds surround by skeletons and terrible forms of the goddess. Most of these works also focus primarily on the goal of desire in its most material aspects, as we see in titles such as *Tantra Mantre Maner Icchā Pūraṇ* (The fulfillment of one's heart's wishes by *tantra* and *mantra*) and *Sarvva Manaskāmanā Siddha Pustak* (The book for the achievement of all one's desires).[38] The last of these has a vivid cover illustration with a *tāntrik* priest making offerings into a fire, above which hovers the face of a three-eyed goddess, while a wife and husband pray beside him. On the back cover, we see a woman holding a plate of offerings, while images of a beautiful home, a loving husband, a nice car, and a stack of money floats dreamily around her. Clearly, this is a text aimed at very this-worldly sorts of desires.[39]

Many of these popular booklets are also explicitly identified with Kāmarūpa as the "land of desire" and the geographic source of magical power. These include titles such as *Kāmarūpī Tantrasāra* (The essence of Kāmarūpa Tantra) and *Ādi o Āsal Kāmākṣyā Tantrasāra* (The original and true essence of Kāmākhyā Tantra).[40] While these booklets do contain some basic discussion of Tantra and the use of *mantras*, their primary focus is almost universally on the six acts of magic, particularly the more malevolent rites such as *vaśīkaraṇa* (subjugation). At least prior to the advent of Bollywood, it has been largely through these inexpensive but widely circulated booklets that the idea of Tantra as "black magic" has spread throughout the Indian popular imagination. With their lurid covers and ubiquitous presence, these cheap publications have clearly helped perpetuate the association of Assam with Tantra and of Tantra with dangerous power.

Witchcraft and the Dark Side of Desire

In addition to its reputation as a "land of magic," Assam has a rich tradition of folk narratives about witchcraft, demons, and the dark side of the supernatural. Many of the popular narratives about witches and haunted sites were cataloged by folklorist Benudhar Rajkhowa in his 1905 book *Assamese Demonology*.[41] Since the publication of Rajkhowa's text, Assam's reputation as the "land of witchcraft" has been increasingly solidified in the popular imagination.

The widespread belief in witches in Assam lies at the complex intersection between broader South Asian Tantric traditions and local folk narratives. The Assamese word *ḍāinī* is derived from the Sanskrit *ḍākinī*, which plays an important role in both Buddhist Tantra and in Śākta Hinduism. While in Buddhism, *ḍākinī* are typically guardians of esoteric knowledge, in Hindu Śākta traditions, the *ḍākinī* are fierce and dangerous attendants of the goddess Kālī, known for feeding upon human flesh: "Her chief characteristic is greediness. She is a cannibal. . . . her mouth waters and the lower lip protrudes as soon as she happens to see a man in front."[42]

Throughout Assam and other parts of northeast India, the term *ḍāinī* is also applied to certain human actors—namely those accused of witchcraft or malevolent magic. Like the *bejs* of Mayong, witches are believed to be able to shift into animal form; however, they are also said to cause all manner of sickness and destruction through their sorcery: "The belief that witches can cause drought, disease, death of children and livestock with a curse is common. It is also believed that . . . the person can change forms, i.e., from human to animal and vice versa."[43]

Today, Assam holds the dubious distinction of having the greatest number of witchcraft accusations and witch killings in India. According to a study from 2020, 107 individuals were killed because of witchcraft accusations in the years since 2011.[44] It is also important to note that witchcraft accusations are highly *gendered* in Assam (as in most parts of the world). While most of the *bejs*, *ojhās*, and practitioners of *tantra-mantra* that we find in places such as Mayong are male, by far the majority of those accused of witchcraft are women. The former are believed to *learn* their craft, while the latter are said to be *born* with their malevolent powers. As Anjali Daimari notes, "When a woman practices [traditional medicine] it's considered to be something evil."[45] Much of the way witch-accusations work, Daimari argues, is by isolating a woman from her community, her family, and her fellow women—thereby allowing other material interests to come into play, such as driving the woman off or stealing her land.[46]

The greatest number of witch-accusations come from largely tribal areas, particularly in the Bodoland districts of Kokrajhar, Baksa, Udalgiri, and Chirang. They also tend to be in areas that generally have less economic development, few educational opportunities, and little access to health care. According to a detailed study by the Partners for Law Development, "What distinguishes areas where witch hunting is practiced from areas where it is not are the development indicators, economic prosperity, access to education, basic needs and healthcare. . . . Poor performance in these areas combine to make the beliefs the dominant lens through which reality, mishaps, and conflicts are viewed."[47]

In most cases, the same study found, witchcraft accusations are triggered by a few common factors. On the one hand, accusations are often sparked by some sudden calamity, such as illness, tragedy, or the unexpected death of a human or animal; on the other hand, they are often closely tied to more personal conflicts over material resources. Most often, these conflicts involve "disputes over land, intentions to grab land or houses, attempts to offset legitimate claims to property, jealousy over the prosperity of the victim's family due to their economic entrepreneurship or holding more property."[48] In other words, these accusations are also often about *desire*—most often, a desire for land, a desire for wealth, a desire for revenge, a desire to silence those who question the status quo, or sometimes just a desire to find a simple explanation for the misfortunes of human life.

Not surprisingly, the instigators of witchcraft accusations are usually known to the victim, especially to neighbors, relatives, and co-workers. And it is often unusually assertive, independent, and outspoken women who tend to be the most common targets of the accusations, particularly those who challenge authorities or ask uncomfortable questions: "The personality of the victim, particularly her assertiveness and characteristics that set her apart as different or transgressive, also become a reason for labelling. . . . An outspoken woman who challenges . . . rather than accepts male dominance . . . tends to get silenced through witch hunting."[49]

Meanwhile, the mostly male *ojhās* and *bejs* are often involved in the accusations and brought in to help confirm the reality of a "witch." Given their expertise in *tantra-mantra*, they are frequently consulted expert witnesses to support one faction's claim that the accused is indeed a practitioner of malevolent magic and sorcery: "Anxieties and grief in these situations play into existing tensions between the parties, or are manipulated by *ojhas, deodhanis* (local or indigenous priests), or such local healers, who confirm the accusations. The *ojhas* do not introduce the idea of a 'witch'; they confirm the idea and perform or reinforce the accusation."[50]

For example, one accused witch was a middle-aged married woman from the Rongdani Rabha community (a scheduled tribe) of the Goalpara district. She and her accuser had an amicable relationship until the accuser's wife became sick and blamed the woman for the illness. An *ojhā* was then brought in to confirm the suspected witchcraft: "The perpetrator's wife fell ill for a while, and she would often say that she used to see the victim in her dreams. This made the perpetrator and his wife suspect that the victim was a witch and that she was responsible for the disease. The perpetrator consulted an ojha about the issue, and the ojha backed up their suspicion."[51]

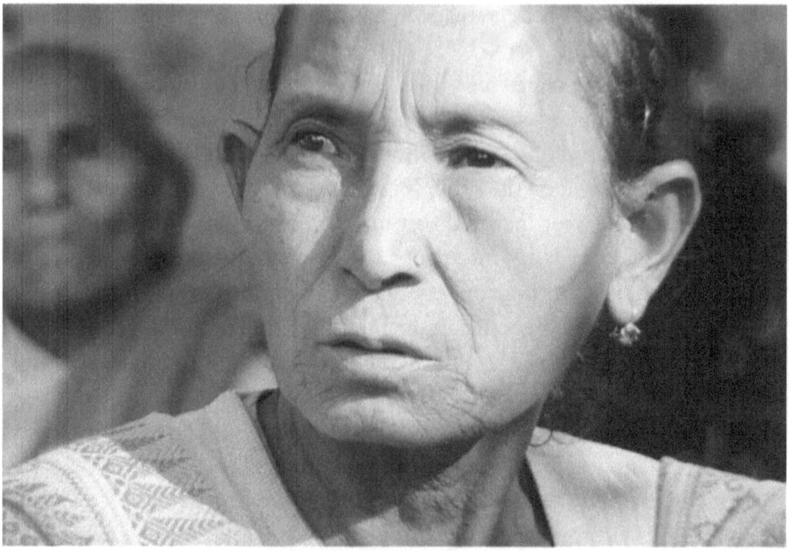

FIGURE 2.4. Birubālā Rābhā, Goalpara, Assam. Photo by Arjitsenmail. CC BY-SA 4.0, https://creativecommons.org/licenses/by-sa/4.0.

When the wife of the accuser finally passed away, the victim was kidnapped and killed by three men wearing army uniforms.

In another case—this one among a Boro community in the Goalpara district—a woman was accused of witchcraft by two of her relatives. During a marriage ceremony, the bride lost consciousness twice, and the wedding guests attributed this misfortune to the evil powers of a witch. Again, they called for an *ojhā*, who, "after performing some rituals and uttering some mantras," claimed that he was able to identify the witch behind this misfortune. The accused witch then fled for her life. But her house was burned down, and she was never allowed back into village.[52]

In recent years, there have also been efforts to combat the epidemic of witchcraft accusations that have spread across the northeast. Perhaps the most powerful figure in this struggle is Birubālā Rābhā, a humble woman from the village of Thakurvila in the Goalpara district. As Rābhā recalls, she herself once believed in the reality of witchcraft and in the power of *ojhās* to identify witches. But in 1985, her son fell seriously ill, and an *ojhā* diagnosed him as possessed by evil spirits. Meanwhile, one of her own relatives accused her of causing the illness herself by means of witchcraft.[53] When her son did not in fact die, she had a kind of awakening and decided that these so-called healers were charlatans who were deceiving and exploiting poor people like herself: "I realised that innocent villagers were being duped."[54] In the years that followed, she traveled to many other villages in Assam and Meghalaya where women were being accused, tried, and beaten as suspected *ḍāinīs*. Thus she recalls traveling to Lakhipur, Assam, where five women were accused of witchcraft: "That is when I woke up. I went to the village and found that the women had been abused and were on the verge of being thrown out. I met the local leaders. . . . I told them there were no witches in this world, and that women should not be harassed."[55]

In 2011, she also created an organization called "Mission Birubālā," which is dedicated to spreading information and protecting the rights of individuals accused of witchcraft across the region. It was largely through Birubālā's efforts that the Assam Witch Hunting (Prohibition, Protection and Prevention) Act was proposed in 2015 and passed in 2018.[56] Although Birubālā herself has no social media skills and says she has never even seen a movie, her organization now has an active online presence, with its own Facebook page and YouTube channel, which circulate videos, press releases, and other content. While these sites may not be as titillating as the many YouTube videos advertising "Mystic Mayong," they have played an important role in spreading awareness of the rampant problem of witch hunting across India.[57]

Significantly, however, Rābhā sees her work not only as a struggle against ignorance and prejudice but also a battle against patriarchy and the use of superstition to oppress women. Like many of the scholarly observers quoted above, she astutely notes the fact that the vast majority of those accused of witchcraft are women, while the majority of the *ojhās* involved in identifying them as witches are men: "I believe in my fight for womanhood against patriarchy," she said, adding: "The quacks, who are mostly men, brand the women as witches."[58]

Despite the best efforts of Rābhā and others, however, witch-accusations continue to plague Assam and other states in the northeast. In October 2020, for example, a woman in Assam's Karbi Anglong district was lynched, beheaded, and set on fire by an angry mob after she and a man were accused of using black magic to cause a girl's illness.[59]

Tantra-Mantra and Magic in Mayong

The small town of Mayong is just one of many sites for the popular practice of *jādu* and *tantra-mantra* today, but it has become easily the most famous in the last century through scholarly literature, media reports, and more recently, YouTube videos.[60] The historical and mythological origins of Mayong are the subject of much speculation and narration. As Rameś

Candra Nāth notes, there is a wide variety of opinion as to the etymology of the name itself, some tracing it to the Sanskrit term *māyā* (magic, illusion), some tracing it to *mār aṅga* ("limb of the mother," meaning one of the severed limbs of the Goddess that fell to different parts of the earth, forming the network of *śākta pīṭhas*), and others tracing it to the indigenous Tiwa word *miyaṅg*, meaning "place of elephants."[61] Much of the contemporary literature on Mayong attempts to link it to older historical sources, particularly to the great epic the *Mahābhārata* and the character of King Ghaṭotkaca, who was known for his magical powers.[62]

While many claim that Mayong's status as the "land of black magic" can be traced back to the ancient past, it seems likely that it is a more recent creation. *Tantra-mantra* and magic are practiced in many sites all along the Brahmaputra valley, but Mayong began to be singled out in the twentieth century, particularly with the publication of texts such as Benudhar Rajkhowa's early book *Assamese Demonology,* mentioned above.[63] As Rajkhowa put it in his 1905 text, "Mayong . . . has been noted for witchcraft for years. The people keep *daini* [witches] and other spirits in their houses. They send them to any man whom they want to injure. They bring good things from other houses by sending a *daini.* The emissary is offered a *pooja* and is sent out of her mission with these words: 'Back when I bid you. Away with my enemy unless he calls on me and satisfies my demand.' The people have places reserved in the dark secluded parts of their houses for pooja to the ghosts."[64]

Today, as Sean Dowdy observes, Mayong has a national if not international reputation as a realm of sorcery and dangerous power, where its many *bejs* and practitioners of *tantra-mantra* offer all manner of benevolent and malevolent magic. Ironically, this reputation is now one of the main drivers in the small but rapidly growing Mayong tourism economy:

> Sorcery is something Mayong is . . . most famous for. Rumors circulate across Northeast India—and now across much of the sub-continent—of Mayong being a center of dangerous black magic, inhabited by sorcerers (*bej*) who can inflict harm or manipulate one's intentions from a distance. In Assam, it is not uncommon to hear Mayong referred to as *jadur dex* (country of magic) or *bhoyonkor dex* (country of fear/danger), a place where anyone could be a potential victim or practitioner of sorcery. . . . Mayongians are quick to remark that whether or not one *believes* in sorcery, it nevertheless *exists* as a social-cum-economic reality, efficacious and easily caught up in. Indeed, throughout Assam, healing and harming through preternatural means is one of the fastest growing industries.[65]

Particularly through the power of the internet and the "ubiquity of cell phones," Dowdy notes, "the clientele of Mayong's bej have grown 100-fold over the past decade."[66]

Today, there are an estimated three hundred or so *ojhās*, *bejs*, and other practitioners of *tantra-mantra* in the Mayong region. While by far the majority of these individuals are male, folklorist Utpal Nāth has also documented several female *bejanīs*, such as Mohani Devī, Bhadrā Devī, Anumāyā Devī, and Cucilā Devī. According to Nāth's account, we should note, virtually all these women practice arts of healing and preparation of traditional medicine from plants and herbs, rather than the more occult and malevolent magic practiced by some of the male *bejs*.[67]

Like the members of the Kulācāra Tantra Mārga at Kāmākhyā, these folk healers have their own complex bodies of secret knowledge, which they carefully guard and transmit from generation to generation. As Ülo Valk notes, based on his research in the region: "I can only guess how much is kept hidden from me in these interviews, because of certain restrictions concerning the secrecy of magic. I have recorded many *mantras* but I know that many of them have not been recited completely in order to maintain their power. Some *bejes* have not been willing to show me their ancient magical manuscripts (*mantra-puthi*) that have been handed down within the family circles."[68] Indeed, the secrecy surrounding the magical knowledge of the *bejs* and *ojhās* is surely a large part of their aura of mystery and power, as well as their continuing authority as ritual specialists.[69]

There is a large body of legend, folklore, and gossip surrounding the practice of magic in Mayong. One of the oldest and most persistent narratives is that the *bejs* of Mayong have control over animals, particularly tigers, which were (at least until recently) a real presence in the region. Thus, Rameś Candra Nāth tells the story of a famous healer named Curābej, who was active around 1960 and was able to stop and even kill tigers through the power of *mantra*. He also had various other abilities to control snakes, dispel ghosts, and so on: "Using *mantras* for binding tigers and counteracting poison, he was able to kill tigers. In his lifetime, he was famous for killing about forty tigers. . . . Wherever a tiger began causing trouble by killing animals, they would call for Curābej to kill the tiger. Apart from tiger-binding *mantras* and poison *mantras*, Curābej also practiced infatuation mantras . . . snake charming *mantras* . . . *mantras* for controlling ghosts and spirits, and others. People used to come from Bihar, Bengal, Orissa, and Uttar Pradesh to learn *tantra-mantra* from him."[70]

Another key belief about the magical practitioners in Mayong is that they can capture and manipulate certain spirits called *bīrās*. Powerful yet ambivalent entities, *bīrās* come in many different forms—such as spirits of people who died unnatural deaths—and can theoretically be caught and controlled. Through the power of *mantra*, the *bīrā* can be deployed for a wide range of practical purposes, such as "collecting information from faraway places, [or] stealing something from other households to attack rivals and enemies physically—beating them, pulling their hair or disturbing them."[71] Valk interviewed a number of *bejs* in Mayong who claimed to have employed *bīrās*, including one who said that he had up to five in his service. However, *bīrās* are dangerous and fickle beings who also need to be fed and honored in their own way, typically with blood sacrifice. According to *bej* Jatin Deka, "for some *biras* human beings should be offered, for some *biras* goats should be offered."[72] We should note that (like other parts of Assam), Mayong also has a long reputation for the practice of human sacrifice. A large cave in the Mayong hills is alleged to have been a site of human sacrifice, and, in 2009, a number of huge sacrificial swords were discovered, with speculation that they were used for human offerings.[73]

The actual practice of magic in Mayong today, however, is generally a good deal less spectacular than lycanthropy or human sacrifice. Rather, as Utpal Nāth explains, it is mostly concerned with healing and protection from illness: "Almost all of the practice and application of *mantras* by residents of Mayong village are used in the desire to cure various illnesses."[74] As in the *Kāmaratna Tantra*, much of the practice at Mayong centers on sexual issues. But again, these are issues that have little to do with sexual pleasure (à la the *Complete Idiot's Guide*) but instead with more practical sexual problems, such as pain during menstruation, vaginal infections, and difficulties conceiving a child. As one *ojhā*, Khogen Nāth, explains, "I prepare medicine for leukorrhea [vaginal discharge] from the roots of seventeen different plants. My mother prepares medicine for couples who are unable to conceive for a long time after marriage."[75]

"Welcome to Mystic Mayong": Tantra, Magic, and Tourism

While Mayong has a widespread reputation as a land of mystery and magic that dates at least as far back as Rajkhowa's 1905 book, there has been a concerted effort to promote that reputation just in the last decade or so. When I first began to research Mayong, I was initially struck by the number of tourism websites promoting Mayong as "India's Black Magic Capital" and even as "India's Own Hogwarts—And It's Not Even Fictional!"[76] Meanwhile, I was even more surprised by the number of videos circulating on YouTube with titles such as "Witchcraft, Tantra, and Black Magic in

India," most of which amplify this reputation of mysterious power, danger, and tantalizing allure.[77] Indeed, there is even a campy music video based on the song "Māyaṅgare Bej," which features a comical, black-clad *tāntrik* who conjures a troupe of singers and dancers from his magic bottle.[78] As Dowdy notes, there has clearly been a kind of "hyping of Mayong as a tourist spot (with *tantra-mantra* as a focus)" along with an odd sort of "shared auto-Orientalism"; that is to say, many Mayongians have not only internalized the Western perception of the "mystic Orient" but also promoted their own image as a land of exotic magic.[79]

When I first visited Mayong in 2017, I went to see the newly constructed Mayong Museum, which was just down the road from my hotel. Built directly across from the area's primary tourist attraction, the Pobitora Wildlife Sanctuary, the museum is quite strategically located. Since 2017, the museum has been expanded and refined, though it retains its clear focus on magic and *tantra-mantra*. When I visited again in 2022, I noted that the garish, Bollywood-style poster "Welcome to Mystic Mayong" was no longer on display, yet most of the museum's exhibits still prominently featured the region's various *bejs* and *ojhās*, along with stories about their magical deeds. The majority of these deeds are acts of healing, such as curing back pain, stomach pain, and eye problems with *mantras*; treating snake bites; applying a *mantra* to salt to cure indigestion; preparing juice from herbs to expel tapeworm; and so on. Other magical rites are more a kind of defensive magic, such as counteracting the effects of black magic, locating an occult object that had been hidden on someone's property in order to destroy the owner, or rites of exorcism for the expulsion of ghosts and spirits (*bhūt-pret khediboloi*). Finally, some examples include acts of malevolent magic, such as preparing an amulet to cast the *mohinī* (enchantment) spell on opponents or hurling charmed duck eggs to attack a person in the dark of night.[80]

The museum also documents a wide variety of animal and plant species used by the *bejs* in their work. These include, for example, cobra fang, tigress vagina, tortoise nail, cow heart, rhino hide, bat flesh, porcupine tail, owl heart, deer antler, butterfly scale, rattlesnake head, stem of black arum plant, root of Amari tree, and various other barks, roots, and leaves.[81]

The primary individual behind the creation of the Mayong Museum and this push to develop the region as a tourist destination is Dr. Utpal Nāth, the local folklore enthusiast mentioned above. As Dowdy observes, Nāth "has definitely played a huge role in making *tantra-mantra* a centerpiece of Mayong tourism—and attracting capital."[82] The author of several essays and books on the history of magic in Assam, Nāth is quite up-front about his desire to promote Mayong as a new kind of spiritual tourist destination and source of economic development: "These days, many people are turning to alternative medicines and faith-healing. Our practitioners have been doing this for generations, and we can use this . . . to woo tourists. We also plan to showcase scriptures on sorcery and rituals associated with magic."[83]

Nāth observed that tourists were already coming to Mayong to visit the wildlife sanctuary, so it only made sense to begin promoting the town itself as a tourist destination due to its long history of magic, mystery, and folk methods of healing: "To promote tourism in Mayong, we can put up magic shows and offer treatments for various ailments through our traditional folk medicine. . . . Today, most of the tourists visit Mayong for Pobitora. But we want to promote Mayong for itself. If we add some magic to its rich past and heritage, it will throw open a brand new tourism opportunity."[84]

In fact, Nāth even went so far as to write his own play about Mayong that prominently featured its magic and *ojhās*, which was performed in Guwahati and was clearly designed to attract tourist interest in the region.[85] His play was also performed at the Mayong Festival held in 2011, which was explicitly designed to promote tourism by highlighting both the region's natural resources and its Tantric reputation. As one Morigaon district officer put it, "Our intention is to promote tourism through Mayong's culture, tradition and wildlife. This festival is one of a series to attract tourists. Mayong has the potential to become a popular tourist attraction."[86]

This push toward tourism and economic development has even been embraced by the figure known as the "King of Mayong" himself. To this day, Mayong retains an honorary seat for a local king that is currently held by Taraṇī Siṅgha, who was coronated in 2005. King Siṅgha suggests that the involvement of Assam's youth could also be an important factor in reviving the magical traditions of Mayong, since there will be a need for future generations to continue these ancient practices and present them to new, more contemporary, and perhaps global audiences: "There has to be active involvement from the young people if we are to revive our ancient magical practices and showcase it to the outside world."[87]

When I returned to Mayong for a second research trip in 2022, I found that the push to develop the touristic and economic potential of the region had not only continued but grown exponentially. I was immediately struck by the number of new hotels in the region—which had at least quadrupled since 2017—and particularly the construction of six or seven new beach resorts along the Brahmaputra River. While some locals have welcomed this new influx of tourist income, others have lamented it as yet another example of state and national politicians conspiring with corporate interests to drive out indigenous communities (in this case, the local Miyas, a community of Muslims who migrated from Bengal and now live along the river). In Dowdy's opinion, this development reflects a confluence of corporate, nationalist, and economic interests that were already in play under the previous Assamese state prime minister (Tarun Gogoi) and were just now coming: "Private interests had been pushing the development of resorts like these for a long time, it's just that by 2018 there was enough intense xenophobic political capital that could force the issue and kill two birds with one stone. Tarun Gogoi's government definitely paved the way for all of this, especially in equating tourism with development (the extension of nationwide neoliberal policies promoted and encouraged by the state)."[88]

There is now a growing body of good scholarship on the complex dynamics of "ecotourism," which is a widespread phenomenon in most parts of the globe today, with often controversial social, political, and environmental effects.[89] But perhaps we could use the phrase "eco-magico-tourism" to describe yet another new form of global travel to sites such as Mayong, where the forces of religion, capitalism, and nationalism all intersect, specifically around the reputation of exotic magic. Moreover, as we will see below in chapter 5, these efforts at advertising and promoting *tantra-mantra* and magic are not unique to the town of Mayong; indeed, they are part of a broader push to develop tourism in the region around the allure of magic, mystery, and Tantra, which is perhaps most obvious in recent attempts to promote the main festival at Kāmākhyā, Ambuvācī Melā.[90] For better or for worse, this "touristification" is one of the prominent themes of modern Tantra as it enters the age of globalization and neoliberalism.

The Varieties of Magical Experience: Three Healers in Contemporary Mayong

During my research in Mayong in 2017 and 2022, I was able to spend some time with several well-known practitioners of magic and *tantra-mantra*. Three of these in particular stand out—Tilak Hāzarikā, Prabīn Śaikīyā, and Phaṇīdhar Nāth—because they reveal the broad spectrum of Mayong's magical practices, which range from the more philosophical and "bookish" to the more occult and fearsome. They have also received some of the most widespread media attention through YouTube films and numerous journalistic accounts.

A friendly, soft-spoken, middle-aged man, Tilak Hāzarikā does not actually self-identify as a *bej* or *ojhā* but rather as someone who is simply very knowledgeable in the realm of *tantra-mantra*. As he explained in a mix of Assamese and English, "*tantra* is an 'Indian philosophy.' It is based on the idea that 'All is God.' God is in everything, so *tantra* is a way of using that divine power. It works through the power of *mantra* [*mantra-śakti*]."[91] The

FIGURE 2.5. Tilak Hāzarikā, Mayong, Assam, 2017. Photo by the author.

skilled practitioner is able to access this power much like a "radio tower" can access invisible radio waves, and he can then use that energy to effect change in the physical world: "Through meditation and religious devotion, one can access the powers/forces of the universe that we cannot see . . . they concentrate and spiral down through all things into the bej, who if performing the proper rituals and keeping himself free of pollution and sin, can wield that power for other purposes. Actually, for any purpose because [śakti] allows the bej to improvise and use creative thoughts to change reality."[92] In his view, *tantra-mantra* is thus not a matter of superstition but rather a practice rooted in a scientific understanding of how the universe works: "I am a schoolteacher by profession and a person with a reasonably logical bent of mind," he explained, asserting that his spells all have some form of "scientific basis."[93]

Hāzarikā also makes an absolute distinction between *tantra-mantra* and black magic or *jādu*; while the former is based on the Vedas and requires spiritual discipline (*sādhanā*), the latter is at best crude illusion and at worst malevolent sorcery: "The practices of Mayong are not black magic. There is no sorcery whatsoever involved. It is entirely a matter of the power of *mantra*."[94] Whatever black magic practices there ever had been at Mayong, he asserts, were dispelled from the region several decades ago, when the local residents took up all the harmful spells and "drowned" them (that is, immersed them) in the river: "There was a really dangerous *mantra* called the *kal diksha*, which was used to kill people. This too was drowned in the river."[95]

When I visited Hāzarikā's home, I noticed a copy of the *Atharva Veda* on his bookshelf. He explained that Tantra is ultimately based upon the four Vedas—*Ṛg*, *Yajur*, *Sāma*, and *Atharva*—and particularly upon the fourth of these, the *Atharva Veda* (a text that does contain a number of magical rites, including *mantras* for healing, curing snakebites, charming prospective lovers, and so on).[96] Unlike other healers who received their instruction from their fathers or gurus, Hāzarikā claimed to be largely self-taught, finding an interest in the subject at a young age and gradually learning more over time. While he is known for a wide range of healings, curing snake bites is one of his specialties.

Hāzarikā also seemed well aware of the growing reputation of Mayong as the "land of magic." His home—seated right on the main road—has been increasingly visited by journalists, scholars, and curious tourists in recent years. Hāzarikā appeared to be quite proud of his reputation as a master of *tantra-mantra*, though he repeatedly went out of his way to dismiss any association with witchcraft or sorcery, which he described as dark parts of the past that have no place in modern India.

FIGURE 2.6. Phaṇīdhar Nāth with handwritten notebook of *mantras*, Mayong, Assam, 2017. Photo by the author.

In contrast to Tilak Hāzarikā, Phaṇīdhar Nāth much more readily embraces the title of *ojhā*. Indeed, thanks to YouTube and other social media, Phaṇīdhar is among Mayong's more famous *ojhās* today and has been sought out for interviews by numerous filmmakers, journalists, academics, and curious tourists. Although a farmer and a mason by trade, he also comes from a line of *ojhās* and learned his skills from his father, who in turn learned from his own father, and so on. Like other *ojhās*, Phaṇīdhar's practice relies primarily on the use of a wide range of *mantras*, which he collected from his father on scraps of paper and bound together in a small, tattered notebook. However, he also made it clear that mere possession of a text is not sufficient and that one also needs deeper knowledge and skills—particularly knowledge of medicinal plants and the skill to use them correctly—in order to perform an act of healing: "It requires a great deal of concentration," he explained; "the *bej* must focus on a plant or substance and use it to find the cure for the problem."[97] Prior to the dominance of modern secular medicine, he believes, most healing in India was performed by *ojhās* using traditional methods such as *mantras* and herbs, and many locals still rely on these techniques.

Phaṇīdhar claims that his practices can help with a wide variety of physical, social, and supernatural needs; they can cure wounds, alleviate pain, find lost objects, and dispel malevolent magical influences. But he is also adamant that his practice of *tantra-mantra* has nothing in common with black magic: "*Tantra-mantra* is one thing, black magic is quite another [*tantra mantra bastu beleg, jādu to beleg*]. It's difficult to master *tantra-mantra*. But black magic is all a matter of trickery and deception."[98] Like virtually all the current *ojhās* of Mayong, Phaṇīdhar also distances himself very firmly from anything smacking of witchcraft, immediately dismissing the idea that his practice has anything to do with the malevolent work of *ḍāinīs*.

When I talked to him for a second time in 2022, Phaṇīdhar was also quite aware of—though seemingly a bit mystified by—the new interest that the outside world was showing in the magic of Mayong. He commented that many journalists, scholars, and tourists from all over India and even other countries had recently been stopping by to see him.[99] He seemed a bit perplexed by the flood of national and international curiosity about what had previously been a local, private, and not particularly "exotic" practice that mostly involved *mantras* and traditional medicine. Yet he also did not seem to mind the new attention, since it had clearly raised his public profile and added to his status, authority, and symbolic capital—not to mention offering some more immediate material capital to his rather modest finances.

If Tilak Hāzarikā emphasizes the more philosophical aspects of *tantra-mantra* and Phaṇīdhar Nāth emphasizes its benign, healing aspects, Prabīn Śaikīya is more open about its more supernatural, occult, and potentially dangerous dimensions.[100] The grandson of the famous Jalou Bez of Ougori village, Prabīn Śaikīyā is widely known as one of the most fearsome practitioners of the region and generally the most up-front about practices such as exorcism, control of ghosts and spirits, and human-animal transformation.

When I met him in 2022, the seventy-year-old man was in the midst of a complex operation that involved winding and unwinding a bunch of cotton threads around his left big toe. After wrapping the threads in a series of complex patterns multiple times, he divided them into individual threads, tied them with a set of knots, and began reciting a long series of *mantras*. Repeatedly throughout the process, he was also interrupted by his mobile phone ringing, which his wife handed to him to talk to before returning to the ritual. When he was finished, he placed the threads in a plastic bag and explained that they had been prepared in order to protect the bearer from ghosts and spirits (*bhūt-pret khedā*). We then had a lengthy conversation about what it means to be a *bej*, the nature of Tantra, and the power of *mantra*.[101] Prabīn is highly regarded for his mastery of the more esoteric and occult side of *tantra-mantra*, including not only the ability to ward off ghosts and spirits but also to create amulets (*tābji*) charged with the power of *mohanī*, or the ability to enchant or hypnotize one's enemies.[102]

FIGURE 2.7. Prabīn Śaikīyā, Mayong, Assam, 2022. Photo by the author.

In addition to his actual magical practice, Prabīn is also a fascinating repository of stories about the various abilities now or at one time attributed to the *bejs* of Mayong. Among other things, the *bejs* have long been said to be able to not only control but to transform themselves into a variety of animal forms, including pigs, dogs, and others.[103] The most famous stories center on their ability to become were-tigers, and there are numerous accounts that provide at least a partial description of the ritual script used to transform oneself into such a beast. According to Prabīn, the ritual requires a banana leaf on which one makes tiger markings; then, lying naked upon the leaf, one recites the appropriate *mantras* and magically assumes the tiger form: "You need a long, tender, curled banana leaf, one with a black node at the top end. This can be cut only on certain auspicious days. . . . Then lay it on the ground. Put stripes on it with vermillion and mustard oil—making it like a tiger. Place the leaf facing north. You must be in a very lonely place, completely naked, and lie down on the leaf, uttering mantras. You have to keep turning from left to right, suddenly you become a tiger."[104]

Unfortunately, Prabīn did not know the secret *mantra* that was the final key to achieving the full transformation into tiger form. His uncle had apparently died before imparting this last crucial piece to the ritual formula. Prabīn also observed that supernatural practices of this sort used to happen much more frequently in his childhood but had declined in recent years due to changing perceptions of magic and modern life. They stopped, he said, when "the light of civilization came to the village" and people understood that such practices were not good.[105]

Of course, one question soon arises once one begins hearing these various claims to occult powers: To what degree do ordinary lay people actually believe in this sort of magic? Even within the small village of Mayong, opinions about *tantra-mantra* and the power of these *ojhās* vary dramatically. For example, I interviewed one young man who worked in a local hotel near the wildlife sanctuary. An ardent believer in the power of the *ojhās*, he proudly asserted: "I definitely have faith in them. I have seen them heal my family members, and I myself have been healed." He leaned down to show me a spot on his ankle where he had once been bitten by a snake, explaining that it had been cured by Phaṇīdhar Nāth with the help of *mantras* and herbs.[106]

Meanwhile, Anupam, the young man who drove me around town on the back of his motorcycle, was a profound skeptic. A worshipper of Kṛṣṇa himself, he thought all this *tantra-mantra* was a thing of the past, something that had once been important in the region but was now increasingly irrelevant.[107] This skeptical view was echoed by a priest from Kāmākhyā, who happened to be having dinner at the same hotel where I was staying one evening. "You can't get something for nothing," he said. "If you want to eat, you have to work for it. There are no free meals from magic."[108] Other residents of Mayong were even less charitable in their view of the *ojhās*. When I asked one retired schoolteacher about it, he laughed and said, "I'll show you '*tantra-mantra*.'" He then showed me two kernels of corn and asked me to close my eyes. Taking my hand, he crossed my index and middle fingers and rolled them across the kernels in the palm of his own hand. "How many kernels did you feel?" he asked. When I said, "two," he laughed and showed me that it was actually just a single kernel, which had created a perceptual illusion in my crossed fingers that made it feel like two. "There is your magic, your *tantra-mantra*! Now, will you take me to America and make me famous?"[109]

Still other residents of Mayong, however, describe the role of the *ojhā* in more sociological and psychological terms. For example, the manager of the hotel where I stayed in 2017 talked in detail about Tilak Hāzarikā's practice, which he interpreted as more a kind of interpersonal healing. In his opinion, Hāzarikā's chief skill was his ability to resolve interpersonal problems such as marital disputes, family relations, and domestic squabbles. To bring peace or *śānti* to a troubled household, he explained, Hāzarikā might talk to the family members and then give them a locket blessed with *mantras* as a means to resolve the issue.[110] Indeed, this hotel manager's analysis was surprisingly similar to that of some modern anthropologists such as Victor Turner, who used the phrase "social drama" to describe the work of religious rites and magical practices. In Turner's model, ritual practices often function as a kind of dramatic performance through which a community can address a particular interpersonal conflict and provide some form of "redress or reconciliation" between the conflicting parties.[111] In this sense, the *ojhā*'s role seems reminiscent of that of multitasking religious specialists in other traditions, such as Haitian Vodou. As Karen McCarthy Brown describes the role of the Vodou priestess or *manbo*, she "combines the skills of a medical doctor, a psychotherapist, a social worker and a priest."[112] While my hotel manager did not use this exact academic language, that was basically the gist of his intuitive and rather astute indigenous interpretation.

Thus, even in one small village such as Mayong, we encounter a striking example of the "conflict of interpretations" discussed above in the introduction. As we will now see, this conflict seems to be growing even more intense with the advent of new communications technologies such as cell phones and the internet, as information about the magical mysteries of Mayong circulates ever more widely and rapidly to a global audience.

Conclusions: Navigating Tantra, Magic, and Witchcraft in the Age of YouTube

To conclude, I would like to reflect briefly on the complex nature of *tantra-mantra*, magic, and witchcraft in the twenty-first century, particularly in the wake of new forms of economic development and new technologies such as cell phones and social media. As I suggest in the figure 2.8, *tantra-mantra* in modern Assam could perhaps be imagined as the central knot or "node"[113] within a complex web that consists of many conflicting interests, forces, and desires. While many members of the local community see it as a genuine form of healing and as a religious practice, many Indian scholars and European anthropologists view it as an intriguing example of local folk practice continuing in the twenty-first century. Meanwhile, it has also been seized upon by government entities for the purposes of tourism and economic development, in the hopes of capitalizing on the supernatural as a new kind of "eco-magical" tourist destination. It has, in turn, become a widespread media spectacle through the networks of YouTube, Facebook, and other platforms. And finally, all these developments have also brought increased allegations of fraud, chicanery, and perhaps also witchcraft or black magic.

What is perhaps most interesting is the way in which local healers and their critics have tried to navigate all these competing desires. That is, how have local *ojhās* such as Phaṇīdhar Nāth, Tilak Hāzarikā, and Prabīn Śaikīyā—as well as skeptics such as Birubālā Rābhā—negotiated these multiple views of *tantra-mantra* in an age of globalization and social media? After all, these *bejs* and *ojhās* benefit in many ways, in terms of both symbolic and material capital, from the new waves of tourism and from Mayong's YouTube reputation as a "land of black magic." They share in the same sort of "auto-Orientalism" that now pervades much of Mayong, embracing and

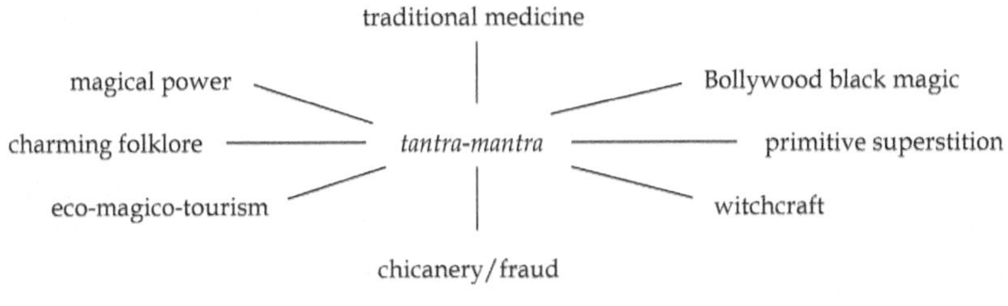

FIGURE 2.8. Diagram illustrating *tantra-mantra* as central node in a complex web of conflicting interests, forces, and desires.

promoting the image of the mystical-magical Orient. Yet at the same time, they also clearly want to distance themselves from the more sensationalist images promoted through tourist websites and videos, which consistently associate them with sorcery, witchcraft, and demonology. And they clearly want to evade the accusations of "quackery" leveled by modern activists such as Birubālā Rābhā, who are increasingly using social media to try to debunk and discredit *tantra-mantra* altogether.

In this sense, I would argue, the *bejs* and *ojhās* of Mayong are attempting to strike a delicate balance that is similar in many ways to that of the Kulācāra Mārga at Kāmākhyā discussed in chapter 1. That is to say, they want to assert their reputation of occult power and "tantricity" while also distancing themselves from witchcraft and black magic. As we see in the magical practice of Phaṇīdhar Nāth, Tilak Hāzarikā, and Prabīn Śaikīyā, there is a clear desire on the part of the practitioners to retain their reputations as healers and wielders of occult power, but there is an equal desire to distance themselves from anything even remotely smacking of witchcraft or of practices that are deemed to be too far outside the pale of "real" religion.

Yet they each strike this delicate balance in a somewhat different way. Tilak Hāzarikā does so primarily by describing his practice as a "science" that is ultimately rooted in the Vedas, a deep understanding of the laws of the universe that has nothing to with superstition or sorcery. Phaṇīdhar Nāth does so more by emphasizing the benevolent and largely innocuous aspects of his work as a traditional healer. Rather than dark or malevolent magic, he describes his practice as a kind of pre-modern folk medicine that simply uses the *mantras* handed down to him along with some basic knowledge of local plants. Finally, Prabīn Śaikīyā is perhaps the most interesting of the three, insofar as he seems to enjoy playing upon his reputation as one who really *does* work in the dark arts, as one who can deal with ghosts, as one who possesses at least part of the ancient powerful magic of Mayong, such as the ability to become a were-tiger.

In short, each of these practitioners is navigating this complex set of tensions in a slightly different way, yet they all seem to reflect a basic ambivalence surrounding their status as practitioners of *tantra-mantra*, with its concomitant risk of association with sorcery. Meanwhile, critics such as Birubālā Rābhā want to fundamentally deconstruct this dynamic altogether, by unmasking the male *ojhās* as frauds while debunking the very idea of witchcraft as a dangerous patriarchal myth. As we will see in the remaining chapters, this ambivalence surrounding the power and danger of Tantra is a recurring theme throughout much of its living practice today.

[CHAPTER THREE]

The Politics of Sacrifice

Blood Offerings and the Struggle over Local and National Identity in Modern India

> Blood that is purified by *mantra* is always praised as nectar. The goddess consumes the head as well as the blood. Therefore, in worship, he should offer the bloody head of the sacrifice.
>
> *Kālikā Purāṇa* (tenth or eleventh century)[1]

> There are many temples across the country where "bali" (sacrifice) is performed but there is no such concept of sacrificing any animal or bird in the name of god in Hinduism. . . . The Vedas do not say anything about this brutal act, and thus this system has to be banned.
>
> Sangeeta Goswami, chairperson of People for Animals, Assam (2010)[2]

In June 2002, King Gyanendra of Nepal visited Kāmākhyā Temple in order to perform the ritual of *pañcabali*, or "five sacrifices." As the offering of a buffalo, a goat, a sheep, a pigeon, and a duck, the rite is not uncommon at Kāmākhyā Temple, where blood sacrifice is a daily occurrence and a large-scale event on major holy days.[3] Yet Gyanendra's visit came in the midst of massive protests against animal sacrifice in his homeland of Nepal and at a time of growing tensions in India, where both Hindu nationalists and animal rights activists had been protesting the practice since the 1990s. Upon Gyanendra's visit, an animal rights group lodged complaints with the local police, arguing that the *pañcabali* is illegal under India's 1960 "Prevention of Cruelty to Animals Act."[4] In light of the protests, the king chose to simply offer a basket of fruit and some prayers to the goddess, and then discreetly left the temple. Shortly after his departure, however, the priests promptly slaughtered the five animals on his behalf.[5]

This incident involving King Gyanendra and the controversy in Assam is just one telling example of a much larger debate surrounding the history, practice, and politics of sacrifice in contemporary India.[6] As Madeleine Biardeau and Charles Malamoud suggest in their classic 1976 work *Le sacrifice dans l'Inde ancienne*, sacrifice is among the oldest, most consistent, and recurring structural themes through the long history of the complex body of texts and traditions that we now label "Hinduism." From the offering of domestic animals in the early *Vedas*, to the internalized sacrifice of yoga and meditation in the *Upaniṣads*, to the offering of devotional love in the *Bhagavad Gītā*, *yajña*, or sacrifice, is one of the most unifying threads in this vast tangle of texts, rituals, and cultural materials over the last 3500 years.[7]

In contrast to Biardeau and Malamoud, however, I will suggest that sacrifice is not simply a deep structural paradigm and symbolic motif that runs through the history of South Asian religions (though it is surely that). Rather, it is *also* a powerful "instrument of struggle" in Bruce Lincoln's sense—that is, a discursive weapon wielded amid a complex field of competing narratives and counter-narratives, in which various communities have sought to construct identities and define themselves against one another in relation to broader material, political, and economic interests.[8]

Historically, of course, ritual sacrifice and dietary practice have been key means of distinguishing one religious community or class of people from another in South Asia—for example, Vedic priests who administered sacrifice and Buddhist and Jain monks who abhorred it,[9] or Hindu Śāktas who worshipped powerful goddesses such as Kālī and Durgā with blood offerings and adherents of Hindu *bhakti* who called for unbloody offerings of devotional love,[10] or indigenous and low-class communities who continue to perform a wide array of sacrifices and modern reformers who have tried to fashion a new kind of Hindu identity that would be cleansed of these bloody practices.[11] In South Asian Tantric traditions, sacrifice has historically been both an important part of ritual practice and a key metaphor for internalized meditative practices (such as *antar-yāga*, inner sacrifice, or *kula-yāga*, clan sacrifice).[12]

Yet in the twentieth and twenty-first centuries, sacrifice—as both a symbolic trope and a literal practice—has taken on a number of new, often volatile political forms in the context of Hindu nationalism and struggles over local identities. Indeed, it has become one of the key markers of both national and regional politics, not only in the northeast states but across India more broadly. Ironically, however, the discourse of sacrifice has assumed several different and often contradictory forms, which I examine in this chapter. First, there is the regular use of the *discourse and symbolism* of sacrifice, which we see throughout Hindu nationalist descriptions of "Mother India" since the nineteenth century and particularly since Independence (such as the "great sacrifice," or *ekātma yajña*, for national unity held in 1983).[13] Second, however, there is the intense criticism of the *practice* of animal sacrifice at sites such as Kāmākhyā—often by the very same Hindu nationalists, who see this as a cruel, barbaric, primitive, and fundamentally "un-Hindu" form of worship.[14] And most recently, there have been efforts by priests at Kāmākhyā to redefine sacrifice, not as a kind of indigenous, Tantric, or non-Hindu practice but rather as a traditional Vedic ritual, in continuity with the cosmogonic *yajña* of the *Ṛg Veda* and the most orthodox rites of the *Brāhmaṇas*.[15] Together, these narratives and counter-narratives surrounding sacrifice represent some of the most volatile fault lines that crisscross the modern "nation and its fragments."[16]

To conclude, I suggest that the particular case of ritual in Assam opens up some larger questions about the politics of sacrifice more broadly, offering key insights into the study of ritual and collective identity. Perhaps mostly importantly, it highlights a central tension concerning desire, blood, and politics in modern India—a tension between the flowing blood of animals offered to the goddess in the hopes of fulfilling various worldly and otherworldly desires, and the nationalist desire to staunch or "territorialize"[17] the flow of blood by imposing a singular ideal of Hindu identity.

Sacrifice, Violence, and the Inner Conflicts of Tradition

If Biardeau and Malamoud are correct that sacrifice is a recurring theme throughout the long history of traditions that we now call Hinduism, the tension, ambivalence, and debate surrounding the practice is no less a recurring theme. As J. C. Heesterman observes in his classic study *The Broken World of Sacrifice*, conflict and contestation are inherent even in the early Vedic ritual, which is itself a complex battleground for a range of competing interests: "Sacrifice, then, is not just an edifying religious ceremony separate from man's worldly affairs. It is the arena of conflict and alliance, the field in which honor and position are to be won, the market for the distribution of wealth. . . . Combining in itself all functions—social, economic, political, religious—sacrifice is the catastrophic center, the turning point of life and death."[18]

Among other things, Heesterman argues, the Vedic sacrifice reflects a deep ambivalence concerning the violence involved in the killing of an animal. Rather than a bloody beheading (the form of sacrifice that we see throughout India today, such as at Kāmākhyā Temple in Assam), the Vedic rite calls for an unbloody suffocation of the victim outside the ritual space. Indeed, the Vedic sacrifice is repeatedly described as an act of "non-harming" that does not involve real death: "You do not die, nor do you come to harm, to the gods you go along paths good to go," the victim is consistently assured.[19] As Heesterman suggests, the Vedic texts reveal an attempt to rationalize the violence of sacrifice amid an abstract system of rules and technical details, while distancing it from popular, non-*brāhmaṇic*, and indigenous forms of slaughter: "What we know as Vedic sacrifice is not sacrifice *tout court*, to be put on par with its normal, popular practice as we find it to the present day in India. . . . Usually the victim is immolated by cutting off the head . . . but the Vedic ritual texts expressly reject this procedure. Instead, they prescribe that the victim be killed by suffocation outside the sacrificial enclosure proper. Vedic sacrifice, as it has been elaborated and systematized by the ritualists, has been resolutely turned away from . . . popular practices."[20]

The ambivalence toward sacrifice is articulated even more clearly in later parts of the Vedic corpus. Thus the *Muṇḍaka Upaniṣad* famously describes sacrifice as a "frail raft" or unsteady boat (*plavā hyete adṛḍhā yajñarūpā*)—an unreliable rite that is ultimately inferior to the path of renunciation for those who seek the true fire of the Self, not in outward ritual but in the interiorized practice of meditation.[21] Similar criticisms of sacrifice were, of course, voiced by Buddhist and Jain communities, which emerged at roughly the same time as the later *Upaniṣads* and rejected the Vedic rite in even more uncompromising terms.[22] As such, the killing and consumption of animals became a key point of debate, division, and negative self-identification among South Asian religious traditions from the fifth century BCE onward.

Blood Sacrifice and the Nation

The ambivalent status of sacrifice as both a discourse and a practice is thus hardly a recent phenomenon, but it has assumed new and intensely politicized forms since the nineteenth century. On the one hand, the use of the imagery and symbolism of sacrifice (*yajña, bali*) has been pervasive throughout Hindu nationalist rhetoric since at least the late nineteenth century. As Imma Ramos notes, the discourse of "sacrifice for the Motherland" was widespread during the late colonial era, particularly among nationalists who "hailed India as Bhārat Mātā and, as her sons, were willing to sacrifice their lives to obtain her freedom."[23] Revolutionary nationalists such as the young Aurobindo Ghose repeatedly used the image of the goddess Kālī as a symbol of Mother India in rage against her colonial oppressors, eager for the blood of sacrificial victims. In the words of the Bengali revolutionary paper *Jugantar* (The end of the age), India should be honored as Kālī, whose anger can only be appeased by blood offerings: "The Mother is thirsty and is pointing out to her sons the only thing that can quench that thirst. Nothing less than human blood and decapitated heads will satisfy her. Let her sons worship her with these offerings and not shrink from sacrificing their lives to procure them."[24] As Christopher Pinney has shown, nationalist art from this period also frequently portrayed the severed heads of freedom fighters offered as sacrificial gifts to the mother goddess, Bhārat Mātā (just as the heads of sacrificial animals were offered to the mother goddess Durgā, to whom she bears a very close resemblance).[25]

At the same time, however, the revolutionary nationalist's image of blood sacrifice was often mocked and dismissed by more moderate voices of the late nineteenth and early twentieth centuries. No less a figure than Bengali poet and Nobel prizewinner Rabindranath Tagore wrote a fictional account of the revolutionary nationalists, finally voicing an extremely negative appraisal of their sacrificial logic. In Tagore's classic novel *At Home and the World*, the character Nikhil expresses his (and the author's own) disillusionment with the nationalists and their bloody rites: "The Bengali contented himself with placing weapons in the hands of the goddess and muttering incantations to her; and as his country did not happen to be a goddess, the only fruit he got was the lopped off heads of the goats of the sacrifice."[26]

The ambivalent nature of sacrifice as both discourse and practice became perhaps even more acute in the decades following India's independence. As Parvis Ghassem-Fachandi argues, the *language* of sacrifice has been widely used by Hindu nationalists since the 1940s to describe the struggle for the purity of the Motherland, and yet the actual *practice* of animal killing has been increasingly denounced as barbaric and un-Hindu. Meanwhile, the ideal of *ahiṃsā* (nonviolence) has been used to highlight the difference between true Hindus (imagined as nonviolent, vegetarian cow-protectors) and both Muslims (imagined as meat-eating cow-killers) and indigenous populations (imagined as carnivorous, uncivilized primitives).[27]

Thus, on one side, we see the rhetorical use of sacrifice in nationalist political programs such as the great "sacrifice for unity" (*ekātma yajña*) sponsored by the Viśva Hindu Pariṣad (VHP) and other nationalist groups in 1983. A massive pan-Indian effort, the sacrifice was intended to ritually embody the unity of the nation by bringing holy water from the river Ganga to temples across India, where it was mixed and circulated in order to create the image of a vast, interconnected, sacred Indian nation as a "geographical unity" and "global social field": "Huge images of Mother India (Bharat Mata) were carried in chariots, and holy water from the Ganges was mixed in pots with water from other sacred rivers and sold to temples. The campaign is alleged to have mobilized some 60 million people, and processions traversing the subcontinent from Hardwar in the north to Kanyakumari in the south . . . covered some 85,000 kilometers."[28]

In 1984, this sacrifice was followed by a major procession of nationalist supporters to Ayodhya, the city believed to be the birthplace of the epic hero and divine *avatār*, Rāma. Again, this procession was described with the language of ritual, as a "sacrifice to liberate the place where Rāma was born" (*Rām janmabhūmi mukti yajña*).[29] In 1989, nationalist groups undertook an even more symbolically charged *yajña*, this time laying the foundation for a temple to Rāma on the site: "Sanctified bricks made of the 'local earth' in multiple places were transported together with *sevaks* to the radial center of Ayodhya, and, in reverse, earth dug in Ayodhya was redistributed to different parts of India."[30] All of this symbolic sacrifice helped lay the groundwork for the much more literal violence that erupted in 1992, when Hindu *sevaks* destroyed the Muslim Babri Masjid, which was believed to lie on Rāma's birthplace, unleashing massive riots and killings across India and Bangladesh.[31]

The nationalist use of sacrificial imagery was even more gruesomely explicit during the anti-Muslim violence that spread across Gujarat following the deaths of fifty-nine Hindu pilgrims on a train in 2002. As Ghassem-Fachandi persuasively argues, the violence in Gujarat followed a consistent sort of "sacrificial script," as both political and media accounts repeatedly described the acts with the language of *yajña*, building on the use of ritual imagery that has become common in nationalist discourse:

> Chief Minister Narendra Modi referred to the ongoing pogrom violence as a legitimate *pratikriya*, a term derived from the domain of ritual action. . . . The newspaper *Sandesh* surpassed these usages by supplementing with diverse other terms—such as *homaya* (ghee oblation into fire), *hutashan* (sacrificial fire), *holi* (ceremonial bonfire), and *katlean* (slaughter) . . . people were not only depicted as "burned alive" but also as . . . "sacrificed as food offerings" (*bhog bani*) . . . in a communally sensitive town like Godhra, which is referred to as the "communal center of sacrificial fires" (*komi hutashanio nu kendra*).[32]

Yet even as the language of sacrifice has been consistently invoked by Hindu nationalists, the *practice* of animal sacrifice has been repeatedly condemned as a violent, primitive, and non-Hindu ritual. Alongside the symbolic idea of "sacrifice for Mother India," the ritual killing of animals has been increasingly disavowed and replaced instead by ideals of *ahiṃsā* and vegetarianism. In the process, vegetarianism has been regularly politicized and used as a rhetorical weapon to critique Muslims, people from lower castes, tribal communities, and others who sacrifice and eat animals. Ironically, Ghassem-Fachandi concludes, the seemingly pacifist ideal of *ahiṃsā* became closely tied to the "aggressive nationalist posturing" that helped fuel the anti-Muslim violence in Gujarat: "Questions of slaughter and carnivorous diet dominate stereotypes and accusations against minorities,

FIGURE 3.1. "Corāsī Devatā Ovālī Gāy," lithograph (Maharashtra: Ravi Varma Press, 1912).

especially Muslims. . . . [V]egetarianism skillfully buttresses a discourse of pronounced stigmatization of Muslims."[33]

Not surprisingly, much of the debate surrounding sacrifice in modern India has focused specifically on the killing of *cows* (Sanskrit: *go*; Hindi: *gāy*; Assamese: *goru*; Linnean: *Bos taurus indicus*). As Rohit De explains in his detailed study of Indian law, "the question of cow slaughter had been a matter of public debate, sporadic violence, and, mass mobilization since the nineteenth century," particularly in response to British colonial rule.[34] The British were generally seen as a beef-eating people, and the cow emerged as a "powerful anticolonial symbol and became the focus of both mobilization and violence through much of north India."[35] For example, a series of popular lithographs from the colonial era depicted the major Hindu gods inside the body of a cow that was in turn giving milk to nourish her people. The body of the nurturing maternal cow thus became a powerful symbol of the collective body of India and specifically of "the greater Hindu community."[36]

In the late nineteenth and early twentieth centuries, however, this image of the cow-nation was often given a more explicitly pro-Hindu and anti-Muslim interpretation. In 1882, the first cow-protection movement (*Gaurakṣiṇī Sabhā*) was founded in Punjab and quickly spread across India. From its origins, as Peter van der Veer observes, the movement had both

Hindu nationalist and anti-Muslim motivations, as a defense of the cow-nation against her oppressors: "The Cow Protection Movement was particularly directed at defining the Hindu community against Muslim sacrificers and British rulers."[37] One of the most controversial images from this period was printed by the Ravi Varma Press in 1912, showing the cow-nation under attack by a hairy, dark-skinned figure while a pleading Hindu beseeched him to refrain. In the eyes of many viewers, the figure was understood to be a "Mohammadan with a drawn sword sacrificing a cow."[38]

With the coming of Indian independence and partition, the debates surrounding cows and sacrifice became even more intense, as did the association of cow slaughter with Muslims. For example, while Article 25 of the Indian Constitution called for the protection of the "right to freely profess, practice, and propagate religion," it only mentioned Hindus, Buddhist, Sikhs, and Jains in its description of religion, quite notably leaving out Muslims and other communities.[39] Article 48 also explicitly called for the prohibition of cow slaughter, insofar as "the State shall endeavor to organize agriculture and animal husbandry on modern and scientific lines and shall . . . take steps for preserving and improving the breeds, and prohibiting the slaughter, of cows and calves and other milch and draught cattle." The ban on cow killing was challenged most famously in 1957 in the case of *Mohd. Hanif Qureshi v. State of Bihar*, when Muslim petitioners argued that it placed both their religious freedom and in many cases their livelihoods in jeopardy. However, the Supreme Court upheld a majority of the cow-protection laws, ruling that "a ban on cow slaughter did not restrict the freedom of religion."[40]

Meanwhile, there were various other efforts in post-independence India to ban the sacrifice of *all* animals, not only cows. One of the first such legal moves was the 1950 "act to prohibit the sacrifice of animals and birds in or in the precincts of Hindu temples in the state of Madras."[41] As Donald Eugene Smith observes, this and other related acts were part of a broader attempt to reform Hinduism and to present a more "respectable" image of the newly established Indian nation to the outside world: "The reform of Hinduism had certain nationalistic as well as religious implications. In the West, the dominant impression of Hindu life still perhaps followed the lines of Katherine Mayo's *Mother India*. It was necessary to eradicate whatever primitive . . . practices tended to confirm this view. The international prestige of Hinduism and India would be raised by such legislation."[42]

Several members of the Madras Legislative Assembly made this point explicitly. As Tenneti Vishwanatham put it, the prohibition of sacrifice was very much a matter of defending the reputation of both Hinduism and of India as a whole: "I do not like any outsider, whether in this country or outside India, to point his finger of scorn and say: 'here are Hindus who kill animals in the name of religion.'"[43]

In more recent decades, debates over animal sacrifice have taken place across India, and laws against the practice have been passed in many states, including Andhra Pradesh, Gujarat, Karnataka, Kerala, Pondicherry, Rajasthan, Tamil Nadu, and Tripura (though sacrifice continues to take place at many temples in these areas).[44] As various observers have noted, the specific targeting of animal sacrifice has been part of a concerted strategy on the part of the BJP and other conservative parties to mobilize voters around notions of Hindu identity.[45]

Some of the most intense conflicts over sacrifice have taken place in Himachal Pradesh. Up through the 1960s, animal sacrifice was a common practice throughout the region, but it became increasingly contentious after 1971 once this geographical space was officially designated a state and brought into the larger body politic of the nation. As Mark Elmore suggests in his study of religion and secularism in the region, "Animal sacrifice became the most critical debate for Himachalis struggling to define themselves, their relations with their pasts, and their relations with Indian national culture."[46] In 2014, the High Court of Himachal Pradesh ordered a complete ban on animal sacrifice within the state, calling the practice "abhorrent and dastardly" and based on "superstitions" that have no place "in the modern era of reason."[47] This court ruling, Elmore argues, has ironically helped reinforce the role of sacrifice as a key marker of local religious identity in the region: "The prevalence of animal sacrifice at many popular tourist sites across the region has become a mark for drawing the lines between religion and state. Governmental administrators and reformers have passed laws prohibiting animal sacrifice, and reformers draw on long traditions . . . to legitimatize substituting the offering of intentions for the offering of live animals."[48]

In 2015, debates surrounding sacrifice reached the Indian Supreme Court, when it was asked to hear a plea to ban the slaughter of animals at religious festivals nationwide. According to the senior advocate in the case, Raju Ramachandran, these sacrifices are gruesome rites where animals are "slaughtered amidst frenzied paranoia" with a "celebration of barbaric and ancient practices that have their foundations in superstition."[49] In this case, however, the justices rejected the plea, concluding that the court "has to balance between the law and religious practices"; ultimately, achieving such balance means respecting the exemption for sacrifices carried out for religious purposes.[50]

Despite the court's ruling, there remains a profound legal stigma around the practice of sacrifice. For example, in the state of Tripura (adjacent to

Assam), animal sacrifice had long been a major part of worship at the key *śākta pīṭha* of Tripureśvarī, where large numbers of goats are typically offered on a daily basis. In 2015, sacrifice was banned by the state's government. In the words of Tripura chief justice Sanjay Karol, "All religions call for compassion, and no religion requires killing. Sacrifice of animals in the temple . . . is seriously morally wrong, for it is an act of illegally taking away of life."[51] When the Indian Supreme Court ordered a stay on the ban, sacrifice was allowed to resume at the temple—but now only behind a curtained area that could not be seen by visitors.[52] Sacrifice could continue, in other words, but only when kept carefully hidden from public view. A similar ruling occurred in the neighboring state of Bangla, where the High Court of Kolkata determined that sacrifices at the famous Kālīghāṭ temple (another key *śākta pīṭha*) could only be performed behind a wall, screening them from the public gaze.[53]

Sacrifice in Assamese History

The conflicts over animal sacrifice that we see throughout modern India have played out in particularly complicated ways in the state of Assam. From the earliest mentions of Kāmarūpa and Prāgjyotiṣapura in Sanskrit literature, this region has been associated with non-Hindu tribal religions and blood sacrifice. Since at least the time of the *Mahābhārata*, this area was described as a land of hill tribes, filled with mountain men (*kirātas*) and ruled by barbarian (*mleccha*) kings.[54] Later Assamese texts such as the *Yoginī Tantra* identify the religion of Assam simply as *kirāta dharma*, or the religion of the *kirāta* tribes, which includes the sacrifice of all manner of both domestic and wild animals.[55] To this day, Assam retains a reputation as a realm of tribal influence and various forms of sacrifice—both animal and human. Almost every year, in fact, there are at least one or two rumors of human sacrifice in the local media.[56]

The mythical origins of Kāmarūpa are themselves tied to a narrative of sacrifice. According to a well-known story found in various retellings in the *Brāhmaṇas*, epics, and *Purāṇas*, Lord Śiva was married to the goddess Satī, the daughter of Dakṣa. However, Dakṣa very much disliked his son-in-law, who was a fierce and frightening deity, so when Dakṣa arranged for a large sacrificial feast, he intentionally did not invite Śiva. The dis-invitation was such a profound insult that Satī committed suicide by throwing herself onto the sacrificial fire. In his rage, Śiva then destroyed the entire sacrifice, beheaded his father-in-law, and carried the corpse of Satī away on his shoulder. Because his fury threatened to destroy the entire universe, the other gods dismembered Satī's body; her severed body parts then fell in various sacred places, which in turn became the *śākta pīṭhas*, or seats of power. Her *yoni* fell in the realm of Kāmarūpa on Nīlācala Hill, where it is now revered in form of the large, vaginally shaped rock inside Kāmākhyā Temple.[57]

Evidence of animal sacrifice in Assam can be found from at least the fifth century CE. According to clay seals and copper-plate inscriptions from the Varman dynasty, King Mahendravarman (470–494 CE) performed two horse sacrifices in order to establish his independence from the Gupta Empire.[58] Royal sacrifices are described throughout the inscriptions and texts of all of the later Assamese kingdoms, from the Pālas (tenth to twelfth centuries) down to the Ahoms (thirteenth to nineteenth centuries). The *Kālikā Purāṇa*—the most important Sanskrit text composed in Assam—contains extensive ritual instructions for the performance of both animal and human sacrifice, as do later Assamese texts such as the *Yoginī Tantra*.[59] As the *Kālikā Purāṇa* declares, male deities such as Gaṇeśa, Śiva, and Kṛṣṇa can be worshipped with sweets, prayers, or religious vows, but the goddess's desire can only be satisfied with blood.[60]

However, the form of sacrifice described in the Assamese texts varies considerably from the ritual described in the Vedas and appears to be a complex mixture of *brāhmaṇic* practices and local practices drawn from Assam's many tribal communities. Historically, Assam and the surrounding northeast region have been home to South Asia's richest diversity of non-Hindu indigenous communities—including the Bodos, Chutiyas, Khasis, Jaintias, Rabhas, and dozens of others—most of whom had their own forms of animal sacrifice.[61] While we do see early references to horse sacrifice (the quintessential royal Vedic rite) in Assam, we far more commonly find sacrifices that are highly un-Vedic and even deeply impure from a *brāhmaṇic* perspective. In the Vedic rite, the animals offered are explicitly identified as "domestic," that is, as animals of the village in direct contrast to wild animals of the jungle: "Sacrifice," Heesterman notes, ". . . is intimately bound up with man's domesticated world. The Vedic ritual texts stress the opposition of *grāma*, 'village,' that is, the domesticated world, and the world of the jungle, *āranya*. Sacrifice typically has its center in the *grāma*."[62] According to the *Śatapatha Brāhmaṇa*, domestic or pure animals include horses, cows, goats, and sheep, while impure or wild animals include the *gaura* (buffalo), the *gavaya* (a species of ox), the wild camel, and the barbarian of the jungle.[63] Indeed, the *Brāhmaṇas* warn that all manner of disaster will ensue if impure, wild animals are offered: "If he were to perform the sacrifice with the jungle animals, father and son would separate, the roads would run apart, the borders of two villages would be far distant, and ravenous beasts, man-tigers, thieves, murderers and robbers would arise in the jungles."[64]

The sacrifices described in the Assamese texts, conversely, involve all manner of wild, non-domestic animals. According to the *Kālikā Purāṇa*, offerings to the goddess include a vast and diverse assortment of animals, including those explicitly listed as impure in the *Brāhmaṇas*, such as alligators, birds, buffaloes, lizards, lions, and elephants.[65] Other Assamese texts such as the *Yoginī Tantra* also recommend sacrifices of yaks, tortoises, and rabbits.[66] As various scholars have observed, this motley assortment of victims has little in common with any Vedic rite but rather reflects the local practices of the northeast hill tribes, such as the Bodos, Khasis, and Mechs, who regularly offered birds, boars, and other wild victims. The Mechs, for example, worshipped a local form of Śiva with buffaloes and pigeons, while the Kacharis presented him with "offerings of ducks . . . buffaloes and swine."[67]

Moreover, the manner in which the animal is killed in sacrifice to the goddess is quite different from any Vedic rite. Whereas the Vedic sacrifice called for an unbloody suffocation of the animal, the Śākta sacrifice centers on a quite bloody act of beheading, and the central focus is on the severed head and blood. "Blood that is purified by mantra," the *Kālikā Purāṇa* explains, "is always praised as nectar. The goddess consumes the head as well as the blood. Therefore, in worship, he should offer the bloody head of the sacrifice."[68] Again, this emphasis on the head and blood is almost identical to the normal practice among the northeast tribes, who typically behead the animal and focus primarily on the offering of the severed heard to the deity. In clear contrast to the unbloody pacification of the Vedic rite, Assamese tribes such as the Kachari offer the heads—"and as a rule only the *heads*"—as gifts to the deity.[69]

I should also note that the museum adjacent to Kāmākhyā Temple contains an impressive collection of hundreds of huge sacrificial swords from a wide range of historical periods, all clearly designed for the beheading of very large animals. This artifactual evidence would seem to confirm that the slaughter of buffaloes and perhaps other large species was practiced here for a very long time.

Desire as Flow: Sacrifice at Kāmākhyā Temple Today

At Assamese temples such as Kāmākhyā today, animal sacrifice is both a central part of the goddess's daily worship and a major event on holy days such as Durgā Pūjā, Kālī Pūjā, and Manasā Pūjā. As Deonnie Moodie notes, sacrifice to the goddess is very much about the circulation of desire through the flow of blood: "Practitioners . . . seek physical and visual access to sacrificed animals and their blood. They believe [the goddess] desires that blood and bestows her power and blessings through it"; and in turn, "devotees . . . offer sacrifices to [the goddess] and believe that it is she who accepts them and, in turn, grants them her immense power to achieve whatever they desire."[70]

Priests at the temple today typically make a distinction between formal *bali-dān*—the sacrifice of animals that are ritually offered to the goddess by *pūjārīs* at specific times inside the temple—and the many other animals that are brought by ordinary devotees and slaughtered at various times throughout the day.[71] The former category includes a he-goat offered every morning as part of the daily worship of the goddess and buffaloes on major holy days, but the latter includes not just goats but also large numbers of pigeons, fish, ducks, and sheep. The actual killing of the animals takes place at two sacrificial sites located just to the west of the temple's dance pavilion (*nṛtya maṇḍapa*). The first is centered on a tall, two-beamed post for the beheading of buffaloes, which looks directly onto the entrance of the *maṇḍapa*, and the second contains a short Y-shaped post for the beheading of goats and other small animals, which is adjacent to the buffalo post. The actual slaughter is performed by a special class of non-*brāhmaṇ* temple functionaries called *bali-kaṭās*, or those who "cut" the sacrificial animal.[72]

The daily worship, or *nityapūjā*, for the goddess begins each morning with the bathing of the *yoni pīṭha*. This is followed by the offering of the *naivedya*, which consists of rice, black gram, mustard oil, vegetables, and the sacrifice of a he-goat. The *pūjārī* first ritually infuses deities into both the sacrificial sword and the goat, after which the *bali-kaṭā* beheads the animal.[73] The blood is then collected in two bowls, and a lamp of ghee and camphor is placed upon the head, which is then offered together with the blood to the goddess. As Navamallika Sharma and Madhushree Das summarize the rite:

> [T]he main door is opened in the morning and at first the temple is cleaned. The red cloth covering the shrine is changed every day by the priests after the "*snana*" (bath) of the shrine. After getting the materials ready for worshipping from the "*bharalghar*" (store room) of the temple, main priest starts the processes of worshipping. A goat is sacrificed (*balidan*), and the blood of that goat is kept in two bowls in front of the goddess and the priest offers it to the goddess. . . . On the separated head of the sacrificed goat a "*Pradeep*" (lamp) of ghee and camphor is lighted and offered to the goddess. After completing the daily puja, the doors of the temple are opened for the pilgrims.[74]

The specific *mantras* used in the offering of the animal inside the temple are highly esoteric and known only to one specific lineage of priests from

FIGURE 3.2. *Bali-kaṭā* sacrificing goat, Kāmākhyā Temple, Guwahati, Assam, 2017. Photo by the author.

FIGURE 3.3. Sacrificial post for buffaloes, Kāmākhyā Temple, Guwahati, Assam, 2022. Photo by the author.

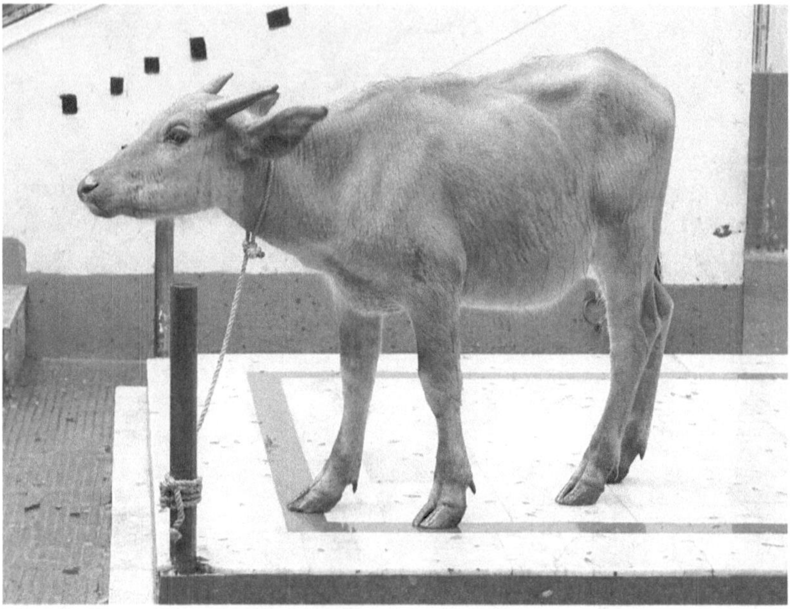

FIGURE 3.4. Buffalo waiting to be sacrificed, Guwahati, Assam, 2022. Photo by the author.

the hereditary Sebait family;[75] however, the general outline of the offering today is similar to what is described in the *Kālikā Purāṇa*, which instructs that a lamp should be placed on the head of the victim, which is then offered together with the blood to the goddess.[76]

While a he-goat is the daily offering, the most important offering to the goddess on major holy days is the buffalo (Sanskrit: *mahiṣa*; Assamese: *mah*; Linnean: *Bos gaurus*), which is sacrificed during key festivals such as Durgā Pūjā. Celebrating the goddess as the slayer of the buffalo demon (Mahiṣāsuramardinī), Durgā Pūjā involves the offering of pigeons, ducks, goats, and up to twenty buffaloes on the eighth (*mahāṣṭamī*) and ninth (*mahānavamī*) days of the festival.[77] The buffalo sacrifices are also typically accompanied by a great deal more fanfare, as crowds ululate and chant along with the crashing of cymbals and pounding of drums.

The central role of the buffalo in Śākta ritual is worth noting for several reasons. Unlike the domesticated cow, the buffalo was considered a wild (and thus impure) offering in Vedic sources such as the *Śatapatha Brāhmaṇa*. And yet, as Biardeau and Malamoud point out, its very impurity makes it the most fitting offering to the Goddess as Śakti, the destroyer of demons and the remover of impurity: "The buffalo . . . is a savage beast . . . a stranger to human society and the sacrificial world. The Vedic literature

FIGURE 3.5. Mahiṣāsuramardinī, Assam State Museum, Guwahati, Assam, 2022. Photo by the author.

does not count it among the permitted animals offered in sacrifice. But it is apt, by this fact, to play the role of the principal that is antithetical to the Goddess, the incarnation of total evil."[78] As we will see below, this complex relationship of similarity and difference between the cow and the buffalo continues to be a point of contention in contemporary debates over sacrifice in Assam.

"Throw Out the Blood": Criticisms of Sacrifice in Assam

As it did in other parts of India, the practice of animal sacrifice also generated intense debate and criticism at various points in Assamese history. The first major attack on the practice began in the sixteenth century during the *bhakti* revival led by the Assamese reformer Śaṅkaradeva (1449–1569). Like his other devotional revivalists, such as Caitanya in Bengal, Śaṅkaradeva championed love of god in the personal form of Kṛṣṇa as the supreme spiritual path, and like other devotional reformers, he targeted the Śākta practice of animal sacrifice as the worst and most dangerous form of spiritual delusion, leading its worshippers not to God but to the worst of punishments: "If he who decapitates animals in sacrifices and makes [the earth] muddy with the bloodshed can go to heaven, who else is destined to hell?"[79]

A second wave of attacks occurred during the British colonial era, when a wide array of Orientalist scholars, administrators, and Christian missionaries began to denounce the bloody rites of the Śāktas, often in vivid and horrifying detail. As Sir Charles James Lyall wrote in his report on "The Province of Assam" in 1903, "the celebrity of the temple of Kamakhya at Gauhati and its importance as a centre of that bloody and sensual form of Śiva and his Consort called *Tantrik* are beyond question. . . . What we know of the religion of the Hinduised aboriginals shows that it conformed generally to this sanguinary type. Human sacrifice was common."[80] The British and American missionaries who came to the region in hopes of converting more souls were even more disparaging in their accounts of these bloody rites. Overall, the inhabitants of this "dark valley" were described as "extremely indolent and lacking in enterprise," not to mention "dirty and bloodthirsty."[81] Missionaries singled out the sacrificial rites as the worst, most disgusting form of superstitious idolatry, and thus as the first things that would need to be abolished in order to bring them to the saving light of Christ. As such, they rejoiced when these primitive tribes finally "discarded earlier practices of propitiating by sacrifices the spirits and demons . . . replacing traditional music for Christian hymns . . . and sacrifices for foreign medicines."[82]

But this critique of sacrifice was by no means voiced only by Orientalists and missionaries; rather, it has also been articulated by many Assamese scholars, who similarly blamed these bloody rites for the decline of their culture and society. Perhaps foremost among these was Banikanta Kakati, who wrote one of the most influential texts on Kāmākhyā and one of the most scathing criticisms of the Tantric form of sacrifice. Before the arrival of the spiritual reformer Śaṅkaradeva, he writes, "society was moth-eaten from within and without any sustaining vitality. . . . The land was infested with the Vāmācāra Tantric schools with their insistence on the philosophy of sex and plate. Amongst religious rites the most spectacular were bloody sacrifices to gods and goddesses amidst deafening noises of drums. . . . Śaṅkara Deva chose the difficult path of living up to his faith in the world. . . . To the exhausted kingdom without inner vitality and external he threw out a gospel of absolute surrender to the One."[83] It is important to note that Kakati emphasizes Śaṅkaradeva's ability to unify a fragmented kingdom (and I think he means not just Assam but also a larger Indian nation) that had been weakened by blood sacrifice, restoring it to a "gospel" of monotheism.

While protests against animal sacrifice had been building in many parts of India since the 1990s, they reached a peak of intensity in Assam after 2005. The Assamese author Indira Goswami (d. 2011) ignited a firestorm of protest with the publication of her novel *Chinnamastar Manuḥṭo* (*The Man from Chinnamasta*), a fictional account of worship at Kāmākhyā that contains a particularly incisive critique of animal sacrifice. Coming from an Assamese family deeply connected to Śaṅkaradeva's devotional movement, Goswami appears to have inherited the reformer's intense dislike of the Śāktas' bloody rites. Indeed, the heart of her novel is really "an impassioned protest against the horror of animal sacrifice."[84]

Interestingly, however, the character who voices the criticism of sacrifice in the novel is neither a Kṛṣṇa devotee nor a Christian missionary but rather a Hindu *sādhu* named Jatadhari. Commenting on the practice of blood sacrifice described in the *Kālikā Purāṇa*, Jatadhari condemns such sacrifices as outdated rituals of the past that should be replaced by unbloody offerings of devotional love: "These are ancient writings and beliefs. You can no longer smell sacrificed limbs burning in the sacrificial fires, can you? . . . The sacred bowls in which blood and lotus flowers were offered to the Mother have all disappeared. Today this terrible history has been confined to the deep recesses of dark caves."[85] Ultimately, the novel calls upon its readers to "throw out the blood" and bury this gory sacrificial past in a "tomb of flowers." Goswami writes: "They drag helpless animals to the sacrifice. The Mother has never said that she would reduce the earth's abundance if she were not offered blood. According to the holy books, flowers are equally acceptable to the Mother. . . . [A]n offering of one *karabi* flower can earn the devotee the virtues of the most arduous *yagna*. . . . The devotees chorused, 'Throw out the blood. Worship the goddess with flowers. Ma . . . Ma . . . Ma!'"[86]

The response to Goswami's novel was intense on both sides of the debate. As Goswami later recounted, the novel initially generated tremendous hostility and even personal threats to the author; however, this reaction was soon followed by an outpouring of support for Goswami and a new wave of protests against the practice of animal sacrifice: "When the novel was serialized in a popular magazine, I was threatened with dire consequences. Shortly after this, a local newspaper, *Sadin*, carried an appeal about animal sacrifice, which resulted in quite an uproar—the editor was gheraoed and a *tantrik* warned me. But when the appeal was published, the response was overwhelmingly in favour of banning animal sacrifice."[87]

Indeed, a number of Assamese critics have taken up the novel's call to end the practice of *bali-dān*. Citing both issues of hygiene and animal cruelty, the chairperson of People for Animals, Sangeeta Goswami, argues that it is the duty of every citizen to reject the practice and embrace the ideals of *ahiṃsā* and universal compassion: "We want a ban on animal sacrifice in public places and places of worship because the archaic ritual involves bloodshed and a problem of hygiene. The directive principles of state policy (Article 51-g) states that as part of our fundamental duties, citizens of India need to have compassion for living creatures."[88]

Significantly, Goswami and other critics flatly reject the idea that animal sacrifice has any grounding in genuine Hinduism or in the Vedas; instead, they regard this notion as a primitive, superstitious corruption of the religion: "There is no such concept of sacrificing any animal or bird in the name of god in Hinduism. . . . The Vedas do not say anything about this brutal act, and thus this system has to be banned."[89] Another critic from Silchar made the case that the practice of sacrifice really derives from the tribal traditions of Assam and as such has nothing to do with the Vedas or any other genuine Hindu scriptures: "If you observe a broad pattern in places where animal sacrifice is practiced you will find they are all from tribal regions or regions where tribal cults were dominant once. . . . It is not a practice of ancient Vedic civilization, nor any Hindu Shruti text recommended it in that sense, so this has to be stopped."[90]

The debates over cow and buffalo sacrifice came to a head in 2021, with the passage of the Assam Cattle Preservation Bill. Initially, the law was designed to prohibit the sale and purchase of beef in any areas inhabited by "non-beef-eating communities" (meaning Hindus and Jains) and "within five kilometers of a temple or *satra*" (Vaiṣṇava monastery).[91] Given the ubiquity of Hindus, Jains, and temples in the region, the law makes it very difficult indeed to sell beef. Still more controversial, however, was the fact that the law originally covered not only cows but *all* bovines (all *bos* species), including "bulls, bullocks, cows, heifers, calves, male and female buffaloes and buffalo calves."[92] In effect, this proscription would have made it almost impossible to continue the usual rites at Assam's many goddess temples, where buffalo offerings are a staple at major holy days. After intense debate and a walkout by opposing members, the Assembly agreed to remove "buffaloes" from the bill, which was then finally approved in August 2021.

This debate and this compromise to allow buffalo slaughter really highlights the complex political dilemma faced by conservative parties such as the BJP. While the BJP has built its identity on Hindutva policies such as cow protection and bans on animal sacrifice, it also risks alienating Hindu voters in regions such as Assam, Tripura, Bangla, and other areas where buffalo and other sacrifices are an integral part of religious life: "The Catch-22 situation for BJP in Assam is that even if it does implement the rule strictly, it is likely to refresh the debate regarding animal sacrifice in the Kamakhya temple, thereby pushing the party in an awkward situation. On the other hand, if it doesn't implement the rule strictly, it would be caught defying the Centre."[93]

The debate has also had wide-ranging economic implications, particularly for anyone involved in the sale and transport of animals for slaughter. As the *Firstpost* reported in 2017, the criticisms of cattle killing and the actions of self-appointed "cow-protectors" (*gaurakṣaks*) have led to a steep decline in the sale of both cows and buffaloes throughout the northeast region. "The rise of cattle vigilantism meant sale and supply of animals was already hit hard in the Northeast. Naeem Khan, who used to earn Rs 20,000 to Rs 30,000 by selling cows and buffaloes in markets in neighboring Meghalaya state and would also supply buffaloes meant for sacrifice at the Kamakhya temple, told *Firstpost* that the cattle trade has almost stopped. Referring to the rise of 'gaurakshaks,' he said, 'I have left the cattle trade, as there is no more "peace" in this business.'"[94]

But the debate over sacrifice and cow protection is far more than a merely economic and political question. Indeed, it is one with quite violent effects across India, as cow vigilante mobs have also attacked, beaten, and even lynched individuals—most of them Muslim—for selling and/or transporting cattle for slaughter. Since 2015, dozens of assaults have occurred in Assam, Bengal, Jammu and Kashmir, Rajasthan, Uttar Pradesh, and other states, resulting in at least forty-four deaths (thirty-six of them Muslim) and hundreds of injuries.[95] Today we see even more clearly than ever that the ideals of *ahiṃsā* and Hindu identity are often forged by means of very real violence against non-Hindu others—above all, Muslims, tribals, people of lower castes, and those on the margins of the imagined nation.

On the other side, however, priests of the temple and other defenders of the tradition are quick to point out the hypocrisy in these attacks on animal sacrifice. Not only do they point to the ample evidence of animal sacrifice in the Vedas, epics, and other classical Hindu literature, but they also observe that animals are killed and eaten everywhere in India today—often in ways that are far less humane than the offering of *bali-dān* at the temple. As Rajib Sarma put it quite bluntly when I asked him about this debate, "Look at any street corner in India today, you'll see meat for sale; goats, chickens, pigs, all kinds of animals are butchered and sold every single day. No one gets upset about that. If you really wanted to end *bali-dān*, you'd have to stop all that other animal killing, too."[96] On another occasion, he added: "Just imagine if they banned the sale of meat—goats, chickens—in the marketplace. There would be rioting in the streets!"[97]

In our various conversations, Rajib and I also discussed some of the parallels to equally complex debates surrounding animal sacrifice in the United States—for example, the debates surrounding Santeria rituals in Florida. In 1987, the city of Hialeah, Florida, passed laws against animal sacrifice that seemed to many observers to be specifically targeted at the local Santeria community.[98] The case ultimately went to the US Supreme Court, which ruled in favor of the Santeria community. In the court's opinion, the laws against sacrifice were not only in violation of the First Amendment's free exercise clause but were specifically "gerrymandered" to target a particular ethic and religious minority, while making exemptions for other secular forms of animal slaughter (such as hunting and slaughterhouses).[99] In Rajib's view, the various attempts to ban sacrifice in India represent a similar a violation of religious freedom, which is enshrined in Article 25 of the Indian Constitution, and they are motivated by similar a combination of religious and ethnic prejudice toward specific minority communities—namely, Muslims, tribals, and those Hindus who do not fit a normative idea of Hindutva.

Another *tāntrik* friend of mine was even more pointed in his critique of the recent attacks on animal sacrifice. Asking to remain anonymous with the acronym "EMI," or "elderly middle-class initiate," he argued that this phenomenon is a clear example of far-right politicians imposing their own narrow ideal of Hinduism onto local cultures. He invoked American sociologist C. Wright Mills in order to critique the coalition of conservative priests and businessmen (*baniyās*) behind these attacks, which he sees as ultimately "fascistic" in nature: "The push against animal sacrifice is being orchestrated by what C. Wright Mills might have called the 'Brahmin-Bania complex' of the RSS and BJP, given that the Brahmins of north and south

India are vegetarians, unlike those of eastern India; so it is a political tactic that feeds into their larger fascist project."[100]

While critics regularly claim that animal sacrifice has no basis in the Vedas or any legitimate Hindu scriptures, defenders of the practice frequently resort to their own reading of the Vedas (which, after all, do contain quite a bit of detailed discussion of animal sacrifice). Thus in 2014, Jadu Sarma, Naba Kanta Sarma, Rajib Sarma, and other members of the Kāmākhyā community formed a collective called the "Vishwa Shanti Devi Yajña Committee." The committee issued a series of publications, with essays in Sanskrit, Assamese, Hindi, and English that emphasized *both* the Vedic origins of *yajña* and the continuities between Vedic ritual and contemporary Tantric practices in Assam. In their view, "A Yanga [Yajna] is one of the oldest rituals in Sanatan Dharma to propitiate the deities. It is the ritual of offerings accompanied by chanting of Vedic mantras. . . . VISHWA SHANTI DEVI YAJNA is going to organize a Yajna in the premises of Kamakhya Temple, Guwahati, where the Goddess Kamakhya Devi will be invoked in the form of Shanti to usher peace and harmony through the performance of the Viswa Shanti Devi Yajna."[101]

Thus, one of the chapters in the volume traces the genealogy of contemporary *yajña* at Kāmākhyā through a wide swath of older Sanskrit literature, including various Purāṇas (*Agni*, *Bhāgavata*, *Matsya*) and the epics (*Mahābhārata*), and leading directly to rites described in the Vedas (*Ṛg*, *Yajur*, etc.).[102] In sum, while critics have virulently denied any connection between *bali-dān* and "real" or "Vedic" Hinduism, the Vishwa Shanti Devi Yajña Committee took the opposite position by attempting to redescribe the practice in the most highly orthodox, *brāhmaṇic* Hindu terms, as a direct continuation of the *yajña* of the Vedas. Not only the concept of "sacrifice" but the very idea of what is "Vedic" and what is "Hindu" has thus become an intense object of both symbolic and physical contestation.

Conclusions: Desire, Blood, and Politics in Modern India

The political debates surrounding sacrifice in Assam—and throughout India—have continued well after King Gyanendra's much publicized visit in 2002. In the summer of 2008, for example, a member of the Legislative Assembly of the Samajwadi Party, Kishore Samrite, again made national headlines when he offered no less than 265 animals at Kāmākhyā. Apparently, the massive offering was made in support of Prime Minister Manmohan Singh's government, while the 265 victims (mostly goats with some buffaloes) represented the voting strength of the combined Samajwadi Party and

United Progressive Alliance. According to an official of the Kāmākhyā Temple Trust Board, this was the largest sacrificial offering for a single cause by a single person in recent memory.[103] However, not all members of the Samajwadi Party were enthusiastic about this massive blood offering, and many top leaders condemned it in the strongest possible terms. As then-party secretary Dr. Sunilam unapologetically put it, "People who sacrifice animals are mentally disturbed. The Party does not believe in it."[104]

To conclude, I would like to make some broader comparative observations about the role of sacrifice as an "instrument of struggle," in Bruce Lincoln's sense of a discursive weapon in contestations over identity, nationalism, and political power. Sacrifice is surely not a singular or homogeneous phenomenon; rather, it represents a kind of dense knot in a complex tangle of religious, social, political, and legal threads that extend both spatially across the region and temporally across many periods of South Asian history. Like the magic and *tantra-mantra* discussed in chapter 2, sacrifice lies at a critical node amid a vast network of conflicting interests. These interests include Vaiṣṇava reformers and Śākta *tāntriks*, animal rights activists and advocates of religious pluralism, Hindu nationalists and indigenous communities, politicians and defenders of local culture, and many, many others.

If warfare has been imagined since the time of the *Mahābhārata* as a "sacrifice of battle," then the metaphor also works in the other direction: sacrifice is itself a "field of battle" and a violently contested space.[105] As Kathryn McClymond observes, "Sacrifice is often an arena in which certain people distinguish themselves from others, community versus community, social rank versus social rank, modern religion versus ancient religion."[106] In this sense, sacrifice is by no means simply a recurring structural theme that runs throughout India's many varied Hindu traditions; it is also a form of ritual that is invested with very real human interests and material desires, a key nexus in struggles over scarce resources, constructions of social boundaries, and competing ideals of the nation.[107] On one side, there are desires for mundane sorts of power, prosperity, and happiness achieved through the offering of blood by Tantric devotees; on the other side, there are desires for another kind of power achieved by staunching the flow of blood and by enforcing a very narrow ideal of Hindutva, as we seen in the discourse of Hindu nationalists in their various forms.

To borrow Deleuze's language once again, we might say the flow of desire embodied in sacrifice has been repeatedly "territorialized" through political and ideological structures, such as religious institutions, political parties, and the nation.[108] In the case of Assam, the flow of desire—carried quite literally through the flow of blood offered to the goddess of desire herself—has been territorialized by the state, through the rise of Hindu nationalism and new laws prohibiting the sale and slaughter of animals. But this "territorialization" is always contested, conflicted, and never complete; the very effort to staunch the flow has only led to new threats of bloodshed. As one devotee named Anirbhan Bhattacharya fiercely declared in an interview in 2013, any attempt to ban sacrifice would only lead to even more blood flowing through the streets: "The government tried to stop us from doing Bali and suggested we replace it with something else, something less violent. . . . Everyone in Assam, tribal and nontribal people, in union said, 'If you ever try to stop us, we will ensure that the streets will be converted into a river of flesh and blood.'"[109]

As such, the "broken world" of sacrifice also highlights the fragmented and contested nature of the modern nation itself. As Thomas Blom Hansen argues, the ideology of Hindu nationalism bears a profound tension and perhaps violent contradiction at its very heart: it is an attempt to impose cultural and political unity onto a vast landscape that is not only incredibly diverse but increasingly divided along regional, linguistic, and religious boundaries: "The Hindu nationalist movement, arguably the most authoritarian movement ever in power in the country, has come to power at a time when the prospects for actually imposing cultural homogeneity, political unity, and uniform governmentality . . . have never been bleaker."[110]

Despite the efforts of nationalist politicians to construct a unified and homogeneous Mother India based on a pristine vision of Hindutva, key sites such as Kāmākhyā refuse to be absorbed into this sanitized ideal. The many scattered limbs of the goddess that constitute the network of *śākta pīṭhas* remain in many ways disconnected and dismembered. They stubbornly persist as fragments of a sacrificial body that cannot be easily assimilated into the narrow confines of the modern nation.

[CHAPTER FOUR]

Dancing for the Snake

Possession, Performance, and Gender in Manasā Pūjā

> The varied powers of the goddess cannot be explained. A childless person gets a child, and a prisoner becomes free, if the goddess is worshiped in the form of a pot in the house.... [O]ne is blessed by the goddess with what is desired.
>
> Durgābar, *Manasā Kāvya* (sixteenth century)[1]

Each summer, Kāmākhyā Temple is the site of two major festivals, which represent in many ways the most exoteric, public, and performative face of this otherwise esoteric Tantric tradition. The lesser-known but perhaps more spectacular of the two is Manasā Pūjā, the worship of the snake goddess Manasā, which takes place on the transition from the month of Śrāvaṇa (July–August) to Bhādra (August–September). An elaborate three-day festival, Manasā Pūjā at Kāmākhyā also involves a performance known as the dance of the *deodhanī* or *debadhanī* (often translated as the "sound" or "echo of the deity").[2] Traditionally a term used for a non-Hindu religious specialist among Assam's many indigenous groups such as the Ahoms, Bodos, and Rabhas, *deodhā* or *deodhāi* here refers to male ritual dancers who become possessed by various deities and engage in an ecstatic, spectacular performance that involves animal sacrifice, consumption of raw meat and blood, and jumping on the blades of swords.[3]

According to her own mythic narratives, Manasā was originally a non-Hindu goddess who was only grudgingly accepted into the Sanskritic Hindu pantheon, and she is today widely worshipped by both indigenous communities and mainstream Hindus.[4] Similarly, the possession performance of the *deodhāis* is a complex, often conflicted, and contested mixture of local practices drawn from Assam's many tribal cultures and the *brāhmaṇic* Hindu institutions of major temples such as Kāmākhyā.[5]

Yet in addition to the bloody and ecstatic performances of the male *deodhāis*, there is another form of dance in honor of the snake goddess, this one performed entirely by women called *deodhanīs*.[6] Today, there are many forms of *deodhanī* dance: some traditional dances are still performed

FIGURE 4.1. Manasā, Assam State Museum, Guwahati, Assam, 2017. Photo by the author.

FIGURE 4.2. Manasā, Mayong, Assam, 2022. Photo by the author.

among indigenous communities such as the Rabhas and Bodos,[7] but more commonly, the female dance is now performed on the stages of major urban centers such as Guwahati.[8] These urban and staged dances represent a clear "domestication" or "folklorization"[9] of the village performance and are strikingly different from the male performances at Kāmākhyā Temple. In contrast to the male dance—which takes place in the yard of the temple at the height of Manasā Pūjā—the women's dance is performed on multiple occasions and often in "secular" spaces, such as halls for popular audiences in downtown Guwahati. Moreover, while the male dance is clearly meant to appear wild, spontaneous, and potentially dangerous, the dance of the *deodhanīs* is far more choreographed, with all the women moving in step to a predetermined script. Although it ostensibly still involves a form of possession, accompanied by the waving of unbound hair and the wielding of swords, it is an unbloody and carefully controlled performance overall.[10] Despite their apparent differences, however, both the male and female dances represent a dramatic, ritualized performance of indigenous identity in its complex, contested, and sometimes violent relationship to the Hindu and Indian identity of the state.

The concept of "possession" (*āveśa* or *samāveśa*) has long been part of many Tantric traditions of South Asia. As Frederick Smith has shown, possession is a key element in even the most elite, philosophical schools such as Kashmir Śaivism. Through initiation and meditation, the *tāntrik* is penetrated and suffused with the power of the deity, realizing his own identity with Lord Śiva: "The *samāveśa* or 'interpenetration' of the individual with the *śakti* or essential energy of Śiva is one of the goals of nondualist meditative practice."[11] However, the sort of possession that we see in the dances of the *deodhāi* and *deodhanī* is at once far less philosophically sophisticated and less esoteric than that of the Kashmir Śaivites; it is a highly public and performative spectacle, combined with significant elements of non-Sanskritic indigenous practices. As such, the possession of the *deodhāis* seems to fall more into the realm of what Smith calls the oracular and "exorcistic practices that survived at the margins of Tantra."[12] The "path of desire" in this case has little to do with elite philosophical discourse but is instead about the power of the possessed *deodhāis* to fulfill the more worldly desires of ordinary devotees, such as healing, soothsaying, and material prosperity.

In my analysis of the goddess and her dancers, I want to make two general arguments. The first is that these possession performances—like much of Tantra in northeast India—represent a complex negotiation between the Sanskritic, *brāhmaṇic* traditions of central India and the many non-Hindu indigenous communities of the northeast states.[13] While many previous scholars have described this kind of popular worship as a thin veneer of Hinduism pasted clumsily over a tribal substratum,[14] I argue that it represents a far more complex process of "interpenetration" and mutual transformation between the *brāhmaṇic* Hindu and local indigenous traditions. Again, to use Doniger's useful term cited in the introduction, it represents as much a process of "*deśī-fication*" as one of Sanskritization—that is, a transformation of the Sanskritic tradition by the local, popular, vernacular culture.[15]

My second argument is that the ecstatic performance of the *deodhāis* has much to tell us about identity as a social, political, and gendered category. While there is a great deal of useful anthropological literature on possession that will be relevant here,[16] I will also borrow some insights from Judith Butler and their widely influential work on performance, gender, and the "subversion of identity."[17] Possession in Assam is indeed a powerful kind of performance that in many ways subverts traditional gender identity, in Butler's sense (men are possessed by female deities, women act in "masculine" ways, and so on). Yet ultimately, I will argue, the deeper "subversion of identity" taking place here is not that between male and female, but first, that between the "Hindu" and the "indigenous"; second, that between the national/Indian and the local/Assamese; and finally, and most profoundly, that between the human and the divine.

Tales of the Serpent: Mythical Narratives of Manasā and Her Dance

The goddess Manasā is the subject of a rich and complex body of mythological narratives in classical Sanskrit texts as well as in vernacular literature of regions such as Bangla and Assam.[18] A complex deity who combines aspects of many different goddesses, she is described as both a fierce and a calm deity, at once dangerous and protective in her poisonous power: "She is at once Sarasvatī and Jāṅgulī, goddess of healing, and one eyed Kadrū, mother of snakes with poison in her empty eye; she is at once the mythic *viṣakanyā*, whose touch is death, and the personification of the ancient idea of homeopathy: With poison do I slay poison."[19] In northeast India, Manasā is worshipped both by mainstream Hindus and by many indigenous communities, such as the Rabhas, Bodos, and other scheduled tribes of the Goalpara, Darrang, and Kamrup districts.[20]

In the case of Manasā Pūjā in Assam, there are two very different sets of narratives that are used to explain the origins of her dance. The first narrative is based on a large body of Bangla and Assamese texts collectively known as *Maṅgal kāvyas* and *Manasā maṅgals*.[21] In Assam, the most important of these are the Manasā songs of the sixteenth-century poets Mankar and Durgābar, and the *Padma Purāṇa* by the seventeenth-century poet Nārāyaṇadeva, which serves as the basis for the *Māroi Ojā* or songs in honor of the snake goddess.[22] As we see in Durgābar's version of the story, Manasā is herself praised as a powerful "goddess of desire"—a dangerous but benevolent goddess who can grant all the desires of those who are truly devoted to her: "The varied powers of the goddess cannot be explained. A childless person gets a child, and a prisoner becomes free, if the goddess is worshipped in the form of a pot in the house. One has to worship her after a day's fast and to offer her five flowers of gold. Then one should bathe in the river Ganga, repeating the saying 'Mānasāi-Māi.' After all these performances, one is blessed by the goddess with what is desired."[23]

The basic story in these vernacular accounts differs somewhat from one text to the next but largely centers on the conflict between Manasā and a powerful merchant named Cāṅd Sadāgar. Initially not recognized as a legitimate goddess, Manasā was determined to win devotees and become respected as a member of the Hindu pantheon. However, Cāṅd Sadāgar was a staunch devotee of Śiva and refused to worship the snake goddess.[24] In her anger, Manasā proceeded to kill Cāṅd's first six sons by snakebite, leaving only his last son, Lakhindar, still alive. Cāṅd arranged a marriage for Lakhindār with a girl named Behulā and then built an iron room for the couple on their wedding night, hoping to protect them from snakebite. Even so, Manasā found a tiny hole in the wall, through which she sent a snake to bite and kill Lakhindar. In her grief, Behulā then carried her husband's corpse all the way to heaven in the hope of bringing him back to life. Once there, she enchanted the gods with her beautiful, sensuous, yet otherworldly dancing: "Her movements were ethereal, she didn't seem to touch feet to the ground but seemed to float and fly and make intricate movements in the air. When her eyes shot a glance at someone, he was at once pierced by love's arrows."[25] As Nārāyaṇadeva described this scene: "In the dance, Behulā's face was radiant. . . . The crown of her head sparkled, as beautiful as an open lotus in the sky. . . . One by one all the gods became enchanted. Gods, demons, heavenly spirits, and faeries all prayed to Padmā, 'Do not delay—go revive Lakhindar!'"[26]

As a reward, the gods promised they would restore her husband's life—but only on the condition that Cāṅd would recognize and worship Manasā. Finally, realizing that doing so was the sole means to restore his son's life, Cāṅd agreed to worship Manasā with his left hand, while continuing to honor Śiva with his right.[27] At last, Manasā was recognized as a true goddess in heaven and in turn brought all of Cāṅd's dead sons back to life.

There are a number of themes at play in this narrative that would later become important for the *deodhāi* dance. The first is that Manasā is clearly presented as a non-Hindu outsider goddess, who has to fight—often by vengeance and treachery—to become recognized as part of the legitimate Hindu pantheon. The second is that, even when accepted as a goddess, she is only recognized with worship by the left-hand (*vāma*) rather than the right (*dakṣiṇa*). Often identified with what is "reverse, contrary, opposite, unfavorable," the *vāma* path is also the path of impurity, transgression, and power in Śākta Tantric traditions.[28]

The second story surrounding the origins of the dance appears to be a narrative unique to Assam itself, which plays upon a more widespread Assamese theme about kings and their complex relationships with goddesses. According to this tale, a great king once promised Manasā the gift of his own head if she would help him sire a son. She did indeed grant the wish, but the king promptly forgot his vow and so had to be reminded through a terrifying vision from the goddess. Finally, the king fulfilled his vow to sacrifice himself by cutting off his own head and then possessed the body of a male devotee, who in turn became the first dancer for the goddess, "thus beginning the *debaddhani* tradition."[29] This first possessed devotee is also said to have become the king's *ghorā*—that is, the "horse" or vehicle upon which the deity "rides" when it possesses a body.[30]

It is worth noting here that the theme of the cursed king is a widespread one in Assamese literature, and one that is often closely tied to tensions between non-Hindu/tribal and Hindu/*brāhmaṇic* traditions. The mythical founder of Kāmarūpa (Assam) itself was the half-god Naraka, who suffered a curse from the goddess because he made a pact with a tribal king;[31] the Koch king who rediscovered Kāmākhyā Temple in the sixteenth century, Viśva Siṅgha, was said to have been born of a *mleccha* (non-Hindu) mother who offended a holy man; and Rudra Siṅgha, one of the greatest Ahom kings, is said to have offended a Hindu priest and died without receiving initiation. All of these narratives point to a complex tension between goddesses and kings, often centered on a deeper tension between *brāhmaṇic* Hindu forms of worship and the non-Hindu, indigenous practices of Assam's many indigenous communities.[32]

Divine Horsemen, Echoes of the Gods: The Dance of the *Deodhāi*

Before examining Manasā Pūjā and its dances in detail, we should first note that *deodhāi* and related terms have a long history in Assamese religious life. For centuries, the words *deodhā*, *deodhāi*, *deudni*, *daudini*, and *deoddhi* have been used to refer to the non-Hindu priests of many of the northeast tribes, such as the Ahoms, Chutiyas, and Bodo-Kacharis, and many scholars believe the contemporary dance to be a direct carryover from non-Hindu traditions into the cycle of the temple.[33]

Moreover, the local *deodhāis* often put up the most resistance to the gradual Hinduization and Sanskritization of Assam's indigenous communities and traditional religious practices. As Edward Gait described the gradual conversion of the Ahoms to Hinduism during the eighteenth century, "Hinduism became the predominant religion, and the Ahoms who persisted in holding to their old beliefs and tribal customs came to be regarded as a separate degraded class. The Deodhais . . . resisted the change with all their might and succeeded for some time longer in enforcing the observance of certain ceremonies."[34] This tension between the Ahom *deodhāis* and the dominant Hindu culture continued well into the late twentieth century. As Yasmin Saikia has shown, the struggle over indigenous/Ahom versus national/Hindu identity saw a powerful resurgence in the 1990s with the Tai-Ahom movement. Much of this movement centered on the unique status of the *deodhāi* as an autonomous religious authority and the "high priest of a religion that is different from Hinduism."[35] As a whole, modern Assamese identity from the colonial to the postcolonial periods has been a complex, often volatile "negotiation and disputation" between the dominant Hindu/Indian and the local/indigenous cultures of the region.[36]

The ambivalence, tension, and complex negotiation surrounding indigenous and Hindu identities is embodied in the celebration of Manasā Pūjā. As Nihar Ranjan Mishra notes, Manasā herself is not worshipped inside the sanctum of the temple but rather in the outer dance pavilion—which again indicates that she is an originally non-Hindu deity only reluctantly and partially allowed into the temple complex: "While the worship of various manifestations of Śakti like Durgā, Vāsantī, are done on the *pīṭhasthāna* of the Kāmākhyā temple, the worship of Manasā is done on a sacred pitcher and is held on the *nāṭamandira* part of the temple which gives us reason to believe that the worship of Manasā is grudgingly adopted into the regular religious service of the temple."[37]

The *pūjā* itself takes place on a pavilion in the *nāṭamandira*, whose floor is decorated with the diagram of a lotus flower, with four plates of various offerings in each of its four corners. A sacred pitcher is placed in the center of the diagram, behind which stands a large image of an eight-hooded snake.

But surely the most spectacular part of Manasā's festival today is the performance of the *deodhāis*, who become the temporary human vehicles of both male and female deities. As Khagera Chandra Mahanta notes, none of the *deodhāis* are *brāhmaṇs* or high class, and most are ordinary men who have other jobs in their normal lives: "Some of them are daily wage earners

FIGURE 4.3. Male *deodhāi*, Manasā Pūjā, Guwahati, Assam, 2017. Photo by Riya Sarma.

or petty shopkeepers. None . . . belong to the priestly caste. . . . Most of them, rather, come from socially low castes. . . . Most of the shamans are illiterate."[38]

The calling of a new *deodhāi* to be the mount of a deity can happen in various ways and at various ages, in some cases in adolescence and in others during adulthood. One dancer named Devīrām (the former mount of Manasā herself) claimed to have been possessed by the goddess around age fourteen, showing various miraculous signs: "He was asked where his

FIGURE 4.4. Male *deodhāi*, Manasā Pūjā, Guwahati, Assam, 2017. Photo by Riya Sarma.

weapons were and could detect their location with no hesitation; moreover, he could handle cobras without being harmed by them."[39]

In the weeks prior to the festival, the dancers prepare themselves by carefully restricting their diet and movements. As Devīrām put it, "For two months we have to control ourselves: what we eat, where we go. We cannot eat anything in restaurants, for example. . . . Two months, we have to keep complete control of ourselves."[40] The *deodhāi* is said to have no choice in the possession, which takes place entirely at the whim of the deity; all he can do is make his body a suitable mount or receptacle for the god's descent: "That is why during the month before the festival the *deodhāi* observe a set of limitations, concerning diet, sexual activity, clothing, etc. . . . anyone who does not follow these limitations, risks causing divine anger and consequently to become crazy (*pāgal hai jābo*)."[41] In some cases, the dancer also develops a "fondness for drinking fresh raw blood of pigeons or he-goats" as the god or goddess exerts more and more influence, eventually placing him "under complete command of the deity."[42]

At the time when they are actually possessed by the deity, the dancers generally claim to feel that the divine power has seized complete control of their bodies and that they lose awareness of their own selves in the embrace of the deity—dying, as it were, to their own identity in order to allow the deity to act through them. As Śivnāth Dās—the dancer and vehicle for the goddess Dakṣiṇa Kālī—described the experience, "During the dance, nothing is the same as before. Do you think I will recognize you? No, I won't be able to. I won't even recognize my loved ones. . . . Dancing is like dying. The dance goes far beyond life and death. If I happen to die, it does not matter, the dance would continue anyway."[43]

The Assamese terms often used to describe this state are *gā lay*, "to take the body"; *lambhi*, "to possess"; and *śarīrod jāi*, "to go into [someone's] body."[44] As Devīrām Dās described the state of possession, he becomes wholly taken over by Manasā, the specific goddess who has chosen him. Even though he has lost all his teeth, he is still able to eat the raw flesh of the sacrificial animals when possessed by the goddess: "When the goddess takes me, I will only be aware of her. I will be like her. . . . I will only be aware of Manasā. She will take this body, and I will dance. I have no teeth. . . . One by one, my teeth have all fallen out. But I can eat the meat of the sacrifice. . . . I eat everything, both the raw meat and blood."[45]

In this sense, the possession experienced by the *deodhāi* is related to but quite distinct from the sort of possession experienced in more esoteric forms of Tantric practice. As we noted above, the possession (*āveśa*) of the human adept by a deity is a key part of many Tantric rituals.[46] Still today at the main Kāmākhyā temple complex, the priestly ritual specialist, or *pūjārī*, is also said to infuse divine energies into his body when he worships the goddess. Through the rite of *prāṇa-pratiṣṭhā* (literally "establishing" or "consecrating" the "breath" or "vital energy"), the body of the *pūjārī* becomes suffused with the power of the deity, which in turn allows him to worship the god or goddess. As Majo Garigliano notes, this rite is in fact a mark of "Tantric" as opposed to merely "Vedic" practice: "Certain ritual operations . . . aim at imposing divine energies onto the boy of the *pujārī* who throughout the ritual 'is no longer just like a human being' . . . the quasi-divine status he acquires make him a *tāntrika*."[47] Yet while both the *deodhāi* dancer and the Tantric *pūjārī* experience a direct, personal encounter with the divine, there are some key differences between the two. Most importantly, the former is completely overtaken and controlled by the deity—losing all awareness and agency—but the latter is never fully identical with the deity and retains his individual consciousness and identity during worship: "The *deodhai* is the arrival point of a movement that starts somewhere else, namely in the deity's will to possess a human body and dance. . . . The contact between the *deodhāi* and the divine

TABLE 4.1. Deities possessing dancers, Manasā Pūjā, 2017

MALE DEITIES	FEMALE DEITIES (ŚAKTIS)
Baragopāla (Kṛṣṇa)	Bagalā (one of the ten wisdom goddesses)
Dhanakubera (local form of Kubera, god of wealth)	Bhairavī (the "terrible" or "awe-inspiring")
Gaṇeśa (elephant-headed god)	Bhuvaneśvarī ("lady of the universe")
Jalakubera (local form of Kubera, god of wealth)	Calantā (movable form of the goddess)
Mahādeva (Śiva)	Cāmuṇḍā (a terrible form of the goddess)
Mahārāja (king who offered head to the goddess)	Chinnamastā (the "severed headed" goddess)
Nārāyaṇa (Viṣṇu)	Ghor Kālī (frightful Kālī)
	Kālī (goddess of time, death)
	Kāmākhyā
	Manasā
	Rakṣa Kālī (protective Kālī)
	Śītalā (goddess of smallpox)
	Śmaśānakālī (Kālī of the cremation ground)
	Tārā ("savior" or "protector")

is total and almost violent, while the contact between *pujārī* and the deity is induced and controlled."[48]

The number and identity of the dancers changes a bit from year to year. As it was performed in 2017, for example, the dance consisted of twenty-one *deodhāis*, each possessed by a distinct male or female deity with his or her own unique characteristics and personalities. As we see in the table 4.1, the ratio of female deities (Śaktis, or embodiments of the goddess's power) to male deities was two to one, with a clear emphasis on the more fearsome, independent, and aggressive goddesses.

On the first day of the dance, the *deodhāis* assemble in the temple complex and undergo an initial rite of purification (*prāyaścitta*). Donning fresh clothes, they listen to the sacred songs (*nām gān*) sung by the women of the temple in honor of the various gods and goddesses who will become present during the dance.[49]

On the second day, they then begin to enter more visibly into states of ritual possession, dancing to the beat of the drummers and becoming mounted in turn by their respective deities. Devotees at this time come to offer a variety of animal sacrifices (*bali-dān*) to the dancers, including goats, pigeons, and ducks, along with gifts of clothing and garlands.[50] In turn, the *deodhāis* take a break from dancing for some time to sit in the *bali-ghar* (sacrificial space), in order to consult with the devotees and offer their advice regarding their problems. As Mahanta suggests in his sociological study of the *pūjā*, devotees come in hopes of receiving assistance with a wide array of different needs and desires: these range from various physical maladies, such as physical and mental illness, barrenness, and bowel disorders to the desire for success in business, school, and politics.[51] The dancers embodying various forms of the goddess (the Śaktis or goddesses of power, especially Kāmākhyā, Manasā, and Kālī) are particularly popular and considered ritually more potent in their ability to offer advice, prophecy, and healing: "Under conditions of trances they are believed to be capable of divining and revealing the cases of illness or maladies and of suggesting their eventual cure or remedies by virtue of their possession."[52] At times, a *deodhāi* may also give a devotee a small piece of ritually consecrated herbal medicine or an amulet filled with dry herbs as the vehicle of her power and healing. As Maity notes in his thorough study of the Manasā tradition, these sorts of practices aimed at fulfilling very worldly desires likely derive from local indigenous traditions (much as the goddess herself does): "Manasā had her origin outside the domain of Brahmanical Hinduism, so this practice may have crept into her worship at an early stage of her evolution."[53]

Finally, on the last day, the festival reaches its height as the dancing increases dramatically in intensity and theatricality. The performance now comes to a climax as the *deodhāis* "shriek, howl and jump, creating a sense of terror among the visitors. At times [they] rush out from the temple premises into the open front yard jumping and shrieking frantically."[54] The dance culminates with a series of ecstatic acts, mostly performed by the Śaktis or embodiments of the goddesses—though undertaken at the direction of the male ringleader of the dance, Mahādeva or Śiva. These acts include dancing on the blades of the large sacrificial swords, drinking the blood from the heads of sacrificed animals, and biting the heads off live birds. As Dold describes this portion of the dance,

> Late in the afternoon, the leader of the Deodhas, the Mahārāj (a deified devotee of Bhairavī) emerges from the sacrificial hall carrying a large sword, a *khadga*, normally used to decapitate buffalo in sacrifice. . . . Two Deodhas hold each end of this sword, cutting edge up, as one after another of the goddess Deodhas, the Śaktis, climb upon and then dance on the sharp edge of the blade. . . . [A] priest appears carrying a live pigeon. As the bird flaps its wings, the priest lifts its head to the mouth of the

> Deodha now standing on the edge of the sword. With a dramatic chomp of his teeth and shake of his head, each Deodha bites the head off two or three birds . . . the Deodha chews, swallows and then spits out clumps of flesh and feathers.[55]

In fact, a *deodhāī*'s ability to consume the raw flesh and to dance on the swords is taken as evidence that he truly is possessed by a deity. If he fails to swallow the flesh, or if his feet are cut by the sword-blade, this fallibility is understood to be a sign that he is not really the vehicle of the god or goddess.[56]

Recently, however, some members of the Kāmākhyā community have actually complained that the dance has become a bit *too* exaggerated in its performance of wildness, bloodshed, and spectacle. As we will see in chapter 5, other festivals such as Ambuvācī Melā have been increasingly transformed into major tourist spectacles and symbols of Hindu nationalism.[57] Some local Kāmākhyāns worry that Manasā Pūjā might suffer the same fate. As Bandana Sarma and her daughter Riya commented in a conversation over tea with me in 2022, the younger dancers seem today to engage in ever more "theatrical" and exoticized displays of ecstatic behavior aimed less at the local community than at tourists and journalists armed with cameras: "There is too much 'acting,'" Riya complained.[58] As Rajib Sarma similarly commented, "Unlike the older dancers, many of the younger ones today are much more 'exhibitionist.' We worry that *debadhanī* will simply become another Ambuvācī, which has been completely commercialized and ruined by tourist spectators."[59]

The gender dynamics of the *deodhāis*' dance are also quite complex. On the one hand, like the priesthood of Kāmākhyā Temple itself, the *deodhāis* are all males, while the central and most authoritative of the *deodhāis* is the one embodying the male god, Mahādeva or Śiva.[60] Yet on the other hand, the dancers become the vehicles of both male and female deities, and it is generally the female deities or Śaktis who attract the most attention and perform the most ecstatic feats. As Majo Garigliano notes, "The *deodhāis* possessed by ferocious (*ṭāna*) deities (like Kālī and Chinnamastā, for instance) dance in a particularly frantic and wild way, while those possessed by cooler deities (mainly male ones) dance in a comparatively calmer way."[61]

While the dancers who embody male deities partake of vegetarian food, it is primarily the Śaktis who consume the meat of sacrificial animals and drink fresh blood, and it is the Śaktis who are believed to have the most power for healing, fulfilling desires, and so on.[62] Moreover, as Patricia Dold suggests, the very act of possession is dependent on the women who sing vernacular songs called *nām* in praise of the goddesses and other deities. Because all women are inherently identified with Śakti, the power or energy

TABLE 4.2. Gender dynamics in the male *deodhāi* dance

	MALE	FEMALE
Singers' gender		X
Dancers' pre-possession gender	X	
Dancers' gender during possession	X	X
Gender of chief deity	X	
Gender of most powerful/ecstatic/healing deities		X

of the goddess, their songs are a key part of the ritual, in which that divine energy suffuses the bodies of the *deodhāi*: "The Deodhas become embodiments of deities and the women, whose voices help transform ordinary men into 'voices of the gods' (*deodhas*) have this ability because they are natural embodiments of *śakti*, the feminine divine principle of power."[63]

In sum, the *deodhāi* performance represents a complex "dance" not only through space but also through gender categories. While the dancers themselves begin, the power that helps invoke the deities into their bodies is the *śakti* of the female singers. While the dance takes place, the chief deity may be Śiva, but the most powerful in terms of their ecstatic abilities and healing potential are the female *śaktis*. Finally, at the close of the dance, the *deodhāis* return to their original male identities, and the female singers return to their usual roles within the temple complex. In tabular form, these complex gender dynamics and inversions could perhaps be rendered as in table 4.2.

The *Deodhanī* Dance: From Ecstatic Possession to Domesticated Folk Performance

While the dance of the male *deodhāis* is the central focus of the annual celebration of Manasā Pūjā, the dance of the female *deodhanīs* is performed at various times and places throughout Assam, among both indigenous village communities and the more urbane Hindus of cities such as Guwahati. However, as the dance has moved from its indigenous village settings to the urban stages of the city, it has also undergone an increasing domestication, becoming less of a violently ecstatic and more of an unbloody staged sort of performance. That is, it appears to have undergone what Smith calls a "domestication" of possession[64] as well as a kind of "folklorization." As Susan Reed notes in her study of dance and nationalism in Sri Lanka, this sort of folklorization is a common pattern in many modern contexts, as traditional cultural forms are refashioned into national folk symbols: "Dances that originated in the village and temple have been adapted and transformed to carry secular meanings and serve national purposes. In stage performances and dance competitions, dances become an emblem of ethnicity and an index of cultural identity."[65]

Female possession performances are widely documented in a number of the indigenous communities of Assam. In his early account of the Bodo-Kachari tribes of western Assam, Sidney Endle described the ecstatic performance of the female *deoddni* (*deodhanī*), who was called upon during extreme circumstances in order to appeal to the gods with dance and blood sacrifice. While Endle's narrative surely needs to be read critically as a product of the British Empire and colonial obsessions with the exotic Orient,[66] it does provide some useful insights into the indigenous ritual practices of Assam in the early twentieth century:

> In times of special emergency, e.g., plague, pestilence, famine, etc., the services of the possessed woman, the Deoddni, are called into action for a special puja. . . . [A] number of figures . . . bearing a rude resemblance to the outlines of the human form are placed in an upright position. . . . Before each figure is placed a layer of the plantain tree with its concave side upwards, and in this are deposited the heads of slaughtered goats, pigeons, chickens, with salt, sugar cane, plantains, gazi (a mixture of rice and pulse), etc., the whole being freely sprinkled with blood. . . . The Deoddni, a somewhat weird looking figure with disheveled hair, and vermillion stained forehead, wearing a long petticoat, dances up and down, to and fro before these figures keeping time roughly with the music of cymbals and tom-toms played by four or five men. . . . [T]he Deoddni, whose faculties are apparently quite absorbed in what she is doing and who seems for the time to be lifted above the world of time and sense, gradually works herself up into a stage of excitement bordering on frenzy. At this stage, which is only slowly attained, a goat is brought forward and taken up before one of the figures . . . when the Deoddni, with one stroke of the long sacrificial sword . . . severs the victim's head from its body. Most of the blood is held to be offered to the maddi [deity]. . . . It is at this stage of climax of the puja, i.e., the sacrificial slaughter of the goat, that the Deoddni is supposed to become possessed of the knowledge she is in search of.[67]

Specifically on the occasion of Manasā Pūjā, ecstatic female performances continue to take place among indigenous communities such as the Rabhas. As Kishore Bhattacharjee notes in her study of the festival celebrated by the Rabhas on the north bank of the Brahmaputra River, the *deodhanī* "occupies a very important role in the performances and rituals. She not only makes predictions but enters in climax situation and dances."[68] During a long dramatic performance of the Manasā narrative, the *deodhanī* enters repeatedly into states of possession known as *dak*, which is said to be derived from the Sanskrit word *daṃśa* (snake bite); thus she is possessed in turn by Durgā (who is bitten by Manasā) and then by Śiva (who drinks the poison that flows from the churning of the cosmic ocean).[69]

The final state of *dak* takes place during the narrative of the death of Behulā's husband, Lakhindar. At this point, the dancer enters into a deep trance state lasting several hours before bursting forth again in one last, wildly ecstatic dance: "Finally when Lakhindar dies in the night time on the marriage day, the deodhani is possessed for long duration . . . and it needs special skill on the part of the deodhani to learn to remain in such a position. At the time of last possession the deodhani jerks her body and in jerking reaches a frenzied state and she comes to normal stage gradually reducing her trembling."[70] This climactic performance is followed by a goat sacrifice, during which the *deodhanī* dances with the sword and follows the priests to the shrine of the local deities.

Like many other traditional Assamese dances, the *deodhanī* dance is now performed for large public audiences in major urban centers such as Guwahati, where it is typically accompanied by the traditional musical form of Ojā pāli in honor of Manasā. Not surprisingly, the dance has also been transformed in a number of important ways. In contrast to the dance among communities such as the Rabha, the contemporary performance of the *deodhanī* dance is (a) staged (that is, performed literally on stages or sports fields for large public audiences), (b) highly choreographed, and (c) unbloody (involving only symbolic, not literal, violence and sacrifice).

The figure most often credited with the modern "revival of the dying art form" of Ojā pāli and *deodhanī* dance was Lalit Candra Nāth, a.k.a. Lalit Ojā.[71] Born in the Darrang district in 1923, Lalit mastered Ojā pāli as a young man and began recruiting women to perform the *deodhanī* dance for Manasā. According to the documentary film based on his life, Lalit Ojā initially had difficulty finding women who were willing to perform the dance, since it brought with it such a negative stigma: "No girl of any decent household would volunteer to be a *deodhanī* dancer. The few who did came from the weaker sections of the society. *Deodhanī* dancers were not only looked down upon, they were considered ineligible for marriage."[72]

Thus, Lalit Ojā recalled a girl named Rādhikā, who was in fact the first one he trained in this dance: "It's an irony. The people like the dancer. They enjoy the dance performance. However, after the dance is over, they show their dislike for the girl who performed the dance."[73]

FIGURE 4.5. Female *deodhanī* dancers, Darrang, Assam, 2017.
Photo by Mostafizur Rahman.

Eventually, however, Lalit succeeded in attracting widespread attention to his revival of the art form, bringing it to a national stage in 1974. After first being invited to perform in Punjab during the governorship of Mahendra Mohan Choudhury, he went on to perform at the Asian Games in New Delhi, the International Trade Fair, and various other high-profile venues. Later, Lalit Ojā would be given a series of major awards for his resuscitation of this folk art form, including the prestigious Sangeet Natak Akademi award from India's National Academy of Music, Dance, and Drama, and the Rabindranath Tagore award, in honor of India's most famous modern poet.[74]

The form of *deodhanī* dance that was revived and reconstructed by artists such as Lalit Candra Nāth is a very different sort of performance than the trance possession described by early scholars such as Endle or the Rabha form of Manasā Pūjā described by ethnographers such as Bhattacharjee. Indeed, it would not be difficult to see this staged form of national dance as a fairly explicit example of the domestication and folklorization of local practices. At least in the eyes of the many state and local promoters of tourism in the region, however, this domestication of the dance is actually a *welcome* phenomenon. As the Assam State Portal describes the dance, in rather telling terms, "There are actually two types of Deodhani. One is a semi classic dance and the other is a trance (not a dance). The Deodhani Dance [is] prevalent in Mangaldoi and southwest Kamrup area, which is linked to the Sukanani Oja-Pali. It is nice to see that the present promoters of this dance have refined it to a readily acceptable beauty."[75]

While this iteration of the dance is still understood to be a form of possession, it is a highly choreographed and scripted performance overall. On the one hand, the performance is modeled on the ecstatic dance of Behulā before the gods, and the dancers dress as warriors, taking up swords to engage in a "virile war dance."[76] As Lalit Ojā explained to his dancers, it is really their gestures and movements that will persuade the gods to intervene and bring Lakhindar back to life: "You should know this: It's here in these hand gestures, looks, *mudrās*, the steps. It is through this dance that Behulā could appeal to the gods and bring him back to life."[77] Yet on the other hand, women are carefully trained in precise, synchronized steps, which involve neither spontaneity nor violence. Performed in a line or in a circle, with the male Ojā pāli musicians playing behind them, the dance involves a choreographed swordplay and ends in a notably unbloody strike of the blades onto the ground (rather than into the neck of an animal). Even the moments of seeming "wildness," such as waving unbound hair and bearing sacrificial swords, are carefully enacted according to a predetermined script and never involve anything more than a gesture toward violence. While it is still clearly a performance of "wildness," the possession here has also been domesticated almost to the point of innocuous anachronism.

The gender dynamics among the *deodhanī* are equally as complex as—but in many ways almost symmetrically inverse images of—those of the male *deodhāis*. While the male dancers are inspired by female singers in their possession, the *deodhanīs* are inspired by the male Ojā pālis; while the male *deodhāis* inhabit a number of feminine roles—particularly those of the powerful *śaktis* such as Manasā, Kāmākhyā, and Kālī—the female *deodhanīs* enact exaggeratedly "masculine" roles, such as wielding swords and simulating animal sacrifice. The two dances are almost mirror images of one another and are rendered in rough tabular form in table 4.3.

However, more than just mirror images, the two dances are also profoundly different in several key ways. First, while the dance of the male *deodhāis* is performed with exaggerated wildness and spontaneity within the Kāmākhyā temple complex, the dance of the *deodhanīs* is either excluded from the temple complex and relegated to indigenous villages or, more commonly today, limited to highly choreographed and folklorized performances on urban stages. Second, while the male *deodhāis* each embody a distinct, individual deity with his or her own personality, characteristics, and dynamics, the *deodhanīs* all collectively embody the same deity

TABLE 4.3. Comparative gender dynamics in the male *deodhāi* and female *deodhanī* dances

	Deodhāi dance		*Deodhanī* dance	
	MALE	FEMALE	MALE	FEMALE
Singers' gender		X	X	
Dancers' pre-possession gender	X			X
Gender of primary possessing deity/leader	X			X
Gender roles enacted by dancer	X	X	X	X
Dancers' post-possession gender	X			X

and act in synchrony as a group without separate personalities. In the performance of the *deodhanīs*, then, the dance has been not simply domesticated but also homogenized and singularized in a fundamental way.

Conclusions: Possession, Performance, and the Subversion of Identity

The possession performances of both the male *deodhāis* and female *deodhanīs* represent important continuities with the broader Tantric "path of desire" as well as some clear departures in this local context. Possession here is not so much a matter of Tantric initiates becoming infused with the deity through controlled meditation in esoteric ritual contexts but rather of public performers becoming ecstatic vehicles of a kind of divine invasion. "Desire" in this case is far more worldly and human—the desire for healing and material prosperity promised by the male dancers, or Behulā's impassioned desire for the return of her husband's life performed by the female dancers.

To conclude, I would like to make some broader comparative comments on the role of possession in relation to individual collective identity in Śākta Tantra and in Assam more broadly. There is, of course, a great deal of fine anthropological literature on the phenomenon of possession, both in India and cross-culturally, that would be relevant here.[78] As Karen McCarthy Brown suggests, for example, the spirits who possess human beings are rarely simple or one-dimensional beings; rather, they are more often "characters defined by contradiction," with a profound "ability to contain conflicting emotions and to model opposing ways of being."[79] We can clearly see this sense of contradiction and conflicting emotion in the case of possession in Assam, where dancers embody both male and female, healing and destructive, Hindu and indigenous, pan-Indian and local, urban and village identities in a single ecstatic performance.

Similarly, as Paul C. Johnson eloquently argues, possession can be a powerful way of negotiating not only different modes of being but also different temporal and historical identities, a means of remembering the past in the present. As religious traditions and communities travel from one place to another and from one generation to the next, possession is often the site where those different spaces and times are relived in the here and now: "Those horizons are recalled and reactivated through rituals that return the spirits of those places to the present through the bodies of priests possessed."[80] In the case of possession in Assam, we can clearly see that the dancers are performing not only their connection to other spatial identities (such as villages and indigenous communities) but also their connection to different historical eras (such as older, pre-Hindu tribal traditions). Like the goddess Manasā herself, the indigenous religions of Assam have been absorbed—albeit in partial and complex ways—into the body of Sanskritic Hinduism. Yet in their dances, the *deodhāis* recall and reactivate older forms of pre-Hindu practice, such as possession, trance, and ecstasy, which are grudgingly permitted on the outer edges of the main temple.[81]

While I do find these and other anthropological perspectives useful, in this specific case I also want to borrow but critically modify some of Judith Butler's influential work on performativity, gender, and the subversion of identity. As Butler suggests, all identity—including gender identity—is neither static nor substantive, but rather an effect that is "performatively produced" through a "stylized repetition of acts"—that is, a constant reiteration of normative social roles carried out in myriad mundane acts, gestures, and ritualized behaviors.[82] However, certain kinds of bodily performances—such as drag, for example—can also open the "possibility of subverting and displacing those naturalized and reified notions of gender," by highlighting their arbitrariness and fragility.[83] While Butler was not particularly interested in religious forms of performance, many of their readers have been, and many have identified similar kinds of ritual and subversive performances at work in other contexts, including the Śākta traditions of northeast India.[84]

The performances of the *deodhāi* and *deodhanī* do indeed involve various forms of gender subversion, in Butler's sense, by crossing over, questioning, and "queering" the categories of masculinity and femininity. Males are mounted by female deities, women perform traditionally masculine roles, and power circulates back and forth dynamically between male and female singers, dancers, and divinities. But ultimately, I would argue, the subversion of *gender* identity is not really the primary or ultimate aim. Indeed, the dances could also be said to *reinforce* gender roles in some ways, insofar as the gender-bending only takes place in very specific, temporally limited, and spatially confined ritual contexts, and the dancers all return to their prescribed gender roles at the conclusion of the dances. This reinforcement is particularly evident in the case of the female dancers whose performance is much more clearly circumscribed, domesticated, and largely rendered non-threatening.[85] Rather, the sort of "subversion of identity" at work in the dance of the *deodhāi* and *deodhanī* is at once broader and more profound than that imagined by contemporary theorists such as Butler.

This larger subversion, I would suggest, is at least twofold. The first I would call the subversion of religious and national identity—and specifically, the subversion of any notion of a singular, homogeneous, or monolithic Hindu or Indian identity. The dance of both the *deodhāi* and *deodhanī* is a powerful reminder of the deep indigenous roots of Assamese religion and culture, highlighting the fact that many of its deities—such as Manasā and Kāmākhyā herself—have indigenous histories quite apart from their Sanskritic and *brāhmaṇic* aspects. So, too, do their worshippers. As Sharma points out in her study of Assam during the colonial and postcolonial periods, the forging of a modern Assamese identity has been a "constant process of negotiation and disputation" between dominant-caste Hindus and the many local Bodo, Rabha, Ahom, and other indigenous cultures.[86] The possession performance of the *deodhāi* and *deodhanī* appears to be a powerful site at which this negotiation and disputation of identity is being enacted—indeed, literally embodied in the very physical movements of the dancers themselves.

Second and perhaps most profoundly, however, the dances of the *deodhāi* and *deodhanī* point to a more radical *subversion of human identity* itself. That is, they enact a transgression of the boundary between the human and the divine, performing a kind of divine invasion of the self by powerful, frightening, sometimes violent and unpredictable deities. While Deleuze and Guattari wrote rather abstractly about the idea of "becoming woman" and "becoming non-human,"[87] these possession performances are quite literally about becoming transformed into suprahuman beings, both male and female. In this sense, these dances trouble not just the limits of gender and sex; rather, they trouble the very limits of subjectivity, agency, and personhood, by suggesting a notion of the self that is not homogeneous or singular but instead open to a multiplicity of voices, to a profound *loss* of self, and to a radically nonhuman otherness.[88]

[CHAPTER FIVE]

"The Cradle of Tantra"

Modern Transformations of a Tantric Center from Nationalist Symbol to Tourist Destination

> Kāmākhyā, the place of the *yoni-maṇḍala*, the place of the beautiful [goddess] Tripura Bhairavī, is the best of all places and the original home of [the goddess] Mahāmāyā. There is no better place on earth. The goddess appears there every month during her menstrual period.
>
> *Devī Bhāgavata Purāṇa* (tenth or eleventh century)[1]

> Prayed to Maa Kamakhya for the development of our nation and the well-being of our citizens.
>
> Twitter statement by Prime Minister Narendra Modi (2016)[2]

In June 2017, I made my third trip to the celebration of Ambuvācī Melā, the largest and most famous festival held at Kāmākhyā Temple. As we saw in the introduction, Ambuvācī Melā coincides roughly with the onset of the monsoon season and celebrates the annual menstruation of the goddess Kāmākhyā herself, whose blood is believed to bring life to the world and blessings to her devotees, just as the rains (*ambu*) bring life and fertility to the earth.[3]

While Kāmākhyā Temple and Ambuvācī Melā have long been revered in Sanskrit literature, both the temple and its primary festival have undergone a series of profound transformations in the modern era. As I made my way up the steep stone staircase on the western side of the temple complex in 2017, I noted a series of striking changes in the celebration of the festival. Not only was the crowd that summer *much, much* larger than in my previous trips, but the entire hillside and the surrounding city of Guwahati were plastered with slickly designed billboards advertising Kāmākhyā as the "Cradle of Tantra" where one can "Discover the Supreme Power." Meanwhile, huge posters featuring none other than Indian prime minister Narendra Modi and then-state minister Sarbananda Sonowal lined the main road running through Guwahati, encouraging pilgrims to come "Come, seek the blessings

FIGURE 5.1. Billboard, Kāmākhyā Temple, Guwahati, Assam, 2017. Photo by the author.

FIGURE 5.2. Billboard, Guwahati, Assam, 2017. Photo by the author.

of Maa Kamakhya." Prominent celebrities and Bollywood stars had also begun appearing on national airways, urging citizens to visit the seat of the goddess.[4] Many of my friends from the local Tantric community, however, were dismayed by these developments, lamenting that the authentic celebration of the goddess's annual menses had been largely destroyed by the rampant commercialization of the event and that their best hope lay in preserving other, more obscure, and still esoteric traditions.[5]

While I was initially somewhat baffled by these transformations, I later realized that these are only the latest in a long series of changes to the Kāmākhyā temple and its festivals that date back to at least the nineteenth century and have often been closely tied to larger political dynamics. As art historian Imma Ramos has persuasively argued, Kāmākhyā Temple became part of a larger effort to establish a sense of cultural unity amid the emerging Indian nationalist movements of the late nineteenth and early twentieth centuries. For nationalist authors, the major seats of the goddess (*śākta pīṭhas*) became key symbols of collective identity, imagined as a network of power centers that might bind this diverse landscape together in both spiritual and political terms.[6] As the site of the goddess's *yoni*—and thus the ultimate seat of creative power—the region of Assam was often an integral part of the broader attempt to reimagine the sacred landscape of a unified Hindu nation.

Much more recently, however, Kāmākhyā Temple and Ambuvācī Melā have also become part of an aggressive push by the national and state governments to promote tourism and economic development in the northeast region. This initiative began as early as 2014, with the election of the conservative prime minister Modi, who had already undertaken a plan to promote the *pīṭhas* and other pilgrimage sites as symbols of Indian national unity.[7] But in the last several years, it has been taken to far more ambitious lengths with the promotion of Ambuvācī in Assam, where the festival is now widely advertised as a means to develop the northeast region and to strengthen a sense of national unity. Together with Modi, Assam's chief minister has made explicit efforts to develop the festival as a symbol of national pride, a driver of economic development, and a center of "religious and spiritual tourism."[8]

Of course, the concept of "spiritual tourism" is neither new nor unique in the twenty-first century.[9] Similar attempts to develop temple and pilgrimage sites have taken place across India, as we see perhaps most clearly in the example of the Vaiṣṇo Devī complex near Jammu, which has seen its number of visitors increase from a few thousand a year in the 1950s to over ten million by 2012.[10] However, this recent move to promote Ambuvācī Melā is remarkable for several reasons. After all, as we have seen throughout this book, Kāmākhyā Temple is a key center of Tantra in its most left-hand forms, which include the consumption of alcohol, meat, and other explicitly transgressive rituals. At its core, Ambuvācī is a Tantric festival, one that focuses centrally on the goddess's menstrual blood; moreover, as we saw in chapter 3, it also involves a tremendous amount of blood sacrifice, with large-scale offerings of goats, pigeons, fish, sheep, ducks, and buffaloes. All these Tantric elements seem profoundly at odds with the agendas of Modi's BJP and other conservative parties—particularly in their attitudes toward purity and sexuality.[11]

After a brief discussion of the mythical and historical origins of Ambuvācī Melā, I examine its changing role in the context of emerging Hindu nationalism during the nineteenth and twentieth centuries. I then discuss the new efforts to promote spiritual tourism and economic development in the region. These efforts, I suggest, have created deep tensions due to the commercialization of the Melā and the government's attempts to downplay or sanitize the more controversial aspects of this Tantric center, which include not only animal sacrifice (discussed above) but also the sexual imagery that surrounds the temple. To conclude, I argue that the case of Ambuvācī further highlights the deep slippage between the nationalist ideals of the BJP and the actual practices that we find at sites such as Kāmākhyā. While the former seek to create a purified, homogeneous vision of a unified Hindu India, the latter remain intimately bound to the powers of sexuality and transgressive ritual. From the blood flowing from the menstruating *yoni* to the throngs of chillum-smoking *sādhus* and the Aghorīs performing corpse rituals, they reveal the lingering presence of heterogeneous, local, and non-*brāhmaṇic* traditions that do not fit easily into the sanitized ideal of a singular Hindu nation. The recent attempts to repackage Ambuvācī as a commercial tourist spectacle have revealed even more profound fissures and in fact created deep divisions within the local community itself.

The Place of Desire: Mythical and Historical Origins of Ambuvācī Melā

As we saw in chapter 3, the mythic origins of Kāmarūpa and Kāmākhyā are closely tied to narratives of bloodshed, desire, power, and sacrifice. Like the other *pīṭhas* throughout South Asia, the *yoni pīṭha* of Kāmākhyā is said to have been born from the sacrifice of the goddess Satī, the wife of Śiva, whose dismembered body parts fell to earth and became the various seats of power throughout South Asia. Historically, however, it is very difficult to date the origins of Kāmākhyā Temple, due to the many layers of sculptural fragments that currently lie scattered all over Nīlācala Hill. The oldest stratum appears to date to at least the seventh century, and the numerous sculptural pieces found around the complex suggest that there was a major temple complex here during the Pāla dynasty (tenth to twelfth centuries, the Assamese counterpart to the Pāla Empire of Bengal and Bihar).[12] The most important text composed in Assam, the *Kālikā Purāṇa*, also dates to the Pāla era and contains extensive descriptions of Kāmākhyā, the region of Assam, and the *yoni pīṭha*. However, the original temple complex was destroyed at some point after the decline of the Pāla Empire and was later rediscovered and rebuilt by the Koch kings in the sixteenth century.[13] The present temple embodies this complex history, with fragments of older sculptural pieces from various historical periods cemented into the walls or onto surrounding structures. Many of these older images, we should note, prominently feature themes of sexuality, reproduction, nursing, and childbearing. Probably the most famous of these is the large *Lajjā Gaurī* (the "modest" goddess), a pregnant figure depicted in a birthing position, which is displayed on the north outer wall of the temple. Until quite recently, pilgrims used to regularly touch her wide-open *yoni* and adorn it with bright red vermillion paste, clearly highlighting the close association between the goddess, the *yoni*, and the generative power of blood. As we will see below, however, the image is now covered most of the time.[14]

The heart of the temple is the *yoni* itself—a rock with a vaginal cleft covered by water from an underground spring—that lies inside the main "womb chamber" or *garbha-gṛha*. As Frédérique Apffel-Marglin and Julia Jean note, it is primarily by touching the *yoni* that devotees enter into direct

FIGURE 5.3. Lajjā Gaurī, Kāmākhyā Temple, Guwahati, Assam, 2017. Photo by the author.

contact with the power and grace of the goddess: "The male *shakta* Tantric brahmin priests who tend the main shrine . . . are never shy to tell those who might hesitate to get on their knees and reach down into the rock cleft: 'Touch it! You must touch it!'"[15]

Like the complex, multilayered historical origins of Kāmākhyā Temple itself, the historical roots of Ambuvācī Melā are by no means clear.[16] Probably the earliest reference to the festival comes from the *Devī Bhāgavata Purāṇa* (tenth or eleventh century), where it is described as the aftereffect of the love-play between Viṣṇu and the goddess Earth. Assuming his boar (Varāha) incarnation, Viṣṇu made love to Earth for a year of the gods (360 human years). At the end of their dalliance, he worshipped Earth as the supreme goddess and declared that she would be honored on several auspicious occasions: "On the day the Ambuvācī ceremony closes, when laying the entry at the start of building a house, at the start of digging a well, and tilling the soil, everyone should worship you with wine, etc."[17] The same text also links the Earth's menstrual cycle specifically to the *pīṭha* of Kāmākhyā, which is praised as the greatest of all temples and the most powerful place in the world. Thus, it is to Kāmākhyā, as the seat of the *yoni*, that the goddess comes each during her menses: "Kāmākhyā, the place of the *yoni-maṇḍala* . . . is the best of all places and the original home of Mahāmāyā. There is no better place on earth. The goddess appears there every month during her menstrual period."[18] By the time of later texts such as the *Kubjikā Tantra* (post–sixteenth century), Kāmākhyā was praised as the greatest *pīṭha* for this last and darkest age, the *kali yuga*, where taking a piece of the goddess's bloody menstrual cloth would lead to liberation and satisfy all desires: "The great *pīṭha* of Kāmarūpa fulfills all one's desires [*kāmarūpaṃ mahāpīṭhaṃ sarvvakāma-phalapradaṃ*]. In the *kali* age, prayer in Kāmarūpa is said to bear quick results. Taking Kāmākhyā's [menstrual] cloth, one should perform prayer and worship. One will attain all desires, without doubt [*pūrṇakāmaṃ labdhed*]."[19]

As it is celebrated in Assam today, Ambuvācī takes place for four days, from the seventh to the tenth days of the month of Āsāḍha (June–July).[20] Occurring at the beginning of monsoon season, with the coming of the cooling rains after the heat of summer, Ambuvācī marks the flow of the goddess's life-giving blood to the earth and the flow of divine grace to her devotees. As one young priest put it, "Blood is the main *shakti* [generated during *Ambuvaci*]. It is *shakti*. Kamakhya is the Mother of the Universe and Her blood is discharging . . . and it is powerful."[21] But Ambuvācī is also a celebration that reflects the profound ambivalence of the goddess's blood and the power it embodies, a power that is tied to impurity and to the dangerous potency of sexual fluids. As David Shulman observes, "Power is . . . derived from forces that are contaminating; these forces belong to the violent substratum of chaos out of which the world emerged."[22] And the goddess's menstrual blood is the very essence of this powerful yet contaminating force. To use the terms of Apffel-Marglin, menstrual blood is perhaps the epitome of the category of the *auspicious*—a substance that is *both* dangerously impure *and* extremely powerful, as the mark of fertility and potential creation of new life. It is as once "sacred and accursed."[23]

Thus, when Kāmākhyā menstruates for three days each year, she is considered to be in a state of impurity, and the temple must be closed to all visitors for three days. As Śrī Gaṅga Śarmā, explains, "Mother Goddess Kāmākhyā becomes impure due to menses, just like an impurity of woman due to her menstruation. . . . During this period . . . the temple doors are closed, and no pilgrim is allowed inside the temple."[24] But this same impure yet powerful blood of the goddess is also believed to bring life to the earth and blessings to her devotees. Thus, on the fourth day, the goddess is a given a "grand bath" (*mahāsnāna*), and the temple doors are reopened for the thousands of pilgrims—many of whom have waited twelve hours or more. Small strips of red cloth representing the bloody flow are distributed to the pilgrims, who thereby receive the power and grace of the goddess. As

Śarmā explains, the red cloth represents the *nirmālya* of the goddess's flow, that is, the sacred "remains" of an offering: "As the sacred remains of this festival, the goddess' red garments (the cloth she was wearing while in her menstrual period) are very fruitful, and the pilgrims wear them as amulets, considering them to be very holy. . . . If ordinary people wear this bloody garment on their own bodies, benefits come from all directions."[25]

As Patricia Dold aptly observes, the goddess's annual menstruation represents a complex mix of both transgression and orthodoxy, of impurity and purity; while the flowing menstrual blood is considered highly polluting and reflects the Tantric roots of the festival, the fact that the temple is off limits during the three days of its flow also reasserts traditional Hindu ideas of purity and rules limiting contact with women: "That menstrual blood is received as *prasad* is therefore transgressive. However, that the temple is closed during the goddess's annual menstruation affirms orthodox standards of purity in that it isolates the menstruating female."[26] This is much the same tension between transgressive power and "respectability" that we noted in chapter 1 regarding the Kulācāra Mārga's complex attitude toward sexuality.

In addition to the goddess's annual menstruation, the impure but auspicious power of blood plays a significant role in many other aspects of Kāmākhyā's worship. As we saw in chapter 3, blood is central to the offering of sacrifice (*bali-dān, yajña*), which is an integral part of the goddess's daily offerings and a major event at large-scale festivals such as Durgā Pūjā. In many ways, sacrifice represents the ritual counterpart to the celebration of Ambuvācī; just as the goddess's power spreads to the earth through her annual menstruation, so too power runs back to her through the blood of animals offered by devotees.[27] Thus, at the close of Ambuvācī, once the temple doors are reopened on the fourth day, countless goats, pigeons, fish, and other animals are brought by pilgrims to be slaughtered. To return to Deleuze's metaphor of "desire as flow," the blood flowing from the menstruating "Goddess of Desire" flows back to her through the many animals offered by her devotees, who come filled with their own various desires for both spiritual and material well-being.[28]

The festival attracts thousands of pilgrims from all over the northeast states and also now increasingly from other parts of India, including Hindus of all classes as well as scheduled castes and tribes and many non-Hindus. In the course of my own interviews, I have found that the reasons pilgrims make the trip are varied and include a wide range of both spiritual and material desires—the general grace of the goddess, spiritual power and protection, physical healing, fertility and the welfare of children, auspicious marriages, good crops, success in business, and so on. As one pilgrim from Rajasthan responded when I asked why he had come, "Kāmākhyā is the mother of everyone, the mother of the whole world. You have a physical mother in your home; Kāmākhyā is the spirit of all mothers, the mother of everyone. She can give you whatever you desire. She only asks for your love."[29]

For example, in June 2022, I met a middle-aged farmer from Jalpaiguri, Bengal, named Rām Gosvāmī, who explained that he had been coming to the Melā for years seeking the goddess's grace; he even stripped off his shirt to show me the many scars on his back where the goddess had cured his wounds. His newly married daughter had just come for the first time in 2022, hoping for blessings to start a new family.[30]

For perhaps obvious reasons, Ambuvācī has a particular attraction for women; as Mishra notes in his detailed sociological study of Kāmākhyā, the female lay pilgrims generally "far outnumber" the males at the Melā.[31] As one woman put it in an interview, women have a natural connection to the goddess insofar as they are inherently part of that same divine energy that flows through all things: "That is where *śakti* comes in. . . . [T]hat special divine force is kind of encompassed in me because I am a woman, and that whole energy is existent in me, and it's up to me to tap it and link it up with the larger force. . . . I am a chip of that energy."[32]

As another woman recalled, she had first come to Ambuvācī at the onset of puberty, and her own first menstruation happened to coincide quite auspiciously with the goddess's annual menstruation. Still today, she performs her *pūjā* using the red cloth that her mother gave her from Ambuvācī: "This is my power [*śakti*]," as she put it. "I forget everything. All troubles, all problems in my life."[33]

The festival is also a favorite pilgrimage site for holy men and women of every variety from all over India, including red-clad Śāktas, black-clad Aghorīs, naked Nāgas, singing Bāuls, chanting Vaiṣṇavas, and myriad others. For example, in just a couple of hours wandering around the festival space, I have shared a chillum of hashish with a friendly group of young disciples from the Bholānāth ashram in Bengal, discussed the practice of corpse rituals with a couple of Aghorīs from Uttar Pradesh, listened to a riotous group of Bāul performers, interviewed an elderly woman from Nagaland who claimed to have supernatural powers, and watched a naked Nāga perform "feats of strength" with his penis.[34] When I asked one older *sādhu* from Rishikesh named Nārāyaṇ Nāth why he had come such a long way to attend the festival, he simply said, "For *śakti* [power], for *prāpti* [the power to obtain anything]. Kāmākhyā is the *yoni*, the source of all power. So, of course I come here!"[35] As another Tantric *sādhu* named Tyāgībābā put it, "The *yoni* is the land. We are the land, trees, wind, mountains. All are from the *yoni*. We all come from *yoni* and *liṅgam*. . . . [There is] no male, no female, no religion, no nation, no separateness, only Goddess."[36]

FIGURE 5.4. Vendor from Bengal selling various goods, Kāmākhyā Temple, Guwahati, Assam, 2022. Photo by the author.

Like most festivals in South Asia, Ambuvācī is also very much a kind of vast, chaotic marketplace—a teeming spiritual/secular bazaar in which more or less any sort of religious artifact, food, clothing, and jewelry can be purchased.[37] Pilgrims can buy not only all the flowers, incense, candles, fruit, sweets, and other items that might be offered to the deities, they can also find *mālās* (rosaries), *liṅgams*, *yantras*, sacred stones, and other religious objects, not to mention quite "secular" merchandise such as earrings, necklaces, hats, plastic toys, stuffed animals, and more or less anything else one might desire. Many vendors also offer an array of magical items. In 2022, I met some *tantra-mantra* merchants who offered a wide range of roots, herbs, rings, amulets, and animal skulls that were said to heal various parts of the body, along with a very scary-looking black doll that was to be used for more malevolent magic.[38] Another elderly vendor named Sunil Sarkar hailed from the infamous "land of magic," Mayong, and sold wooden objects shaped like a snake. "This is called Naag Panchami," he explained. "You keep it dipped in water overnight and the water turns red the next day. If a woman were to drink this water, she will never complain of menstruation-related trouble ever. It's medicine that works miraculously."[39] Innumerable other products, both magical and mundane, are on offer throughout the festival space.

However, this mass of pilgrims arriving at the temple each year also generates a certain amount of tension with the local Kāmākhyā community, many of whom do not appreciate the crowds, noise, and mass amounts of waste filling up their living spaces.[40] As we will see below, these tensions have only intensified in recent years as the Melā has grown exponentially.

Imagining Mother India: The *Pīṭhas* and the Politics of Indian Nationalism

As a key seat of power and the locus of the goddess's sexual organ, Kāmākhyā Temple and the broader region of Kāmarūpa have long been closely tied to political power, kingship, and territory. The key Assamese text the *Kālikā Purāṇa* was likely composed during the reign of King Dharmapāla (1035–1060) or his predecessor Indrapāla (960–990), and it spends a great deal of time discussing the importance of kingship, the nature of political power, and the structure of the ideal state. Above all, by honoring the rites of sacrifice and the major *pūjās*, the king maintains his power and conquers his enemies: "By performing sacrifices and offering gifts, one becomes a king in this world. Therefore, to have a kingdom one should follow *dharma*. By means of these rites and by performing sacrifices, your enemies are destroyed, and you will achieve kingship, without doubt."[41] Copper-plate inscriptions from the Pāla era also highlight the close relationship between the king, as the embodiment of the supreme Kāmeśvara (Lord of Desire), and the goddess, as the embodiment of the kingdom and his counterpart, Kāmeśvarī (Lady of Desire).[42]

Long after the collapse of the Pāla dynasty, Kāmākhyā continued to be closely tied to kingship and territory. The temple was rediscovered in the sixteenth century by the Koch king Viśva Siṅgha (1515–1540) and then rebuilt in its present form by his son Naranārāyaṇa (1540–1586). Later, the most powerful Ahom kings such as Rudra Siṅgha (1697–1714) and Śiva Siṅgha (1714–1744) continued to patronize Śākta Tantra as the "cult of strength" and brought important *brāhmaṇs* from Bengal to care for the temple.[43]

However, if Kāmākhyā has long been intimately linked to the power of the state, it assumed a new significance in the nineteenth and twentieth centuries, in the context of emerging Indian nationalist movements. As Ramos persuasively argues in her study of the *śākta pīṭhas*, the once obscure and remote region of Assam became increasingly important to many Indians (particularly Bengalis) during the nineteenth century amid the politics of British colonial rule. In part because of their concerns about the spread of nationalist movements across northeast India, the British authorities separated Assam from Bengal in 1874, placing it under its own chief commissioner. In turn, many Bengalis began to strongly assert the connection between the two regions, highlighting their cultural, linguistic, and religious links with Assam—links embodied, above all, in *pīṭhas* such as Kāmākhyā: "The renewed interest in the Shakti Pithas as symbolic of the motherland was a clear response to the colonial fragmenting of territory. . . . Establishing a relationship between Bengal and Assam (and the rest of India) was crucial to the Bengali literati's anti-imperialist discourse. They sought to transcend the cartographic boundaries imposed by the British by uniting these . . . neighboring territories, emphasising their shared culture, especially through pilgrimage sites."[44]

Many authors also began to encourage Bengalis to learn more about the region and make their own pilgrimage to Kāmākhyā. Among them was Halirām Phukkan (1802–1832), an Assamese official who worked for the colonial administration. In 1830, Phukkan published a text in Bengali script entitled *Kāmākhyā Yātra Paddhati* (Procedure for pilgrimage to Kāmākhyā) and distributed it widely to help his countrymen make the journey to this holy site. As he put it in his history of Assam, *Āsām Burañjī*, "Many are vaguely aware that there is a country called Assam, Kāmarūpa, etc. But leave alone proper information or news, the people from other countries hardly know how that country is or even where it is located."[45]

The ties between Assam, Bengal, and the rest of India were also fostered in the late nineteenth and early twentieth centuries by improved travel networks. In 1899, two new travel routes were opened to Guwahati through rail and river, which also facilitated more pilgrimage to and publicity for Kāmākhyā Temple.[46] Thus we find a number of travel narratives by prominent Bengalis during this period, recounting their arduous journey to this powerful seat of the *yoni*. Swāmī Vivekānanda visited the site with his mother in 1901 as part of a tour of India's pilgrimage sites, as did Debendranath Tagore (father of the great poet Rabindranath Tagore).[47] Many of these authors explicitly linked pilgrimage to these holy sites with the ideal of India as a sacred landscape and thus with the burgeoning nationalism of the late nineteenth and early twentieth centuries. In 1904, the famous Western disciple of Swāmī Vivekānanda, Sister Nivedita, published a key essay on "Indian Pilgrimage," in which she describes India's spiritual centers as the knots in a complex web woven by the many threads of pilgrimage routes, which bind this landscape together into a singular religious whole, unified by "love for the Motherland."[48] She continues: "All over India, away from her ancient high roads, and thrown like a network across her proudest Himalayas, are little thread-like paths. . . . Assuredly a deep and conscious love of place pervades the whole of the Indian scheme. It has never been called patriotism, only because it has never been defined by boundaries of contrast; but the home, the village, the soil, and in a larger sense the rivers, the mountains and the country as a whole, are the objects of an almost passionate adoration."[49]

In sum, both the *śākta pīṭhas* and the concept of pilgrimage became key parts of the emerging nationalist spirit that first spread in the nineteenth century and then burst forth powerfully in the early twentieth century. It is not difficult to see why. As Peter van der Veer suggests, pilgrimage is inherently a ritual that at once mobilizes large communities and marks out boundaries of sacred space; as such, it is often a vital component in various forms of religious nationalism, particularly in South Asia: "Movement and the definition of space and territory are central elements in religious nationalism. . . . Given that pilgrimage is, by definition, a ritual of the larger community, it is easily incorporated into religious nationalism."[50]

Likewise, the *pīṭhas* easily lend themselves to a nationalist imagining of India as a divine territory united by a network of power centers, each embodying the great goddess. As Diana Eck notes, "The recognition of India as a sacred landscape, woven together north and south, east and west, by the paths of pilgrims, has created a powerful sense of India as Bhārat Mātā—Mother India."[51]

From Nationalist Symbol to Spiritual Tourism and Economic Development

If Kāmākhyā and other *pīṭhas* became important parts of an emerging nationalism in the nineteenth and twentieth centuries, they have become central to a new plan for tourism and economic expansion in the twenty-first century. Much of this plan has been led by the ruling nationalist party, the BJP, and by Prime Minister Modi himself. As then-candidate Modi put it in a speech in 2014, pilgrimage sites such as the *pīṭhas* should be regarded as a means of both unifying the body of Mother India and building the Indian economy. Just as pilgrimage to Mecca has helped boost the economy of Saudi Arabia as a holy nation, *yātra* to the *pīṭhas* should do the same for India: "The pilgrimage—*yatras*—to religious places are very important for 125 crore Indians and thus, developing them as tourist spots could strengthen the Indian economy, but the rulers of this country have . . . ignored development of the Indian religious places as tourist spots. . . . The development of Mecca and Medina as religious places has strengthened the economy of that country, but we have ignored the values of our cultural heritages."[52]

One of the most striking uses of the *pīṭhas* as a symbol of both nationalism and tourism was the creation of a new sort of spiritual theme park in

Gujarat called the "51 Pīṭhs at Ambājī." Located near the traditional *pīṭha* of Ambājī—the site of the goddess's heart—this new project is designed to re-create all fifty-one *pīṭhas* in microcosmic form, with replicas of each of the temples located around Gabbar Hill. The Gujarat Tourism website promises that visiting the site, with its convenient co-location of all of the nation's *pīṭhas*, will be equivalent to performing the greatest Vedic rites: "To give devotees of Goddess Shakti a once-in-lifetime opportunity to get the blessings of all the forms of the Goddess, a unique project is created here. The Shakti Peethas bestow holy achievements and spiritual welfare on the devotees."[53] In the words of Prime Minister Modi himself, "The yatra of these Shaktipeeths manifest the unity of Bharat Mata," which is a boon to both national pride and local economic development.[54]

As Ramos suggests, the creation of this spiritual tourist site with all fifty-one *pīṭhas* is clearly tied to the larger ideals of Hindu nationalism championed by conservative parties such as Modi's BJP. However, the very act of bringing all the *pīṭhas* together in one place and representing them all in similar ways (uniform concrete reconstructions) also obscures their individuality and uniqueness, reducing them all to a singular Hindu nationalist narrative: "The bringing together of these Pithas in one location invariably homogenizes the immensely nuanced diversity of each individual site, encouraging the establishment of a single monolithic tradition that risks silencing . . . local forms of religious syncretism."[55] At the same time, these sterile modern replicas are also quite "sanitized," noticeably free of the messier aspects of many actual goddess temples, such as animal sacrifice—a practice fiercely rejected by most conservative factions today.[56]

The recent push to develop Ambuvācī Melā is clearly part of this broader effort to use the *pīṭhas* as symbols of nationalism, tourism, and economic development. This fact was evident to me as soon as I arrived in Guwahati in June 2017 and was greeted by huge billboards erected along the main A. T. Road, which prominently featured Prime Minister Modi, then–chief minister Sonowal, and then–tourism minister Himanta Biswa Sarma, inviting visitors to "seek the blessing of Maa Kamakhya."[57] The State Tourism Department has been quite explicit about the fact that this promotion is part of a larger economic development plan. According to a statement by Minister Sarma featured in the promotional booklet for the Melā, the government's aim is simply to "propagate religious and spiritual tourism in Assam."[58] In an interview in 2017, then–chief minister Sonowal laid out the plan in much greater detail, describing his vision of creating "a centre of religious tourism, set around Ambubachi Mela."[59] Sonowal's argument here is quite telling, connecting the economic development of Assam directly to the power of Kāmākhyā herself—the goddess of desire, who can bring all manner of material and spiritual gifts to her people: "Asserting that the people of Assam should have been one of the economically advanced communities in the country as they have the goddess' blessings, Sonowal said this has, however, not happened because no concerted effort was made to harness the tourism potential of the temple. 'Kamakhya Temple should be the source of light and enlightenment for the world.'"[60]

Sonowal's plans are indeed ambitious. While the festival drew an estimated ten *lakh* (one hundred thousand) visitors in 2016, he hoped that it would bring twice as many in 2017, ultimately making Kāmākhyā "one of the biggest centres of spiritual culture" in India.[61] The state government has a number of new proposals to vastly expand access to the temple, which include widening existing roads and constructing a new road from the western side of the temple. Following Modi's lead, Sonowal hopes to use the festival not just as a symbol of the region's spiritual greatness but as the center of a plan for the aggressive development of the northeast as the economic powerhouse of twenty-first-century India: "In light of renewed thrust of Act East Policy, Guwahati would turn into the gateway of South East Asia in the future and state capital region has also been planned expanding into the nearby areas of the city. . . . Referring to Modi's quote of 'the north east being the new engine of growth for a new India,' Sonowal said all sections of society must join hands for developing the state and the region."[62] Such an ambitious plan to redevelop the temple is, of course, tremendously expensive and has therefore required significant investments not only from state and national governments but also from the private sector. Thus, energy giant Oil India Limited (OIL) has planned to partner with the Tourism Department and spend some 250 million rupees for the development and maintenance of the temple.[63]

In their efforts to promote the Melā, the state government has even called upon some of India's most famous and highly paid celebrities to encourage their fellow citizens to make the pilgrimage. As *India.com* reported, "While Assam Government leaves no stone unturned in developing Assam Tourism, popular actresses like Devoleena Bhattacharjee, Mahika Sharma and Parineeta come forward imploring their fans to visit Assam this monsoon."[64] Thus Bhattacharjee, a well-known TV actress and dancer, implored her fans not just to come to Kāmākhyā but to go further by exploring the spiritual and touristic richness of Assam as a whole: "Assam is one among the centre of religious and spiritual tourism, set around Ambubachi Mela and Kamakhya Temple. Goddess Kamakhya's temple has established the state as one of the great spiritual destinations in the country, and all efforts are being made by the government to highlight this great place of worship on the world stage. I believe people should try visiting the mela and explore Assam. They will for sure feel the presence of Devi Maa."[65]

However, perhaps the most creative plan to promote the Melā was a nationwide, cross-country "bike road show." Accompanied by an intensive campaign on social media, three bikers were sent riding across India for thirty-seven days to spread the message about Ambuvācī to every corner of the nation: "Himanta Biswa Sarma flagged off a bike rally on Tuesday, which will cover most north Indian states to interact with minsters and common people of different states in a bid to draw more tourists to Kamakhya during the mega-event in the city . . . The minister said there will be a focus to make the state a place for religious tourism."[66] At least in terms of sheer numbers, these efforts at mass publicity appear to have been effective. While an estimated one hundred thousand people made the pilgrimage in 2016—already far more than I observed during my first visit in 2000—over 250,000 attended in 2017.[67]

If changes to the temple and its festivals had developed rapidly after 2015, they only accelerated in the years between 2017 and 2022. Thus in 2020, the billionaire businessman Mukesh Ambani—considered by many to be the wealthiest man in Asia—made a large gift of some nineteen kilograms of gold to the temple in order to construct a new gold dome (at an estimated cost of 100,000,000 rupees [= $1,317,000 USD]).[68] There is also now a multistory parking garage on Nīlācala Hill along with various structures and covered walkways to facilitate the rapid flow of large numbers of visitors. Meanwhile, a huge new ferry landing and road are under construction on the west side of the temple complex, along with a flyover that will lead directly from the airport interchange to the main Kāmākhyā gate. While the COVID-19 pandemic led to the temporary cancellation of the large-scale public festivities in 2020 and 2021,[69] the massive promotion of the temple and Ambuvācī kicked back into high gear with the reopening of the Indian economy in 2022.

Not everyone is excited about these new development plans for the Melā, however. On the contrary, there have been intense criticisms of these rapid changes, which reveal a deeper fissure within the Kāmākhyā community itself. Many of the recent changes at the temple have followed in the wake of a protracted legal dispute and a split within the community between two opposing factions.[70] Prior to 1998, the affairs of the complex were run by the Bardeurīs, or the family of *brāhmaṇs* with hereditary rights over the main Kāmākhyā temple. In 1998, the affairs of the complex were transferred to a group called the Kāmākhyā Debutter Board, which was intended to be a more democratic association with representatives from many temples, not only those from Kāmākhyā, and which also included non-*brāhmaṇ* members.[71] A lengthy legal battle ensued, in which the Bardeurīs fought to regain control of the complex. While the Kāmākhyā Debutter Board invoked the rhetoric of "democracy" in their claim to authority, the Bardeurīs made their claim based on "customary rights," which they trace all the way back to the early *brāhmaṇs* brought from Kannauj, mentioned in chapter 1.[72] The battle was waged first in the Kamrup courts, then in the Gauhati High Court, and ultimately in the Indian Supreme Court. Finally, in July 2015, the Supreme Court ruled in favor of the Bardeurī Samāj, ordering the Kāmākhyā Debutter Board to turn over control of the complex and its finances.[73]

Most of the recent changes to the complex and the rapid "touristification" of Ambuvācī have taken place in the wake of this decision, as the Bardeurīs appear to be working closely with the Assam state government, the Department of Tourism, and numerous corporate interests to expand Kāmākhyā's profile as a center of both religious and economic development.[74] This cooperative relationship is clearly evidenced by the many billboards around the complex, which feature corporate sponsors such as Dalmia Cement, Star Cement, Indian Oil, Assam Oil, News Live, and BIG FM Radio, among various others.[75]

Meanwhile, most of the complaints have come from supporters of the Kāmākhyā Debutter Board, many of whom lament the loss of the more traditional features of the complex and the devastation to the natural environment and ecology of Nīlācala Hill.[76] Indeed, critics have been vocal and often quite pointed in their views about the recent changes to the temple, which they regard as a "distortion' of a heritage structure"[77] and a crass push to bring in more tourism revenue. As one Tantric initiate and resident complained to me, the spiritual core of Ambuvācī has basically been lost, and he no longer has any desire to go near the temple during the week of tourist hordes, blatant consumerism, and crass festival displays. Instead, he prefers to wait until the crowds have left and the place has quieted down to perform his *pūjās* at the hill's various temples. He was actually relieved when the COVID-19 crisis hit Assam, because it forced the temple to cancel the massive public festival in 2020 and 2021; instead, he said, the community could for once focus on the internal meaning of Ambuvācī, which is an esoteric Tantric practice that has nothing to do with the tourist spectacle.[78] Similarly, as the *tāntrik* who asked to be called "EMI" put it, "I haven't been to Kāmākhyā for many years, ever since the Assam government began to promote it aggressively as a tourist site, resulting in its becoming excessively crowded." In his view, this promotion is yet another example of "the philistine Brahmin-Bania caste-coalition" that has attempted to impose its Hindutva ideology and economic agenda on all of India.[79] Bandana Sarma, a woman who has long been active in the preservation and protection of the temple's traditions, was even more pessimistic in her view of the current state of the Melā, which she believes has been essentially destroyed and replaced by a hollow tourist spectacle: "Ambuvācī is finished. It started going downhill around 2009, and now it is totally commercialized. It is done."[80]

"Sanitized Tantra": Efforts to Clean Up the Space and the Symbolism of Ambuvācī

A key part of the plan to develop the Melā and Kāmākhyā Temple is a highly visible program of cleanliness and hygiene. Like most large festivals, Ambuvācī can produce massive amounts of garbage and all manner of human and animal waste. By encouraging thousands more devotees to attend, while also transforming the Melā into a national tourist destination, the state's plans are obviously exacerbating this problem, and efforts have therefore been made to at least create the image of a space of purity and hygiene. Throughout the temple complex and surrounding parts of the city, we now find numerous billboards that read "Cleanliness Is Next to Godliness," proclaiming the area to be a litter-free, plastic-free, and tobacco-free zone, while garbage collectors can be seen running baskets of waste up and down the steps.[81] Yet despite the rhetoric of hygiene, mountains of garbage continue to accumulate on many parts of the hill, including an enormous plastic landslide below the Bagalā temple.

These tensions over hygiene were further intensified by the COVID-19 pandemic, which interrupted the Melā for two years. In 2022, the administration took measures to limit the masses of pilgrims gathering in "mega-camps" and waiting in long lines for free food distribution in an effort to avoid turning the festival into a new COVID hotspot.[82] Yet given the huge numbers of visitors coming from all parts of India and sitting, eating, and singing in close proximity for several days, the efforts seemed quite limited, and the effects almost impossible to trace.

At the same time, the current administrators of the temple have also made a number of efforts to clean up the temple space itself, often in ways that have outraged many of the older priests and *tāntriks*. These efforts include, for example, covering over many of the original stone steps and gates with slick marble facing. Even though the temple grounds are scattered with remarkable sculptural pieces from the Pāla era and earlier, they have also erected new but cheaply made concrete images around the grounds. Meanwhile, on the south side of the main temple, a large new set of images of Śiva and Kāmākhyā has been installed—but placed behind glass and metal bars. This sequestration seems oddly out of place at a temple where, as we saw above, touching, rubbing, and making contact with the images

FIGURE 5.5. New images of Śiva and Kāmākhyā behind glass and metal bars, Kāmākhyā Temple, Guwahati, Assam, 2017. Photo by the author.

is a basic part of daily worship. As several of my *tāntrik* friends have commented (at times in horror), this development clearly reflects a north Indian influence and has little in common with local Assamese traditions.[83]

However, these efforts to "clean up" Ambuvācī are not only focused on the physical space but also on the symbolism of the festival itself. When I realized that the Melā was becoming a huge focus of economic development promoted by the BJP, I was curious to see how this conservative administration would deal with the fact that this place is a Tantric center and the seat of the goddess's sexual organ, where the entire focus is divine menstruation. I was impressed to see that the promotional materials printed by the state Department of Tourism all use language that is at once provocative and alluring while also extremely vague and full of ambiguous euphemisms. As we see in the official tourist booklet for the Melā, the government clearly wants to highlight the economic potential of the area, while carefully downplaying the explicit sexuality of the site (for example, by never mentioning menstruation or the sexual aspect of the *yoni*):

> Snuggled atop the Nilachal Hill on the western flank of the Guwahati city, is the temple of Goddess Kamakhya, haloed with an air of mysticism that resonates with ancient legends. Considered the most sacred and the oldest of the 51 Shakti Peeths on Earth, the temple overlooks the ever-burgeoning city. . . . One of the biggest congregations of Eastern India, Ambubachi Mela is the most important festival of the Kamakhya Temple. . . . It is believed that Maa Kamakhya goes through her annual

holy cycle, and the temple doors are shut for these three days. . . . Mystics believe the festival period to be the best time for meditation.[84]

Beyond mere euphemisms, however, the government has also tried to remove some of the more embarrassing and potentially (for tourists) uncomfortable aspects of the Melā. Among other things, they asked the Nāga *sannyāsīs*—who are naked and traditionally parade quite visibly through the festival—to discontinue their annual procession: "'We respect the tradition of the Naga sanyasis who remain naked. But then since people from all walks of life and of all ages flock to Kamakhya temple during the Ambubachi Mela, we don't want other devotees to feel embarrassed or awkward,' said Mohit Chandra Sarma, doloi of the temple."[85]

However, one of the most striking examples of the attempts to "sanitize" the temple space is the covering of the famous image of Lajjā Gaurī on the north face of the *nāṭamandira*. As noted above, this image had long been a favorite object of devotion by pilgrims who used to touch her *yoni* and rub her with vermillion and other substances. Beginning in roughly 2018, however, the image began to be covered from the neck down with a cloth (*kāpor*). When I asked several priests about this striking development, they explained that there was a concern that some visitors would be upset by the image, and so now it is kept hidden or "secret" (*gopanīya*) most of the time.[86] While the priests I spoke to seem to accept this decision without much comment, other members of the community with who I spoke were shocked and outraged by this move, since in their the whole point of the image is to be not only seen but physically touched.[87] Moreover, the decision to cover the image seems quite ironic indeed, since the entire temple is centered on a *yoni* that pilgrims come specifically to touch.

The ambivalence surrounding Lajjā Gaurī and her *yoni* is reminiscent of the ambivalence that surrounds the *liṅgam* in much of modern Hinduism. As Wendy Doniger notes, one of the oldest *liṅgams* in India is the famous Gudimallam *liṅgam* in Andhra Pradesh, which is also one of the most anatomically correct. Unmistakably phallic in shape, the Gudimallam *liṅgam* features a full-length relief image of Śiva, who in turn has his own smaller *liṅgam*. Today, however, the lower part of the small Śiva image is covered by cloth that conceals his genitals—even as, ironically, the much larger *liṅgam* itself remains quite uncovered.[88] As Donger notes, this example seems to reflect a broader ambivalence toward the *liṅgam* that has existed since at least the Mughal era, and particularly since the British colonial period. British Orientalist scholars, Christian missionaries, and colonial administrators regularly expressed their shock and disgust at the open worship of the *liṅgam*, and this disgust was internalized by many Hindu reformers of the

FIGURE 5.6. Lajjā Gaurī covered, Kāmākhyā Temple, Guwahati, Assam, 2022. Photo by the author.

nineteenth and early twentieth centuries. Today, many Hindus—especially those leaning toward the conservative policies of the BJP, VHP, and RSS (Rashtriya Swayamsevak Sangh)—vehemently deny that the *liṅgam* has anything to with a phallus at all and censor and silence those who say it does: "The Muslims . . . attacked lingams, and the British made the Hindus ashamed of them. This set the stage for the final blow, when yet another political movement, the twentieth-century Hindutva faction, condemned . . . what they regarded as unacceptable aspects of their own religion, such as the sexual aspects of the Shiva lingam."[89]

The move to cover the *yoni* of Lajjā Gaurī, I think, reflects a similar sense of shame surrounding sexuality and is likely influenced by many of the same conservative religious and political sentiments. It also reflects the broader emphasis on sexual purity—and specifically *women's* sexual purity—that runs through much of contemporary Hindu nationalist discourse. As Chetan Bhatt observes, Hindu fundamentalists consistently focus on the female body as a symbol of the nation ("Mother India"), one whose sexuality is not to be celebrated and embraced but rather disciplined, controlled, and concealed: "The obsession with the body is strikingly repressive. . . . There is little celebration in revivalist discourse of the real erotic traditions of . . . Hinduism or the sexual pleasures of the human body. The sexual body is instead to be disciplined, contained, silenced, obscured, or erased. . . . In this symbolism, the woman's body often becomes the privileged site of revivalist agitation."[90]

And yet, much like the efforts to remove physical impurity, these symbolic efforts to clean up the image of Ambuvācī have largely failed. As we saw in chapter 3, the quite bloody and messy practice of animal sacrifice remains a central part of worship here, particularly during major festivals. Despite the ban on the procession of the Nāgas, the festival remains replete with all manner of other phenomena that will likely make many tourists uncomfortable. From the ubiquitous groups of *sādhus* smoking chillums of hashish, to the black-clad Aghorīs displaying human skulls, to the hundreds of goats milling around waiting to be slaughtered, Ambuvācī remains a stubbornly untidy, uniquely Assamese, and ultimately quite *tāntrik* sort of event. In the end, a thin cloth placed over Lajjā Gaurī does little to conceal the fact that Kāmākhyā is a temple centered on a wet, flowing *yoni* whose blood thousands of pilgrims come to see, touch, feel, and carry home with them. Unlike the sterile cement replicas of Kāmākhyā and other *śākta pīṭhas* erected at the Ambājī tourist attraction in Gujarat, the actual worship of the goddess performed at her local sites cannot easily be assimilated into the sanitized ideal of Hindutva.

The persistent messiness, bloodiness, and ambivalence of the festival is captured very effectively by the Assamese poet and academic Nitoo Das. In her 2017 poem "Ambubasi," Das vividly describes the Goddess, who "(unlike us regular women) had the luxury of bleeding only once a year." Meanwhile, the "long-haired fanmen" flock to the Melā hunting for "a quick high in the hills, amid the bloodshitpiss" of sacrificial animals and fluids running from a long-dead *yoni*:

she sat wide-bottomed, spread-thighed
behind closed doors and bled
from a very dead vagina
. . . .
They chanted and sang and fed her and made much of her
and the priests waited
to see the waters in the sewers turn red.[91]

Conclusions: Tourism, Neoliberalism, and the Territorialization of Desire

To close, I would like to make some broader comparative comments on the implications of the changing shape of this particular festival for our understanding of religious nationalism and neoliberal development more broadly. We could analyze the contemporary transformations of this festival in many different ways. It would not be difficult, for example, to read the contemporary Ambuvācī Melā as yet another example of religious tourism in the context of globalization, commodification, and consumer culture, which we see at Vaiṣṇo Devī and other pilgrimage sites in South Asia. As Michael Stausberg notes, religion and tourism are intimately interwoven in the contemporary world. As a result, religious festivals, pilgrimage sites, and rituals tend to become enmeshed in the same processes of commodification as do virtually all aspects of culture amid the ever-expanding networks of the neoliberal world order: "Tourism is an inherent part of (global) consumer culture. The tourism sector sells travel, and in order to generate the necessary interest and desire, its advertisements promise unique travel experiences, sometimes with images grounded in mythological and religious tropes (e.g., 'paradise') used as strategies of branding and packaging. Moreover, tourism offers many sites of consumption. By merging into the experience industry and the tourism sector, aspects of religions become a matter of consumption by more than their local users."[92] In the process, Stausberg observes, religious traditions tend to become both "exoticized and Orientalized"—that is, made to appear more tantalizing, alluring, and Other—as well as "simplified"—that is, made more easily digestible for general tourist consumption.

Surely, we can see all these processes at work in the contemporary celebration of Ambuvācī Melā. According to the Assam state government's own rhetoric, the Melā is now viewed as both a key form of "cultural heritage" and a vitally important economic resource. As we have seen above, the Melā has also been at once exoticized and "auto-Orientalized" (billed as "the cradle of Tantra"), as well as simplified and sanitized in order to be made more palatable to a broad audience of tourists.

But what is perhaps most striking about the contemporary celebration of Ambuvācī is that it represents a powerful but also deeply conflicted confluence of three major interests: the religious institution (the Kāmākhyā temple management), the state (national and local governments), and business (various private corporate interests). As we saw in chapter 3, there have been various attempts by conservative political factions to "territorialize" the Tantric flow of desire by banning or marginalizing practices such as blood sacrifice throughout India. In the case of Ambuvācī Melā, I think we can say that there is yet another attempt to "territorialize" this tradition, not just by nationalism but now also by the expanding networks of neoliberalism and global capitalism.[93] The multiple forces of the religious institution, the state, and various corporate interests are all working in concert to try to create a new sort of pilgrimage site that weds a Hindu nationalist ideal with India's larger economic goals of development on a global stage. We might say the object here is not just to create a form of "ecotourism" or even of "eco-magico-tourism," of the sort that we see in Mayong; rather, it is perhaps an attempt at a kind of "eco-magico-nationalist-tourism."

And yet, as we can see in this weird mishmash of hyphenated terms, there are also deep fissures, tensions, and contradictions between these different interests. As Sabina Magliocco has shown in her study of Catholic performances in modern Sardinia, the "touristification" and commodification of festivals in the global context often generates intense conflicts within local communities; it raises profound disagreements about the ways in which these communities perceive themselves and wish to represent themselves to outsiders: "The entry of festivals into the consumer economy has brought about a number of resulting changes in festival structure, in the function and meaning of festival. . . . The same qualities which have enabled festivals to become consumer products also make them vehicles for the playing out of conflicts."[94]

We have seen precisely these sorts of conflicts play out in the recent touristification of Ambuvācī Melā, as groups such as the Kāmākhyā Debutter Board and the Bardeurī Samāj have articulated profoundly different views of the temple, the festival, and the entire tradition. As we saw in chapter 3 in our discussion of animal sacrifice, there are deep tensions between the ideals of Hindu nationalism and local traditions such as Śākta Tantra in Assam. While the former tries to present an idealized notion of religious purity and political unity, the latter remains stubbornly messy, bloody, and non-homogeneous. As Christophe Jaffrelot suggests, the very project of Hindu nationalism is thus in many ways a conflicted and perhaps impossible one. For it is an attempt to impose an ideal of religious unity and national homogeneity onto an incredibly diverse body of texts, rituals, and traditions that have evolved over 3500 years, articulated in dozens of different languages and myriad local cultures.[95] Similarly, I would argue, the neoliberal attempts to absorb more and more local traditions into a global system of economic development are equally riddled with internal tensions and conflicting interests. They reveal not only the contested nature of the modern Indian "nation and its fragments"; they also what reveal what Daniel Bell famously called the "cultural contradictions of capitalism"—or what some have recently called the "cultural contradictions of neoliberalism,"[96] as global market forces attempt to absorb wildly heterogeneous cultures and traditions into a monolithic system based on the "commodification of everything."[97]

Perhaps nowhere are these cultural contradictions more apparent than in the case of Ambuvācī Melā and, above all, in the more extreme Tantric elements that are integral to this tradition. A festival centered on the annual menstrual cycle of a powerful Tantric goddess, a temple where blood sacrifice is an integral part of daily worship, a tradition embedded in the ritual use of impurity and sexuality—none of these elements fits particularly well with the brand of Hindutva promoted by Modi, Sonowal, Sarma, and other BJP leaders. Nor does it fit very well with the sanitized vision of ecotourism promoted by state and national governments in India today. Despite many attempts to purify or "deodorize" the festival for touristic and commercial purposes, it remains at its core a Tantric menstruation festival. Like the open *yoni* of the Lajjā Gaurī on the outer wall of the temple, it can perhaps be covered over with a thin veil of Hindutva slogans and tourist advertisements, yet the powerful, messy, and "auspiciously impure" blood of the goddess continues to seep through in various transgressive ways.

[CHAPTER SIX]

"Sinister *Tāntriks*"

Tantra in Popular Culture, Fiction, and Film

> A tantrik suddenly appeared before them—it was as if he rose from a ditch under a broken post. . . . His face was dirty. Its expression vicious like a serpent about to strike. The students whispered, agitated: "That tantric drinks the blood of slaughtered animals. . . . He rubs his body with blood instead of ashes."
>
> Indira Goswami, *The Man from Chinnamasta* (2005)[1]

> They are frauds, those who call themselves God. They are so base they are not worthy of being called criminals. If God is an ocean, they are not even a millionth drop of that ocean. . . . There is only one God. But these men are Satans who pose as God. Satans!
>
> Prakash Mehra, director, *Jādūgar* (Magician, 1989)[2]

In January 2000, I was wandering around the streets of downtown Cuttack, Orissa, trying to find my way to one of the many goddess temples of the city, when I was confronted with a massive billboard for a new film entitled *Śaitān Tāntrik* (Satanic *tāntrik*).[3] The billboard featured a wild-eyed, fiendishly grinning, bald *tāntrik* priest, surrounded by images of skulls, human sacrifice, terrifying forms of Kālī, and beautiful women in various states of panic and undress. I also couldn't help noticing that the *tāntrik* priest in the film looked suspiciously like the bald, laughing priest of Kālī in Stephen Spielberg's 1984 blockbuster film *Indiana Jones and the Temple of Doom.* In turn, Spielberg's film was itself based on a long genealogy of earlier cinematic and fictional tropes that includes the Beatles' 1975 film *Help!* (which featured comically evil *tāntriks* performing human sacrifice to the goddess "Kālīyā"), the 1939 American film *Gunga Din* (which featured another sinister bald *tāntrik* priest performing human sacrifice to Kālī Mā and was in turn based on Rudyard Kipling's 1890 poem "Gunga Din"), and many British and American novels of the late nineteenth and early twentieth centuries, such as *Secrets of the Kaula Circle, The Swami's Curse*, and countless others.[4]

In sum, this low-budget, poorly made B-movie, *Śaitān Tāntrik*, was really a kind of microcosm of the crisscrossing play of imaginings, representations,

FIGURE 6.1. Billboard for *Śaitān Tāntrik,* Cuttack, Orissa, 2000. Photo by the author.

and misrepresentations at work between India, England, and America over the last century. The image of Tantra has bounced back and forth between nineteenth-century Orientalists, British colonial administrators, Indian and American novelists, twentieth-century Bollywood filmmakers, and twenty-first-century television producers, resulting in the now-stock trope of the "sinister *tāntrik*." Appearing ubiquitously throughout Indian popular culture, the sinister *tāntrik* is a sort of modern counterpart to the figure of the "sinister *yogi*" that David Gordon White has traced throughout earlier Sanskrit literature.[5] As we saw in chapter 2, there is a striking difference between the representation of Tantra in the Western popular imagination and its representation in the Indian popular imagination. While North American and European popular audiences almost universally associate Tantra with sex and optimal orgasm, Indian audiences associate it largely with black magic and occult power.[6] What became "the art of sexual ecstasy" in the Western imagination became "the art of dark magical power" in the Indian imagination. The former imagines Tantra as the "path of desire" in the sense of eroticism, while the latter imagines Tantra as the "path of desire" in the sense of greed, power, and domination.

This chapter examines the figure of the sinister *tāntrik* and his various representations in popular media. I could easily spend an entire book exploring this theme in fiction (such as the Assamese novel *The Man from Chinnamasta*), in comic books (such as the *Bhūt-Pret-Tantra-Mantra* series from Manoj Comics), or in cyberspace (such as the many Tantric black magic websites based in Assam).[7] For the sake of this chapter, however, I focus primarily on the representation of Tantra in modern film and television. Here I also pan back out, discussing not just northeast India but the broader South Asian representation of Tantra. While magical, occult, and Tantric themes feature prominently in Assamese films such as *Kathānadī* (2019),[8] they are ubiquitous throughout the broader landscape of Indian film since at least the 1980s. The sinister *tāntrik* appears in hundreds of films released in Hindi, Bangla, Telugu, Tamil, and other languages, ranging from extremely low-budget productions such as *Śaitān Tāntrik* or *Khūnī Tāntrik* (Bloody *Tāntrik*, 2001) as well as high-end action films such as *Nāṉ Kaṭavuḷ* (I am God, 2017), and web series such as *Tantra (Black Magic)* (2018–2019).[9]

For the sake of space, I will limit my focus to just six examples, each of which draws heavily upon the traditional image of the "sinister *tāntrik*" while also rearticulating it in a modern Indian context. These include three well-known Hindi films—*Gahrāī* (Depth, 1980), *Jādūgar* (Magician, 1989), and *Saṅgharṣ* (Struggle, 1999)—one Telugu film—*Ammoru* (Goddess, 1995)—one Bangla web series—*Tārānāth Tāntrik* (2019)—and one proposed web series for which I served as a reluctant academic consultant—*Tāśrī* (in progress).[10] Like the medieval *yogīs*, these cinematic *tāntriks* are deeply ambivalent characters, possessing tremendous powers but also engaged in acts of sorcery, exorcism, and human sacrifice. However, these films also rearticulate the image of the sinister yogī through a variety of contemporary idioms—for example, by referencing American horror films or mixing in non-Indian black magic tropes such as Haitian Vodou. The sinister *tāntrik*, we will see, is also recast in contemporary scripts drawn from modern Indian debates over caste politics and land disputes, fake gurus and their Western disciples, psychiatry and mental illness, globalization, and corporate power.

To conclude, I make some broader theoretical comments, drawing upon but also critically rethinking some contemporary approaches to horror, such as those of Julia Kristeva and Judith Butler.[11] The sinister *tāntrik* is in many ways the embodiment of the "abject" in Kristeva's sense of the "cast off," particularly the horror of death, perversion, transgression, and taboo that is rejected by the social body. As Vijay Mishra argues in *Bollywood Cinema: Temples of Desire*, much of modern Indian film is shaped by the desire to project a kind of "shared national community and a pan-Indian popular culture."[12] The sinister *tāntrik*, however, is precisely what does *not* fit into and must be cast out of that national community and pan-Indian culture.[13] In Indian film, this abjection is always conquered in the end: the sinister *tāntrik* is ultimately defeated—in some cases by a "good" yogī, in some cases by a deity representative of pure, normative, non-*tāntrik* Hinduism, and in rare cases by another *tāntrik* wielding an even more powerful but equally "abject" sort of dark magic. Yet his lingering presence in popular culture reflects a dark desire that can perhaps never be fully cast away.

Skull-Bearers and Human Sacrifice: Tantra in Sanskrit and Vernacular Fiction

Throughout Sanskrit drama and narrative, Tantra has long been associated with black magic, sorcery, and trickery. As we saw in the introduction, one of the first references to texts called *tantras* is in Bāṇabhaṭṭa's classic fantasy tale *Kādambarī* (seventh century), which comically describes a power-hungry, demented old *sādhu* from South India. With his collection of *tantras* and *mantras*, the perverted *sādhu* is said to be obsessed with love spells, the "madness of alchemy," and a "yearning to enter the world of demons."[14] Later Sanskrit literature often focuses on the infamous Kāpālikas or "skull bearers," an early *tāntrik* lineage devoted to Śiva in his terrible form that may have been carried over into modern sects such as the infamous Aghorīs (who also carry human skulls as their begging bowls).[15] Thus, the eleventh-century author Kṛṣṇamiśra includes a detailed satire of a Kāpālika in his drama *Prabhodacandrodaya*. Inhabiting cremation grounds, drinking wine from skulls, and offering human sacrifices, the Kāpālika is portrayed here as the epitome of the most frightening powers of impurity, violence, and transgression:

> I who am adorned with a garland of human bones, who live in the cremation ground and who eat out of a human skull, with an eye purified by the instrument of yoga, see the world having differences within itself but being non-different from God. . . . We who offer oblations in the fire in the form of human flesh, brains, entrails and marrow break our fast with alcohol help in the skull of a *brāhmaṇa*. Mahābhairava [*Śiva* in his terrible form] has to be worshipped with human offerings, lustrous streams of blood flowing from the stiff throat which is freshly cut.[16]

The figure of the perverse and cruel *tāntrik* Kāpālika reappears throughout modern Indian fiction, for example in the works of nineteenth-century Bangla authors such as Bankimcandra Caṭṭopādhyāy (1838–1894). Born into a *brāhmaṇ* family and working as a deputy collector for the British government, Bankimcandra was part of a broader movement in the colonial period that sought to reform and reimagine Hinduism for the modern era, while also cleansing it of its more embarrassing elements, such as Tantra.

As Wilhelm Halbfass summarizes Bankimcandra's reformed ideal of Hinduism (or "neo-Hinduism"): "The 'truly' religious elements of Hinduism had to be . . . separated from the multifarious forms of superstition, from local popular cults. Such a purified Hinduism . . . could be placed above Islam and Christianity."[17] Bankimcandra's most famous work, *Kapālakuṇḍalā* (1866), continues the stereotype of the sinister skull-bearer, here performing the infamous *tāntrik* rite of *śava sādhanā*, or worship with and upon a human corpse. As the character Nabakumār describes him, "The form with matted hair was seated on a putrid corpse. With even greater fear he saw that a human skull lay before him, and inside it was some red liquid. On all sides, bones were strewn. . . . He knew that this person must be a terrible Kāpālika."[18] The cruel Kāpālika then traps Nabakumār and plans to offer him as a human sacrifice to Kālī—a trope that later reappears throughout Bollywood (and American) horror films.

In short, the image of the *tāntrik* as a dangerous, power-hungry, and corrupting figure was clearly in place as a widespread trope in Indian literature by the end of the nineteenth century. However, it would also be taken up, amplified, and often wildly exaggerated by British novelists of the early twentieth century, where the sinister *tāntrik* became the ultimate embodiment of everything they thought was wrong with modern India.[19] As we see in works such as F. E. F. Penny's *The Swami's Curse* (1929), Flora Annie Steel's *The Law of the Threshold* (1924), and Elizabeth Sharpe's *Secrets of the Kaula Circle* (1936), the *tāntrik* was equated with not just black magic but also sexual perversion and even subversive political activities. For example, in Penny's novel *The Swami's Curse*, we are told that "the follower of the Tantric cult professes no austerities. He seeks to kill desire by an unlimited indulgence which brings satiety and extinction of emotion. The indulgence is enjoined by his so-called religion; and his depravity is commended as a great virtue."[20]

By no means a relic of the colonial era, however, the figure of the sinister *tāntrik* has continued well into the twenty-first century, as we see in recent Assamese novels such as Indira's Goswami's award-winning book *The Man from Chinnamasta* (2005). As we noted in chapter 3, one of the primary themes in Goswami's novel is an intense critique of animal sacrifice in Assam, which is described as the main obsession of the *tāntrik* and his cruel rites. Here, the *tāntrik* is portrayed as not only sinister but as quite "serpentine" and monstrously evil: "The tantrik slithered out from the cracks of a tumbled down monument, like a poisonous serpent of doom," while his crazed disciples shrieked hysterically and cried out for blood offerings to the goddess. "You fools!" the *tāntrik* screamed, "The Goddess Kamakhya has quenched her thirst for thousands of years with blood of both humans and animals."[21] In their mindless bloodlust, the *tāntrik* and his followers actually end up cutting their own flesh as an offering to the goddess—only to find all their wasted blood washed away by heavy rains the next morning.

In sum, the sinister *tāntrik* has been a recurring figure in both the Indian and Western imaginations for at least the last 150 years—a figure of ultimate danger and transgressive power who embodies the potential subversion of not simply the individual self but of society and the body politic.[22]

The Varieties of *Tāntrik* Experience: Fraudulent, Sinister, and Pure *Māntriks* in *Gahrāī*

In the late twentieth century, fictional representation of the sinister *tāntrik* was inevitably carried over into the realm of cinema and soon became a standard trope throughout Bollywood and other Indian film industries. For example, Vikas Desai and Aruna Raje's 1980 film *Gahrāī* (Depth) is a particularly interesting variation on the sinister-*tāntrik* theme. Centered on a mysterious case of spirit possession involving a young girl in a wealthy Bangalore family, the film presents three different versions of the *tāntrik* character—one a charlatan, one a power-hungry fiend, and one a pure, selfless devotee of Lord Gaṇeśa. As such, it covers the spectrum of imaginative representations of the yogī in Indian popular culture, from the ridiculous purveyor of mumbo-jumbo to the sinister black magician to the true knower of powerful esoteric knowledge. At the same time, however, the film also asserts the triumph of the pure, truly "Hindu" yogī as devotee of Gaṇeśa over the wicked *tāntrik*.

The father in the film, Cennābasappā, is a successful manager and a hard-nosed rationalist who initially has little patience for things supernatural. When he needs money to build a new home in Bangalore, he decides to sell his plantation in his ancestral village to a soap company. The plantation's caretaker, Baswā, becomes deeply agitated, viewing the selling of one's ancestral lands as analogous to the rape of one's own mother. Meanwhile, the young daughter Umā begins to behave strangely, going into trance states and uttering cryptic revelations about the past. The most terrible of these revelations is that Cennābasappā had once seduced and impregnated Baswā's wife, who later committed suicide.

After trying every possible medication to no avail, the family decides to bring in a *māntrik* ("knower of *mantras*," a term often used interchangeably with *tāntrik*) to try to exorcise whatever spirit, ghost, or other entity has possessed the girl. As we saw in chapter 4, spirit possession and exorcism have a long history both in traditional South Asian Tantra and in popular representations of *tāntrik* magic. The ability to possess or dispossess bodies has long been part of Tantric literature, and it clearly survives as a trope in the Indian popular imagination.[23]

Unfortunately, the first *māntrik* they call upon turns out to be a ridiculous charlatan, a buffoon who embodies the stereotype of the *tāntrik* as a mere fraud. Performing his *pūjā* with absurd and pompous display, he invokes the goddess Mahā Kālī while chanting *mantras*, slapping the girl across the face, smashing coconuts, and of course collecting a large fee. Disgusted with this huckster, the son suggests another, more powerful *māntrik* named Puṭṭācārī. This one appears to possess more genuine abilities but also seems suspiciously concerned with knowing whether or not Umā is a virgin. After learning that she is indeed, he abducts her and takes her to perform a secret *tāntrik* ritual in a cemetery, hoping to use her virginal potentiality in order to awaken the power of the goddess. As he chants and waives her *āratī* lamp before a fire, the girl sits naked in a trance, surrounded by *mantras*, *yantras*, and various offerings. The *tāntrik* is performing his *pūjā* before a stone image and a *yoni*, invoking the deity with the words "*darśanaṃ kuru, darśanaṃ kuru!*" When the brother interrupts the ritual to save the girl, the *tāntrik* cries out, warning that they will incur the goddess's wrath and be cursed forever: "Stay back! You cannot interrupt the worship of the goddess! You will be ruined. The goddess will never forgive you. . . . She cannot be freed now. And you cannot take her away. . . . I have waited for this moment for fifteen years. . . . Your daughter has all the right qualities, because of which the goddess has agreed to come. You have angered the goddess. You will be ruined!"[24]

Finally, after rescuing the girl, the family decides to consult one last yogī to exorcise the spirit—this time, the sincere, powerful, yet humble Śāstrī. Immediately upon visiting the house, Śāstrī discovers two cursed objects that have been hidden around the grounds: a lemon and a small sort of "Voodoo doll" with pins in it. He burns the evil objects and then confronts the spirit inside the girl. Sitting before an altar bearing the image of Lord Gaṇeśa, Śāstrī forces the spirit to confess that it had been trapped through black magic by another *māntrik*, who had been hired by none other than the disgruntled caretaker, Baswā. All of this was Baswā's vengeance against the family for selling the ancestral plantation.

When the family thanks the Śāstrī and offers to pay him for his efforts, he refuses any compensation, humbly attributing his abilities not to himself but rather to Lord Gaṇeśa, whose grace alone can bind or free such spirits: "No, please don't bow your head to me. All this is the grace of Lord Gaṇeśa. Bow to him. I am a human just like you. . . . You don't need to give me any charity or anything. I don't do all this to earn wealth. It is all the grace of Lord Gaṇeśa. He is the one who does all this."[25]

Here we see the ultimate contrast with the sinister *tāntrik*: instead of a mere charlatan or a power-hungry sorcerer who harnesses dark forces for material gain, Śāstrī embodies the ideal of the pure yogī who is devoted only to God in in the loving and generally quite non-*tāntrik* form. While the power-hungry *tāntrik* performs his secret rituals in the cemetery before the goddess's *yoni,* the selfless Śāstrī performs his healing *pūjā* before the flowered-covered image of Gaṇeśa. As such, the film also portrays the triumph of a kind of mainstream, normative Hinduism over the dangerous path of the *tāntrik.*

Magic—Real, Fake, and Really Fake in *Jādūgar*

Prakash Mehar's 1989 film *Jādūgar* (Magician) continues the theme of the malicious and fraudulent *tāntrik,* though with an interesting twist of its own. Here the villainous *tāntrik* is conquered not by a more powerful, genuine yogī but rather by a kind of "genuine fake"—the flamboyant *jādūgar* named Gogā.

The story opens when Śaṅkar Nārāyaṇ returns from America to discover that his father—formerly a businessman and convict—has set up shop as a miracle-working guru with a large and lucrative *āśram.* Bearing an elaborate handlebar mustache, shaven head, and ponytail, Mahāprabhu performs a variety of cheap stage tricks, such as materializing small objects and manifesting sacred ash (*vibhūti*) from his hands, in order to dupe his gullible devotees. His followers include not only Indian disciples but a large number of wealthy white foreigners who are pouring millions in cash, gifts, gold, and jewelry into his coffers. Thus, Śaṅkar overhears the guru's Indian disciples gambling at night, with several white female devotees hanging on the side: "He lost today's earnings," one jokes, "but it doesn't matter. He'll trap ten more rich foreigners tomorrow."[26] Here we should note that the film is surely parodying some of the hugely prosperous Hindu mega-gurus of the 1980s, such as Sathya Sai Baba—also famous for materializing small objects and sacred ash—and Bhagwan Shree Rajneesh—who was quite infamous for both his large following of Western white hippies and his outrageous wealth and conspicuous consumption.[27] The cheating guru offers Śaṅkar the massive riches from his treasury, but the son refuses with disgust and leaves the *āśram.*

Hoping to unmask his father, Śaṅkar decides to call upon a famous and flamboyant stage magician named Gogā (played by Amitabh Bachchan). The plan is for Gogā to confront the charlatan Mahāprabhu, reveal his cheap tricks for what they are, and so dethrone him once and for all. This Gogā easily does, but then he too is seduced by the power of guru-ship and takes over the god-man role himself, assuming the title of "Gogeśvara" or Lord Gogā. Still determined to retake his *āśram*, the fallen Mahāprabhu tries to unmask and/or kill Gogā in various ways, first attempting to poison him and then sending in his minions to attack the magician. This attack leads to a farcical fight scene, in which Gogā demonstrates a mixture of martial arts, stage magic, and seemingly genuine *tāntrik* powers—sometimes tricking opponents with magic handkerchiefs, sometimes turning guns into bananas, and sometimes magically removing his foes' clothing. Indeed, the fight scene is one of several telling moments in which the film plays upon the boundary between stage magic and real spiritual power, hinting that Gogā may possess more of the latter than we first assume.

Finally, another of Mahāprabhu's minions is sent with an axe to chop off Gogā's hands and so prevent him from working his magic. In response, Gogā freely offers up his hands to the butcher and then delivers an impassioned speech about the difference between true and false religion. "Stop dancing to the tune of frauds," he tells the axman. "They are frauds, those who call themselves God. They are so base, they are not worthy of being called criminals. If God is an ocean, they are not even a millionth drop of that ocean. There's only one God, whether they call him Bhagwan, Allah, Karim, or God. There is only one God. But these men are Satans who pose as God. Satans!"[28]

Deeply impressed, the axman finally accepts the truth that his guru is a fraud who has been exploiting his followers with his lame magic tricks: "Mahāprabhu Jagatsāgar Cintāmaṇi is not God but an ordinary mortal, a cheap magician who is selling God's name in every home and misleading people." Instead of taking Gogā's hands, he returns to his former master and chops off Mahāprabhu's hands instead, thus depriving the charlatan of his means of deception.

In the end, Gogā completely exposes Mahāprabhu in front of everyone and then also reveals himself to be, not a god, but simply an ordinary man who has merely played the role of "Gogeśvara" in order to expose the fraud. "Then where is God's true form?" the people ask him. "Look inside yourself!" Gogā sternly replies, launching into another impassioned speech about the difference between true religion and the chicanery of these false *gurus*: "God exists in every being. Man cannot become God by displaying fake miracles. If anyone can do a real miracle, it is the Supreme Lord, whom we call Allah, Jesus, Bhagwan. . . . Have faith in yourself, but don't have blind faith. . . . Worship whatever God you like, but don't have blind faith. . . . Or you will come across many Mahāprabhus on every street corner, who will continue to loot you."[29]

In this closing oratory, we can clearly see that Gogā is articulating a kind of "feel-good pluralist secularism" that is also expressed in other classic Bollywood films, most notably *Amar Akbar Anthony*, which likewise celebrates the validity of diverse religious faiths.[30] At the same time, he is articulating a very modern, neo-Hindu or neo-Vedāntic universalism that has become commonplace since the nineteenth century, particularly through the works of Rāmmohun Roy, Bankimcandra, Swāmī Vivekānanda, and other reformers: God is One, though He is known by many names, dwelling in the heart of every being,[31] and this universal, pure faith in the One True God has nothing to do with the gross superstition and *guru*-worship of the ignorant masses, who so easily fall for trickery and chicanery—above all, for the occult deceptions of the *tāntriks*.

In sum, like *Gahrāī*, *Jādūgar* narrates the ultimate defeat of the sinister *tāntrik*. But in this case, the victory is accomplished not by a "good" or "real" yogī but rather by a kind of "authentic fake," a stage magician who uses his trickery to unmask the pretender. Yet the end result is ultimately much the same: "true" religion and a "real" understanding of God triumphs over the deceptive, exploitative, and indeed "Satanic" imitation of religion concocted by the false *guru*. The former is a kind of neo-Hindu universalist faith in the Supreme Lord who is found in all religious traditions, while the latter is the blind faith and fraud of the sinister *tāntrik*.

The Silence and the Struggle: Blending Hollywood and Bollywood Horror in *Saṅghars̩*

Like most Bollywood films, many in the sinister-*tāntrik* genre make oblique references to American Hollywood productions. As we saw above, many low-budget productions such as *Śaitān Tāntrik* contain clear imitations of Hollywood classics, such as Spielberg's classic work of Orientalist excess, *Indiana Jones and the Temple of Doom* (1984). And some viewers have noted that films such as *Gahrāī* show the influence of the American horror classic *The Exorcist* (1973), with its possession-and-exorcism narrative.

However, the 1999 film *Saṅgharṣ* is a more interesting blend of American and Indian themes, with both clear references to and complex reworkings of Jonathan Demme's 1991 film *The Silence of the Lambs*.[32] The film begins with a series of child-abduction and murder cases that have remained unsolved by the police and so are turned over to a trainee in the Central Bureau of Investigation named Rīt Oberāy. Rīt's investigations lead her to suspect Lajjā Śaṅkar Pāṇḍey, yet another embodiment of the sinister-*tāntrik* figure, who also brings in an added dimension of psychological and sexual perversion.

Like myriad *tāntrik* characters before him in both Indian and Western narratives,[33] Lajjā Śaṅkar is hoping to achieve immortality through the rite of human sacrifice, using the blood of children to engender his own eternal life.

Meanwhile, Detective Rīt suffers psychological traumas of her own, having witnessed the death of her brother—a Sikh separatist—at the hands of the police when she was a child. Tortured by her childhood memories and by this complex criminal case, she seeks advice from Professor Aman Varma, a brilliant man who has been unjustly imprisoned. The professor is initially rude and unresponsive but eventually agrees to help her, guiding her through her childhood traumas and ultimately tracking down the villain. Rīt discovers that the killer has been offering to buy street-beggar children for his rituals and so lays a trap for him, using a beggar's son as bait. The fiendish Lajjā Śaṅkar does indeed arrive to buy the boy, but he is wearing the disguise of a woman with a *sāṛī* and makeup—thus adding a new, gender-bending twist to the sinister-*tāntrik* motif. When Rīt and her team confront Lajjā Śaṅkar, he displays superhuman strength, throws them around, and survives a seemingly fatal gunshot before escaping.

Back in his forest home, Lajjā Śaṅkar exhibits psychotic and fanatical symptoms, beating his own head with a rock and engaging in a conversation with the goddess Kālī like a child speaking to his mother. The goddess instructs him to slay the father who had lured him into the trap, which he does, and as he is strangling the man, he reveals that he has been offering blood sacrifices to the goddess since he was eleven years old—"satisfying the Mother's hunger"—in the attempt to cheat death and achieve immortality: "I went to a shed and butchered eleven buffaloes. The god of death has been afraid of me since then. I'll keep fighting death until I defeat it!"'[34] Meanwhile, Rīt finds an old video tape of Lajjā Śaṅkar recorded back when he was held in a mental institution, in which he claims to have been speaking to his mother Kālī since he was a tiny child: "She orders me, and I obey all her orders," he says, chanting *mantras* and going into a trance. "Look into these eyes. These are the eyes of a messenger of God. . . . Small kids can peep into them and find heaven."[35]

Lajjā Śaṅkar's next child victim is none other than the son of the home minister himself, whom he plans to offer as his ultimate gift to the Mother—a child sacrifice on the last day of a solar eclipse—which will at last bring him immortality. The sacrifice is to take place in a secret underground cave temple, which very much recalls the cave temple in Spielberg's *Indiana Jones and the Temple of Doom* (as does Lajjā Śaṅkar himself, who has now shaved his head and resembles the bald priest of Kālī in Spielberg's film). "I am going to be freed of this cycle of life and death today!" he declares, asserting his superhuman status as the all-powerful *tāntrik* who has now mastered death itself: "This child is my last gift to goddess Kālī. . . . I am not a human being. Life and death are part of the lives of ordinary beings like you."[36] Fortunately, Rīt and the professor (now escaped from prison) have tracked him down in time to prevent the heinous act. Just as Lajjā Śaṅkar is about to deliver the fatal blow to the child, the professor leaps across the temple and engages in a bloody fight, during which Lajjā Śaṅkar repeatedly bites him, leaving his mouth dripping blood (recalling images of Kālī, Tārā, and other *tāntrik* goddesses). While the professor beats down the *tāntrik*, Rīt finally overcomes her childhood traumas and rescues the child.

Probably most readers have recognized the similarities between the basic plot and characters of *Saṅgharṣ* and those of Demme's *Silence of the Lambs*. Both films center on a female investigator who is pursuing a cross-dressing serial killer with some form of mental illness, and in both, the key to solving the case comes from an imprisoned genius, who reluctantly agrees to offer his insight (the special maximum-security prison cell in which the professor is placed in *Saṅgharṣ* is even visually very similar to Hannibal's cage in *Silence of the Lambs*). In both films, the investigator has suffered some childhood trauma that has permanently shaped her character—witnessing the death of her brother, in Rīt's case, and witnessing the screaming lambs, in Starling's. And in both cases, the villain is seeking some kind of personal transformation through bloodshed—the quest for immortality in Lajjā Śaṅkar's case, and the quest for a woman's body in Buffalo Bill's.

Saṅgharṣ, however, translates these themes through the uniquely South Asian idioms of the sinister *tāntrik*. Here the villain is not a man tormented by his gender identity crisis and failed sex change, but rather one driven by the more classically South Asian spiritual goal of freedom (*mokṣa*) from death and rebirth. And he pursues this goal through the means not of mere slaughter and skinning his victims but of human sacrifice, a practice that has had a long and intensely controversial reputation—both real and imaginary—in *tāntrik* traditions for over a millennium. Human sacrifice and its tremendous material rewards are described in a number of Śākta and Tāntrik texts, such as the *Kālikā Purāṇa*, *Muṇḍamāla Tantra*, and others;[37] the eighteenth-century *Yoginī Tantra* even explicitly calls for the offering of a male child (*narasya kumāra*).[38] Yet the specter of mixed horror and power embodied in human sacrifice was clearly amplified and exaggerated wildly through British and American novels and films from the nineteenth century to the present, culminating in the bloody offerings to Kālī that we see in *Gunga Din* (1939), the Beatles' film *Help!* (1965), and, most famously, *Indiana Jones and the Temple of Doom* (1984).[39] *Saṅgharṣ* has clearly been informed by all these various historical influences, weaving them together with the narrative structure and psychological dynamics of modern American films.

The Great Goddess and the *Tāntrik* Demon in *Ammoru*

The figure of the sinister *tāntrik* is not, of course, limited to Hindi films or to Bollywood; indeed, he is in some ways an even more colorful character in other South Asian–language films in Telugu, Malayalam, Bangla, and Assamese, among many others. In some cases, he even becomes a kind of unexpected antihero, as in the case of the kickboxing martial-artist *tāntrik* Aghorī in *Nāṉ Kaṭavuḷ*. And in others, he is a terrifically evil figure of pure sorcery and malice who can only be defeated by the great goddess (*devī*) herself, as in the 1995 Telugu film *Ammoru*.[40]

Directed by Kodi Ramakrishna, *Ammoru* centers on the character Bhavānī, a beautiful young lower-caste orphan and devotee of the goddess Ammoru. A local form of the great goddess (*devī*), Ammoru is worshipped in her temple in the form of a pillar with three eyes and lolling tongue that looks much like the famous Kālī image at Kālīghāṭ in Kolkata. The villain in the film, meanwhile, is a criminal black magician named Gorakh, who in many ways embodies the ultimate stereotype of the sinister *tāntrik*—at once tremendously powerful and yet filled with malice and hatred, using his occult knowledge for vengeance and material gain. Bhavānī is responsible for Gorakh being imprisoned, and so he vows to take terrible revenge upon her, upon her husband, and upon their infant child. Gorakh's mother, Līlāmma, first tries to kill Bhavānī, but the goddess Ammoru protects her by assuming the form of a young maidservant. Upon his release from jail, Gorakh uses his dark *tāntrik* magical arts to invoke an evil spirit and so finally kills the child and tortures the husband.

In the climactic final scene, Bhavānī takes her wounded husband into the temple of Ammoru and locks the gate. Gorakh then deploys his full powers as a sinister *tāntrik*, creating a *yantra* diagram, uttering *mantras*, and invoking a terrifying, hideous spirit in order to create a kind of Voodoo doll. Sticking pins into the doll, he tortures the helpless husband while Bhavānī screams in terror. As Gorakh finally bursts through the temple gate, Bhavānī places her hand on the spikes of the trident that stands in front of Ammoru's image. Invoking a classic scene from the *Mahābhārata* (the disrobing of Draupadī by Duḥśāsana), Gorakh grabs Bhavānī's sāṛī and tries to disrobe her; however, the act rips her hand across the points of the trident and sprays her blood across the temple, splashing it on the face of Ammoru. The blood is enough to awaken the goddess, who rises up in a spectacular display of CGI effects, morphing through all the various forms of the goddess (Durgā, Lakṣmī, Sarasvatī, Parvatī, etc.) before finally assuming a terrible Kālī-like manifestation. Grabbing the trident and performing a ferocious dance, she impales the evil Gorakh, beheads him, and finally annihilates him completely. The impalement and beheading, we should note, are clearly reminiscent of the classic myth of the great goddess (Durgā or Caṇḍī) slaying the buffalo demon (Mahiṣāsura) as narrated in the *Devī Mahātmyā* and countless other Sanskrit and vernacular texts. In the end, the goddess returns to her childlike maidservant form and restores Bhavānī's lost baby to life, as the whole village cheers and rejoices.

Once again, *Ammoru* narrates the ultimate defeat of the sinister *tāntrik*. In this case, however, the *tāntrik* is conquered not by another yogī or by a magician, but directly by the awesome power of the goddess herself. As such, the film is not only invoking classic Hindu myths such as the slaughter of the buffalo demon; it is also depicting the defeat of the evil black magic of the *tāntrik* by the good and true religion of the *devī*, the Hindu great goddess.

Sinister and (Reluctantly) Heroic *Tāntriks*: *Tārānāth Tāntrik*

If the *tāntrik* appears as a kind of stock villain in countless Bollywood and other South Asian films, he does occasionally assume a more complex and sometimes even heroic role. For example, in the Tamil film *Nāṉ Kaṭavuḷ* mentioned above, the *tāntrik* is portrayed as a frightening yet oddly heroic figure, using his great power as an Aghorī to defeat cruel villains. However, perhaps the most famous example of the *tāntrik* in a heroic role—albeit a sort of reluctant and ambivalent one—is the character of Tārānāth Tāntrik. First appearing in two stories by famed Bangla author Bibhūtibhūṣaṇ Bandyopādhyāy, and then continued in six more stories by his son, Tārādās Bandyopādhyāy, Tārānāth is portrayed as an aging astrologer living in Kolkata (then called Calcutta) of the 1930s who has amazing tales to tell of his earlier life as a *tāntrik*.[41] The stories were made into a popular graphic-novel series in 2015 and later into a web series in 2019.[42]

Unlike most Bollywood films, the *Tārānāth Tāntrik* series highlights the more complex and ambivalent nature of Tantra, emphasizing both its sinister and spiritual dimensions. This difference in representation is likely due to the fact that Tantra has a long and rich history in northeast India, and the worship of powerful Śākta goddesses such as Kālī, Kāmākhyā, Tārā, and others is still widespread throughout Bangla and Assam. The *Tārānāth Tāntrik* series clearly invokes earlier Bangla representations of the darker

FIGURE 6.2. Advertisement for *Tārānāth Tāntrik* web series, 2019.

side of Tantra, such as *Kapālkuṇḍalā*, but it combines these depictions with a more complicated portrayal of the *tāntrik* as someone who can use his great power for both good and evil purposes. The TV series also combines imagery from colonial Calcutta of the 1930s—shot in black and white—with campy drawings of frightening goddesses, rituals, skulls, and ghouls that are clearly borrowed from comics and graphic novels (and probably also from recent Netflix series such as *The Chilling Adventures of Sabrina* and others).

The series begins with two friends in old Calcutta who decide to go visit aging Tārānāth Tāntrik, who is known for his weird and fascinating tales of the supernatural. Tārānāth has apparently lost most of his former power as a *tāntrik* and now advertises himself merely as an astrologer (*jyotirvidyāvinod*). But he obliges his visitors with a series of lively stories about his earlier life as a student of the occult. Thus, he tells them how he roamed the countryside in search of a guru and finally made his way to an eccentric and frightening female *tāntrikā* named Mātu Pāglī (crazy mother). Mātu reluctantly took him on as a student and led him through terrifying practices, such as a corpse ritual in which the goddess Ṣoḍaśī appeared to him, taking possession of the dead body of young woman.[43]

Perhaps the most explicit account of the ambivalent nature of Tantra appears in episode five of the first season, entitled "Betāl" (from the

Sanskrit *vetāla*, a demon or vampire). Loosely based on a story by Tārādās Bandyopādhyāy,[44] the episode begins when the two friends visit the aging Tārānāth and ask him about the infamous skull-bearing Kāpālikas, wondering how they compare to *tāntriks* like himself: "I mean, what's the difference between a Kāpālik and a *tāntrik*?" (*āre, kāpālik, tāntrik eder madhye pārthakya ki?*). In reply, Tārānāth tells the story of how he was once called to the home of one of his disciples, a widower named Madhu whose household was suffering from a terrible curse. It seems that another powerful named Locan Kāpālik had visited him some weeks before. Locan had demanded that Madhu give him his daughter to become his consort (*sādhikā* or *bhairavī*) in *tāntrik* practice. When Madhu angrily refused and drove him away, Locan cursed him, causing his cow and cat to die and his daughter to begin coughing up blood. Tārānāth then tracked the evil Locan down and pretended to be seeking him out in order to become his disciple. Locan accepted him as a student and proceeded to show him the secret rite of invoking a *betāl*—a hideous, bald, vampiric ghoul who rose up from the fire, possessed the Kāpālik, and then flew off invisibly toward Madhu's home. Running back to Madhu, Tārānāth performed his own *tāntrik* rite that caused the *betāl* to become visible. Although the *betāl* launched a ferocious attack, Tārānāth remained firm in his meditation and ultimately destroyed the snarling demon.[45]

In sum, the Tārānāth episode presents Tantra as a far more ambiguous and unpredictable sort of power. While still very much tied to the frightening realm of death, darkness, and demons, it is an ambivalent practice that can be wielded for both good and evil ends. In Tārānāth's narrative, the sinister *tāntrik* or Kāpālik can only be defeated by an equally fearsome *tāntrik*—just as, in Tantric literature, it is often said that a thorn can only be removed by a thorn, and poison can only be counteracted with poison. It seems significant, however, that all of Tārānāth's *tāntrik* stories take place in the distant past of the British colonial era, long before the birth of the modern Indian nation, and he himself appears as a tired, weak old astrologer living out his last days in the decaying city of 1930s Calcutta.

"Don't Look into Her Eyes": The Scholar as Consultant in *Tāśrī*

The final representation of the sinister *tāntrik* that I would like to discuss in this chapter is one in which I happened to have a peculiar personal involvement—and this surely marks one of the oddest and most surreal twists in my research for this book. In the summer of 2019, I was contacted by Sameer Pitalwalla, the head of a digital media company in Mumbai called

FIGURE 6.3. Pitch deck for *Tāśrī*. Art by Ekta Bharti, 2021.

Culture Machine. Pitalwalla was in the early stages of creating an original Netflix-style web series based on a popular Hindi novel by Sumit Menāriyā entitled *Tāśrī*.[46] Like *Tārānāth Tāntrik*, *Tāśrī* plays upon the ambivalent nature of Tantra as an occult force that can be wielded for both benign and sinister ends. Combining elements of Bollywood with American films and series such as *Inception*, *The Matrix*, and *Westworld*,[47] the novel had enjoyed wide success in India particularly in digital format and was then being developed by Pitalwalla's team to be pitched as a web series. I had been contacted to see if I would be interested in serving as a consultant for his team, advising them specifically on the representation of Tantra and related symbols, practices, yogic techniques, and so on. After some debate, I reluctantly agreed to take the job—though mostly out of pure curiosity and a sort of anthropological desire to see what the process would look like from the inside, as it were. I realized that, in so doing, I would be ironically inserting myself into the popular representation of Tantra—for better or for worse—and would be "collaborating" in a way that I had never imagined when I first began this book. In the interests of full disclosure, I should also note that I was offered the fee of $863 USD for my services.[48]

The original novel centers on a young woman named Tāśrī who happens to have been born a kind of natural *tāntrik* with the innate ability to read minds by looking into a person's eyes (in Menāriyā's story-world, one is born a *tāntrik*, much as one is born a wizard in the *Harry Potter* universe, and there is a kind of secret worldwide network of these hereditary *tāntriks*). The primary antagonist in the story is the powerful but corrupt

Mṛtyuṅjaya, who is described much like a stereotypical Aghorī, dressed in black and adorned with skulls. As Tāśrī first describes him in an opening dream sequence, he appears as an "old *tāntrik* wearing a black robe with a long beard. A garland of human skulls around the neck, a small trident in his hand, and very red eyes."[49]

Mṛtyuṅjaya is currently the head of a secret *tāntrik āśram* to which Tāśrī's own father had once belonged. Hungry for power, Mṛtyuṅjaya had killed Tāśrī's father and taken control of the *āśram*. But it seems that Mṛtyuṅjaya is also a successful and ruthless businessman, who sits atop a vast empire of corporations that include Ayurvedic pharmaceuticals, media, exports, and cryptocurrencies. Mṛtyuṅjaya's final aim is to perform a great ritual called a *sūtra sādhanā* in order to achieve ultimate power, but he needs the gifted Tāśrī as the final key to complete the rite. At the end of the novel, however, the reader encounters a final plot twist (clearly influenced by films such as *Inception*): it turns out that Tāśrī has actually been in a coma the entire time, and all of these events are actually an elaborate series of dreams orchestrated by a doctor using a "dream machine" to try to guide Tāśrī out of her unconscious state.

In their plan for the web series, Pitalwalla and his team decided to stretch the story out over seven episodes, each one loosely structured around one of the seven *cakras* of the *kuṇḍalinī* yoga system. In their pitch for the series, they also made explicit reference to popular American series, such as *Stranger Things*, *Sacred Games*, *Watchmen*, and *American Gods*,[50] and they brought in some well-known writers, such as Saurav Mahopatra. Now based in the United States, Mahopatra has written a number of popular graphic novels based on Hindu mythology (produced by none other than Deepak Chopra), such as *Myths of India: Shiva*, *Myths of India: Kali*, and many others. In Mahopatra's narrative for the series, Tantra is represented as a kind of underground network of masters with superpowers, all of whom still exist secretly just beneath the surface of the world, often holding positions of great influence in modern society, politics, and business: "Far from the stereotype of skull-holding, unkempt hair, black robed charlatans, our practitioners of Tantra have kept pace with the evolving face of India, embedded into the tapestry of the Indian milieu. From their fragmented and persecuted history, they've realized the value of remaining incognito, as well as accruing power in the mundane world. Some of them occupy high positions in the world of business and politics."[51]

Here we see that Tantra has been very much incorporated into a contemporary twenty-first-century image of India and its growing economic and geopolitical power. Yet the conclusion to the proposed series still follows the familiar script of the sinister *tāntrik*. In the end, Tāśrī masters the *cakras* and *kuṇḍalinī*, while her own supernatural abilities grow to the point that she can not only read minds but actually injure and kill with the power of her mind. In a final battle, she defeats the evil Mṛtyuñjaya, who flees the *āśram* (presumably to return in a future season).

My own role in all of this was to help the team with some of the basic historical background, texts, and contemporary practice of Tantra, as well as to try to correct any egregious errors in their representation. In a kind of bizarre way, however, the writers had also inserted me into the narrative; in one scene in the script, Tāśrī is browsing through the shelves of her college library to do some research on Tantra: "She flips the pages as she begins to peruse through *The Power of Tantra: Religion, Sexuality, and the Politics of South Asian Studies* by Hugh B. Urban as well as *The Serpent Power: The Secrets of Tantric and Shaktic Yoga* by Arthur Avalon."[52] Adapting a phrase from Tantric scholar and practitioner Agehananda Bharati, we could perhaps describe this phenomenon as a kind of "academic pizza effect"—that is, a scholarly version of the cross-cultural play of representations and influences between India and "the West."[53]

The job turned out to be both fascinating and often frustrating. From the outset, the novel and the series were portraying Tantra in ways that have essentially no basis in any text or historical tradition—for example, by making one's identity as a *tāntrik* genetic, making Tāśrī's primary *tāntrik* power mind-reading, and imagining *tāntriks* to be the secret influence behind modern corporate power. Overall, their version of Tantra seemed more influenced by American and British productions such as *X-Men, Harry Potter, Watchmen,* and *Inception* than by any South Asian tradition. I provided Pitalwalla's team with as much historical information as I could, suggesting specific texts, images, and practices that might be incorporated, such as representations of the *cakras* in South Asian texts and artwork. I also consulted at length with Mahopatra on the development of the *tāntrik* world and on a backstory that would make some kind of sense and have at least some grounding in South Asian history. Because of the COVID-19 pandemic, all of our work had to be conducted via Zoom, which involved complex calls at odd hours in multiple time zones, often with very sketchy internet connections. All these logistical difficulties only compounded the general sense of frustration surrounding the project.

Yet in the end, while my suggestions were all welcomed enthusiastically, I fear they had relatively little impact on the final product. A few of my comments on the historical development and diversity of Tantra were incorporated into the storyline, as were some of my thoughts on using traditional

Tantric art and architecture, but otherwise, I seemed to have little visible influence. Nonetheless, I was credited prominently as a "Research & Story Consultant" in the professionally designed pitch deck for the series.[54]

As of the writing of this book, the series has yet to be picked up for production. Yet it offers yet another example of the "sinister *tāntrik*" in a new, very modern Indian context. Now the *tāntrik* is not simply a cartoonish villain but a powerful businessman who heads an empire of pharmaceuticals and cryptocurrencies. While earlier films had invoked themes from classic American productions such as *Indiana Jones* and *Silence of the Lambs*, *Tāśrī* is much more plugged into the global circulation of binge-watched web series such as *Stranger Things*, *Westworld*, and *American Gods*. Meanwhile, the scholar himself has become an odd sort of reluctant participant-observer and unexpected collaborator in the popular representation of Tantra as it circulates promiscuously between India, America, and other points across the globe.

Conclusions: Horrors of Power—Tantra and Abjection in Modern "Hinduism"

To conclude, I would like to make some broader comments on the place of the sinister *tāntrik* in the contemporary imagining of "Hinduism." In many ways, the *tāntrik* of Bollywood film appears to embody much of what Kristeva means by the "abject"—that is, the death, defilement, or impurity that violates the boundaries of individual identity and so generates the most intense feelings of dread, disgust, and horror: "The corpse (or cadaver: *cadere*, to fall) . . . is cesspool and death; it upsets even more violently the one who confronts it as fragile and fallacious chance. . . . [A]s in true theater, without makeup or masks, refuse and corpses *show me* what I permanently thrust aside in order to live."[55] The abject, she suggests, is at once seductive and repulsive, attracting our desire even as it disgusts and frightens: "It lies there, quiet, close, but cannot be assimilated. It beseeches, worries, and fascinates desire. . . . Apprehensive, desire turns aside; sickened, it rejects."[56]

From his first description in Sanskrit literature, as we saw above, the *tāntrik* has been associated precisely with this kind of abjection in the form of corpses, skulls, severed heads, cremation grounds, impurity, and transgression. These themes of abjection are all clearly carried over into modern Indian horror. The sinister *tāntrik* is not simply a criminal con man (as in *Jādūgar*), but also a power-hungry practitioner of secret rituals, offering a virgin before a *yoni* in the cemetery (as we see in the figure of Puṭṭācārī in *Gahrāī*); he is a cross-dressing, psychologically damaged pervert, seeking immortality through child sacrifice (as we see in *Saṅgharṣ*); and he is a black magician, invoking hideous spirits in order to torture and kill his enemies (as we see in *Ammoru* and *Tārānāth Tāntrik*). In each case, he is the very embodiment of abjection in Kristeva's sense—the death, blood, impurity, sickness, and perversion that gives horror its power and power its horror. Again, he is the embodiment of desire (*kāma*)—but in this case, a perverse and corrupt kind of desire. Though seductive and fascinating, it is a desire that only seeks power and is ultimately deformed by its own lust and greed.

Yet the sinister *tāntrik*, I would argue, is "abject" not simply in relation to the individual body; he is also abject in relation to the larger social body and to the construction of modern "Hinduism" in the twentieth and twenty-first centuries. As Douglas Brooks suggests, Tantra has consistently been seen as the "Other within" Hindu traditions, the uncomfortable presence of esoteric and transgressive traditions that do not fit tidily into the modern imagining of Hinduism as a world religion.[57] Like the terms *tantra* and "Tantrism," the term "Hinduism" is neither an indigenous nor a singular category but rather a modern construction used to label a vast and diverse array of texts, traditions, rituals, deities, and communities.[58] And since the nineteenth century, both Western Orientalist scholars and various Hindu reformers have attempted to define the boundaries of this unruly body of traditions. In so doing, they have typically excluded those aspects of Indian tradition that seemed to violate the sensibilities of modern civilized society.[59] Perhaps above all, both Western scholars and Hindu reformers singled out the Tantric tradition as the worst, most debased and degenerate mixture of black magic and sexuality, and thus the first thing to be jettisoned in the reimagining of Hinduism in the modern world.[60] As we saw in chapter 1, many Hindu reformers such as Swāmī Vivekānanda warned that Tantra in its perverse "left-hand" (*vāmācāra*) form was corrupting modern India like a disease and must therefore be purged in order to restore the true teachings of the Vedas. In his view, Tantra was originally a non-Indian, non-Aryan practice that first infected Buddhism and then later Hinduism, resulting in the "terrible abominations of Vamachara."[61] Now, he warned his fellow Hindus, "see how this Vamachara (immoral practice) of the Tantras has entered into your very marrow. . . . We must stem the tide of Vamachara, which is contrary to the spirit of the Vedas."[62] In short, he exhorted his fellow Hindus to "give up this terrible Vamachara which is ruining your country!"[63]

This attempt to purge the abjection of Tantra from the realm of legitimate Hinduism is replayed throughout modern Indian cinema. However, more than just the latest reiterations of an older trope, these films each rework this theme in different ways in a modern Indian context. Thus, in the case of *Saṅgharṣ*, the film not only borrows heavily from American films; it also recasts the sinister *tāntrik* in terms of modern psychiatry and mental illness. *Jādūgar*, in turn, reflects on the modern ubiquity of fraudulent *gurus* (along with their gullible Western disciples). In the case of *Ammoru*, the film also grapples with the tensions and complexities of caste politics, which are central to much of Tamil and Telugu cinema. *Tārānāth Tāntrik* presents a more ambivalent picture of Tantra as having both sinister and benign aspects. Indeed, only the latter is capable of destroying the former: only the heroic Tantra of Tārānāth can defeat the malevolent Tantra of Locan. Even here, however, Tantra is largely relegated to the realm of the "abject"—the world of corpses, darkness, and death. Moreover, Tantra survives only in the waning days of colonial Calcutta of the 1930s, a last vestige of pre-modern India before Independence. Tārānāth himself is reduced to a shadow of his former power, just as Tantra is reduced to a quaint series of ghost stories from an earlier age before the dawn of the modern Indian nation. Finally, *Tāśrī* recasts the sinister *tāntrik* in perhaps the most interesting way, as a kind of malevolent force lurking beneath the surface of contemporary India in the twenty-first century. He is not only a black-clad, skull-bearing Aghorī but also a businessman and CEO who embodies the secret, subterranean power that flows just out of sight through the global economy itself.

In short, the *tāntrik* is not simply a stock villain representing all that is "other" to the ideology of Hindu nationalism. He is also a complex figure who is creatively recast in many different ways in relation to a wide array of contemporary religious concerns, cultural anxieties, and historical changes.

Yet despite this diversity of various castings and performances, the final scene for the sinister *tāntrik* in each of these films is fairly consistent. Time and again, the villainous *tāntrik* is conquered and destroyed—sometimes by a "good" yogī who is devoted to a non-*tāntrik* deity such as Gaṇeśa; sometimes by the goddess herself, who slays him like Durgā slaying the power-hungry buffalo demon; and sometimes by another, more powerful *tāntrik*. In the end, the *tāntrik* is defeated, and proper order is re-established.[64] Yet the perpetual recurrence of the sinister *tāntrik* in Indian cinema, fiction, comics, and other popular media suggests that he remains a haunting presence, a troubling form of abjection that can never fully be cast away—a dark desire that can never be completely overcome.

[CONCLUSIONS]

The Path of Desire in an Age of Capital

Living Tantra in the Context of Globalization and Neoliberalism

> Desire, indeed, takes various forms. Everything is pervaded by the principle of Desire. A man outside the pale of Desire never is, was, or will be, seen in this world.
>
> *Mahābhārata, Śānti Parva*[1]

> The world is a big place. There's all kinds of magic in it.
>
> Bhāskar Hāzarikā, director, *Kathānadī* (2015)

In early July 2017, I was having a cup of tea with my friend Rajib in a small restaurant just outside the main Kāmākhyā temple. I happened to have with me a few of the many cheap paperbacks on *tantra-mantra* and popular magic that I had just purchased from one of the stalls on the path up to the temple. Seeing them, Rajib immediately dismissed them with a chuckle as not "real Tantra," but simply as trashy pamphlets produced mainly for tourists. In his view, they have as little in common with "genuine" Tantra as do the various American paperbacks such as *The Complete Idiot's Guide to Tantric Sex*. In response, I argued that, as a historian of religion, I am interested in *all* forms of Tantra in its complex variety—not just the Sanskritic tradition that we see in the Kulācāra Mārga but also the more vernacular and lowbrow forms that we see in the *tantra-mantra* practices of Mayong, the possession performances in villages of Assam, and the popular representations in film and comic books. I explained that I was even interested in the commercialization and "touristification" of Tantra, which I see as yet another fascinating—if perhaps sad and regrettable—chapter in the complex history of this tradition.

I am not sure that he found my arguments very persuasive.

And yet, this exchange between Rajib and me highlights several key threads in the complex fabric of Tantra that I have tried to pursue throughout this book. First, it emphasizes the complex relationships, partial overlaps, and key differences between "insider" and "outsider," practitioner's and scholar's perspectives on Tantra.[2] While Rajib and I are friends and have helped each other in various ways over the last five years, we also approach the material very differently and have many critical disagreements on what Tantra is and how it should be studied. While for Rajib, "real Tantra" is an esoteric lineage passed down from guru to disciple in carefully controlled ritual contexts, for me as a historian of religions, it *also* includes all the other messy vernacular, lived, and popular forms of practice, such as magic, dance, fiction, films, and TV series.

Second, this exchange highlights the complex, ambivalent, and often conflicted relationship between the more elite Sanskritic forms of Tantra and its more popular manifestations and representations. While practitioners such as Rajib clearly emphasize a fundamental distinction between the two, the historian and ethnographer in me sees them as inextricably intertwined. For example, when we view a performance such as the *deodhanī* dance at Manasā Pūjā, I would argue, we can clearly see a vernacular, tribal-influenced possession performance that has been rather grudgingly accepted into the largely *brāhmaṇ*-controlled space of the temple (much as Manasā herself was only grudgingly accepted into the Hindu pantheon). And even then, it is largely held at bay, performed as it is outside rather than inside the main temple sanctum. But I would also add that I don't see my critical scholarly perspective as superior to or more accurate than that of the insider-practitioners; rather, I would argue for the necessity of *both*—that is, the perspectives of both contemporary practitioners and critical historians. In my view, these approaches are best understood not as binary opposites but rather as partially overlapping and already mutually entangled frameworks of understanding.

Finally, this exchange also highlights the complex entanglement of Tantra (and, today, arguably all religious traditions) in the expanding webs of globalization, economic development, and neoliberalism.[3] As we have seen throughout this book, there is almost no aspect of Tantra that has not been impacted by the forces of modernity, colonialism, nationalism, consumer capitalism, and tourism. But of course, these forces have also impacted different parts of the world in very different ways, leading to massive asymmetries of wealth, power, and influence that cannot be ignored. While the cheap books on *tantra-mantra* in the stalls of Kāmākhyā sell for forty rupees (less than a dollar), the slickly designed paperbacks on *Tantric Sex* at Barnes and Noble typically sell for at least twenty to thirty dollars (more than 1500–2300 rupees). Or, to use a more pointed comparison: While a tenured American professor can easily afford to fly to India, travel widely, and access almost any library in South Asia, Europe, or around the world, ordinary Tantric practitioners may be unable to travel far even within India and may be prevented from accessing archival sources that are central to their own traditions. These asymmetries can neither be easily resolved nor whitewashed; they can perhaps at best be addressed by some of the collaborative and reflexive approaches described in the introduction and in the remainder of this conclusion.

Living Tantra and Global Capital: Knots and Nodes in the Webs of Desire

In this book, I have focused on the Tantric traditions of Assam not only because these represent some of the oldest and most important currents of Tantra in South Asia; perhaps more importantly, they are also a kind of microcosm of the complex tensions that we see in the many contemporary forms of Tantra today. They embody in a very acute way the dynamics between the Sanskritic and the vernacular, the elite and the popular, the national and the local, and the embrace of capitalist development and the defense of tradition. We saw this latter impact perhaps most explicitly in the transformations of Ambuvācī Melā and the recent efforts to develop this Tantric celebration into a symbol of national identity, tourism, and economic development. But it now pervades almost every aspect of the tradition.

In this sense, Tantra today is perhaps best imagined as a kind of dense knot—to return to the original meaning of *tantra* as a "loom" or "weaving device"—within a tangled network of different religious, cultural, and economic interests. Or, to use Michel Foucault's metaphor, it represents a kind of linchpin that lies at the complex intersection of many difference forces. Some of these tensions were, of course, already present in the earliest Tantric literature. Tantra itself is often defined as the conjunction of *yoga* (spiritual discipline) and *bhoga* (sensual enjoyment), or as the use of desire (*kāma*) for the aim of spiritual liberation (*mokṣa*). Similarly, Alexis Sanderson famously described the historical tension between the ideals of "purity and power" in his classic study of the Śaivite traditions of Kashmir.[4] Yet these tensions have taken on a new valence in the twenty-first century, in the context of globalization, economic development, tourism, and nationalism. Indeed, we might say that one of the greatest tensions surrounding Tantra today is that between the desire to preserve a (real or imagined) idea of the traditional past and the aggressive neoliberal desire for capital and development. The current dispute over the new roads, ferry landing, and general "touristification" at Kāmākhyā is a clear example of this deep tension, which is likely to grow more intense in the years to come.

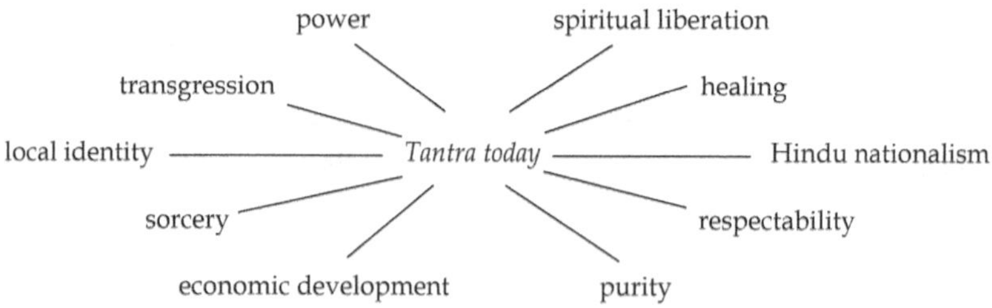

FIGURE 7.1. Diagram illustrating the place of Tantra today.

In structural terms, we could perhaps represent these tensions in figure 7.1, which is a more complex variant of the diagram that I proposed in chapter 2 in order to describe the place of magic and *tantra-mantra* in Assam. While this schema is obviously overly simplistic, I want to try to capture at least something of the complex dynamics between the goals of power and the ideals of purity, spiritual liberation, and respectability; between the assertion of local identity and the claims of a sort of national, Hindutva community; and between the goals of rapid economic development and the attempt to preserve ancient tradition.

As I noted at the beginning of this book, there is now a great deal of excellent scholarship on the history of Tantra as a textual tradition, but there is still a general paucity of work on Tantra as a living, popular, vernacular tradition. Fortunately, some very good scholarship on living Tantra has begun to emerge in recent years, such as the work of Mani Rao, Sukanya Sarbadhikary, June McDaniel, and a few others. Yet what is perhaps most needed today, I would argue, is not simply more good ethnographic research on Tantra; rather, we also need to seriously rethink contemporary Tantra in relation to the complex forces of globalization, nationalism, and neoliberalism.[5] How has Tantra been affected and transformed by the dynamics of late capitalism, with its transnational flows of people, ideas, and capital; the politics of economic development; and the impact of social media? As we see in the touristification of Mayong or the economic development of Kāmākhyā and other sites, Tantra is now very much a part of the expanding webs of nationalism, tourism, and global capitalism. By no means simply an obscure esoteric tradition practiced in the secret corners of Bangla or Assam, it is also very much a part of new mediascapes such as YouTube, Facebook, and Twitter.[6]

Surely, some traditional practitioners and many scholars will regard this phenomenon more as evidence of "dying Tantra" than of "living Tantra," as these traditions have become increasingly overtaken by the forces of globalization and capitalism, and surely there will be ongoing debates over the legitimacy of these new forms of Tantra. Yet that makes them no less worthy of study by historians of religion today.

Indeed, these new forms of Tantra and magic may also give us a telling insight into the strangely "enchanted" nature of contemporary capitalism itself. Many early sociologists such as Max Weber predicted that the modern world would become increasingly rationalized, bureaucratized, and disenchanted—that is, progressively evacuated of its magical and mysterious qualities.[7] And yet, we seem to see plenty of evidence that the exact opposite has happened, that the modern world has become in many ways weirdly "re-enchanted," and that capitalism itself may be ironically compatible with even the most extreme forms of religion and magic—including many forms of living Tantra.[8]

Talking Back to Contemporary Theory: The Alchemy and Territorialization of Desire

I began this book by reflecting on some of the deep methodological, ethical, and epistemological problems involved in the study of esoteric traditions such as Tantra. These problems are particularly acute when one happens to be a white, male, American scholar working on traditions of South Asia, where there is already a long history of colonialism and imperial domination, as well as of Orientalist scholarship that has often helped advance the project of empire. In the eyes of many critics today, the United States has taken Britain's place as the new global imperial power, with American scholars serving as the new agents of cultural colonization. Indeed, over the last two decades, many American scholars have been accused of perpetuating a kind of exoticized, sexualized neo-Orientalist view of India in general and of Tantra in particular.[9]

There is no easy solution to these problems, which are long-standing, profound, and historically complex. Yet perhaps one of the most useful ways of thinking about scholarship in the contemporary context is offered in Anna Tsing's sensitive ethnographic account, *The Mushroom at the End of the World*. I especially appreciate Tsing's discussion of the inevitable fact of global "contamination" and the need for a "collaborative" approach to scholarly work. In the twenty-first-century global context, she suggests, all cultures are already "contaminated" with one another. There is no pristine, untouched tradition (if, indeed, there ever was one). Perhaps the only means of survival today is a practice of collaboration—that is, an attempt to acknowledge our mutual contamination and to struggle together toward some sort of livable future: "Staying alive—for every species—requires livable collaborations. Collaboration means working across difference, which leads to contamination. Without collaborations, we all die. . . . Collaboration means working across difference . . . we are mixed up with others even before we begin any new collaboration."[10]

In the case of academic research on topics such as Tantra, I think such collaboration means recognizing that scholars and their objects of study are already entangled in complex ways—already "contaminated"—through the inevitable processes of globalization. Rather than retreating into some notion of either "pure tradition" or "scholarly objectivity," perhaps the only viable response is a collaborative one, by working with members of traditions toward some sort of mutual understanding. As of the writing of this book, for example, I have been working on a collaborative project with Rajib Sarma, Bandana Sarma, Prem Saran, Sundari Johansen Hurwitt, and others that aims to create a Center for Tantric Studies. Intended to be global and interdisciplinary, this center would bring together scholars, students, and practitioners from multiple fields, while creating a large digital library of manuscripts, texts, images, and other resources.

Collaborating in this way does not, however, mean that one has to renounce a critical scholarly approach or become a "cheerleader" or an "advocate" (as Bruce Lincoln put it).[11] It simply means adopting a basic attitude of respect toward those whom one hopes to understand, viewing them not as resources to be plundered for academic gain or subjects to be colonized in neo-imperialist fashion but as real people with their own complex lives, histories, and perspectives to offer. Moreover, genuine collaboration—rather than simple advocacy or cheerleading—not only allows for but *requires* a critical perspective. In this book, for example, I have discussed many aspects of living Tantra—magic, folk practice, popular representations, and so on—that many of my friends such as Rajib Sarma and Prem Saran would likely dismiss as illegitimate or as "pseudo-Tantra." Moreover, I have also adopted a more critical and historical view of the tradition that problematizes its own self-representation in ways that Rajib and others would probably not agree with. The point is that we must always acknowledge and remain sensitive to the clear asymmetries of power that exist between scholars and those whom they hope to represent—particularly in the case of traditions that have a history of colonialism, imperialism, and Orientalist misrepresentation, as South Asian Tantra clearly does.

At the same time, and perhaps more importantly, the criticism must be allowed to flow in both directions. Here I find Saba Mahmood's metaphor of allowing other cultures to "speak back" to contemporary theory very helpful.[12] Rather than simply plopping our Foucault or Butler down on another culture and running it through the academic theory-grinder, a more ethically responsible—and ultimately more interesting—approach is to also allow other ways of thinking, doing, and being to talk back to our theoretical perspectives, forcing us to critically rethink, reframe, and revise some of our own most taken-for-granted positions. Doing so requires a critical self-reflexivity and a paradoxical sort of "self-parochialization," as Webb Keane points out: "It is an ethic of self-displacement or self-parochialization; that is, of taking on another's perspective, not just to understand them, but also in the service of a political, cultural, or moral critique of one's own society, even of one's own values. For, among other goals, this ethic engages with alternative visions of political life, social well-being, and human flourishing—without necessarily advocating them—as affording positions from which to see things in a new light."[13]

In the case of Tantra in northeast India, I have suggested that the concept of *kāma* opens up a particularly fruitful critical dialogue. On the one hand, I do think Deleuzian ideas of desire, flow, and territorialization offer some useful insights into the Tantric idea of *kāma* (and perhaps also into other Asian concepts such as Tao in Chinese thought).[14] Following Deleuze, we could say that desire in this case is by no means limited to sexuality but encompasses all forms of desire, pleasure, enjoyment and need, ranging from the most physical desires for material well-being and prosperity to the most transcendent desires for spiritual liberation. Again, desire is not a lack or absence in a Freudian sense, but rather a productive power, the creative, pervasive, and dynamic energy of the goddess that flows through all aspects of the cosmos, the social order, and the human body alike.[15] Yet desire is also continually "territorialized" and "re-territorialized" in various ways: through religious institutions, through ritual practice, through the dynamic performance of gender, through nationalist politics, and more recently through the networks of globalization, tourism, and neoliberalism.[16] Today, the flow of desire is perhaps most obviously territorialized by the power of *capital*, which is flowing ever more rapidly into northeast India and quite literally "territorializing" the landscape through the construction of new roads, new ferry landings, and new conceptions of waste, cleanliness, and physical purity.[17]

Yet there are also many ways in which a Tantric understanding of *kāma* forces us to rethink or reframe contemporary theorizations of desire. As many feminist critics have noted, Deleuze and Guattari's understanding of *désir*—as fascinating and productive as it is—largely "fails to take into account sexual difference" and seemingly "by-pass[es] gender altogether."[18] As Rosi Braidotti argues, even Deleuze and Guattari's key concept of "becoming woman" is largely uninformed by any actual woman's perspective or by contemporary feminist thought; it seems to dissolve sexuality into a kind of play of "generalized becoming" that arguably undermines a feminist project and erases the very real historical struggles in which women have been engaged:

> One cannot deconstruct a subjectivity one has bever been fully granted control over; one cannot diffuse a sexuality which has historically been defined as dark and mysterious. In order to announce the death of the subject, one must first have gained the right to speak as one. . . . Deleuze gets caught in the contradiction of postulating a general "becoming woman" which fails to take into account the historical and epistemological specificity of the female feminist standpoint. A theory of difference which fails to take into account sexual difference leaves me as a feminist critic in a state of skeptical perplexity.[19]

The Tantric concept of *kāma*, conversely, is inextricably tied to notions of gender and to constructions of masculinity and femininity.[20] Embodied in the goddess of desire herself (Kāmākhyā or Kāmeśvarī), desire is imagined as a divine feminine energy that creates, sustains, and flows through all of existence. The power of the goddess is in turn embodied most clearly in the *yoni*, whose annual menstruation is believed to bring life to the earth and grace to devotees. If Deleuze is correct that modern philosophy has been dominated by the phallus—that is, by masculine, hierarchical forms of reason—then the Śākta Tantric tradition offers an alternative vision in which the *yoni* is not only equal to but in some ways more powerful than the *liṅgam*.[21] And "becoming woman" in this tradition is not simply a philosophical concept or a rhetorical maneuver; it is an actual *practice* that involves techniques of meditation, yoga, and possession performances in which human practitioners become the vehicles of a variety of powerful deities, both male and female. Surely, when discussing the idea of "becoming woman," we should also talk to *actual women*, such as the countless female devotees who make the annual pilgrimage to Ambuvācī Melā, or the female members of the Kula lineage, or the many women who see themselves as intimately linked to and even identical with the goddess as power.

But at the same time, as we saw in chapter 1, it would be difficult to read Śākta Tantric traditions as "feminist" in any modern sense of the term. They may have some interesting intersections with certain forms of contemporary feminist thought, but they clearly diverge in critical ways, as well.[22] For example, the idea that women are inherently identified with the goddess and that women's bodies are vehicles of divine creative power does align partially with some forms of second-wave feminism—such as some French feminist theorists and many in the women's spirituality movement in North America.[23] Thus, authors such as Frédérique Apffel-Marglin and Julia Jean have argued that Śākta Tantra offers "avenues for women's enlightenment, social liberation and a revisioning of oppressive social and cultural systems."[24] Yet even here it is difficult to read the tradition as exactly "feminist" in a modern sense, since it remains largely dominated by male *brāhmaṇs* who control both the Tantric lineage and the temple management, and it does little to offer women power in the public realm or political sphere, outside of family or esoteric ritual contexts.[25]

The tradition would seem even more at odds with recent third-wave and post-feminist approaches, which are generally deeply suspicious of any universalistic or essentializing claims about women and women's bodies.[26] Like most Tantric traditions, the Śākta traditions of Assam remain quite essentialist in their view of masculinity and femininity, which are modeled on the universal binary of god and goddess, Śiva and Śakti, *liṅgam* and *yoni.* The powers of women here remain largely tied to the powers of the *yoni*—the powers of fertility, reproduction, and motherhood.[27]

Historically, moreover, the divine power of the goddess has been repeatedly rechanneled and reterritorialized by male interests—by male-dominated religious institutions, by various empires, and by the modern political state. Through another kind of "alchemy of desire," the female power of the goddess and the *yoni* have been repeatedly transmuted into the male power of the guru, the priest, the king, and (most recently) the prime minister. The problem of patriarchy and its various territorializations has in fact been articulated by some Assamese women, such as the poet Nitoo Das cited in chapter 5, who cynically observed that the Goddess has the "luxury of bleeding only once a year" (unlike "regular women").

However, this question of gender is precisely where a more complex, mutual, and multi-sided dialogue between South Asian, European, and North American perspectives could be productive. It would seem that Tantric understandings of desire and sexuality ought to be of real interest to feminists and other critical theorists, offering new ways to think about the body, power, and femininity—new perspectives rooted in the *yoni* rather than the phallus. And yet, these South Asian perspectives are also not completely immune to critique. Allowing other traditions to "speak back" to modern theory should not mean that the conversation simply ends in the silence of the latter, but rather that it opens a more complex dialogical exchange in which *both* sides are subject to criticism. Again, such exchange is a matter of "engag[ing] with alternative visions of political life, social well-being, and human flourishing—*without necessarily advocating them*—as affording positions from which to see things in a new light."[28]

But perhaps most importantly, an approach that allows other cultures to speak back to contemporary theory would also force us to reflect critically upon our own "desires" as scholars. It would ask us to remain "relentlessly self-consciousness"—as Jonathan Z. Smith famously put it[29]—about our own motivations in the study of others' religions. Why do we even want to study these traditions in the first place? If the desire to do so is not simply an updated form of colonialism and cultural imperialism, then what *does* lead us to travel across the world and study complex esoteric traditions like these? Is it simply to further our academic careers and add a new line to our CVs? Is it mere curiosity or cross-cultural voyeurism? Or—less cynically, as I have suggested here—could it perhaps be an attempt to work toward a more collaborative, mutually beneficial, and broader understanding of human cultures that might help all of us navigate the strange new world of late capitalism in a more sustainable way?

Reimagining Religion through Vernacular Practice

Lastly and most ambitiously, I would hope that this book about living Tantra in northeast India might have some broader implications for our contemporary understanding of religion itself. To return to Primiano's key point, the study of living and vernacular forms of practice is not just another way of asserting the "folk" in opposition to the "official" religion; on the contrary, it calls into question the very idea that there even *is* an "official" religion and asks us instead to think about *all* religions as living traditions in which vernacular practice is always already entangled with orthodox institutions.[30] As we have seen in this book, even the most elite Sanskritic forms of Tantra are inextricably intertwined with all manner of "folk," indigenous, vernacular practices, expressed through Assamese, Bangla, Bodo, Hindi, and countless other languages. Major festivals such as Ambuvācī and Manasā Pūjā and ritual practices such as animal sacrifice are replete with local, non-*brāhmaṇic* practices, so much so that the very idea of a "high" form of Tantra in opposition to a "low" or "folk" variety ultimately makes little sense.

Much the same is surely true of all religion. The lived practice of Catholicism is hardly a simple binary of the priestly Latin versus the local folk traditions, but an incredibly messy tangle of practices drawn from many different cultures, languages, and regional negotiations; it involves festival, popular magic, and exorcism as much as theological debates over the Trinity or the person of Christ.[31] The lived practice of Buddhism is saturated with all manner of local practices that have little to do with the Four Noble Truth and Eightfold Path but are very much about the immediate needs and desires of ordinary laypeople; it involves amulets, relics, divination, and possession performances as much as philosophical debates on the nature of the self or emptiness.[32]

In his classic essay on the definition of "Judaism," Jonathan Z. Smith famously suggested that religions are best described not as neatly defined, tidy, and bounded categories but instead as something more like "heaps of rubbish" or "hotch-potches."[33] That is to say, there is a vast array of different texts, rituals, and identities, some of which scholars have decided to sweep together and collectively label as a particular religion such as "Judaism." But these categories are always messy and ambiguous, and they always bleed into and overlap with other categories in all sorts of complex ways.

Much the same is true of the messy and ambiguous "hotch-potch" category of "religion" itself, which has no clear boundaries and continues to be debated by scholars, students, and practitioners to this day. To return to the etymology of Tantra, which is derived from *tan-*, meaning to "weave" or "stretch," we might think of religion as a dense knot in which myriad threads are not so much neatly woven together as frayed, snarled, and tangled. Scholars and students are themselves entangled in these threads, struggling to draw the boundaries around the hotch-potch, even as they participate in its very "hotch-potchiness." Like the living forms of Tantra described in this book, the category of religion is itself a dense knot of the past and the present, the elite and the folk, the spiritual and the material, the global and the local, the spiritual and the commercial, the practitioner and the scholar. In this sense, religion might best be reimagined as a messy tangle of conflicting desires, ranging from the most spiritual and transcendent to the most worldly and mundane.

Acknowledgments and Entanglements

Anyone who attempts to study another religion and culture inevitably becomes entangled in complex, often intimate, and sometimes conflicted relationships with their objects of study. To try to understand anything other than oneself is to become enmeshed in dynamic, often messy networks of knowledge, exchange, and power that determine both the limits and the possibilities of one's work. In her remarkable book *The Mushroom at the End of the World*, anthropologist Anna Tsing compares the research and writing of a book to the dense networks of fungal mycelia that spread beneath the forest floor of most ecosystems, connecting plants and trees and periodically producing the fleshy "fruit" of mushrooms: "Below the forest floor, fungal bodies extend themselves in nets and skeins, binding roots and mineral soils, long before producing mushrooms. All books," she concludes, "emerge from similarly hidden collaborations."[1] This book has likewise emerged from a complex network of deep relationships in ways that are, I hope, mostly symbiotic and mutually beneficial rather than parasitic.

My topic is, after all, Tantra, which is an extremely complex and multifaceted tradition that spread widely throughout the Hindu, Buddhist, and Jain communities of Asia from at least the sixth century onward. The term *tantra* itself derives from the Sanskrit root *tan-*, "to weave" or "to stretch," and many of the earliest meanings of *tantra* are related to looms and to weaving.[2] Tantra, in its most basic meaning, is simply a text or a tradition that is "woven" of the many threads of discourse. Those who study and write about Tantra are themselves inevitably entangled in these threads of discourse—though in deeply complicated ways that also reflect the violent histories of colonialism and imperialism and the persistent imbalances of power between South Asia, Europe, and North America in the twenty-first century.[3] As I argued in the preceding pages, these intricate, often uncomfortable entanglements are now inescapable, yet they need not be solely a source of neocolonial exploitation and postcolonial guilt, but rather may also be occasions for more productive sorts of cross-cultural collaboration.

Among the many entanglements that have made this book possible are the following friends, colleagues, and mentors who have generously assisted me in my research and writing: Utpala Borah, Sravana Borkataky-Varma, Paul Courtright, Anjali Daimari, Wendy Doniger, Sean Dowdy, Kati Fitzgerald, Prema Goet, Shaman Hatley, Glen Hayes, Tilak Hāzarikā, Sundari Johansen Hurwitt, Andrea Jain, Paul C. Johnson, Padma Kaimal, Jeffrey Kripal, Jeffrey Lidke, Bruce Lincoln, Kimberly Masteller, Ila Nagar, Phaṇīdhar Nāth, Utpal Nāth, Ganesh Ojhā, Imma Ramos, Prabīn Śaikīyā, Prem Saran, Bandana Sarma, Nandi Sarma, Paban Sarma, Rajib Sarma, Raman Sarma, Riya Sarma, Bruce Sullivan, Aaron Ullrey, Ülo Valk, Kyle Wagner, and David Gordon White—among many others.

Support for this book has been provided by generous grants from the American Academy of Religion, the Fulbright Foundation, and the National Endowment for the Humanities.

Notes

INTRODUCTION

1. B. N. Shastri, ed., *Kālikā Purāṇa* (Delhi: Nag Publishers, 1991), 62.133: "*ksāmastham kāmamadhyastham kāmadevapuṭīkṛtam, kāmena kāmayet kāmo kāmaṃ kāme niyojayet.*"

2. Madeleine Biardeau, *Hinduism: The Anthropology of a Civilization* (Paris: Flammarion, 1981), 149–50.

3. Gilles Deleuze and Félix Guattari, *Anti-Oedipus: Capitalism and Schizophrenia* (Minneapolis: University of Minnesota Press, 1983), 5.

4. Kāmarūpa is listed as one of the oldest *śākta pīṭhas* in texts such as the *Tantrasadbhāva Tantra* (eighth century) and *Hevajra Tantra* (eighth to tenth century). See Hélène Brunner-Lachaux, Gerhard Oberhammer, and André Padoux, eds., *Tāntrikābhidhānakośa: Dictionnaire des termes techniques de la littérature hindoue tantrique* (Wien: Verlag der Österreichischen Akademie der Wissenschaften, 2004), 2:87; D. C. Sircar, ed., *The Śākta Pīṭhas* (Delhi: Motilal Banarsidass, 1973), 12. On Kāmākhyā Temple and Assamese Tantra, see Hugh B. Urban, *The Power of Tantra: Religion, Sexuality, and the Politics of South Asian Studies* (London: I. B. Tauris and Palgrave MacMillan, 2010); Hugh B. Urban, "The Womb of Tantra: Goddesses, Tribals, and Kings in Assam," *Journal of Hindu Studies* 4 (2011): 231–47; Loriliai Biernacki, *Renowned Goddess of Desire: Women, Sex, and Speech in Tantra* (New York: Oxford University Press, 2007); Nihar Ranjan Mishra, *Kamakhya: A Socio-Cultural Study* (New Delhi: D. K. Printworld, 2004); Apurba Chandra Barthakuria, *The Tantric Religion of India: An Insight into Assam's Tantra Literature* (Kolkata: Punthi Pustak, 2009); Paulo Rosati, "The Yoni Cult at Kāmākhyā: Its Cross-Cultural Roots," *Religions of South Asia* 10, no. 3 (2016): 278–99; Pranav Deka, *Nīlācala Kāmākhyā: Her History and Tantra* (Guwahati: Lawyer's Book Stall, 2004).

5. On Ambuvācī Melā, see Hugh B. Urban, "The Cradle of Tantra: Modern Transformations of a Tantric Centre in Northeast India, from Nationalist Symbol to Tourist Destination," *South Asia* 49, no. 2 (2019): 256–77; Frédérique Apffel-Marglin and Julia A. Jean, "Weaving the Body and the Cosmos: Two Menstrual Festivals in Northeastern India," *Worldviews* 24, no. 3 (2020): 245–84; Patricia Dold, "Pilgrimage to Kamakhya through Text and Lived Religion: Some Forms of the Goddess at an Assamese Temple Site," in *Studying Hinduism in Practice*, ed. Hillary P. Rodrigues (New York: Routledge 2011), 46–61; Brenda Dobia, "Śakti Yātrā—Locating Power, Questioning Desire: A

Women's Pilgrimage to the Temple of Kāmākhyā" (PhD diss., University of Western Sydney, 2008).

6. See Prema Goet, *The Path of Śakti* (Oxford: Oxford Center for Hindu Studies, 2019); Prema Goet, "Aghora Tantra in Kāmākhyā," paper presented at the Oxford Center for Hindu Studies, Oxford, September 20, 2020.

7. PTI, "Religious Tourism Centre to Be Built around Ambubaci Mela and Kamakhya Temple Says Assam CM Sarbananda Sonowal," *Financial Express*, June 22, 2017, http://www.financialexpress.com/india-news/religious-tourism-centre-to-be-built-around-ambubachi-mela-and-kamakhya-temple-says-assam-cm-sarbananda-sonowal/729948/. See Directorate of Tourism, *Ambubachi Mela* (Guwahati: Directorate of Tourism, 2107); Assam Tourism Development Corporation, *Celebrate the Fertility of Mother Nature: Ambubachi 2017* (Guwahati: Assam Tourism Development Corporation, 2017). See also Urban, "Cradle of Tantra."

8. See Hugh B. Urban, "Death, Nationalism and Sacrifice: Ritual, Politics, and Tourism in Northeast India," in *Irreverence and the Sacred: Critical Studies in the History of Religions*, ed. Hugh B. Urban and Greg Johnson (New York: Oxford University Press, 2018), 156–84.

9. See Judy Kuriansky, *The Complete Idiot's Guide to Tantric Sex* (New York: Alpha, 2001); Barbara Carrellas, *Urban Tantra: Sacred Sex for the Twenty-First Century* (Berkeley, CA: Ten Speed Press, 2017). On New Age or Neo-Tantra, see Hugh B. Urban, *Tantra: Sex, Secrecy, Politics and Power in the Study of Religion* (Berkeley: University of California Press, 2003), ch. 6.

10. See David Gordon White, *Kiss of the Yoginī: "Tantric Sex" in Its South Asian Contexts* (Chicago: University of Chicago Press, 2003); Ronald Davidson, *Indian Esoteric Buddhism: A Social History of the Tantric Movement* (New York: Columbia University Press, 2002); Alexis Sanderson, "Purity and Power among the Brahmins of Kashmir," in *The Category of the Person: Anthropology, Philosophy, History*, ed. Michael Carrithers, Steven Collins, and Steven Lukes (Cambridge: Cambridge University Press, 1985), 190–216; Geoffrey Samuel, *The Origins of Yoga and Tantra: Indic Religions to the Thirteenth Century* (Cambridge: Cambridge University Press, 2008); André Padoux, *Vāc: The Concept of the Word in Selected Hindu Tantras* (Albany, NY: SUNY Press, 1990); Gavin Flood, *The Tantric Body: The Secret Tradition of Hindu Religion* (London: I. B. Tauris, 2005); Shaman Hatley, "Tantra, Overview," in *Hinduism and Tribal Religions*, ed. Jeffery D. Long, Rita D. Sherma, Pankaj Jain, and Madhu Kanna (New York: Springer, 2022).

11. See Urban, *Power of Tantra*; Biernacki, *Renowned Goddess*; Mishra, *Kamakhya*; Rosati, "Yoni Cult." Other notable exceptions include E. Sundari Johansen Hurwitt, "The Voracious Virgin: The Concept and Worship of Kumārī in Kaula Tantrism" (PhD diss., California Institute of Integral Studies, 2019); Irene Majo Garigliano, "The Brahmans of the Kāmākhyā Temple Complex: Customary Rights, Relations with Pilgrims, and Administrative Power" (PhD diss., Istituto Italiano di Studi Orientali, 2015).

12. Mani Rao, *Living Mantra: Mantra, Deity and Visionary Experience Today* (New York: Palgrave MacMillan, 2018); Sukanya Sarbadhikary, *The Place of Devotion: Siting and Experiencing Divinity in Bengal Vaishnavism* (Berkeley: University of California Press, 2015). The few other exceptions include David Gordon White, ed., *Tantra in Practice* (Princeton, NJ: Princeton University Press, 2000); June McDaniel, *Offering Flowers, Feeding Skulls: Popular Goddess Worship in West Bengal* (New York: Oxford

University Press, 2004); Andrea Acri and Paolo E. Rosati, eds., *Tantra, Magic and Vernacular Religions in Monsoon Asia: Texts, Practices, and Practitioners from the Margins* (London: Routledge, 2022).

13. Biardeau, *Hinduism*, 149–50. See Padoux, *Vāc*, 40; Flood, *Tantric Body*, 84.

14. Hugh B. Urban, *The Economics of Ecstasy: Tantra, Secrecy, and Power in Colonial Bengal* (New York: Oxford University Press, 2001); Urban, *Tantra*; Urban, *Power of Tantra.*

15. André Padoux, "A Survey of Hindu Tantrism for the Historian of Religions," *History of Religions* 20, no. 4 (1981): 350. See also Padoux, *Vāc*, 31.

16. David Gordon White, "Tantrism," in *The Encyclopedia of Religion*, ed. Lindsay Jones (New York: MacMillan, 2005), 13:8984.

17. Padoux, "What Do We Mean by 'Tantrism?,'" in *The Roots of Tantra*, ed. Katherine Ann Harper and Robert L. Brown (Albany, NY: SUNY Press, 2002), 17.

18. Interviews with author, Kāmākhyā Temple, February 11, 2004. Interviews for this project were conducted in multiple languages, including Assamese, Bangla, English, and Hindi, often in a mix of all of the above.

19. Heman Sarma, quoted in Majo Garigliano, "Brahmans," 80. Another Tantric from Bengal named Svapan Giri defined it as follows: "Tantra comes from the union of Śiva and Śakti, the male and female energies that create the universe; Tantra is the way of tapping into that power and using it" (interview, Kāmākhyā Temple, Guwahati, Assam, June 17, 2022).

20. Muktināth Śarmā, "Tantra," in *Souvenir Viswa Shanti Devi Yajña*, ed. Sri Jadu Nath Sarma, Rajib Sarma, and Sri Naba Kanta Sarma (Guwahati: Viswa Shanti Devi Yajña Committee, 2014), 4. See also Prem Saran, *Yoga, Bhoga and Ardhanariswara: Individuality, Wellbeing, and Gender in Tantra* (New York: Routledge, 2008), 14. Saran defines Tantra as "the centuries-old South Asian cults of erotic yoga (mystical union) which use ritualized sexual intercourse, either physically or only visualized as a means to attain to the mystical experience."

21. See Hugh B. Urban, "Horrifying and Sinister *Tāntriks*," in *Bollywood Horrors: Religion, Violence and Cinematic Fears in India*, ed. Ellen Goldberg, Aditi Sen, and Brian Collins (New York: Bloomsbury Academic, 2020), 78–93.

22. See Carol Salomon, "Bāul Songs," in *Religions of India in Practice*, ed. Donald Lopez (Princeton, NJ: Princeton University Press, 1995), 187–208.

23. Śrī Gopāl Dās Bāul, interview with author, Guwahati, Assam, June 22, 2017.

24. Interview with author, Kāmākhyā Temple, July 4, 2017. This view was echoed by a number of Aghorīs whom I interviewed at Kāmākhyā Temple from June 16 to June 27, 2022.

25. Puṅjābī Bābā, interview with author, Kāmākhyā Temple, January 8, 2022.

26. Ronald L. Barrett, *Aghor Medicine: Pollution, Death, and Healing in Northern India* (Berkeley: University of California Press, 2005), 11. Other groups such as the Nāths—whom scholars often call "Tantric"—show similar ambivalence toward the label. See Adrián Muñoz, "Matsyendra's 'Golden Legend': Yogi Tales and Nāth Ideology," in *Yogi Heroes and Poets: Histories and Legends of the Nāths*, ed. David Lorenzen (Albany, NY: SUNY Press, 2012), 109–27: "Most of the Nāth yogis that I met in India and Nepal . . . claimed to be different from, and even opposed to, tantrics."

27. Perhaps the most practical way to define Tantra more broadly is with a "polythetic" definition; that is, rather than focusing on one particular feature, a polythetic definition identifies a number of common attributes or "family resemblances." If a given phenomenon shares a reasonable number of them, it is useful to label it "Tantra." For a good discussion of this polythetic approach and a list of ten common features of Tantra, see Douglas R. Brooks, *The Secret of the Three Cities: An Introduction to Hindu Śākta Tantra* (Chicago: University of Chicago Press, 1990), 55ff. For other definitions, see Urban, *Power of Tantra*; White, *Tantra in Practice*; André Padoux, *The Hindu Tantric World: An Overview* (Chicago: University of Chicago Press, 2017); Alexis Sanderson, "Śaivism and the Tantric Traditions," in *The World's Religions*, ed. Stewart Sutherland, Leslie Houlden, Peter Clarke, and Friedhelm Hardy (New York: Routledge, 1988), 660–704.

28. Biardeau, *Hinduism*, 149–50. See also John Woodroffe, *Shakti and Shākta* (New York: Dover, 1978), 633: "All Hindu schools seek the suppressions of mere animal worldly desire. What is peculiar to the Kaulas is the particular method employed for the transformation of desire. The *Kulārṇava Tantra* says that man must be taught to rise by means of those very things which are the cause of his fall. 'As one falls on the ground, one must lift oneself by aid of the ground.'"

29. Francesca Fremantle, trans., *A Critical Study of the Guhyasamāja Tantra* (London: University of London, 1971), 46.

30. Sir Monier Monier-Williams, *A Sanskrit-English Dictionary* (Oxford: Clarendon Press, 1995), 271. As Wendy Doniger observes, "*Kama* represents desire and pleasure . . . not merely sexual but more broadly sensual—music, good food, perfume and so forth" (introduction to Wendy Doniger and Sudhir Kakar, trans., *Vatsyayana, Kamasutra: A New Translation* [New York: Oxford University Press, 2009], xiii).

31. Padoux, *Hindu Tantric World*, 87: "A principle means of transcending the empirical self and uniting with the Absolute is through the use of *kāma* (Eros, passion)."

32. *Ṛg Veda*, 10.129.3–4, in *The Rig Veda*, trans. Wendy Doniger (New York: Penguin, 2005), 25.

33. Puṇyānandanātha, *Kāmakalāvilāsa*, ed. and trans. Arthur Avalon (Madras: Ganesh and Co., 1958), verse 54: "*kāmalaṅganāvilāso'yaṃ / paraśivabhujaṅgabhāvākarṣ aṇaharṣāya kalpate nityaṃ.*"

34. Arthur Avalon, introduction to Puṇyānandanātha, *Kāmakalāvilāsa*, xv.

35. *Kālikā Purāṇa*, 62.133. For a similar play on the multiple meanings of *kāma* in relation to the region of Kāmarūpa and the goddess Kāmeśvarī, see Teun Goudriaan and J. A. Schoterman, eds., *The Kubjikāmatatantra: Kulālikāmnāya Version* (Leiden: Brill, 1988), 2.89–90: "She has obtained the fruit of the bliss of passion [*kāma*], for which reason she shall be called Kāmeśvarī. Out of compassion, the form of desire [*kāmarūpa*] has been fashioned before me in manifold ways. For that reason, the great seat of Kāmarūpa will come into existence in the Kali age."

36. Tārānātha Vidyāratna, ed., *Kulārṇava Tantra* (Delhi: Motilal Banarsidass, 1975), 4.20.

37. Interviews with author, Dhūmāvatī Temple, July 9, 2017. Another devotee from Assam defined Tantra as "the power that flows through everything and the way of tapping into that power. It is a way of focusing your mind through meditation to

access that power. Then you can achieve anything you desire" (interview with author, Bhuvaneśvarī Temple, June 23, 2022). As a female devotee similarly put it, "Tantra is a divine power, a god-gifted power" (*Shakti: The Performance of Gender at Kamakhya Assam*, directed by Tracy Wares [2001; Berkeley: Department of Anthropology, University of California, Berkeley]). See also Jeffrey S. Lidke, *The Goddess within and beyond the Three Cities: Śākta Tantra and the Paradox of Power in the Nepāla-Maṇḍala* (New Delhi: D. K. Printworld, 2017), 151: "For Nepalese *Śākta tāntrikas*, the Devī is synonymous with power in all of its manifold aspects."

38. Ariel Glucklich, *The End of Magic* (New York: Oxford University Press, 1997), 148.

39. Gwendolyn Layne, trans., *Kādambarī: A Classic Sanskrit Tale of Magical Transformation* (New York: Garland, 1991), 226. See also Urban, *Tantra*, 37. On other fictional representations of Tantra, see David Lorenzen, *The Kāpālikas and Kālamukhas: Two Lost Śaivite Sects* (Delhi: Motilal Banarsidass, 1991), 16–23, 54–55.

40. I borrow this idea of allowing other cultures to "talk back" to modern theory in part from Saba Mahmood, *The Politics of Piety: The Islamic Revival and the Feminist Subject* (Princeton, NJ: Princeton University Press, 2011); see also Saba Mahmood, "Feminist Theory, Embodiment, and the Docile Agent: Some Reflections on the Egyptian Islamic Revival," *Cultural Anthropology* 16, no. 2 (2001): 202–36.

41. See Deleuze and Guattari, *Anti-Oedipus*; Michel Foucault, *The History of Sexuality, Volume 1: An Introduction* (New York: Vintage, 1978); Judith Butler, *Subjects of Desire: Hegelian Reflections in Twentieth Century France* (New York: Columbia University Press, 1987).

42. Gilles Deleuze, "Désir et plaisir," *Magazine littéraire* 325 (October 1994): 59–65. For other discussions of Deleuze's work in relation to Indian and East Asian thought, see Ian Buchanan, George Varghese K., and Manoj N. Y., eds., *Deleuze, Guattari, and India: Exploring a Postcolonial Multiplicity* (New York: Routledge, 2022); Ronald Bogue, Hanping Chiu, and Yu-lin Lee, eds., *Deleuze and Asia* (Newcastle upon Tyne, UK: Cambridge Scholars Publishing, 2014).

43. Deleuze and Guattari, *Anti-Oedipus*, 27. See Butler, *Subjects of Desire*, 205. See also William Deal and Tim Beal, *Theory for Religious Studies* (New York: Routledge, 2004), 63: "Desire, as conceived of in psychoanalysis, is something to be repressed and contained. Seeking to liberate desire from this negative charge, Deleuze and Guattari develop an understanding of desire as a flow of libido that exists prior to any representation of desire in psychoanalysis. Desire becomes 'territorialized' through political and ideological structures like family, religion, school, medicine, nation, sports, and media."

44. Jihai Gao, "Deleuze's Conception of Desire," *Deleuze and Guattari Studies* 7, no. 3 (2103): 406. See Hannah Stark, *Feminist Theory after Deleuze* (New York: Bloomsbury Academic, 2016); Philip Goodchild, *Deleuze and Guattari: An Introduction to the Politics of Desire* (London: Sage, 1996); Cheri Carr and Janae Scholtz, eds., *Deleuze and the Schizoanalysis of Feminism* (New York: Bloomsbury Academic, 2019); Claire Colebrooke, *Gilles Deleuze* (New York: Routledge, 2001).

45. Butler, *Subjects of Desire*, 206. See Daniel Smith, "Gilles Deleuze," *Stanford Encyclopedia of Philosophy*, May 23, 2008, revised June 3, 2022, https://plato.stanford.edu/entries/deleuze/: "'Desire' in desiring-production is not oriented to making up a lack, but is purely positive. Desiring-production is autonomous, self-constituting, and creative: it is the *natura naturans* of Spinoza or the will-to-power of Nietzsche."

46. Stark, *Feminist Theory after Deleuze*, 2. See Jerry Aline Flieger, "Becoming Woman: Deleuze, Shreber and Molecular Identification," in *Deleuze and Feminist Theory*, ed. Ian Buchanan and Claire Colebrook (Edinburgh: Edinburgh University Press, 2000), 39: "Deleuze's strange world of abstract machines, apparatuses of capture, tribal despots, and ambulant war machines seems to be pretty much a male realm. . . . [H]is nomad, his smith, his warrior chief are all seemingly masculine constructs, armoured, aggressive."

47. Stark, *Feminist Theory after Deleuze*, 29. See also Tamsin Lorraine, *Irigaray and Deleuze: Experiments in Visceral Philosophy* (Ithaca, NY: Cornell University Press, 1999), 186: "The kind of sexuality that Deleuze and Guattari concern themselves with is a masculine one with a masculine bias."

48. Todd May, *Gilles Deleuze: An Introduction* (Cambridge: Cambridge University Press, 2005), 150. See Gilles Deleuze and Félix Guattari, *Thousand Plateaus: Capitalism and Schizophrenia* (Minneapolis: University of Minnesota Press, 1987), 275; Patty Sotirin, "Becoming Woman," in *Gilles Deleuze: Key Concepts*, ed. Charles J. Stivale (Montreal: McGill-Queen's University Press, 2005), 98–109.

49. See Rosi Braidotti, "Discontinuous Becomings: Deleuze on the Becoming-Woman of Philosophy," *Journal of the British Journal for Phenomenology* 24, no. 1 (1993): 44–55. She argues that Deleuze's notion of "becoming woman" fails to engage with feminist perspectives or the history of women's struggles: "One cannot deconstruct a subjectivity one has never been fully granted control over; one cannot diffuse a sexuality which has historically been defined as dark and mysterious. . . . Deleuze gets caught in the contradiction of postulating a general 'becoming woman' which fails to take into account the historical and epistemological specificity of the female feminist standpoint" (48).

50. See Urban, *Power of Tantra*; Biernacki, *Renowned Goddess*.

51. On the development of the idea of *kuṇḍalinī* and its role in Tantric practice, see White, *Kiss*, 221–23; Lilian Silburn, *Kuṇḍalinī: The Energy of the Depths* (Albany, NY: SUNY Press, 1988).

52. See Saran, *Yoga, Bhoga, and Ardhanariswara*.

53. See Hugh B. Urban, "Dancing for the Snake: Possession, Gender, and Identity in the Worship of Manasā in Assam," *Journal of Hindu Studies* 11, no. 3 (2018): 304–27.

54. Mark Dyczkowski, *A Journey into the World of the Tantras* (Varanasi: Indica Books, 2004), 103–4: "The original name of this place, known to both early Hindu and Buddhist sources, is Kāmaru. The Sanskritized form 'Kāmarūpa' is easily derivable from it." Many have suggested that the name may originally derive from local indigenous languages. See Kali Prasad Goswami, *Kamakhya Temple: Past and Present* (New Delhi: A. P. H. Publishing Corporation, 1998), 12.

55. The earliest references to Prāgjyotiṣapura appear in the *Mahābhārata*, where it is said to have been the kingdom of the demon king Naraka. Throughout the epics and in the later Sanskrit literature, this region is said to be inhabited by "mountain men" (*kirātas*) and barbarians (*mlecchas*)—that is, by indigenous, non-Hindu hill tribes. See J. A. B. van Buitenen, trans., *The Mahābhārata, Volume 3, Book 4: The Book of Virāta and Book 5: The Book of Effort* (Chicago: University of Chicago Press, 1978), 140; J. A. B. van Buitenen, trans., *The Mahābhārata, Volume 2, Book 2: The Book of the Assembly, Book 3: The Book of the Forest* (Chicago: University of Chicago Press, 1975), 78, 89, 103, 117, 247,

265; Nirode Boruah, "Pragjyotisapura—The Capital City of Early Assam," *Proceedings of the Indian History Congress* 64 (2003): 337–47.

56. Various scholars have suggested that the name Kāmākhyā may be a Sanskritization of older indigenous goddesses of the northeast region. Some trace the name to the Khasi goddess *Ka Meikha*, or "old cousin mother." Many Khasi and Garo folk tales claim that Kāmākhyā was originally a site of their own deities. One narrative describes Kāmākhyā Hill as "the place at which the Khasis halted during their journey from . . . the Himalayas to their present home," and the hill is still referred to as *U Lum Ka Meikha* by many Khasis (Hamlet Bareh, *The History and Culture of the Khasi People* [Gauhati: The Author, 1967], 18–38). Alternatively, Banikanta Kakati suggests that it may come from other indigenous terms such as *Kamoi, Kamoit*, or *Kamru*. See Kakati, *Assamese, Its Formation and Development* (Guwahati: Lawyer's Book Stall, 1962), 53. Mishra links Kāmākhyā to a number of indigenous goddesses of the northeast, including Khānkhām of the Ahoms, Āi Kāmākhyā of the Bodos, and Kā Meikhā of the Khasis (*Kamakhya*, 15–18).

57. Brunner-Lachaux, Oberhammer, and Padoux, *Tāntrikābhidhānakośa*, 2:87; David Snellgrove, ed., *The Hevajra Tantra: A Critical Study* (London: Oxford University Press, 1959), 1.7.12.

58. Dyczkowski, *Journey*, 104: "This place is of great importance for the early Śākta—technically called Kaula—Tantras. . . . This is largely because of its association with Matsyendranātha, the reputed originator of the Kaula Tantric traditions. . . . Abhinavagupta praises him first, before all the other teacher he venerates." See Prabodh Chandra Bagchi, ed., *Kaulajñānanirṇaya and Some Minor Texts of the School of Matsyendranātha* (Calcutta: Metropolitan Printing and Publishing House, 1934), 16.7b–8a, 22.9–11. For the broader body of legends surrounding Matsyendranātha, see Muñoz, "Matsyendra's 'Golden Legend.'"

59. Agehananda Bharati, *The Ochre Robe: An Autobiography* (New York: Ross-Erikson, 1980), 248. Bharati is said to have received Tantric initiation in Assam from a well-known guru, Ramani Kanta Sarma (Prem Saran, personal communication, July 4, 2021). See also Jeffrey J. Kripal, "Remembering Ourselves: On Some Countercultural Echoes of Contemporary Tantric Studies," in *Transformations and Transfer of Tantra in South Asia and Beyond*, ed. István Keul (Berlin: De Gruyter, 2012), 449.

60. K. R. van Kooij, *Worship of the Goddess According to the Kālikā Purāṇa* (Leiden: E. J. Brill, 1979), 35. See Albert Grünwedel, *Der Weg nach Sambhala* (München: J. Roth, 1915), 18ff.

61. Paul Olaf Bodding, quoted in Imma Ramos, *Pilgrimage and Politics in Colonial Bengal: The Myth of the Goddess Sati* (London: Routledge, 2017), 56. Likewise, Reverend Robinson described the region as a place where "the most abominable rites are practiced, and the most licentious scenes exhibited, which it is hardly possible to suppose the human mind, even when sunk to the very lowest depths of depravity, could be capable of devising" (Ramos, *Pilgrimage and Politics*, 56).

62. Sir Charles Eliot, *Hinduism and Buddhism: An Historical Sketch* (London: Routledge and Kegan Paul, 1921), 66.

63. See, for example, Mayukh Majumdar, "The Land That Even Mughal Generals Feared—Mayong, India's Black Magic Capital," *Mirror Now News*, January 13, 2018,

https://www.timesnownews.com/mirror-now/society/article/mayong-black-magic-witchcraft-mughal-aurangzeb/188418.

64. Partners for Law Development, *Witch Hunting in Assam: Individual, Structural and Legal Dimensions* (Guwahati: Northeast Network, 2015), 5.

65. See Urban, "Horrifying and Sinister *Tāntriks*."

66. See Robert Orsi, *Between Heaven and Earth: The Religious Worlds People Make and the Scholars Who Study Them* (Princeton, NJ: Princeton University Press, 2006), 158. Orsi defines lived religion as "religion as people actually do and imagine it in the circumstances of their everyday lives."

67. Leonard Primiano, "Vernacular Religion and the Search for Method in Religious Folklore," *Journal of Western Folklore* 54, no. 1 (1995): 44. See Leonard Primiano, *Vernacular Religion: Collected Essays of Leonard Norman Primiano*, ed. Debora Dash Moore (New York: New York University Press, 2022); Marion Bowman and Ülo Valk, eds., *Vernacular Religion in Everyday Life* (New York: Routledge, 2014), 4–5.

68. Leonard Primiano, "Afterword," in *Vernacular Religion in Everyday Life*, ed. Bowman and Valk, 382–94.

69. Frederick M. Smith, *The Self Possessed: Deity and Spirit Possession in South Asia* (New York: Columbia University Press, 2006), 19.

70. Wendy Doniger, *The Hindus: An Alternative History* (New York: Penguin, 2009), 6: "The opposite of Sanskritization, the process by which the Sanskritic tradition simultaneously absorbs and transforms those same popular traditions, is equally important, and that process might be called oralization or popularization, or even, perhaps, Deshification. . . . The two processes of Sanskritisation and Deshification beget each other."

71. Dold, "Pilgrimage to Kamakhya," 49.

72. For sociological approaches, see Georg Simmel's seminal work, "The Secret and the Secret Society," in *The Sociology of Georg Simmel*, ed. Kurt Wolff (MacMillan: New York, 1950), 345–78; and Stanton Tefft, *The Dialectics of Secret Society Power in States* (Atlantic Highlands, NJ: Humanities Press, 1992). For anthropological perspectives, see Paul C. Johnson, *Secrets, Gossip, and Gods: The Transformation of Brazilian Candomblé* (New York: Oxford University Press, 2002); Ian Keen, *Knowledge and Secrecy in an Aboriginal Religion* (New York: Oxford University Press, 1998); Gilbert Herdt, *Secrecy and Cultural Reality: Utopian Ideologies in the New Guinea Men's House* (Ann Arbor: University of Michigan Press, 2003). On Western esotericism, see Antoine Faivre, *Access to Western Esotericism* (Albany, NY: SUNY Press, 1994); Wouter J. Hanegraaff, *Western Esotericism: A Guide for the Perplexed* (New York: Bloomsbury Academic, 2013). For a range of different perspectives, see Hugh B. Urban and Paul Christopher Johnson, eds., *The Routledge Handbook of Religion and Secrecy* (New York: Routledge, 2022); Hugh B. Urban, *Secrecy: Silence, Power, and Religion* (Chicago: University of Chicago Press, 2021).

73. See Hugh B. Urban, "The Torment of Secrecy: Ethical and Epistemological Problems in the Study of Esoteric Traditions," *History of Religions* 37, no. 3 (1998): 209–48.

74. On this question, see James Clifford, *The Predicament of Culture: Twentieth Century Ethnography, Literature, and Art* (Cambridge, MA: Harvard University Press, 1988), 55–91; Urban, "Torment of Secrecy."

75. Padoux, *Hindu Tantric World*, 16. See also Padoux, *The Heart of the Yoginī: A Sanskrit Tantric Treatise* (New York: Oxford University Press, 2013), 25: "Secrecy is always

insisted upon in Tantric traditions, which are initiatory. The teaching is therefore transmitted secrecy by the master, the guru, to a carefully chosen disciple, intent on acquiring the esoteric knowledge."

For other scholars who grapple with the problem of secrecy in Tantra, see also Brooks, *Secret of the Three Cities*; Davidson, *Indian Esoteric Buddhism*; Urban, "Torment of Secrecy."

76. "Thus, O Goddess! I have told you the imposition, a most secret [*guhyatama*] procedure. It is indeed to be performed by you most secretly. O Praised by the heroes! It is to be entrusted only to those who follow the rule [of Kula], never to anyone who is not [the initiated] disciple of a master of this tradition. This [ritual] is more secret than any secret [*guptād guptataraṃ*] I have revealed to you today" (*Yoginī Hṛdaya*, 67–68, trans. Padoux, in *Heart of the Yoginī*, 110).

77. Jyotirlāla Dāsa, ed., *Kāmākhyātantram: mūla, ṭīkā o baṅgānubāda sameta* (Calcutta: Navabhārata, 1978), 118–19. See also Puṇyaśīla Śarmā, ed., *Gupta-sādhana Tantra* (Prayāga: Kalyāṇa Mandir, 1970), 1.6; Vidyāratna, ed., *Kulārṇava Tantra*, 11.82–85: "Just as one must protect his wealth from thieves, O Beloved, so too, one must protect this Kula worship from bestial men (*paśu*). . . . This Kula ritual should always be kept secret, as a woman does not reveal her pregnancy by her lover. The Vedas, Purāṇas, and Śāstras display themselves like prostitutes, but this wisdom is secretive like a daughter in law."

78. On the conflict of interpretations as a hermeneutical problem, see Paul Ricoeur, *The Conflict of Interpretations* (New York: Continuum, 2004); Urban, "Torment of Secrecy."

79. Shaman Hatley lists at least seven different interpretations of sexual practices in Tantric literature, which range from love magic to ritualized orgasmic coitus to the internalization and sublimation of the sexual fluids. Hatley, *The Brahmayāmalatantra or Picumata, Volume 1: Revelation, Ritual, and Material Culture in an Early Śaiva Tantra* (Pondicherry: Institut Français de Pondicherry, 2018), 199–209. For two very different interpretations of *maithuna* in Tantric literature, compare White, *Kiss*, and Christian Wedemeyer, *Making Sense of Tantric Buddhism: History, Semiology, and Transgression in the Indian Traditions* (New York: Columbia University Press, 2012).

80. See White, *Kiss*; Urban, *Power of Tantra*, ch. 3.

81. See Sarbadhikary, *Place of Devotion*, 144–45.

82. The *Kāmākhyā Tantra*, for example, recommends others' wives, prostitutes, and menstruating women as the best partners in *maithuna*: "Having approached the *yoni* of another man's wife, the wise man should especially make offerings. The *yoni* of a prostitute [*veśyāyoni*] is the best. . . . With a woman in her menstrual cycle [*ṛtuyuktalatā*], he will attain manifold pleasures" (Śāstrī, ed., 3.59–60).

83. See Urban, *Power of Tantra*, chs. 3–4; Sarbadhikary, *Place of Devotion*, 145.

84. On this point, see also Urban, "Torment of Secrecy"; Urban, *Secrecy*, introduction.

85. Rajib Sarma, interview with author, Guwahati, Assam, June 21, 2017.

86. Rajib Sarma, "Kamakhya Temples' Complex: A Socio-Religious Perspective," unpublished PDF on file with author, June 2, 2017.

87. Rajib Sarma, personal communication, May 14, 2017. See Majo Garigliano, "Brahmans," 87.

88. See Ülo Valk, "Conceiving the Supernatural through Variation in Experience Stories: Assistant Spirits and Were-Tigers in the Belief Narratives of Assam," *Shaman* 23, nos. 1–2 (2015): 141–64, at 146: "I can only guess how much is kept hidden from me in these interviews, because of certain restrictions concerning the secrecy of magic. I have recorded many mantras but I know that many of them have not been recited completely in order to maintain their power." See also Utpal Nāth, "Māyaṅgar Jāduvidyār Sādhanā: Vijñān, Viśvās āru Andhviśvās," in *Kālśilā: Smṛtigrantha*, ed. Utpal Nāth (Jagirod, India: Abhinab Offset Printers, 2010), 120–26.

89. Kāmākhyā community members, conversations with author, Kāmākhyā Temple, June–July 2017 and January 2022. I should add that I have great respect for scholars who do choose to take initiation, provided they do so in an ethically responsible and academically critical way. A good example is E. Sundari Johansen Hurwitt, who is both a solid scholar and an initiate in the Kāmākhyā tradition. Her dissertation, "Voracious Virgin," is a good example of work by a scholar-practitioner who walks the line in a responsible and productive way.

90. On the idea of an "economy of secrets," see Daniel Jütte, *The Age of Secrecy: Jews, Christians, and the Economy of Secrets, 1400–1800* (New Haven, CT: Yale University Press, 2015); Lamont Lindstrom, *Knowledge and Power in a South Pacific Society* (Washington, DC: Smithsonian Institute, 1990); Urban, *The Economics of Ecstasy*; Urban, "Torment of Secrecy"; Urban, *Secrecy*.

91. I have known and interviewed Prem Saran since 2008 and Rajib Sarma since 2016. For information on Sarma and his work, see "Nīlācala Kāmākhyā," *Kamakhya.org*, accessed February 28, 2022, https://kamakhya.org/author/rajib/. On Saran, see "Dr. Prem Saran," *Knowledge Management Online*, accessed February 28, 2022, http://www.knowledge-management-online.com/dr-prem-saran2.html. The practitioners who asked to remain anonymous will be quoted without names or other identifying attributes in this book.

92. Karen McCarthy Brown, *Mama Lola: A Vodou Priestess in Brooklyn* (Berkeley: University of California Press, 2011). Similar kinds of ethnographic projects that involve this sort of entanglement include Anna Tsing, *The Mushroom at the End of the World: On the Possibility of Life in Capitalist Ruins* (Princeton, NJ: Princeton University Press, 2017), and Tanya Erzen, *Straight to Jesus: Sexual and Christian Conversions in the Ex-Gay Movement* (Berkeley: University of California Press, 2006).

93. Anna Tsing, *Friction: An Ethnography of Global Connection* (Princeton, NJ: Princeton University Press, 2005), 245–46; see Tsing, *Mushroom at the End of the World*, viii.

94. Over the last ten years, I have collected dozens of manuscripts for Sarma and Saran, many from the British Museum Library and the Nepalese-German Manuscript Collection in Hamburg. I have also shared with them numerous recordings of South Asian folk songs and hundreds of my own research photos. We have also been discussing the idea of creating a collaborative "Center for Tantric Studies" that would bring together scholars and practitioners from around the world.

95. Sameer Pitalwalla, producer, "Tashree Original Series Bible," June 15, 2020, PDF on file with author. See also Saurav Mahopatra and Aditya Bhattacharya, "Tashree Pitch Deck," March 11, 2021, PDF on file with author.

96. On the impact of neoliberalism on religion, see Andrea R. Jain, *Peace, Love, Yoga: The Politics of Global Spirituality* (New York: Oxford University Press, 2020); Jeremy

Carrette and Richard King, *Selling Spirituality: The Silent Takeover of Religion* (New York: Routledge 2004); Hugh B. Urban, *Zorba the Buddha: Sexuality, Spirituality, and Capitalism in the Global Osho Movement* (Berkeley: University of California Press, 2016). In my understanding of neoliberalism, I follow David Harvey, who defines it as essentially "the commodification of everything"; see Harvey, *A Brief History of Neoliberalism* (New York: Oxford University Press, 2007).

97. Primiano, "Vernacular Religion," 44. See Bowman and Valk, eds., *Vernacular Religion*, 4–5.

CHAPTER ONE

1. B. N. Shastri, ed., *Kālikā Purāṇa* (Delhi: Nag Publishers, 1991), 74.204–5.

2. Georges Bataille, "Attraction and Repulsion," in *The College of Sociology (1937–39)*, ed. Denis Hollier (Minneapolis: University of Minnesota Press, 1988), 121.

3. On the terms *kula* and *kaula*, see Hélène Brunner-Lachaux, Gerhard Oberhammer, and André Padoux, eds., *Tāntrikābhidhānakośa: Dictionnaire des termes techniques de la littérature hindoue tantrique*, vol 2. (Wien: Verlag der Österreichischen Akademie der Wissenschaften, 2004), 120–21: "*Kula* is used in the early Śaivite tradition of the Vidyāpīṭha to describe the group of *yoginīs*, divine female powers, group in families or clans, each directed by a divine Mother (*mātṛkā*)." *Kaula* then refers to texts and traditions belonging to or derived from the *kula* (142). See also Sanjukta Gupta, Teun Goudriaan, and Dirk Jan Hoens, *Hindu Tantrism* (Leiden: Brill, 1979), 44.

4. Prabodh Chandra Bagchi, ed., *Kaulajñānanirṇaya and Some Minor Texts of the School of Matsyendranātha* (Calcutta: Metropolitan Printing and Publishing House, 1934), 16.7–8. See Hugh B. Urban, *Power of Tantra: Religion, Sexuality, and the Politics of South Asian Studies* (London: I. B. Tauris and Palgrave MacMillan, 2010), 39–41.

5. See David Gordon White, *Kiss of the Yoginī: "Tantric Sex" in Its South Asian Contexts* (Chicago: University of Chicago Press, 2003); Alexis Sanderson, "Śaiva Texts," in *Brill's Encyclopedia of Hinduism*, vol. 6, ed. Knut A. Jacobsen (Leiden: Brill, 2015), 10–42, at 28.

6. See Brunner-Lachaux, Oberhammer and Padoux, *Tāntrikābhidhānakośa*, 3:78–79: "Whereas *dakṣiṇācāra* refers to Vedic rites based on standards of purity, *vāmācāra* refers to the very opposite, that is, to the use of the impure left hand in ritual practice. The pair *dakṣiṇācāra* and *vāmācāra* come to distinguish, respectively, the way of ritual performed in congruity with *vaidika* purity norms . . . and the . . . transgression thereof. . . . Often *vāmācāra* is synonymous with the *kulācāra* itself." See also Gupta, Goudriaan, and Hoens, *Hindu Tantrism*, 44; Douglas R. Brooks, *Secret of the Three Cities: An Introduction to Hindu Śākta Tantra* (Chicago: University of Chicago Press, 1990), 28; Mark S. G. Dyczkowski, *The Canon of the Śaivāgamas and the Kubjikā Tantras of the Western Kaula Tradition* (Albany, NY: SUNY Press, 1988), 59–67.

For a discussion of *dakṣiṇācāra* and *vāmācāra* in the context of Assamese Tantra, see Adhyapaka Śrī Umākānta Deva Śarmā, "Asame Tantrasādhanā," in *Souvenir Viswa Shanti Devi Yajña*, ed. Sri Jadu Nath Sarma, Rajib Sarma, and Sri Naba Kanta Sarma (Guwahati: Viswa Shanti Devi Yajña Committee, 2014), 28.

7. See André Padoux, *Vāc: The Concept of the Word in Selected Hindu Tantras* (Albany, NY: SUNY Press, 1990), 40; Gavin Flood, *The Tantric Body: The Secret Tradition*

of Hindu Religion (London: I. B. Tauris, 2005), 84: "In the tantric traditions of the left, *kāma* is not an end in itself but a means to an end; desire is used to transcend itself as a thorn can be removed by a thorn, or perfection attained by those things that would normally lead one to fall from the path."

8. On territorialization and deterritorialization, see Gilles Deleuze and Félix Guattari, *Anti-Oedipus: Capitalism and Schizophrenia* (Minneapolis: University of Minnesota Press, 1983), chs. 2–3; Eugene Holland, *Deleuze and Guattari's Anti-Oedipus: Introduction to Schizoanalysis* (New York: Routledge, 1999), 19–20; on connections between Deleuze and esoteric traditions such as alchemy, see Joshua Ramey, *The Hermetic Deleuze: Philosophy and Spiritual Ordeal* (Durham, NC: Duke University Press, 2012), 29–30.

9. See Rajib Sarma, "Kamakhya Temples' Complex: A Socio-Religious Perspective," unpublished PDF on file with author, 2017; Muktināth Śarmā, "Tantra," in *Souvenir Viswa Shanti Devi Yajña*, ed. Sri Jadu Nath Sarma, Rajib Sarma, and Sri Naba Kanta Sarma (Guwahati: Viswa Shanti Devi Yajña Committee, 2014); Prem Saran, *Yoga, Bhoga and Ardhanariswara: Individuality, Wellbeing, and Gender in Tantra* (New York: Routledge, 2008), 14–15.

10. See Hugh B. Urban, *Economics of Ecstasy: Tantra, Secrecy, and Power in Colonial Bengal* (New York: Oxford University Press, 2001); Hugh B. Urban, *Tantra: Sex, Secrecy, Politics and Power in the Study of Religion* (Berkeley: University of California Press, 2003), 134–64.

11. See Urban, *Tantra*, 134–64; Urban, *Economics of Ecstasy*.

12. On this point, see Śarmā, "Tantra"; Irene Majo Garigliano, "The Brahmans of the Kāmākhyā Temple Complex: Customary Rights, Relations with Pilgrims, and Administrative Power" (PhD diss., Istituto Italiano di Studi Orientali, 2015).

13. See Ronald L. Barrett, *Aghor Medicine: Pollution, Death, and Healing in Northern India* (Berkeley: University of California Press, 2005), xii–xiii.

14. See Prema Goet, "Aghora Tantra in Kāmākhyā," paper presented at the Oxford Center for Hindu Studies, Oxford, September 20, 2020; Prema Goet, *The Path of Śakti* (Oxford: Oxford Center for Hindu Studies, 2019).

15. I borrow the term "tantricity" from E. Sundari Johansen Hurwitt in her paper "The Inconvenience of History: The Politics of Myth and the Construction of Public Tantric Identity." Paper presented at the annual meeting of the American Academy of Religion, San Antonio, TX, November 21, 2021.

16. White, *Kiss*, 17. Sanderson lists five main features of Kaula traditions: (1) erotic ritual with a female companion; (2) sanguinary practices for the propitiation of the fierce gods, Bhairava and Cāmuṇḍā; (3) the notion that supernatural powers may be attained through the extraction by yogic means of the vital essences of living beings; (4) initiation through the consumption of consecrated liquor; and (5) the centrality of states of possession ("Śaiva Texts," 28).

17. Tārānātha Vidyāratna, ed., *Kulārṇava Tantra* (Delhi: Motilal Banarsidass, 1975), 3.5. See also Dyczkowski, *Canon*, 67.

18. Dyczkowski, *Canon*, 59. See Alexis Sanderson, "Śaivism and the Tantric Traditions," in *The World's Religions*, ed. Stewart Sutherland, Leslie Houlden, Peter Clarke, and Friedhelm Hardy (New York: Routledge, 1988), 660–704, at 680.

19. Dyczkowski, *Canon*, 60. See Jeffrey S, Lidke, *The Goddess within and beyond the Three Cities: Śākta Tantra and the Paradox of Power in the Nepāla-Maṇḍala* (New Delhi: D. K. Printworld, 2017), 2.

20. White, *Kiss*, 18. See Sanderson, "Śaivism and the Tantric Traditions," 680ff; Lidke, *Goddess*, 2.

21. Bagchi, ed., *Kaulajñānanirṇaya*, 22.9–11. See Dyczkowski, *Canon*, 65; Shaman Hatley, *The Brahmayāmalatantra or Picumata, Volume 1: Revelation, Ritual, and Material Culture in an Early Śaiva Tantra* (Pondicherry: Institut Français de Pondicherry, 2018), 19–21.

22. Bagchi, ed., *Kaulajñānanirṇaya*, 16.7b–8a: "*sādhvikaṃ yogasaṃyukto kāmākhyaṃ pīṭhamāsmṛtam / tasmin melāpakaṃ labdhvā yoginīsiddhiḥ tatsamam.*" For other narratives associated with Matsyendra and Assam, see Adrián Muñoz, "Matsyendra's 'Golden Legend': Yogi Tales and Nāth Ideology," in *Yogi Heroes and Poets: Histories and Legends of the Nāths*, ed. David Lorenzen (Albany, NY: SUNY Press, 2012), 109–27.

23. See White, *Kiss*; Sanderson, "Śaivism and the Tantric Traditions," 671; Urban, *Power of Tantra*, 31–42.

24. Abhinavagupta, *Tantrāloka*, translated by Dyczkowski, in *Canon*, 170. See also Dyczkowski, *A Journey into the World of the Tantras* (Varanasi: Indica Books, 2004), 103–4: "The original name of this place, known to both early Hindu and Buddhist sources, is Kāmaru. The Sanskritized form 'Kāmarūpa' is easily derivable from it. This place is of great importance for the early Śākta—technically called Kaula—Tantras. . . . This is largely because of its association with Matsyendranātha. . . . Abhinavagupta praises him first, before all the other teachers he venerates."

25. Interviews with author, Guwahati, Assam, January 11, 2022; see E. Sundari Johansen Hurwitt, "The Voracious Virgin: The Concept and Worship of Kumārī in Kaula Tantrism" (PhD diss., California Institute of Integral Studies, 2019), 428.

26. Shastri, ed., *Kālikā Purāṇa*, 81.19–23; see Urban, *Power of Tantra*, 102–4; Nihar Ranjan Mishra, *Kamakhya: A Socio-Cultural Study* (New Delhi: D. K. Printworld, 2004), 146.

27. Shastri, ed., *Kālikā Purāṇa*, 74.204–5.

28. Shastri, ed., *Kālikā Purāṇa*, 74.136–38; see Urban, *Power of Tantra*, 102–4.

29. André Padoux, *The Hindu Tantric World: An Overview* (Chicago: University of Chicago Press, 2017), 16.

30. See Urban, *Power of Tantra*, ch. 1.

31. Majo Garigliano, "Brahmans," 139.

32. One of the most important archeological sites in Assam is the so-called Madan Kāmdev temple complex (actually a Śiva temple), which dates to the tenth or eleventh century—around the time of King Dharmapāla. Among the more impressive images there is Vaikuṇṭha Vaiṣṇavī, a female figure with three faces—a human in the center, a lion on right, and a boar on left. This image is a rare female version of Vaikuṇṭha Viṣṇu, who is also depicted with three or four faces, including those of a human, lion, and boar. Vaikuṇṭha Viṣṇu was in turn the center of the Tantric Pāñcarātra Vaiṣṇava tradition that once flourished in Kashmir. One of the most famous images of Vaikuṇṭha Viṣṇu was said to have been brought from Kannauj to the Lakṣmaṇa temple of

Khajurāho (tenth century). See Kalpana Desai, *Iconography of Visnu* (Abhinav Publications, 2013), 37–47; Pratapaditya Pal, *Art and Architecture of Ancient Kashmir* (Bombay: Marg Publications, 1989), 85; Sanderson, "Śaivism and the Tantric Traditions," 701.

According to art historian Kimberly Masteller, who consulted with me on this image, it seems likely that the Vaikuṇṭha Vaiṣṇavī image in Assam is a kind of double appropriation of the Vaikuṇṭha Viṣṇu figures from Kashmir and Kannauj (personal communication, July 6, 2017). It is also worth noting that Vaiṣṇavī is one of the seven *mātṛkās* (divine mothers) and is listed as a primary *yoginī* in the *Kālikā Purāṇa.*

33. Interview with author, January 11, 2022. See Johansen Hurwitt, "Voracious Virgin," 428; S. C. Banerji, *A Companion to Tantra* (New Delhi: Abhinav Publications, 2007), 15.

34. Sarma, "Kamakhya Temples' Complex," 2–3; Majo Garigliano, "Brahmans," 65.

35. See Sarma, "Kamakhya Temples' Complex."

36. Johansen Hurwitt, "Voracious Virgin," and personal conversations, December 2021.

37. Johansen Hurwitt, "Voracious Virgin," 428–29. On Kālīkula and Śrīkula see Teun Goudriaan and Sanjukta Gupta, *Hindu Tantric and Śākta Literature* (Wiesbaden: Harrassowitz, 1981), 75–86.

38. Rajib Sarma, interviews with author, Guwahati, Assam, June 24, 2017 and July 3, 2020.

39. See Johansen Hurwitt, "Voracious Virgin," 428–29; Majo Garigliano, "Brahmans," 80; with some clarification from Rajib Sarma, interview with author, Guwahati, Assam, July 3, 2020.

40. Śarmā, "Tantra,"9.

41. See Arthur Avalon, introduction to *The Tantra of the Great Liberation (Mahānirvāna Tantra)* (New York: Dover, 1972), lxxiv–lxxv.

42. Majo Garigliano, "Brahmans," 88.

43. Heman Sarma, quoted in Majo Garigliano, "Brahmans," 88.

44. One initiate described a priest who began to introduce new practices into the tradition and eventually went mad and leapt out of a window. Others have allegedly been cursed by the goddess for their greedy and unscrupulous behavior (personal communication, July 14, 2022).

45. Majo Garigliano, "Brahmans," 101. Moreover, the Kulācāra lineage at Kāmākhyā is also not radically egalitarian. Although it claims to allow members of all classes, religions, and ethnicities, it retains a clear hierarchy, in part based on class. As one initiate explained to me, the lineage is a kind of series of concentric circles, with outsiders on the outermost ring, followed by initiates, initiates from Kāmākhyā, then *brāhmaṇ* initiates, and finally the guru's family. In sum, class definitely plays a role, despite the rhetoric of egalitarianism (personal correspondence, December 2021).

46. Brooks, *Secret of the Three Cities*, 70: "Tantrism . . . does not intend to be revolutionary in the sense of establishing a new structure of social egalitarianism. . . . It opens its doors only to a few who . . . seek to distinguish and empower themselves." See also Gupta, Goudriaan, and Hoens, *Hindu Tantrism*, 32; Hugh B. Urban, "The Conservative

Character of Tantra: Secrecy, Sacrifice, and This-Worldly Power in Bengali Śākta Tantra," *International Journal of Tantric Studies* 6, no. 2 (2002); Debendranāth Bhaṭṭācārya, *Asamat Śaktipūjā* (Guwahati: Bāṇī Prakāśa, 1977), 68–72.

47. On the question of women in Tantra, see Urban, *Power of Tantra*, 125–46; Loriliai Biernacki, *Renowned Goddess of Desire: Women, Sex, and Speech in Tantra* (New York: Oxford University Press, 2007); Agehananda Bharati, "Making Sense Out of Tantrism and Tantrics," *Loka: A Journal from the Naropa Institute* 2 (1976): 53; Miranda Shaw, *Passionate Enlightenment: Women in Tantric Buddhism* (Princeton, NJ: Princeton University Press, 1994), 12–13; Madhu Khanna, "The Goddess-Woman Equation in the Tantras," in *Gendering the Spirit: Women, Religion, and the Post-Colonial Response*, ed. Durre S. Ahmed (New York: Zed Books, 2002), 35–69.

48. J. A. Schoterman, ed., *Yoni Tantra* (Delhi: Manohar, 1980), 7.17b and 1.6. See also Biernacki, *Renowned Goddess*; Sanjukta Gupta, *Cosmic Play of Power: Goddess, Tantra, and Women* (Delhi: Motilal Banarsidass, 2013), 395: "On the strength of their potentiality to be mothers, women are considered closer to *śakti* than men. Many Śākta religious texts stipulate kind and respectful treatment of women. . . . Although Tantrics see the entire phenomenal world as mere manifestations of *śakti*, they worship virgins and married women both as symbols of the Goddess and as beings in which *śakti* is manifest with the least concealment. Such gestures instill a sense of self-respect and confidence in those and other women of the community."

49. Śāstrī, ed., *Kāmākhyā Tantra*, 3.42–43. On this point, see Biernacki, *Renowned Goddess*; Urban, *Power of Tantra*, ch. 4.

50. See Biernacki, *Renowned Goddess*; Avalon, introduction to *Tantra of the Great Liberation*, lxxviii.

51. Sarma, "Kamakhya Temples' Complex," 12. See also the interviews with Assamese women in Tracy Wares' film *Shakti*; for example: "I am Devi, I am Shiva, I am everything. I am so powerful like Devi, mother goddess. I have to do puja for myself. I pray to myself, I have to love myself. She exists inside, not outside . . . Because I am looking at myself as a goddess" (*Shakti: The Performance of Gender at Kamakhya Assam*, directed by Tracy Wares [2001; Berkeley: Department of Anthropology, University of California, Berkeley]).

52. Majo Garigliano, "Brahmans," 90. "Hemen Sarma stressed the role of the wife of the initiate during the *dīkṣā*. The wife has a supervisory role over her husband and administers alcohol to him during. Apart from that, however, Hemen Sarma's words suggest that the woman plays a fundamental role as the unique source of *śakti*" (Majo Garigliano, "Brahmans," 101).

53. Women as gurus are mentioned in several texts. See Śītalā Prasāda Upādhyāya, ed., *Tripurārṇava Tantra* (Varanasi: Sampurnanand Sanskrit University, 1992), 1.196–97: "There are no rules for women; all are said to be gurus. Merely by receiving an authoritative mantra, she is the supreme guru. She can teach by means of the authoritative mantra and obtain books. A man does not have such authority, for woman is the supreme deity." See also Brahmānandagiri, *Śāktānandataraṅgiṇī* (Varanasi: Sampurnanand Sanskrit University, 1987), 2.31–32.

54. See Johansen Hurwitt, "Voracious Virgin," 437: "The ideal expressed to me by both senior and junior practitioners is that women may be full and active participants in most rituals performed by the kula. In practice, however, there are quite a few

restrictions on women's participation. Without a doubt, the primary practitioners of the Kāmākhyā kula are men. Men are . . . the primary decision-makers on the place, time, and content of rituals."

55. Johansen Hurwitt, "Voracious Virgin," 433–37.

56. Johansen Hurwitt, "Voracious Virgin," 439; see Majo Garigliano, "Brahmans," 93.

57. In her study of late Tantric texts from northeast India, Biernacki argues that these offer positive and often empowering roles for women (*Renowned Goddess*). Frédérique Apffel-Marglin and Julia A. Jean make a similar argument regarding female sexuality in Ambuvācī Melā ("Weaving the Body and the Cosmos: Two Menstrual Festivals in Northeastern India," *Worldviews* 24, no. 3 [2020]: 245–84). For positive views of women in Buddhist Tantra, see Shaw, *Passionate Enlightenment*.

58. Sravana Borkataky-Varma argues that the tradition is generally more limiting to women's agency than empowering: "While there are small groups of . . . women Tantric adepts who have successfully navigated and challenged their social norms, the majority of women experience deep exploitation and receive utilitarian treatment" ("In the Tea Light of Tantra: An Ethnographic Study of *Kuṇḍalinī* Rising in Women's Bodies" [PhD diss., Rice University, 2016], iv). For other critical views of women in Tantra, see Gupta, Goudriaan, and Hoens, *Hindu Tantrism*, 34; White, *Kiss*, 270–71.

59. I addressed the question of feminism and Tantra at length in *Power of Tantra*, ch. 5. I argue that the tradition is not exactly "feminist" in any modern sense of the term, but it does open at least some space for women to maneuver in new ways and in some cases assume roles of leadership and status that are otherwise unavailable.

60. David Gordon White argues that, in the earliest texts, *mudrā* "signifies the vulva of the consort and is as such a code word for the more conventional terms *bhaga* and *yoni*" (*Kiss*, 81); in this sense, he argues that it is similar to the Tantric Buddhist use of the term *karmamudrā* to refer to a physical "sealing partner" in sexual rituals. Other scholars such as Shaman Hatley reject White's argument as a misreading of the texts (personal correspondence, January 20, 2022). Major Tantric digests from Bengal such as the *Bṛhat Tantrasāra* clearly identify *mudrā* as edible substances such as spelt (*kṛṣara*) and roasted or fried grains (*bhraṣṭa-dhānya*). See Kṛṣṇānanda Āgamavāgīśa, *Bṛhat-Tantrasāra*, ed. Śrīrasikamohana Caṭṭopādhyāya (Calcutta: Navabhārata Publishers, 1996), 698. Likewise, texts from Assam such as the *Yoginī Tantra* clearly identify *mudrā* as roasted or fried grains that are "to be chewed" (*bharja-dhānyādikaṃ yad yac carvaṇīyaṃ pracakṣate / Sā mudrā kahitā*). See B. N. Shastri, ed., *Yoginī Tantra* (Delhi: Bhāratīya Vidyā Prakāśana, 1982), 1.6.36. As Rajib Sarma explained to me, *mudrā* typically includes legumes such as chickpeas and pigeon peas, which can be eaten uncooked (interview with author, Guwahati, Assam, June 22, 2017).

61. Padoux, *Hindu Tantric World*, 119. The list of three *makāras* appears in texts such as Abhinavagupta's *Tantrāloka*, and the list of five *tattvas* or *makāras* appears in many later works such as the *Kulārṇava Tantra, Gupta-sādhana Tantra, Kāmākhyā Tantra, Yoni Tantra*, and others. See Brunner-Lachaux, Oberhammer, and Padoux, eds., *Tāntrikābhidhānakośa*, 3:208.

62. Śarmā, "Tantra," 6.

63. Majo Garigliano, "Brahmans," 90.

64. Rajib Sarma stated that whiskey is the most common form of alcohol used. He mentioned that there is a tribal form of alcohol that is sometimes used but said it is "too strong." He noted that he and others had experimented with different kinds of whiskey and found that the variety didn't make much difference (interview with author, Guwahati, Assam, June 22, 2022).

65. Sarma, interview with author, June 22, 2017.

66. Saran, interview with author, March 18, 2022. See Kulasundari Devi, "Dancing with Devotion towards Liberation: Intersections and Theological Exploration of Society, Orthodoxy and the Shakta Tantric Ideal," in *Souvenir Viswa Shanti Devi Yajña*, ed. Sri Jadu Nath Sarma, Rajib Sarma, and Sri Naba Kanta Sarma (Guwahati: Viswa Shanti Devi Yajña Committee, 2014), 97.

67. Śarmā, "Tantra," 6. Evidence of the danger of drinking in the name of Tantra is not difficult to find. One afternoon I was walking down the footpath on the east side Kāmākhyā Hill when I stopped to look at the images outside the Śmaśān Kālī temple. I asked the men sitting outside if I could take a photo, and, when they said no, a disheveled, long-haired man came forward and insisted that I go ahead and take a photo. "Take it!" he said, and then blessed my camera: "Everything is pure, the image is pure, the camera is pure, of course you can take a photo!" Calling himself Betal Nath Baba, he was clearly intoxicated. When I asked him about his *puja* and *sādhanā*, he declared that his practice was *tāntrik* and pulled a bottle of whiskey from his pocket to prove the point: "This is *tāntrik sādhanā*!" (July 10, 2017).

As Rajib Sarma complained, many of the so-called Tantric gatherings that one finds today in Bengal, Assam, and other areas are not much about real *sādhanā* but are mostly just "drinking parties" (personal correspondence, June 22, 2017).

68. Rajib Sarma, interview with author, Guwahati, Assam, July 10, 2017. Other Tantric texts from the northeast similarly confirm that the meat can be of many kinds. According to the *Bṛhat Tantrasāra*, meat can be of eight varieties, including cow, sheep, horse, buffalo, lizard, goat, camel, and deer (Āgamavāgīśa, *Bṛhat-Tantrasāra*, 698).

69. Shastri, ed., *Yoginī Tantra*, 1.6.69–73.

70. Śarmā, "Tantra," 7. We should note that this part of Śarmā's text is very close to Avalon's account of the five Ms in his introduction to the *Tantra of the Great Liberation*: "'Wine' is that intoxicating knowledge acquired by yoga of the Parabrahman, which renders the worshippers senseless as regards the external world. Meat (*māngsa*) is not any fleshly thing, but the act whereby the *sādhaka* consigns all his acts to Me (*mām*). *Matsya* (fish) is that *sāttvika* knowledge by which through the sense of 'mineness' the worshipper sympathizes with the pleasure and pain of all beings. *Mudrā* is the act of relinquishing all association with evil which results in bondage and *maithuna* is the union of the Shakti Kundalinī with Shiva in the body of the worshipper" (cxix).

71. See White, *Kiss*, 1–26; Christian Wedemeyer, *Making Sense of Tantric Buddhism: History, Semiology, and Transgression in the Indian Traditions* (New York: Columbia University Press, 2012).

72. Hatley outlines at least seven different forms of sexual practice in Tantric texts: love magic; love magic for nonhuman beings; ritualized orgasmic coitus wherein sexual fluids are given ritual function and meaning; highly regulated coitus that may form an element of the secret assembly; initiation; highly ritualized ecstatic gnosis;

sexual yoga as a sublimation of bliss; and yogic techniques involving sex without seminal loss. He suggests that sexual union while refraining from ejaculation—the "sword's edge observance" (*asidhārāvrata*)—may be one of the oldest sexual techniques (*Brahmayāmalatantra*, 1:199–208). See Urban, *Power of Tantra*, ch. 3.

73. Sukanya Sarbadhikary, *Place of Devotion: Siting and Experiencing Divinity in Bengal Vaishnavism* (Berkeley: University of California Press, 2015), 114.

74. Sarbadhikary, *Place of Devotion*, 114.

75. See Carol Salomon, "Bāul Songs," in *Religions of India in Practice*, ed. Donald S. Lopez (Princeton, NJ: Princeton University Press, 1995), 195–96.

76. Saran, *Yoga, Bhoga*, 14; personal conversations, June 22, 2022, and June 24, 2022. See also Lidke, *Goddess*, 51–54.

77. Saran, *Yoga, Bhoga*, 136.

78. Borkataky-Varma, "In the Tea Light of Tantra," 245.

79. Interviews with author, Kāmākhyā, January 2022; interview with author, Mayong, June 27, 2017.

80. Śarmā, "Tantra," 7.

81. Shastri, ed., *Yoginī Tantra*, 1.6.69–73. See also Bhaṭṭācārya, *Asamat Śaktipūjā*, 83–86.

82. Rajib Sarma, interview with author, Guwahati, Assam, January 11, 2022.

83. Quoted in Majo Garigliano, "Brahmans," 90.

84. Saran, email communication, March 8, 2020. In June 2022, Prem, Rajib, and I had a lengthy conversation about the different lineages and the status of initiation from various gurus in Assam. They disagree on this point.

85. See Urban, *Power of Tantra*; Dyczkowski, *Canon*, 59.

86. Majo Garigliano, "Brahmans," 92–93.

87. Majo Garigliano, "Brahmans," 92. "Alcohol is the main thing," explained Bipul Kumār De, a *tāntrik* from Bengal who was residing on the western side of Kāmākhyā (interview with author, Kāmākhyā Temple, June 21, 2017).

88. On this point, see Urban, *Tantra*, 44–72, 134–64; Urban, *Power of Tantra*, 147–64. As Muñoz argues, by the sixteenth century "there was a 'tantric reform' taking place in Bengal . . . some religious leaders were trying to mould a sterilized form of tantra easier to admit by Brahmins and maybe even by Muslims" ("Matsyendra's 'Golden Legend,'" 114).

89. See Hugh B. Urban, "Śaṅkaradeva and Mādhavadeva," in *Brill's Encyclopedia of Hinduism*, vol. 4, ed. Knut Jacobson (Leiden: Brill, 2012), 397–404.

90. Śrīmanta Śaṅkaradeva, *Kīrtana Ghoṣā* (Nagaon, India: Śrīmanta Śaṅkaradeva Saṅgha, 2010), 23.

91. See Urban, *Power of Tantra*, 147–54; Urban, "Śaṅkaradeva and Mādhavadeva," 4.

92. Mishra, *Kamakhya*, 73n. See Muñoz, "Matsyendra's 'Golden Legend,'" 114.

93. Sir Monier Monier-Williams, *Hinduism* (London: Society for Promoting Christian Knowledge, 1894), 122–23; Barnett, quoted in John Woodroffe, *Principles of Tantra: The Tantratattva of Śrīyukta Śiva Candra Vidyārṇava Bhaṭṭācārya Mahodaya* (Madras: Ganesh and Co., 1960), 3–5. See Urban, *Tantra*, ch. 1.

94. Raja Rammohun Roy, "A Defense of Hindoo Theism," in *The English Works of Raja Rammohun Roy*, vol. 1, ed. Jogendra Chunder Ghose (New Delhi: Cosmo Publications, 1982), 89–100.

95. Vivekānanda, *The Complete Works of Swami Vivekananda* (Calcutta: Advaita Ashram, 1984), 7:174.

96. Vivekānanda, *The Complete Works of Swami Vivekananda* (Calcutta: Advaita Ashram, 1984), 3:340.

97. See Hugh B. Urban, "The Strategic Uses of an Esoteric Text: The *Mahānirvāṇa Tantra*," *South Asia* 18, no. 1 (1995): 55–81; Avalon, trans., *Tantra of the Great Liberation*.

98. John Duncan Martin Derrett, "A Juridical Fabrication of Early British India: *The Mahānirvāṇa Tantra*," in John Duncan Martin Derrett, *Essays in Classical and Modern Indian Law* (Leiden: Brill, 1977), 197–242.

99. John Woodroffe, *Shakti and Shākta* (New York: Dover, 1978), 594.

100. *Mahānirvāṇa Tantra*, 7.24–27, in Avalon, trans., *Tantra of the Great Liberation*.

101. The *Kāmākhyā Tantra* recommends others' wives, prostitutes, and menstruating women as the best partners in *maithuna*: "Having approached the *yoni* of another man's wife [*parastrīyoni*], the wise man should especially make offerings. The *yoni* of a prostitute [*veśyāyoni*] is the best. He should perform worship there, O goddess. . . . With a woman in her menstrual cycle [*ṛtuyuktalatā*], he will attain manifold pleasures" (Śāstrī, ed., 3.59–60).

102. *Mahānirvāṇa Tantra*, 6.14, in Avalon, trans., *Tantra of the Great Liberation*. See Avalon, introduction to *Tantra of the Great Liberation*, cxvii-cxviii: "As regards *maithuna*, this Tantra states that men in this Kali age are by their nature weak and disturbed by lust. . . . It accordingly ordains that when the *Kaliyuga* is in full sway, the fifth *tattva* shall only be accomplished with . . . the worshiper's own wife . . . it prescribes in lieu of *maithuna* meditation by the worshiper upon the lotus feet of the Devi."

103. Woodroffe, *Shakti and Shākta*, 594; Avalon, introduction to *Tantra of the Great Liberation*, xi–xii: "This Tantra is . . . one which is well known and esteemed, though perhaps more highly so amongst that portion of the Indian public which favours 'reformed' Hinduism than amongst some Tāntrikas, to whom . . . certain of its provisions appear to display unnecessary timidity." See also Urban, *Tantra*, 64–67.

104. Rachel McDermott, *Singing to the Goddess: Poems to Kālī and Umā from Bengal* (New York: Oxford University Press, 2001), 20.

105. See Urban, *Economics of Ecstasy*, 161–206.

106. Woodroffe, *Shakti and Shākta*, 619.

107. Reza Aslan generated intense outrage when he filmed a highly exoticized episode about Aghorīs for his CNN series on religion. See Michael Safi, "Reza Aslan Outrages Hindus by Eating Human Brains in CNN Documentary," *Guardian*, March 10, 2017, https://www.theguardian.com/world/2017/mar/10/reza-aslan-criticised-for-documentary-on-cannibalistic-hindus/.

108. Jonathan Parry, *Death in Banaras* (Cambridge: Cambridge University Press, 1995), 258–59. See also Jonathan Parry, foreword to Barrett, *Aghor Medicine*, xii–xiii: "In recent decades . . . the association between the Aghori ascetic and these extreme practices . . . has been deliberately downplayed. The sect has undergone significant

reform, and today the dominant strand in its ideology focuses on social services to the truly disadvantaged over the quest for individual salvation."

109. See Goet, *Path of Śakti*, and Goet, "Aghora Tantra."

110. Although these transgender individuals are widely known as *hijṛās* (eunuchs) today, the communities in north India prefer to be called *kinnaras*, referring to the celestial *kinnaras* of Hindu and Buddhist mythology who are known for their song and dance.

111. Goet, "Aghora Tantra."

112. See Shastri, ed., *Kālikā Purāṇa*, 38.130; Urban, *Power of Tantra*, 45.

113. See Schoterman, ed., *Yoni Tantra*, 2.10–25; Urban, *Power of Tantra*, 110.

114. *Śava sādhanā* is an important part of many Tantric traditions, particularly in Bengal and other parts of northeast India. The practice involves meditation while seated upon a fresh human corpse, and it can be performed in the pursuit of both otherworldly and this-worldly desires—both to achieve ultimate spiritual liberation (beyond duality and death) and to acquire magical powers (including control over the ghost of the deceased). For descriptions of the practice, see Āgamavāgīśa, *Bṛhat-Tantrasāra*, 438–44; June McDaniel, *Offering Flowers, Feeding Skulls: Popular Goddess Worship in West Bengal* (New York: Oxford University Press, 2004), 124–38; S. C. Banerji, *A Companion to Tantra* (New Delhi: Abhinav Publications, 2007), 28–30.

115. Goet, "Aghora Tantra."

116. Goet, "Aghora Tantra."

117. Georges Bataille, *The Accursed Share* (New York: Zone Books, 1999), 2:183–84; see Georges Bataille, *Erotism: Death and Sensuality* (San Francisco, CA: City Lights, 1986), 39; Urban, *Power of Tantra*, 120.

118. Agehananda Bharati, *The Ochre Robe: An Autobiography* (New York: Ross-Erikson, 1980), 99.

119. See Urban, *Tantra* and Hugh B. Urban, *Zorba the Buddha: Sexuality, Spirituality, and Capitalism in the Global Osho Movement* (Berkeley: University of California Press, 2016).

120. Johansen Hurwitt, "Inconvenience of History."

121. Michel Foucault, *History of Sexuality, Volume 1: An Introduction* (New York: Vintage, 1978), 17–49. See Urban, *Tantra*, 2.

CHAPTER TWO

1. Phaṇīdhar Nāth, interview with author, Mayong, June 27, 2017.

2. Vaibhavi Tiwari, "Real-Time Hogwarts of India—Mayong Village!" *Indian Express*, January 7, 2020, https://theindianness.com/real-time-hogwarts-of-india-mayong-village/.

3. See Rameś Candra Nāth, "Māyaṅgar Bej āru Bejāli: Ji Dekhilo Ji śunilo," in *Kālśilā: Smṛtigrantha*, ed. Utpal Nāth (Jagirod, India: Abhinab Offset Printers, 2010), 33; Utpal Nāth, "Māyaṅgar Jāduvidyār Sādhanā: Vijñān, Viśvās āru Andhaviśvās," in *Kālśilā: Smṛtigrantha*, ed. Nāth, 120–26; Sean Dowdy, "*Goroka*: Cosmography and the Shared Account in Assam" (PhD diss., University of Chicago, 2017). For popular

accounts, see: "Mayong—the Land of Black Magic," Pobitora Wildlife Sanctuary, November 13, 2016, https://pobitorawildlifesanctuary.wordpress.com/2016/11/13/mayong-the-land-of-black-magic/; Abir Gupta, "India's Black Magic Capital: The Little Known Story of the Mayong Village in Assam," *Storypick*, July 28, 2016, http://www.storypick.com/mayong-black-magic/; Daulat Rahman, "New Light on Land of Black Magic," *Telegraph*, May 14, 2009, https://www.telegraphindia.com/north-east/new-light-on-land-of-black-magic-huge-swords-unearthed-at-mayong-in-assam-point-to-human-sacrifice/cid/629252.

4. See Ülo Valk, "Conceiving the Supernatural through Variation in Experience Stories: Assistant Spirits and Were-Tigers in the Belief Narratives of Assam," *Shaman* 23, nos. 1–2 (2015): 141–64; Dowdy, "*Goroka*"; Nāth, "Māyaṅgar Jāduvidyār Sādhanā."

5. The Mayong Museum has a collection of about fifty manuscripts on *mantra* and magic, and the secretary of the museum, Dr. Utpal Nāth, stated that there are at least four hundred more contained in private homes around the area (interview with author, Mayong, Assam, June 26, 2017).

6. See Sean Dowdy, "Reflections on a Shared Name: Taboo and Destiny in Mayong (Assam)," *SAMAJ: South Asia Multidisciplinary Academic Journal* 12 (2015), https://journals.openedition.org/samaj/4027; Valk, "Conceiving the Supernatural."

7. Naresh Mitra, "Taboo Tourism to Cast Spell on Outside World," *Times of India*, August 21, 2010, http://timesofindia.indiatimes.com/india/Taboo-tourism-to-cast-spell-on-world-outside/articleshow/6386819.cms. As Kaustuv Saikia notes, "the idea of Mayong as a 'dangerous place' is accepted by the community as part of the grand narrative of Assam" ("Demystifying Black Magic: Mayong Village Museum and Research Centre," *Critical Collective*, 2020, https://criticalcollective.in/Museums.aspx?tid=28).

8. Valk, "Conceiving the Supernatural," 142.

9. Phaṇīdhar Nāth, interview with author, Mayong, June 27, 2017. For videos of the copper-plate back-pain ritual, see *Mayong: Myth/Reality*, directed by Utpal Borpujari (2013; Guwahati: Darpan Cine Production).

10. Ariel Glucklich, *The End of Magic* (New York: Oxford University Press, 1997), 148. See also Ülo Valk and Neelakshi Goswami, "Generic Resources and Social Boundaries of Magic in Assam: Fieldwork Notes from Assam," *Journal of Folkloristics* 1 (2013): 5–13, at 7: "Tantra-mantra, however, is different from this kind of *jadu*. It can be called the true magic, and both practitioners and their patients seem to share equal belief in its power."

11. See Hugh B. Urban, *Tantra: Sex, Secrecy, Politics and Power in the Study of Religion* (Berkeley: University of California Press, 2003), conclusion.

12. K. N. Sarma, ed., *Kāmaratna Tantra* (Guwahati: Lawyer's Book Stall, 1998). On the six acts of magic, see Aaron Michael Ullrey, "Grim Grimoires: Pragmatic Ritual in Magic Tantras" (PhD diss., University of California, Santa Barbara, 2016).

13. See Hugh B. Urban, *Power of Tantra: Religion, Sexuality, and the Politics of South Asian Studies* (London: I. B. Tauris and Palgrave MacMillan, 2010), ch. 6.

14. Partners for Law Development, *Witch Hunting in Assam: Individual, Structural, and Legal Dimensions* (Guwahati: North East Network, 2015). See also Madhu Mehra and Anuja Agrawal, "'Witch-Hunting in India': Do We Need Special Laws?," *Economic and Political Weekly*, March 26, 2016: 51–57; Lekha Borah and Madhushree Das,

"Witch-Hunting in Assam: Myth or Reality?," *Space and Culture India* 7, no. 3 (2019): 99–114.

15. See Nāth, "Māyaṅgar Jāduvidyār Sādhanā," 122. See also Valk and Goswami, "Generic Resources and Social Boundaries," 5–13; Valk, "Conceiving the Supernatural," 141–64.

16. On "auto-Orientalism" and "self-Orientalism," see Harumi Befu, *Hegemony of Homogeneity* (Melbourne: Transpacific Press, 2001); Al Shilabi Ahmed, *Postcolonial Libyan Novel: Self-Orientalism and Occidentalism* (Saarland, Germany: Lambert Academic, 2015). On Orientalist discourse on India and its association with magic, see Chris Goto-Jones, *Conjuring Asia: Magic, Orientalism and the Making of the Modern World* (Cambridge: Cambridge University Press, 2016); Richard King, *Orientalism and Religion: Postcolonial Theory, India, and the Mystic East* (New York: Routledge, 1999); Ronald Inden, *Imagining India* (London: Blackwell, 1990).

17. The few studies of Tantric magic include Teun Goudriaan, *Māyā, Divine and Human: A Study in Magic and Its Religious Foundations in Sanskrit Texts* (New Delhi: Motilal Banarsidass, 1978); Gudrun Bühnemann, "The Six Rites of Magic," in *Tantra in Practice*, ed. David Gordon White (Princeton, NJ: Princeton University Press, 2000), 447–62; Glucklich, *End of Magic*; André Padoux, *The Hindu Tantric World: An Overview* (Chicago: University of Chicago Press, 2017), 124–25; Ullrey, "Grim Grimoires"; Andrea Acri and Paolo E. Rosati, eds., *Tantra, Magic and Vernacular Religions: Texts, Practices, and Practitioners from the Margins* (London: Routledge, 2022).

18. Padoux, *Hindu Tantric World*, 124.

19. Padoux, *Hindu Tantric World*, 124.

20. Bühnemann, "Six Rites of Magic," 447–48. See also Goudriaan, *Māyā*, 255–56. Ullrey examines another important group of magical texts in "Grim Grimoires."

21. Ullrey, "Grim Grimoires," 1.

22. Lakṣmaṇadeśikendra, *Śāradātilakatantram* (Delhi: Caukhambā Saṃskṛta Pratiṣṭhāna, 2001), 22.121–22: "*athā abhidhāsye tantre asmin samyak ṣaṭkarmalakṣaṇam |sarvatantrānusāreṇa prayogaphalasiddhidam śāntivaśyastambhanāni vidveṣoccāṭane tataḥ|māraṇāntāni śaṃsanti ṣaṭkarmāṇi manīṣiṇaḥ.*"

23. For example, this verse is quoted exactly in Tāntrikācārya Śrībhairava Śāstrī, *Siddha Śābarar Tantra-Mantra* (Kolkata: Sajal Publishers, n.d.), 43, and in many other popular texts.

24. Goudriaan, *Māyā*, 259.

25. Bühnemann, "Six Rites of Magic," 448.

26. Sarma, ed., *Kāmaratna Tantra*, i-iii. See Nāga Bhaṭṭa, *Kāmaratna Tantra: Vā Vaśīkaraṇa Tantra* (Calcutta: Calcutta Town Library, 1952); Nāga Bhaṭṭa, *Indrajālavidyāsaṃgraha* (Calcutta: J. Vidyasagar's Sons, 1915).

27. *Kāmaratna Tantra*, 3.

28. *Kāmaratna Tantra*, 11.

29. *Kāmaratna Tantra*, 37, 48, 76–78.

30. Faivre, *Access to Western Esotericism* (Albany, NY: SUNY Press, 1994), 10.

31. *Kāmaratna Tantra*, 57.

32. *Kāmaratna Tantra*, 68, 104.

33. *Kāmaratna Tantra*, 7.

34. *Kāmaratna Tantra*, 52–64.

35. *Mohinī*. manuscript, acc. no. MMAY/LOK/14, Mayong Central Museum, Mayong, India; *Mantra Puthi*, manuscript, acc. no. MMAY/LOK/38, Mayong Central Museum, Mayong, India; *Mantra*, manuscript, acc. no. MMAY/LOK/09, Mayong Central Museum, Mayong, India.

36. Utpal Nāth, interview with author, Mayong, June 27, 2017. See also Utpal Nāth, ed., *Māyār Rājya Māyaṅgar Kāhinī* (Mayong, India: Studio Nath Brothers, 2013); Nāth, "Māyaṅgar Jāduvidyār Sādhanā," 120.

37. I showed some of these newer texts to Aaron Ullrey, and he is of the opinion that they are mostly in continuity with older Sanskrit texts on magic, though with some added elements from modern life and folk magic (personal communication, September 30, 2021).

38. See Tāntrika Śrīkāmadeva Pujāri, *Sarva Manokāmana Siddhi Tantramantra* (Guwahati: Āmār Prakāśa, 2003); Kālabhairava, *Camatkārī Yantre Sarva Manoskāmanā Siddhi* (Kolkātā: Sajal Pustakālay, n.d.); Tantrikācārya Svāmī Virajānanda Gṛhī Brahmacārī, *Mantra Śaktite Maner Icchā Pūraṇ* (Kolkātā: Mantraśakti Prakāśanī, n.d.); Śrītrailokyanātha Śāstrī, *Tantra Mantre Maner Icchā Pūraṇ* (Kolkātā: Rājendra Library, n.d.); Tāntrikācārya Śrībrahmānanda, *Sarvva Manaskāmanā Siddha Pustak* (Calcutta: Rajendra Library, n.d.)

39. Śrībrahmānanda, *Sarvva Manaskāmanā Siddha Pustak*. The text defines Tantra as follows: "In Sanskrit it is defined as: '*tan-tra*.' The word '*tan*' is '*tanu*,' that is, the body [*deha*] or physical form [*śarīra*]. And '*tra*' is '*trāṇa*' or protection [*raksa*]. *Tan-tra* is the union of these two words, that is, *tan* and *tra*. The meaning in Bangla would be: 'What protects the body, that is, what preserves the physical self, is called 'Tantra'" (1).

40. Tāntrikācārya Śrībhairava Śāstrī, *Kāmarūpī Tantrasāra* (Kolkātā: Rājendra Library, n.d.); Śrīmanta Cakravartī, *Ādi o Āsal Kāmāksyā Tantrasāra* (Kolkātā: Sacendra Prakāśana, n.d.); Ratneśvara Tantrajyotisaśastri, *Kāmākṣyā Tantrasāra* (Kolkātā: Orient Library, n.d.); Śrī Kṣudirām, *Kāmākṣa Tantra Sāra Ādi o Prācin* (Kolkātā: Sajal Pustakālay, 2008). This close association of magic with Kāmākhyā in popular literature has spread far beyond the boundaries of northeast India. Publishers from Delhi and other areas have also promoted the mystery and power surrounding Kāmarūpa. One of the most slickly produced of these is the Hindi text *Kāmarūpa Kāmākhyā kā Tāntrik Rahasya*, by Tāntrik Bahal (Delhi: Rājā Pocket Books, 2017). In contrast to the cheaply printed Bangla and Assamese texts, Bahal's features a glossy cover and high-quality paper. Yet like its cheaper counterparts, the text advertises itself as "the ultimate, secret discussion of the Tantric mysteries of Kāmākhyā practice for the complete fulfillment of one's heart's desires."

41. Benudhar Rajkhowa, *Assamese Popular Superstitions and Assamese Demonology* (Guwahati: Gauhati University Press, 1973). On the impact of Rajkhowa's book, see Dowdy, "*Goroka*," 177.

42. Rajkhowa, *Assamese Popular Superstitions*, 130.

43. Partners for Law Development, *Witch Hunting in Assam*, 6. See also Mehra and Agrawal, "'Witch-Hunting in India'"; Borah and Das, "Witch-Hunting in Assam."

44. Rokibuz Zaman, "Getting to the Roots of Decades-Old Problem of Witch-Hunting in Assam," *Times of India*, October 18, 2020, https://timesofindia.indiatimes.com/city/guwahati/getting-to-the-roots-of-decades-old-problem-of-witch-hunting-in-assam/articleshow/78731380.cms.

45. N.O., "Witchcraft in Assam: Toil and Trouble," *Economist*, April 2, 2012, https://www.economist.com/banyan/2012/04/02/toil-and-trouble. See Partners for Law Development, *Witch Hunting in Assam*, 14.

46. Anjali Daimari, interview with author, Guwahati, Assam, January 10, 2022. See Daimari, "Witch-Hunting and Resistance to the Formation of Women's Community," in *Communities of Women in Assam: Being, Doing and Thinking Together*, ed. Nandana Dutta (London: Routledge, 2015), 41–66, at 52–53: "It is a common belief . . . that a witch's charm can only be countered by the ojha or medicine man. Ojhas practice the art of healing. They are said to possess special knowledge about folk medicine. . . . He/she is supposed to possess the power to counter the activities of the witches. The ojhas too collect herbs, roots, barks of trees and flowers to prepare their medicines . . . they are believed to possess secret magical powers. . . . The ojhas are believed to have the power to identify witches and destroy their evil powers. So while the daina is considered evil the ojha is considered a good spirit."

47. Partners for Law Development, *Witch Hunting in Assam*, 6. See also Simashree Daimari, "Beliefs in Witchcraft among the Tribes of Goalpara District of Assam," PhD diss., Gauhati University, 2007.

48. Partners for Law Development, *Witch Hunting in Assam*, 27–29.

49. Partners for Law Development, *Witch Hunting in Assam*, 29.

50. Partners for Law Development, *Witch Hunting in Assam*, 28.

51. Partners for Law Development, *Witch Hunting in Assam*, 56.

52. Partners for Law Development, *Witch Hunting in Assam*, 57–58.

53. Hrishita Rajbangshi, *The After Effects of Witch-Hunting: Trauma, Struggle, and Revolution* (New Delhi: Zubaan, 2018), 21–22. See also Joya Chakraborty, "Witch Hunting in Assam: Strategising Alternative Media for Women Empowerment and Overcoming Superstition," *Journal of North East India Studies* 3, no. 2 (2013): 15–24.

54. Tora Agarwala, "Why the Road Has Been Long and Hard for Padma Shri Awardee Birubala Rabha, Assam's Crusader against Witch-Hunting," *Indian Express*, January 31, 2021, https://indianexpress.com/article/express-sunday-eye/why-the-road-has-been-long-and-hard-for-padma-shri-awardee-birubala-rabha-assams-crusader-against-witch-hunting-7167091/.

55. Kashish Khanna, "Meet Padma Shri Birubala Rabha, Assam's Anti-Witch Hunt Crusader," *Femina*, February 18, 2021, https://www.femina.in/trending/achievers/meet-padma-shri-birubala-rabha-assams-anti-witch-hunt-crusader-186796.html.

56. Agarwala, "Why the Road Has Been Long." See also Jehirul Islam and Afruz Ara Ahmed, "Witch Hunting in Assam: Practices, Causes, Legal Issues and Challenges," *Unitedworld Law Journal* 1, no. 2 (2017): 135–45.

57. Mission Birubala, "Mission Birubala," 2022, https://www.facebook.com/missionirubala/; Mission Birubala, "#mission_birubala," 2022, https://www.youtube.com/hashtag/mission_birubala.

58. IANS, "A Witch-Hunting Survivor Crusades to Save Assamese Women," *Hindustan Times*, June 14, 2016, https://www.hindustantimes.com/india-news/a-witch-hunting-survivor-crusades-to-save-assamese-women/story-IjRG4KvjMiT289X9kMaxuN.html. See also Chakraborty, "Witch Hunting in Assam."

59. PTI, "Two Lynched, Beheaded, Set on Fire over Witchcraft Suspicion, Assam," *Times of India*, October 2, 2020, https://timesofindia.indiatimes.com/city/guwahati/two-lynched-beheaded-set-on-fire-over-witchcraft-suspicion-in-assam/articleshow/78444001.cms.

60. See Borpujari, dir., *Mayong: Myth/Reality*; B.R.A.N.D. Production, *Mayong* (2016; Guwahati: B.R.A.N.D. Production). There are dozens of YouTube videos in Hindi and other languages, such as: Dakota of Earth, "Witchcraft, Tantra, and Black Magic in India," posted February 27, 2020, 10:43, https://www.youtube.com/watch?v=JfoER0061QA; "Mayong: Traditional Black Magic," Jadu Samrat Vikram, posted August 24, 2020, 36:31, https://www.youtube.com/watch?v=DGCq3SDGQfI; The Lallantop, "Capital of Black Magic," posted April 3, 2021, 32:52, https://www.youtube.com/watch?v=vbm5teqV_zA; Travrist, "Mayong Village: Famous for Black Magic," posted March 22, 2022, 15:35, https://www.youtube.com/watch?v=I3SJGJBoyuM; Honiya Dakpe, "Inside India's Black Magic Capital," posted March 14, 2021, 16:35, https://www.youtube.com/watch?v=GaYXuO9oLGc.

61. Nāth, "Māyaṅgar Bej āru Bejāli," 33. See also Avantika Bhuyan, "The Tantrik Town," *Open*, August 20, 2010, https://openthemagazine.com/art-culture/the-tantrik-town/.

62. See B.R.A.N.D. Production, *Mayong*. This narrative also currently appears on the Wikipedia page for Mayong, for example: Wikipedia, s.v. "Mayong (Assam)," last modified February 15, 2023, 17:19, https://en.wikipedia.org/wiki/Mayong_(Assam)#:~:text=Mayong%20(or%20Mayang%2C%20also%20known,attraction%20because%20of%20its%20history.

63. Sean Dowdy, personal communication, January 23, 2022: "I think Benudhar Rajkhowa's 1905 book *Assamese Demonology* was really the first instance of Mayong's fetishization as some sort of hotbed of magic/tantra/etc. . . . This, I think, made a huge difference in isolating Mayong in the public imagination as somewhat disconnected from (or exceptional to) the other tantra cults and circuits along the river."

64. Rajkhowa, *Assamese Popular Superstitions*, 145–46.

65. Dowdy, "Reflections on a Shared Name." See Dowdy, "*Goroka*," 83; Nāth, "Māyaṅgar Bej āru Bejāli," 33–38. As Valk comments, "Mayong has a special attraction for visitors who come with the intention of meeting the local healers, semi-professional experts in magic (*bejali, tantra-mantra*). People from several regions . . . visit these *bejs* for magical treatment, to find solution to problems in marriage and relationships, to deal with mental and psychological imbalances, to search for lost objects, get predictions about their personal futures and many other reasons. Some *bejs* specialize in certain fields of expertise, such as snakebites, love magic or exorcism" ("Conceiving the Supernatural," 142).

66. Dowdy, personal communication, January 23, 2022.

67. Photos from Mayong Museum taken by Utpal Nāth, January 17, 2022.

68. Valk, "Conceiving the Supernatural," 146. Nāth, "Māyaṅgar Jāduvidyār Sādhanā," 121–22.

69. On secrecy and religious authority, see Hugh B. Urban, *Secrecy: Silence, Power, and Religion* (Chicago: University of Chicago Press, 2021), introduction.

70. Nāth, *Māyār Rājya Māyaṅgar Kāhinī*, 51.

71. Valk, "Conceiving the Supernatural," 147.

72. Jatin Deka, quoted in Valk, "Conceiving the Supernatural," 147.

73. B.R.A.N.D. Production, *Mayong*. See Rahman, "New Light on Land of Black Magic."

74. Nāth, "Māyaṅgar Jāduvidyār Sādhanā," 122.

75. B.R.A.N.D. Production, *Mayong*. In the film, Khogen Nāth's mother, Muhoni Devī, also describes the uses of a particular preparation that is useful for a number of female sexual issues: "It is used to get pregnant. This medicine is also for girls who face stomach cramps during periods."

76. Gupta, "India's Black Magic Capital"; Rahman, "New Light on Land of Black Magic"; Namrata Dhingra, "India's Own Hogwarts—And It's Not Even Fictional!," *Make My Trip* (blog), September 24, 2019, https://www.makemytrip.com/tripideas/blog/mayong-village-in-assam.

77. Dakota of Earth, "Witchcraft, Tantra, and Black Magic"; Borpujari, dir., *Mayong: Myth/Reality*.

78. *Māyaṅgare Bej*, directed by Sikandar (2016; Guwahati).

79. Dowdy, personal communication, January 23, 2022. On "auto-Orientalism," see Befu, *Hegemony of Homogeneity*. As Chris Goto-Jones observes, Orientalist discourse of the late nineteenth and early twentieth centuries commonly portrayed India and other distant lands of the "Mystic East" as the "home of magic" and so also as "repositories of the West's magical fantasies" (*Conjuring Asia*, 4). Many Mayongians appear to have embraced that Orientalist narrative and happily declare the town to be the "home of magic" par excellence.

80. Photos from Mayong Museum taken by Dr. Utpal Nāth, viewed January 17, 2022.

81. Objects and photos from the Mayong Museum, viewed January 17, 2022; photos taken by Dr. Utpal Nāth.

82. Dowdy, personal communication, January 23, 2022.

83. Mitra, "Taboo Tourism." See Utpal Nath, *Mayong, the Land of Black Magic and Pobitora Wild Life Sanctuary* (Mayong, India: Mayong Village Museum and Research Centre, 2008); Utpal Nath, *Tourism in Mayong: Problems and Prospects* (Rajamayong, India: Mayong Anchalik College, 2019).

84. Mitra, "Taboo Tourism." As Nāth put it in another interview: "Mayong is famous for *tantra-mantra*. . . . Until now there has only been wildlife tourism, but apart from Pobitora . . . river tourism has potential at Mayong on the banks of the Brahmaputra, and it can also be ideal location for cultural tourism" (interview in Borpujari, dir., *Mayong: Myth/Reality*).

85. Nāth, *Mohanīya Māyaṅg* (Mayong, India: Office of the Range Officer, Pobitora Wildlife Sanctuary, 2011). See also Nāth, *Māyār Rājya Māyaṅgar Kāhinī*; Utpal Nāth, ed., *Tantram* (Rajamayong, India: Mayang Anchalik College, 2017).

86. Naresh Mitra, "Mayong Set to Cast Spell on Tourists," *Times of India*, November 26, 2011, http://timesofindia.indiatimes.com/articleshow/10874682.cms?utm_source=contentofinterest&utm_medium=text&utm_campaign=cppst.

87. Mitra, "Taboo Tourism."

88. Dowdy, personal communication, January 23, 2022.

89. See David A. Fennell, *Ecotourism* (New York: Routledge 2020); Robert Fletcher, *Romancing the Wild: Cultural Dimensions of Ecotourism* (Durham, NC: Duke University Press, 2014).

90. See Hugh B. Urban, "The Cradle of Tantra: Modern Transformations of a Tantric Centre in Northeast India, from Nationalist Symbol to Tourist Destination," *South Asia* 49, no. 2 (2019): 256–77; see also ch. 5 below.

91. Tilak Hāzarikā, interview with author, Mayong, January 18, 2022.

92. Tilak Hāzarikā, interview in Dowdy, "*Goroka*," 192. He made similar comments when I interviewed him in Mayong, January 18, 2022.

93. Tilak Hāzarikā, interview in Bhuyan, "Tantrik Town." Elsewhere, too, Hāzarikā asserts: "There is a scientific aspect to this . . . to call it wild medicine (*jungli oxud*), bejali, magic or whatever (*jadu beleg*) is incorrect. It is universal science and religion only (*Eitu sorisorito bigyan aru dhormo okol*)" (interview in Dowdy, "*Goroka*," 182).

94. Tilak Hāzarikā, interviews with author, Mayong, January 18, 2022, and June 26, 2017.

95. Hāzarikā, interview in Bhuyan, "Tantrik Town" and interview with author, Mayong, January 18, 2022.

96. See Kenneth Zysk, *Religious Medicine: History and Evolution of Indian Medicine* (New York: Routledge, 1993), x–xii.

97. Phaṇīdhar Nāth, interview in Bhuyan, "Tantrik Town."

98. Phaṇīdhar Nāth, interviews with author, Mayong, January 18, 2022, and June 26, 2017.

99. Nāth, interview with author, Mayong, January 18, 2022.

100. Tilak Hāzarikā, Phaṇīdhar Nāth, and Prabīn Śaikīyā, interviews with author, Mayong, January 2022. See also Dowdy, "*Goroka*," 392–93.

101. Prabīn Saikīyā, interviews with author, Mayong, January 2022.

102. The Mayong Museum has several photos of Prabīn engaged in these acts.

103. See Nāth, "Māyaṅgar Jāduvidyār Sādhanā," 120–26.

104. Valk, "Conceiving the Supernatural," 154.

105. Valk, "Conceiving the Supernatural," 156.

106. Interview with author, Mayong, June 28, 2017.

107. Interview with author, Mayong, June 27, 2017.

108. Interview with author, Mayong, June 27, 2017.

109. Interview with author, Mayong, June 26, 2017.

110. Interview with author, Mayong, June 27, 2017.

111. Victor Turner, *Dramas, Fields, and Metaphors: Symbolic Action in Human Society* (Ithaca, NY: Cornell University Press, 1975), 39–43.

112. Karen McCarthy Brown, *Mama Lola: A Vodou Priestess in Brooklyn* (Berkeley: University of California Press, 2011), 5.

113. I use the term "nodes" in the sense used by Arjun Appadurai, *Modernity at Large: Cultural Dimensions of Globalization* (Minneapolis: University of Minnesota Press, 1996), 22; see also Michel Foucault, *The History of Sexuality, Volume I: An Introduction* (New York: Vintage, 1978), 103; Hugh B. Urban, *Zorba the Buddha: Sexuality, Spirituality, and Capitalism in the Global Osho Movement* (Berkeley: University of California Press, 2016), introduction.

CHAPTER THREE

1. B. N. Shastri, ed., *Kālikā Purāṇa*, (Delhi: Nag Publishers, 1991), 67.20–21.

2. "Animal Sacrifice Draws Protest in Assam," *Assam Tribune*, October 17, 2010, https://assamtribune.com/animal-sacrifice-draws-protest-in-assam.

3. See Hugh B. Urban, "Death, Nationalism, and Sacrifice: Ritual, Violence, Politics, and Tourism in Northeast India," in *Irreverence and the Sacred: Critical Studies in the History of Religions*, ed. Hugh B. Urban and Greg Johnson (New York: Oxford University Press, 2018), 156–84; Hugh B. Urban, *Power of Tantra: Religion, Sexuality, and the Politics of South Asian Studies* (London: I. B. Tauris and Palgrave MacMillan, 2010), 51–98; Hugh B. Urban, "The Womb of Tantra: Goddesses, Tribals, and Kings in Assam," *Journal of Hindu Studies* 4 (2011): 231–47; Hugh B. Urban, "The Path of Power: Impurity, Kingship and Sacrifice in Assamese Tantra," *Journal of the American Academy of Religion* 69, no. 4 (2001): 597–637.

4. The Prevention of Cruelty to Animals Act 59 of 1960 (December 26, 1960), as Amended by Central Act 26 of 1982. It is important to note that the act makes an exemption for killing animals as part of a religious ritual: "Nothing contained in this Act shall render it an offense to kill any animal required by the religion of any community" (VI.28).

5. Shankhadeep Choudhury, "Nepal King Offers Animal Sacrifice in Kamakhya," *Times of India*, June 27, 2002, http://timesofindia.indiatimes.com/india/Nepal-King-offers-animal-sacrifice-in-Kamakhya/articleshow/14279990.cms.

6. See Mark Elmore, *Becoming Religious in a Secular Age* (Berkeley: University of California Press, 2016), 213–22; Eliza Kent, *Sacred Groves and Local Gods: Religion and Environmentalism in South India* (New York: Oxford University Press, 2013), 16–17.

7. Madeleine Biardeau and Charles Malamoud, *Le sacrifice dans l'Inde ancienne* (Paris: Presses universitaires de France, 1976), 153. See J. C. Heesterman, *The Broken World of Sacrifice: An Essay in Ancient Indian Ritual* (Chicago: University of Chicago Press, 1993), 2–3; J. C. Heesterman, *The Inner Conflict of Tradition: Essays in Indian Ritual, Kingship, and Society* (Chicago: University of Chicago Press, 1985), 98: "[Sacrifice] is the primordial act of creation and establishes the order of the universe. . . . [S]acrifice [is] the organizing principle of the Hindu world order."

8. Bruce Lincoln, *Discourse and the Construction of Society: Comparative Studies in Myth, Ritual, and Classification* (New York: Oxford University Press, 2014), 5. See Bruce Lincoln, *Death, War, and Sacrifice: Studies in Ideology and Practice* (Chicago:

University of Chicago Press, 1991); Kathryn McClymond, *Beyond Sacred Violence: A Comparative Study of Sacrifice* (Baltimore, MD: Johns Hopkins University Press, 2008).

9. Heesterman, *Broken World*, 217; Katherine Ulrich, "Food Fights: Buddhist, Hindu and Jain Dietary Polemics in South India," *History of Religions* 46, no. 3 (2007): 228–61.

10. See Urban, *Power of Tantra*, 147–64; Urban, "Path of Power."

11. See Elmore, *Becoming Religious*; Kent, *Sacred Groves*, 16–17.

12. See Urban, *Power of Tantra*, chs. 2–4. Many *tantras* from the northeast region recommend the offering of a wide range of animals. Thus, the *Kaulajñāna Nirṇaya* suggests offerings of dog, cat, camel, jackal, horse, turtle, tortoise, boar, heron, deer, buffalo, rhinoceros, and fish (11.14–19). The *Yoni Tantra* recommends sacrifices of goat, sheep, antelope, mongoose, cow, jackal, lion, and horse (J. A. Schoterman, ed., *Yoni Tantra* [Delhi: Manohar, 1980], 3.5–8; 3.16–17; 5.24–26). The *Yoginī Tantra* recommends the sacrifice of yak, alligator, and human beings (B. N. Shastri, ed., *Yoginī Tantra* [Delhi: Bhāratīya Vidyā Prakāśana, 1982], 2.7.163–65). As we will see below, these lists include animals that would be considered highly impure by Vedic standards (Urban, *Power of Tantra*, ch. 2).

On the practice of *antar-yāga* and *kula-yāga*, see Raniero Gnoli, trans., *Luce delle sacre scritture (Tantrāloka) di Abhinavagupta* (Milano: Adelphi, 1999), ch. 29; Lilian Silburn, *Kuṇḍalinī: The Energy of the Depths* (Albany, NY: SUNY Press, 1988), 177ff; John R. Dupuche, *Abhinavagupta: The Kula Ritual, as Elaborated in Chapter 29 of the Tantrāloka* (Delhi: Motilal Banarsidass, 2003); Hélène Brunner-Lachaux, Gerhard Oberhammer, and André Padoux, eds., *Tāntrikābhidhānakośa: Dictionnaire des termes techniques de la littérature hindoue tantrique*, 3 vols. (Wien: Verlag der Österreichischen Akademie der Wissenschaften, 2000), 2:127–28.

13. On nationalist uses of sacrificial imagery, see Parvis Ghassem-Fachandi, *Pogrom in Gujarat: Hindu Nationalism and Anti-Muslim Violence in India* (Princeton, NJ: Princeton University Press, 2012); Lise McKean, *Divine Enterprise: Gurus and the Hindu Nationalist Movement* (Chicago: University of Chicago Press, 1996), 40–42; Stanley Tambiah, *Leveling Crowds: Ethnonationalist Conflicts and Collective Violence in South Asia* (Berkeley: University of California Press, 1997), 248–49; Peter van der Veer, "Victim's Tale: Memory and Forgetting in the Story of Violence," in *Violence, Identity, and Self-Determination*, ed. H. D. Vries and S. Weber (Stanford, CA: Stanford University Press, 1997), 197–98.

14. On Hindu nationalist critiques of sacrifice, see Ghassem-Fachandi, *Pogrom in Gujarat*, 17; Michaël Bruckert, "The Politicization of Beef and Meat-Eating in Contemporary India: Protecting Animals and Aliening Minorities," in *Culinary Nationalism in India*, ed. Michelle T. King (New York: Bloomsbury Academic, 2019), 150–72.

15. See Sri Jadu Nath Sarma, Rajib Sarma, and Sri Naba Kanta Sarma, eds., *Souvenir Viswa Shanti Devi Yajña* (Guwahati: Viswa Shanti Devi Yajña Committee, 2014).

16. See Partha Chatterjee, *The Nation and Its Fragments* (Princeton, NJ: Princeton University Press, 1993). On Assamese identity and its tense relation to the nation, see Jayeeta Sharma, *Empire's Garden: Assam and the Making of Modern India* (Durham, NC: Duke University Press, 2011); Yasmin Saikia, *Fragmented Memories: Struggling to Be Tai-Ahom in India* (Durham, NC: Duke University Press, 2004).

17. On the territorialization of desire, see William Deal and Tim Beal, *Theory for Religious Studies* (New York: Routledge, 2004), 63. As Gilles Deleuze and Félix Guattari

write, "If it is true that the function of the modern State is the regulation of decoded, deterritorialized flows, one of the principal aspects of this function consists in reterritorializing, so as to prevent the decoded flows from breaking loose at all the edges of the social axiomatic" (*Anti-Oedipus: Capitalism and Schizophrenia* [Minneapolis: University of Minnesota Press, 1983], 258).

18. Heesterman, *Broken World*, 2–3.

19. *Taittirīya Brāhmaṇa*, 3.7.7.14, quoted in Heesterman, *Broken World*, 34. See Wendy Doniger, *The Hindus: An Alternative History* (New York: Penguin, 2009), 9: "The roots of *ahimsa* may lie in Vedic ritual, in animal sacrifice, in the argument that the priest does not actually injure the animal but merely 'pacifies him'; the primary meaning of *ahimsa* is thus to do injury without doing injury."

20. Heesterman, *Inner Conflict*, 87. "Essential to sacrifice is the immolatory act of violence and destruction. . . . At this point . . . sacrifice collided with the Hindu value of *ahiṃsā*" (98).

21. Juan Mascaro, trans., *The Upanishads* (New York: Penguin, 1965), 10. As Doniger notes, even before the *Upaniṣads*, the *Brāhmaṇas* were also "beginning to reflect uneasiness about eating animals at all" (*Hindus*, 149).

22. Heesterman, *Broken World*, 217; see Hermann Oldenberg, *Die Lehre der Upanishaden und die Anfänge des Buddhismus* (Göttingen: Vandenhoeck and Ruprecht, 1915), 305.

23. Imma Ramos, *Pilgrimage and Politics in Colonial Bengal: The Myth of the Goddess Sati* (London: Routledge, 2017), 9–10.

24. *Jugantar*, quoted in Keshub Choudhuri, *The Mother and Passionate Politics* (Calcutta: Vidyodaya Library, 1979), 46. See Hugh B, Urban, *Tantra: Sex, Secrecy, Politics and Power in the Study of Religion* (Berkeley: University of California Press, 2003), 93–98.

25. Christopher Pinney, *Photos of the Gods: The Printed Image and Political Struggle in India* (London: Reaktion Books, 2004), 116–17.

26. Rabindranath Tagore, *At Home and the World* (London: MacMillan, 1967), 123.

27. Ghassem-Fachandi, *Pogrom in Gujarat*, 20. On the shift to vegetarianism, see Chris Fuller, *The Camphor Flame* (Princeton, NJ: Princeton University Press, 1992), 83–105.

28. Tambiah, *Leveling Crowds*, 248.

29. Tambiah, *Leveling Crowds*, 248–49.

30. Tambiah, *Leveling Crowds*, 249.

31. See Gerald Larson, *India's Agony over Religion* (Albany, NY: SUNY Press, 1995), 266–77.

32. Ghassem-Fachandi, *Pogrom in Gujarat*, 77.

33. Ghassem-Fachandi, *Pogrom in Gujarat*, 20, 15. Danielle N. Boaz makes a similar point, arguing that "laws and litigation protecting animal welfare can often be a guise for racial discrimination and religious intolerance" ("The 'Abhorrent' Practice of Animal Sacrifice and Religious Discrimination in the Global South," *Religions* 10, no. 3 [2019]: 1–20, at 1).

34. Rohit De, *A People's Constitution: The Everyday Life of Law in the Indian Republic* (Princeton, NJ: Princeton University Press, 2018), 123.

35. De, *People's Constitution*, 126.

36. De, *People's Constitution*, 127. See Pinney, *Photos of the Gods*, 108.

37. Peter van der Veer, *Religious Nationalism: Hindus and Muslims in India* (Berkeley: University of California Press, 1994), 95.

38. Pinney, *Photos of the Gods*, 106–9. As Pinney suggests, "the cow became an inclusive symbol that was grounded simultaneously in an exclusional foundational violence which marked out Islam and Untouchable beef-eating practices as incompatible with this new space of the cow-nation" (107).

39. Const. of India (1950), art. XXV, https://www.constitutionofindia.net/constitution_of_india/fundamental_rights/articles/Article%2025. As scholars such as Pramit Singh argue, Article 25 violates the secularism claimed by the Constitution "because of the clearly expressed special interest of the state in favour of 'social welfare and reform' of the Hindu religion" ("Hindu Bias in India's 'Secular' Constitution: Probing Flaws in the Instruments of Governance," *Third World Quarterly* 26, no. 6 [2005]: 909–926, at 915). As such, Singh argues, it is one of many examples that "the secularism of India's constitution is Hindu-tainted . . . its Hindu bias must be read as symptomatic of the depth of institutionalized Hindu communalism in India and the shallowness of the secular foundations of the Indian republic" (909).

40. De, *People's Constitution*, 123–24. Many have argued that the *Hanif Qureshi* decision is an example of how "Hindu majoritarian views were cloaked in the neutral guise of constitutional law and became a reference point in every legal debate over cow slaughter" (De, *Peoples' Constitution*, 124). See Rajeev Devan, "Religious Freedom in India," *American Journal of Comparative Law* 36, no. 1 (1987): 209–54. As Singh argues: "The specific insertion of 'prohibiting slaughter of cows and calves' in the constitution as one of the directive principles of state policy was an unmistakable reflection of the religious preferences and powers of the dominant upper caste Hindus among constitution makers" ("Hindu Bias," 917).

41. Donald Eugene Smith, *India as a Secular State* (Princeton, NJ: Princeton University Press, 1963), 235.

42. Smith, *India as a Secular State*, 235.

43. *Madras Legislative Assembly Debates*, 1950, vol. 4, 113, 629, cited in Smith, *India as a Secular State*, 237. As V. I. Muniswamy Pillai put it, this prohibition was very much a matter of cleansing and reforming the global image of the Hindu religion: "Taking into account how the world views the religion of the Hindus, I think it is high time that these small blemishes that are a blot on the Hindu religion should be removed. . . . It will go a long way to show to the world how sacred our religion is and how pure its worship" (cited in Smith, *India as a Secular State*, 237).

44. Currently, more than twenty states have laws restricting the slaughter of cattle (cows, bulls, and bullocks) and buffaloes to various degrees. See Subham Dutt, "Assam's New Cattle Preservation Law," *PRS India* (blog), August 20, 2021, https://prsindia.org/theprsblog/assam%E2%80%99s-new-cattle-preservation-law.

45. See Bruckert, "Politicization of Beef and Meat-Eating," 150–72.

46. Elmore, *Becoming Religious*, 213.

47. Ramesh Sharma, Mehar Singh, Sonali Purewal, State of Himachal Pradesh, et al., *CWP No. 9257 of 2011, CWP No. 4499 of 2012 and CWP No. 5076 of 2012* (Shimla: High

Court of Himachal Pradesh, September 26, 2014), 95. See Boaz, "'Abhorrent' Practice of Animal Sacrifice," 1–20. According to the court's ruling, "No person throughout the State of Himachal Pradesh shall sacrifice any animal in any place of public religious worship, including all lands and building near such places of religious worship, which are ordinarily connected for religious purposes, or in any ceremony/Yagya/congregation or procession connected with any religious worship" (Satender Chauhan, "Himachal High Court Bans Animal Sacrifice at Religious Places," *India Today*, September 1, 2014, http://indiatoday.intoday.in/story/animal-sacrifice-himachal-pradesh-high-court-puts-a-ban/1/380340.html).

48. Elmore, *Becoming Religious*, 222. For similar debates in Tamil Nadu, see Kent, *Sacred Groves*, 16–17.

49. Krishnadas Rajagopal, "SC Rejects Plea to Ban Animal Sacrifices in Festivals," *Hindu*, September 28, 2015, http://www.thehindu.com/news/national/sc-rejects-plea-to-ban-animal-sacrifices-in-festivals/article7699034.ece.

50. Dhananjay Mahapatra, "Can't Interfere in Animal Sacrifice Tradition: Supreme Court," *Times of India*, September 28, 2015, http://timesofindia.indiatimes.com/india/Cant-interfere-in-animal-sacrifice-tradition-Supreme-Court/articleshow/49144192.cms.

51. Dhananjay Mahapatra, "Tripura HC Bans State-Sponsored Goat Sacrifice at Tripureswari Temple," *Times of India*, September 28, 2019, https://timesofindia.indiatimes.com/india/tripura-hc-bans-state-sponsored-goat-sacrifice-at-tripureswari-temple/articleshow/71343834.cms.

52. Chandan Panday, "Animal Sacrifice Resumes in Tripura Temples as SC Stays HC Order," *East Mojo*, November 25, 2019, https://www.eastmojo.com/news/2019/11/25/animal-sacrifice-resumes-in-tripura-temples-as-sc-stays-hc-order/.

53. The ruling was made in 2006, but it took a several years before the temple complied. Sacrifices now take place behind a seven-foot wall and are largely inaccessible to devotees. See Deonnie Moodie, "Of Blood, Power, and Public Interest: Concealment of Sacrificial Rites under Indian Law," *Journal of Law and Religion* 34, no. 2 (2019): 165–82.

54. J. A. B. van Buitenen, trans., *The Mahābhārata, Volume 2, Book 2: The Book of the Assembly, Book 3: The Book of the Forest* (Chicago: University of Chicago Press, 1981), 2.23.19, 2.31.9–10. See also V. R. Ramchandra Dikshitar, "Administration of East India," in *Discovery of Northeast India: Geography, History, Culture*, ed. S. K. Sharma and Usha Sharma (Delhi: Mittal Publications, 2005), 3:155: "The Vedic people disregarded Assam as a country of the Mlecchas, an impure country unfit for performance of Aryan rites and ceremonies."

55. Shastri, ed., *Yoginī Tantra*, 1.9.13–16.

56. In 2019, a headless body was found near Kāmākhyā at the time of Ambuvācī Melā that led to speculation of human sacrifice. See Arunabh Saikia, "Human Sacrifice in Assam," *Scroll.in*, June 23, 2019, https://scroll.in/article/927875/human-sacrifice-in-assam-a-headless-body-found-near-kamakhya-temple-raises-questions; Urban, *Power of Tantra*, 1–20; Daulat Rahman, "New Light on Land of Black Magic," *Telegraph*, May 14, 2009, https://www.telegraphindia.com/north-east/new-light-on-land-of-black-magic-huge-swords-unearthed-at-mayong-in-assam-point-to-human-sacrifice/cid/629252.

57. See Shastri, ed., *Kālikā Purāṇa*, 18.41–47; Urban, *Power of Tantra*, ch. 1. On the Satī narrative and its iconography, see Paul Courtright, "The Iconographies of Sati," in *Sati: The Blessing and the Curse: The Burning of Wives in India*, ed. John Stratton Hawley (New York: Oxford University Press, 1994), 27–48.

58. Mukunda Madhava Sharma, *Inscriptions of Ancient Assam* (Guwahati: Gauhati University Press, 1978), 8.

59. See Shastri, ed., *Kālikā Purāṇa*, 31.7, 55.3–6; Shastri, ed., *Yoginī Tantra*, 2.9.158 and 2.7.170. Urban, *Power of Tantra*, chs. 2–3; Urban, "Womb of Tantra"; Urban, "Path of Power"; Sravana Borkataky-Varma, "Red: An Ethnographic Study of Cross-Pollination between the Vedic and the Tantric," *International Journal of Hindu Studies* 23, no. 2 (2019): 179–94.

60. See Shastri, ed., *Kālikā Purāṇa*, 55.1–2. As the same text puts it elsewhere, "The gods are pleased by sacrifices; by sacrifice, everything is established. The earth is upheld by sacrifice; sacrifice saves living beings. Creatures live on food, and food grows from rain. Rains come from sacrifice; thus, everything is made of sacrifice" (31.7–8). See Urban, *Power of Tantra*, 57.

61. See Urban, "Womb of Tantra" and "Path of Power."

62. Heesterman, *Broken World*, 29–30. See Charles Malamoud, "Village et forêt dans l'idéologie de l'Inde brâhmanique," *Archives européennes de sociologie* (1976): 3–20.

63. Julius Eggeling, ed., *Śatapatha Brāhmaṇa* (Delhi: Motilal Banarsidass, 1963), 6.2.1.1 and 7.5.2.32.

64. *Taittirīya Brāhmaṇa* 3.9.1.2–4, quoted in Brian K. Smith, *Classifying the Universe: The Ancient Indian Varna System and the Origins of Caste* (New York: Oxford University Press, 1994), 250.

65. Shastri, ed., *Kālikā Purāṇa*, 55.3–6.

66. Shastri, ed., *Yoginī Tantra*, 2.7.163–65: "One goat is better than ten yaks. A single tortoise is equal to ten goats. And a rabbit is better than a hundred tortoises. A boar is worth more than a thousand rabbits. A buffalo is said to be better than two thousand boars. A rhino is better than two thousand buffalos. But the fruit of a human being is equal to a thousand rhinos." See also Pradīp Kumār Rāy, ed., *Muṇḍamālātantram* (Varanasi: Prācya Prakāśana, 2010), 4.9–10: "With the offering of a goat, one becomes eloquent; with the offering of a ram, one becomes a poet. With a buffalo, one becomes wealthy; with a deer, one achieves the reward of spiritual liberation. With a bird, one becomes prosperous; with an alligator, one receives the great reward. With the offering of a human being, one achieves the power that is supreme perfection."

67. M. Neog, *Early History of the Vaiṣṇava Faith and Movement in Assam* (Delhi: Motilal Banarsidass, 1980), 80. See Banikanta Kakati, *The Mother Goddess Kamakhya* (Guwahati: Publication Board, Assam, 1989), 65.

68. Shastri, ed., *Kālikā Purāṇa*, 67.20–21.

69. Sidney Endle, *The Kacharis* (Delhi: Cosmo Publications, 1975), 39–41. See M. Śāstrī, "Dharma āru darśan," in *Asamīya Jātir Itivṛtta*, ed. G. Sarma (Jorhat, India: Assam Sāhitya Sabhā, 1977), 120.

70. Moodie, "Of Blood, Power, and Public Interest."

71. Various interviews with author, Kāmākhyā Temple, June 2017, January 2022, June 2022.

72. In June 2022, I interviewed one of the *bali-kaṭās*, who comes from a long line of *bali-kaṭās*. As he explained, "the goddess gives us everything, all we desire, and we offer her what she desires. She can only be satisfied with blood. We offer her the blood and the head, and then devotees all share in the meat."

73. *Bali-kaṭā* interviews with author, Kāmākhyā Temple, June 18, 2021. See Irene Majo Garigliano, "The Brahmans of the Kāmākhyā Temple Complex: Customary Rights, Relations with Pilgrims, and Administrative Power" (PhD diss., Istituto Italiano di Studi Orientali, 2015), 74.

74. Navamallika Sharma and Madhushree Das, "Priests and Practices: Understanding the Socio-Religious Scenario of Kamakhya Temple," *Clarion: International Multidisciplinary Journal* 4, no. 1 (2015): 120–26, at 122. See Nihar Ranjan Mishra, *Kamakhya: A Socio-Cultural Study* (New Delhi: D. K. Printworld, 2004), 47.

75. Rajib Sarma, personal communication, June 2, 2017.

76. Shastri, ed., *Kālikā Purāṇa*, 55.17–20: "He should carefully perfume the blood of the victim with water, salt, good fruits, honey, fragrance, and flowers and [offer it] with the mantra: 'Oṃ Aiṃ Hrīṃ Śrīṃ. Kauśikī, I am offering the blood to you.' He should put the blood and the head with a lamp on it in the proper place."

77. Mishra, *Kamakhya*, 49. See Oinam Sunil, "At Kamakhya, There's No Stopping Animal Sacrifice," *Times of India*, October 16, 2006, https://timesofindia.indiatimes.com/india/at-kamakhya-theres-no-stopping-animal-sacrifice/articleshow/2172705.cms.

78. Biardeau and Malamoud, *Le sacrifice*, 146–47. See also Madeleine Biardeau, "Devi: The Goddess in India," in *Asian Mythologies*, ed. Yves Bonnefoy (Chicago: University of Chicago Press, 1993), 95–98; Urban, "Path of Power"; Hugh B. Urban, "Matrix of Power: Blood, Kingship and Sacrifice in the Worship of Mother Goddess Kamakhya," *South Asia* 31, no. 3 (2008): 500–34.

79. Bhūṣaṇa Dvija, *Mahāpuruṣa Śaṅkaradeva* (Jorhat, India: Durgādhar Barkataki, 1925), 227. See Hugh B. Urban, "Śaṅkaradeva and Mādhavadeva," in *Brill's Encyclopedia of Hinduism*, vol. 4, ed. Knut Jacobson (Leiden: Brill, 2012), 397–404.

80. James Lyall, "The Province of Assam," *Journal of the Society of Arts* (June 5, 1903): 619.

81. H. K. Barpujari, *The American Missionaries and North-East India (1836–1900 AD): A Documentary Study* (Guwahati: Spectrum Publications, 1986), xxxix.

82. Barpujari, *American Missionaries*, xlviii. See Urban, *Power of Tantra*, ch. 6.

83. Kakati, *Mother Goddess Kamakhya*, 79.

84. Uma Mahadevan-Dasgupta, "Struggle for Change," *Hindu*, April 1, 2007, http://www.thehindu.com/todays-paper/tp-features/tp-literaryreview/struggle-for-change/article2274599.ece.

85. Indira Goswami, *The Man from Chinnamasta* (Delhi: Katha, 2006), 26. See Ruksana Parveen, "Animal Sacrifice in Indira Goswami's *The Man from Chinnamasta*," *Paripex: Indian Journal of Research* 3, no. 9 (2014): 77–78.

86. Goswami, *Man from Chinnamasta*, 128–29.

87. "The Man from Chinnamasta Comes to Chennai," *Katha*, November 19, 2006, http://kathamedia.blogspot.com/2006/11/man-from-chinnamasta-comes-to-chennai.html.

88. "Religion Saves Animal Sacrifice," *Telegraph*, December 5, 2008, https://www.telegraphindia.com/north-east/religion-saves-animal-sacrifice-gauhati-high-court-chickens-out-on-enforcing-ban/cid/520119.

89. "Animal Sacrifice Draws Protest in Assam."

90. "Debate: Animal Sacrifice Is Barbaric and Should Be Stopped," *Barakbulletin*, October 18, 2018, https://www.barakbulletin.com/en_US/debate-animal-sacrifice-is-barbaric-and-should-be-stopped-says-satyagrahi-kalpranab-gupta-a-ritual-as-per-vedic-scriptures-counters-purohit/. Another devotee from Guwahati argued that the true "sacrifice" is an internal offering of the self to the goddess, while the physical practice of animal sacrifice is primarily an institution created by the priests of the temple (interview with author, Silchar, Assam, June 17, 2022).

91. Tora Agarwala, "Assam Cattle Preservation Bill 2021 Passed in Assembly after Opposition Walkout," *Indian Express*, August 14, 2021, https://indianexpress.com/article/north-east-india/assam/assam-cattle-preservation-bill-2021-passed-in-assembly-after-opposition-walkout-7452708/. See also "Assam's Cow Protection Bill Bans Sale of Beef within 5km of Temples," *Hindu*, November 22, 2021, https://www.thehindu.com/news/national/other-states/assams-cow-protection-bill-bans-sale-of-beef-within-5km-of-temple/article61442669.ece.

92. Agarwala, "Assam Cattle Preservation Bill."

93. Kangkan Acharyya, "Cattle Slaughter Ban Comes Up against Tradition in Assam's Kamakhya Temple," *Firstpost*, May 31, 2017, https://www.firstpost.com/india/cattle-slaughter-ban-comes-up-against-tradition-in-assams-kamakhya-temple-bjp-caught-in-catch-22-situation-3500341.html.

94. Acharyya, "Cattle Slaughter Ban." See Apoorva Mandhani, "Centre Bans Sale of Cows for Slaughter at Animal Markets," *Live Law*, May 27, 2017, http://www.livelaw.in/centre-bans-sale-of-cows-for-slaughter-at-animal-markets-restrict-cattle-trade/. As we saw above, the first *Gorakshini Sabha* (Cow Protection Society) was established in Punjab in 1881; the movement has seen a resurgence since the late twentieth century with the growing power of the BJP, VHP, RSS (Rashtriya Swayamsevak Sangh), and other conservative Hindu parties. See De, *People's Constitution*, 126; van der Veer, *Religious Nationalism*, 91.

95. Amrit Dhillon, "'Free Pass for Mobs': India Urged to Stem Vigilante Violence against Minorities," *Guardian*, February 19, 2019, https://www.theguardian.com/world/2019/feb/19/a-free-pass-for-mobs-to-kill-india-urged-to-stem-cow-vigilante-violence. See also Christophe Jaffrelot, "Over to the Vigilante," *Indian Express*, May 13, 2017, https://indianexpress.com/article/opinion/columns/over-to-the-vigilante-gau-rakshak-cultural-policing-beef-ban-4653305/.

96. Rajib Sarma, interview with author, Guwahati, Assam, June 23, 2017.

97. Rajib Sarma, interview with author, January 11, Guwahati, Assam, 2022.

98. On the Hialeah case, see Artemus Ward, "Animal Sacrifice," *First Amendment Encyclopedia*, 2009, https://mtsu.edu/first-amendment/article/30/animal-sacrifice;

Robert B. Flowers, *That Godless Court? Supreme Court Decisions on Church-State Relationships* (Louisville, KY: Westminster John Knox Press, 2005), 44–47.

99. *Church of the Lukumi Babalu Aye, Inc. and Ernesto Pichardo v. City of Hialeah,* 508 U.S. 520 (1993). As Justice Kennedy wrote in his opinion, "The ordinances had as their object the suppression of religion. The pattern we have recited discloses animosity to Santeria adherents and their religious practices . . . the texts of the ordinances were gerrymandered with care to proscribe religious killings of animals but to exclude almost all secular killings" (quoted in Flowers, *That Godless Court*, 46).

100. EMI, interview with author, March 18, 2022.

101. Himanta Biswa Sarma, "Message," in *Souvenir Viswa Shanti Devi Yajña*, ed. Sri Jadu Nath Sarma, Rajib Sarma, and Sri Naba Kanta Sarma (Guwahati: Viswa Shanti Devi Yajña Committee, 2014), n.p. See Śrī Rādhikmohan Bhāgavatī, "Yajña: Iyār Tātparya" in the same volume, 21. This opinion was shared by a priest interviewed in Silchar, who also argued for the Vedic origin of sacrifice: "Where there are many Vedic scriptures, those can be complex . . . we Hindus on auspicious occasions devote edible items to God and then eat it as Prasadam. It can be Payash or it can be meat" ("Debate: Animal Sacrifice Is Barbaric").

102. Śrī Viveka Kumāra Miśra, "Vaidika Yajña," in *Souvenir Viswa Shanti Devi Yajña*, ed. Sri Jadu Nath Sarma, Rajib Sarma, and Sri Naba Kanta Sarma (Guwahati: Viswa Shanti Devi Yajña Committee, 2014), 37–45.

103. Samudra Gupta Kashyap and Milind Ghatwai, "After the Vote, the Poor Goat," *Indian Express*, July 29, 2008, http://archive.indianexpress.com/news/after-the-vote-the-poor-goat-sp-mla-sacrifices-265-for-upa/342323/.

104. Rachel McDermott, *Revelry, Rivalry and Longing for the Goddesses of Bengal* (New York: Oxford University Press, 2011), 215.

105. Heesterman, *Broken World*, 43; see Alf Hiltebeitel, *The Ritual of Battle: Krishna in the Mahabharata* (Ithaca, NY: Cornell University Press, 1976).

106. McClymond, *Beyond Sacred Violence*, 3.

107. Lincoln, *Death, War, and Sacrifice*, 204.

108. See Deal and Beal, *Theory for Religious Studies*, 63; Deleuze and Guattari, *Anti-Oedipus*, 258.

109. Borkataky-Varma, "Red," 179–94.

110. Thomas Blom Hansen, *The Saffron Wave: Democracy and Hindu Nationalism in Modern India* (Princeton, NJ: Princeton University Press, 1999), 237. See Christophe Jaffrelot, *Hindu Nationalism, a Reader* (Princeton, NJ: Princeton University Press, 2007), 6.

CHAPTER FOUR

1. B. K. Barua and S. N. Sarma, eds., *Manasā-Kāvya* (Gauhati: Dattabarya, 1951), 88; Pradyot Kumar Maity, *Historical Studies in the Cult of the Goddess Manasā: A Socio-Cultural Study* (Calcutta: Punthi Pustak, 1966), 122.

2. There is some disagreement about the etymology of *deodhāi* and *deodhanī*. Many trace the terms to a Sanskrit origin, deriving them from *deva* (god) and *dhvani* (sound, echo, reverberation); see Frederick M. Smith, *The Self Possessed: Deity and Spirit Possession in South Asia* (New York: Columbia University Press, 2006), 140–41. However,

the terms are widely used to refer to a variety of indigenous, non-*brāhmaṇic* ritual practitioners among the tribes of Assam, variously called *deodhā*, *daudini*, etc. Hence *deodhāi* could simply be rendered as "one who serves or bears the deity" (*deo*), with *deodhanī* being the feminine form. See Miles Bronson, *A Dictionary in Assamese and English* (Sibsagar: American Baptist Mission, 1867), 298; Sidney Endle, *The Kacharis* (Delhi: Cosmo Publications, 1975), 39–41; Madhurima Goswami, "Folk Dances of Assam: A Short Appraisal," *Indian Folklife* 31 (2008): 21–22.

3. There is not a great deal of scholarly literature on *deodhanī nāc*; the little that exists includes Irene Majo Garigliano, "The Brahmans of the Kāmākhyā Temple Complex: Customary Rights, Relations with Pilgrims, and Administrative Power" (PhD diss., Istituto Italiano di Studi Orientali, 2015); Nihar Ranjan Mishra, *Kamakhya: A Socio-Cultural Study* (New Delhi: D. K. Printworld, 2004); M. C. Goswami, "An Annual Shamanistic Dance," *Journal of the University of Gauhati* 11, no. 2 (1960): 37–58; Patricia Dold, "Pilgrimage to Kamakhya through Text and Lived Religion: Some Forms of the Goddess at an Assamese Temple Site," in *Studying Hinduism in Practice*, ed. Hillary P. Rodrigues (New York: Routledge, 2011), 46–61; Khagen Chandra Mahanta, "Shamanistic Dance and Treatment of Disease in Assam," in *Contemporary Tribal Studies*, ed. George Pfeffer and Deepak Kumar Behera (New Delhi: Concept Publishing Company, 1997), 309–19; Mikel Burley, "Dance of the Deodhas: Divine Possession, Blood Sacrifice and the Grotesque Body in Assamese Worship," *Religions of South Asia* 12, no. 2 (2019): 207–33.

4. See June McDaniel, *Offering Flowers, Feeding Skulls: Popular Goddess Worship in West Bengal* (New York: Oxford University Press, 2004), 148–56. See Maity, *Historical Studies*, 296: "Manasā had her origin outside the domain of Brahmanical Hinduism."

5. See Mishra, *Kamakhya*, 54; Hugh B. Urban, "Dancing for the Snake: Possession, Gender, and Identity in the Worship of Manasā in Assam," *Journal of Hindu Studies* 11, no. 3 (2018): 304–27; Hugh B. Urban, "The Womb of Tantra: Goddesses, Tribals, and Kings in Assam," *Journal of Hindu Studies* 4 (2011): 231–47.

6. See Maity, *Historical Studies*, 295: "When performed by women it is known as Deodhanī, and when by men as Deodhā. Both are performed on the occasion of Manasā worship."

7. As Mishra notes, "The Rabhas also worship the snake deity Manasā. This pūjā is held either for one day or for three days with traditional ritualistic fervor including animal sacrifices. . . . The Rabhas are said to be the originators of Manasā worship in Goalpara and southern part of . . . Kāmarūpa district" (*Kamakhya*, 17). See R. Rabha, *Rabha Jana Jāt* (Jorhat, India: Assam Sahitya Sabha, 1974).

8. Kishore Bhattacharjee, "Constructing Community and Kinship through Epic Singing," *Indian Folklore Research Journal* 6 (2006): 1–12.

9. On the concept of "domestication," see Smith, *Self Possessed*, 11; on "folklorization," see John H. McDowell, "Rethinking Folklorization in Ecuador: The Multivocality in the Expressive Contact Zone," *Western Folklore* 69, no. 2 (2010): 181–209.

10. See *Hāte mudrā mukhe pada mayer sadṛśa nāc*, directed by Prabīn Hāzarikā (2012; Gauhati, India: Krisangi Creation).

11. Smith, *Self Possessed*, 371. See also André Padoux, "Transe, possession ou absorption mystique? *L'āveśa* selon quelques textes tantriques cachemiriens," in *La possession*

en Asie du Sud: Parole, corps, territoire, ed. J. Assayag and G. Tarabout (Paris: École des Hautes Études en Sciences Sociales, 1999), 133–47; Alexis Sanderson, "Śaivism and the Tantric Traditions," in *The World's Religions*, ed. Stewart Sutherland, Leslie Houlden, Peter Clarke, and Friedhelm Hardy (New York: Routledge, 1988), 660–704, at 660; Alexis Sanderson, "Śaiva Texts," in *Brill's Encyclopedia of Hinduism*, vol. 6, ed. Knut A. Jacobsen (Leiden: Brill, 2015), 10–42, at 28. As Mark S. G. Dyczkowski notes, "The deity may be invoked to take possession of the worshiper so that he can gain awesome power through which he perceives the deity's pervasive presence (*vyāpti*) in all things" (*The Canon of the Śaivāgamas and the Kubjikā Tantras of the Western Kaula Tradition* [Albany, NY: SUNY Press, 1988], 59).

12. Smith, *Self Possessed*, 368.

13. See Urban, "Womb of Tantra"; Jayeeta Sharma, *Empire's Garden: Assam and the Making of India* (Durham, NC: Duke University Press, 2011).

14. See Edward Albert Gait, *A History of Assam* (Calcutta: Thacker, Spink, and Co., 1963); Banikanta Kakati, *The Mother Goddess Kamakhya* (Guwahati: Publication Board, Assam, 1989).

15. Wendy Doniger, *The Hindus: An Alternative History* (New York: Penguin, 2009), 6. On this point, see also Urban, "Womb of Tantra"; Sravana Borkataky-Varma, "The Dead Speak: A Case Study from the Tiwa Tribe Highlighting the Hybrid World of Śākta Tantra in Assam," *Religions* 8, no. 221 (2017): 1–15.

16. Among the many anthropological studies of possession, I find the following most useful in this article: Smith, *Self Possessed*; Karen McCarthy Brown, *Mama Lola: A Vodou Priestess in Brooklyn* (Berkeley: University of California Press, 2011); Paul C. Johnson, *Diaspora Conversions: Black Carib Religion and the Recovery of Africa* (Berkeley: University of California Press, 2007); Paul C. Johnson, ed., *Spirited Things: The Work of "Possession" in Afro-Atlantic Religions* (Chicago: University of Chicago Press, 2017); I. M. Lewis, *Ecstatic Religion: A Study of Shamanism and Spirit Possession* (New York: Routledge, 2003); Erica Bourguignon, *Possession* (San Francisco: Chandler and Sharp, 1976); Mary Keller, *The Hammer and the Flute: Women, Power, and Spirit Possession* (Baltimore, MD: Johns Hopkins University Press, 2005).

17. Judith Butler, *Gender Trouble: Feminism and the Subversion of Identity* (New York: Routledge, 1990); see Ellen Armour and Susan St. Ville, eds., *Bodily Citations: Religion and Judith Butler* (New York: Columbia University Press, 2006).

18. See Kaiser Haq, *Triumph of the Snake Goddess* (Cambridge, MA: Harvard University Press, 2015); Edward C. Dimock and A. K. Ramanujan, "The Goddess of Snakes in Medieval Bengali Literature, Part II," *History of Religions* 3, no. 2 (1964): 300–22.

19. Dimock and Ramanujan, "Goddess of Snakes," 300–301.

20. Bhattacharjee, "Constructing Community," 1–12; Maity, *Historical Studies*, 291.

21. See Friedhelm Harvey, "Information and Transformation: Two Faces of the *Purāṇas*," in *Purāṇa Perennis*, ed. Wendy Doniger (Albany, NY: SUNY Press, 1993), 159–84. As Harvey observes, the main sources of these narratives are (1) Sanskrit *purāṇas* such as the *Brahmavaivarta* and *Devībhāgavata*, (2) folktales, and (3) and the *Manasā-maṅgalas*, or stories of the goddess, written in Bangla and Assamese.

22. Nārāyaṇadeva, *Padmapurāṇa: Manasā-Maṅgala*, ed. Tamonash Chandra Das Gupta (Calcutta: University of Calcutta Press, 1947); Mankar and Durgābar, *Manasā-kāvya*,

ed. Kālirām Medhi (Guwahati: Dattabaruwa, 1964). See also Maity, *Historical Studies*, 119–28.

23. Barua and Sarma, eds., *Manasā-Kāvya*, 88; Maity, *Historical Studies*, 122. As the famous folk performer and dance instructor Lalit Ojā put it, "Manasā gives you wealth, blesses everybody, makes it possible to live in peace and happiness. That is why the goddess is worshiped" (interview in Hāzarikā, dir., *Hāte mudrā mukhe pada mayer sadṛśa nāc*).

24. Nārāyaṇadeva, *Padmapurāṇa*, 54–86. See Maity, *Historical Studies*, 121–24.

25. Haq, *Triumph of the Snake Goddess*, 329.

26. *Padmapurāṇa*, 129. Similarly, as Durgābar narrates, "With five great sounds, her graceful body played the cymbals. Like a heavenly courtesan, she made dancing gestures, bearing a peacock feather" (Medhi, ed., *Manasā-kāvya*, 123).

27. Haq, *Triumph of the Snake Goddess*, 335; Nārāyaṇadeva, *Padmapurāṇa*, 130–31.

28. See Hugh B. Urban, *The Power of Tantra: Religion, Sexuality, and the Politics of South Asian Studies* (London: I. B. Tauris and Palgrave MacMillan, 2010), 102–4.

29. Smith, *Self Possessed*, 141; Mishra, *Kamakhya*, 148.

30. Mahanta, "Shamanistic Dance," 263; Goswami, "Annual Shamanistic Dance," 38.

31. See B. N. Shastri, ed., *Kālikā Purāṇa* (Delhi: Nag Publishers, 1991), 36.7; Urban, *Power of Tantra*, 80.

32. See Urban, "Womb of Tantra"; Hugh B. Urban, "Matrix of Power: Blood, Kingship and Sacrifice in the Worship of Mother Goddess Kāmākhyā," *South Asia* 31, no. 3 (2008): 500–34.

33. See Harināth Śarmādalai, *Asamat Śakti-Sādhanā āru Śākta-Sāhitya* (Nalbari, India: Padmapriya Library, 1998), 208; D. Nath, *History of the Koch Kingdom, 1515–1615* (Koch Behar: Mittal Publications, 1989), xi. As Endle notes, *deoddni* is a generic term used among many of the tribes lumped under the Kachari group to refer to non-*brāhmaṇ* religious specialists who are versed in exorcism and other rites (*Kacharis*, 139). Likewise, as Goswami notes, *daudini* is a general Bodo term for a shamanic dancer ("Folk Dances," 21–22).

34. Gait, *History of Assam*, 178. See Padmeshwar Gogoi, *Tai-Ahom Religion and Customs* (Guwahati: Publication Board, Assam, 1976), 41: "The Ahom priesthood (Mo-Shām, Mo-Hung, Mo-Plang or in Assamese Deodhāis, Mohans, and Bāilungs) resisted this change over to Hinduism and even cursed the kings who initiated this change in religious policy. The priests predicted ill of the future and subsequent misfortunes into which the country had fallen."

35. Yasmin Saikia, *Fragmented Memories: Struggling to Be Tai-Ahom in India* (Durham, NC: Duke University Press, 2004), xiv.

36. Sharma, *Empire's Garden*, 11.

37. Mishra, *Kamakhya*, 54.

38. Mahanta, "Shamanistic Dance," 315.

39. Majo Garigliano, "Brahmans," 205n.

40. *Ghora: Waiting for the Goddess*, directed by Alessandro Cartosio and Irene Majo Garigliano (2013; Rome: Sapienza University of Rome).

41. Majo Garigliano, "Brahmans," 96–97.

42. Mahanta, "Shamanistic Dance," 313.

43. Śivnāth Dās, interview, in *Ghora,* dirs. Cartosio and Majo Garigliano.

44. Majo Garigliano, "Brahmans," 96. Deviram Das, the *deodhāi* of Manasā, "insists that Manasā actually takes his body (*gā lay*). *Gā* is the Assamese word for 'body' and is used as a synonym of *śarīr*, which is also employed in everyday parlance. *Lai* is the Assamese equivalent of the Hindi *lenā*; it means 'to take' and is used in several different contexts. Deviram Das also employs the verb *lambhi,* which can be conveniently translated by the English 'to possess.' Unlike *lai, lambhi* is uniquely used to point out the fact that a human becomes possessed by an external, nonhuman force, either a deity or a devil. A third expression Deviram Das uses when talking about the Goddess Manasā is *śarīrod jāi* (to go into [someone's] body)" (Majo Garigliano, "Brahmans," 96).

45. Devīrām Dās, interview, in Cartosio and Majo Garigliano, *Ghora.*

46. See Padoux, "Transe"; Smith, *Self Possessed.*

47. Majo Garigliano, "Brahmans," 61.

48. Majo Garigliano, "Brahmans," 98. "The *deodhāi* is a kind of puppet in the deity's hands. He does not choose to be possessed, he simply accepts becoming the vehicle of the deity. During possession he . . . loses the awareness of his identity; devotees understand his words to be those of the deity and worship him" (Majo Garigliano, "Brahmans," 102). See also D. Vidal, "Des dieux face à leurs specialistes: conditions de la prêtrise en Himachal Pradesh," in *Prêtrise, pouvoir et autorité en Himalaya,* ed. V. Bouillier and G. Toffin (Paris: École des Hautes Études en Sciences Sociales, 1989), 61–78.

49. Dold, "Pilgrimage to Kamakhya," 55.

50. Dold, "Pilgrimage to Kamakhya," 55.

51. Mahanta, "Shamanistic Dance," 317.

52. Mahanta, "Shamanistic Dance," 315. See Majo Garigliano, "Brahmans," 96.

53. Maity, *Historical Studies,* 296.

54. Mahanta, "Shamanistic Dance," 315.

55. Dold, "Pilgrimage to Kamakhya," 55. See Majo Garigliano, "Brahmans," 204.

56. Majo Garigliano, "Brahmans," 205–6.

57. See Hugh B. Urban, "The Cradle of Tantra: Modern Transformations of a Tantric Centre in Northeast India, from Nationalist Symbol to Tourist Destination," *South Asia* 49, no. 2 (2019): 256–77.

58. Bandana Sarma and Riya Sarma, interview with author, Guwahati, Assam, June 22, 2022.

59. Rajib Sarma, interview with author, Guwahati, Assam, July 10, 2017.

60. Mishra, *Kamakhya,* 57–58.

61. Majo Garigliano, "Brahmans," 204.

62. Mishra, *Kamakhya,* 57–58.

63. Dold, "Pilgrimage to Kamakhya," 57.

64. Smith, *Self Possessed,* 11.

65. Susan A. Reed, *Dance and the Nation: Performance, Ritual, and Politics in Sri Lanka* (Madison: University of Wisconsin Press, 2010).

66. See Hugh B. Urban, *Tantra: Sex, Secrecy, Politics and Power in the Study of Religion* (Berkeley: University of California Press, 2003), 44–72; Urban, *Power of Tantra*, 1–19.

67. Endle, *Kacharis*, 40–41.

68. Bhattacherjee, "Constructing Community," 10. As Goswami notes, the traditional *deodhanī* performance is "more of a ritual than a dance" in which "the dancer, who apparently goes into a trance, uses mimetic movements of snakes and goddess Manasa and enacts the popular legend of Behula" ("Folk Dances," 21).

69. "There are different stages of spirit possession. Firstly, Durga who enters the garden of Siva becomes tired and unconscious which is known as Phool Dak, enacted by the deodhani. The deodhani for the second time falls in a trance when Durga is bitten by Manasa in the form of a snake. After that when Siva becomes unconscious after consuming poison found in the churning of the ocean, the deodhani becomes Mahadeva and dies" (Bhattacharjee, "Constructing Community," 10).

70. Bhattacharjee, "Constructing Community," 10.

71. Hāzarikā, dir., *Hāte mudrā.*

72. Hāzarikā, dir., *Hāte mudrā.*

73. Lalit Ojā, interview, in Hāzarikā, dir., *Hāte mudrā.*

74. Naresh Mitra, "All the World's a Stage for Lalit Chandra Nath Ojha," *Times of India*, September 16, 2012, http://timesofindia.indiatimes.com/city/guwahati/All-the-worlds-a-stagefor-Lalit-Chandra-Nath-Ojha/articleshow/16426150.cms?referral.PM.

75. Assam State Portal, "Culture of Assam," *Assam.gov.in*, 2023, https://assam.gov.in/about-us/391.

76. T. Raatan, *History, Religion, and Culture of Northeast India* (Delhi: Isha Books, 2006), 96.

77. Lalit Ojā, interview, in Hāzarikā, dir., *Hāte mudrā.*

78. See note 16 above.

79. Brown, *Mama Lola*, 98.

80. Johnson, *Diaspora Conversions*, 18.

81. For a similar dynamic in Tiwa spirit possession, see Borkataky-Varma, "The Dead Speak."

82. Butler, *Gender Trouble*, 24, 140.

83. Butler, *Gender Trouble*, 33–34.

84. On applications of Butler's work to religious studies, see Armour and St. Ville, eds., *Bodily Citations*. For applications of Butler's work to Tantra, see Urban, *Power of Tantra*, 23–24, 134–36; Loriliai Biernacki, *Renowned Goddess of Desire: Women, Sex, and Speech in Tantra* (New York: Oxford University Press, 2007).

85. On the "domestication" of possession, see Smith, *Self Possessed*, 11.

86. Sharma, *Empire's Garden*, 11.

87. See Gilles Deleuze and Félix Guattari, *A Thousand Plateaus: Capitalism and Schizophrenia* (Minneapolis: University of Minnesota Press, 1987), 275; Patty Sotirin,

"Becoming Woman," in *Gilles Deleuze: Key Concepts*, ed. Charles J. Stivale (Montreal: McGill-Queen's University Press, 2005), 98–109.

88. On this point, see Smith, *Self Possessed*, 594: "Possession reveals the individual to be so porous and indefinite that we must conclude that it is a tenuous social construction. . . . [P]ossession is both self-affirming and radically transformative. . . . [I]t affirms the social self while eclipsing the spiritually isolated self." See also Keller, *Hammer and the Flute*.

CHAPTER FIVE

1. Kṣemarāja Śrī Kṛṣṇdāsa, *Devībhāgavatapurāṇam* (Delhi: Nag Publishers, 1986), 7.38.16–17.

2. Digambar Patowary, "Assam: Modi Starts Day of Poll Campaigning with Temple Visit," *Hindustan Times*, April 9, 2016, https://www.hindustantimes.com/india/assam-modi-starts-day-of-poll-campaigning-with-temple-visit/story-08TZ5LcIogsn7wtfchSvsO.html.

3. For discussions of Kāmākhyā and Ambuvācī, see Nihar Ranjan Mishra, *Kamakhya: A Socio-Cultural Study* (New Delhi: D. K. Printworld, 2004); Frédérique Apffel-Marglin and Julia A. Jean, "Weaving the Body and the Cosmos: Two Menstrual Festivals in Northeastern India," *Worldviews* 24, no. 3 (2020): 245–84; Brenda Dobia, "Śakti Yātrā—Locating Power, Questioning Desire: A Women's Pilgrimage to the Temple of Kāmākhyā" (PhD diss., University of Western Sydney, 2008); Patricia Dold, "Pilgrimage to Kamakhya through Text and Lived Religion: Some Forms of the Goddess at an Assamese Temple Site," in *Studying Hinduism in Practice*, ed. Hillary P. Rodrigues (New York: Routledge, 2011), 46–61; Hugh B. Urban, "The Womb of Tantra: Goddesses, Tribals, and Kings in Assam," *Journal of Hindu Studies* 4 (2011): 231–47; Loriliai Biernacki, *Renowned Goddess of Desire: Women, Sex, and Speech in Tantra* (New York: Oxford University Press, 2007).

4. "Ambubachi Festival 2017: Indian Television Stars Implore Fans to Visit Nilachal Hill, Assam, for Ambubachi Mela," *India.com*, June 22, 2017, http://www.india.com/buzz/ambubachi-festival-2017-indian-television-stars-implore-fans-to-visit-nilachal-hill-assam-for-ambubachi-mela-2259007/.

5. Interviews with author, June–July 2017 and January–March 2022.

6. Imma Ramos, *Pilgrimage and Politics in Colonial Bengal: The Myth of the Goddess Sati* (London: Routledge, 2017), 9–10. See Peter van der Veer, *Religious Nationalism: Hindus and Muslims in India* (Berkeley: University of California Press, 1994), xii; Christophe Jaffrelot, "The Hindu Nationalist Reinterpretation of Pilgrimage in India: The Limits of Yatra Politics," *Nations and Nationalism* 15, no. 1 (2009): 1–19.

7. Ramos, *Pilgrimage and Politics*, 104–6; Narendra Modi, "Shri Narendra Modi Highlights the Need to Develop Tourism in Spiritual Locales," *NarendraModi.in*, February 13, 2014, https://www.narendramodi.in/shri-narendra-modi-highlights-the-need-to-develop-tourism-in-spiritual-locales-and-support-the-poor-5969; PTI, "Narendra Modi Accuses Centre of Ignoring Pilgrimage Places," *Deccan Chronicle*, February 14, 2014, http://www.deccanchronicle.com/140214/news-politics/article/narendra-modi-accuses-centre-ignoring-pilgrimage-places.

8. PTI, "Religious Tourism Centre to Be Built around Ambubaci Mela and Kamakhya Temple Says Assam CM Sarbananda Sonowal," *Financial Express*, June 22, 2017, http://

www.financialexpress.com/india-news/religious-tourism-centre-to-be-built-around-ambubachi-mela-and-kamakhya-temple-says-assam-cm-sarbananda-sonowal/729948/. See Directorate of Tourism, *Ambubachi Mela* (Guwahati: Directorate of Tourism, 2107); Assam Tourism Development Corporation, *Celebrate the Fertility of Mother Nature: Ambubachi 2017* (Guwahati: Assam Tourism Development Corporation, 2017).

9. Michael Stausberg, *Religion and Tourism: Crossroads, Destinations, and Encounters* (New York: Routledge, 2010); Ellen Badone and Sharon Roseman, eds., *Intersecting Journeys: The Anthropology of Pilgrimage and Tourism* (Champaign: University of Illinois Press, 2004); Colin M. Hall and Hazel Tucker, *Tourism and Postcolonialism: Contested Discourses, Identities, and Representations* (London: Routledge, 2004); David L. Gladstone, *From Pilgrimage to Package Tour: Travel and Tourism in the Third World* (New York: Routledge, 2005); Sabina Magliocco, *The Two Madonnas: The Politics of Festival in a Sardinian Community* (Long Grove, IL: Waveland Press, 2005).

10. See Christina A. Joseph, "Hindu Nationalism, Community Rhetoric and the Impact of Tourism: The 'Divine Dilemma' of Pushkar," in *Raj Rhapsodies: Tourism, Heritage and the Seduction of History*, ed. Carol E. Henderson and Maxine Weisgrau (Aldershot: Ashgate, 2007), 203–19; Sandeva Khajuria and Suvidha Khanna, "Tourism Risks and Crimes at Pilgrimage Destinations: A Case Study of Shri Mata Vaishno Devi," *International Journal of Event Management Research* 8, no. 1 (2014): 77–79; Knut Aukland, "Hindu Pilgrimage and Modern Tourism," in *The Oxford History of Hinduism: Modern Hinduism*, ed. Torkel Brekke (New York: Oxford University Press, 2019), 125–40; Knut A. Jacobsen, *Pilgrimage in the Hindu Tradition: Salvific Space* (London: Routledge, 2012); Abha Chauhan, "Sacred Landscape and Pilgrimage: A Study of Mata Vaishno Devi," in *Holy Places and Pilgrimages: Essays on India*, ed. Rana P. B. Singh (New Delhi: Shubhi Publications, 2011), 103–28.

11. See Urban, "Death, Nationalism, and Sacrifice: Ritual, Violence, Politics, and Tourism in Northeast India," in *Irreverence and the Sacred: Critical Studies in the History of Religions*, ed. Hugh B. Urban and Greg Johnson (New York: Oxford University Press, 2018), 156–84.

12. Pranav Deka, *Nīlācala Kāmākhyā: Her History and Tantra* (Guwahati: Lawyer's Book Stall, 2004), 10; Ronald Bernier, *Himalayan Architecture* (Madison, NJ: Farleigh Dickinson University Press, 1997), 23.

13. See Hugh B. Urban, *The Power of Tantra: Religion, Sexuality, and the Politics of South Asian Studies* (London: I. B. Tauris and Palgrave MacMillan, 2010), 31–50.

14. See Urban, *Power of Tantra*, 51–72.

15. Apffel-Marglin and Jean, "Weaving," 258.

16. It should be noted that Ambuvācī Melā is not mentioned in the key Assamese text the *Kālikā Purāṇa*, which is significant since this text discusses so many other aspects of Kāmākhyā and her worship. This omission suggests that the practice was probably not in place at Kāmākhyā at this time (tenth to twelfth centuries). Later texts such as the *Yoginī Tantra* (seventeenth to eighteenth centuries) obliquely refer to Ambuvācī but seem to place its celebration in the month of Karkaṭa (July–August) rather than Āṣāḍha (June–July) (B. N. Shastri, ed., *Yoginī Tantra* [Delhi: Bhāratīya Vidyā Prakāśana, 1982], 2.6.169). Mishra suggests that the difference in the date may be due to calendrical changes (*Kamakhya*, 52). Other texts such as the *Devībhāgavatapurāṇam* and *Kubjikātantram* do not specify a date.

17. Śrī Kṛṣṇdāsa, *Devībhāgavatapurāṇam*, 9.9.35–37.

18. Śrī Kṛṣṇdāsa, *Devībhāgavatapurāṇam*, 7.38.16–18.

19. Jyotirlāl Dās, ed., *The Kubjikātantram: Mūla Saṃskṛta o Bāṅgānuvāda Sameta* (Calcutta: Navabhārata Publishers, 1978), 7.56–58.

20. For good descriptions of Ambuvācī as practiced today, see Mishra, *Kamakhya*; Apffel-Marglin and Jean, "Weaving"; Irene Majo Garigliano, "The Brahmans of the Kāmākhyā Temple Complex: Customary Rights, Relations with Pilgrims, and Administrative Power" (PhD diss., Istituto Italiano di Studi Orientali, 2015), 194ff.

21. Apffel-Marglin and Jean, "Weaving," 258–59. This sentiment was echoed by numerous devotees and *sādhus* whom I interviewed at the festival in 2017 and 2022.

22. David Dean Shulman, *Tamil Temple Myths: Sacrifice and Divine Marriage in the South Indian Śaiva Tradition* (Princeton, NJ: Princeton University Press, 1980), 347.

23. Frédérique Apffel-Marglin, "Female Sexuality in the Hindu World," in *Immaculate and Powerful: The Female in Sacred Image and Social Reality*, ed. Clarissa W. Atkinson, Constance H. Buchanan, and Margaret R. Miles (Boston, MA: Beacon Press, 1985), 44. See also Narendranath Bhattacharyya, *Indian Puberty Rites* (Delhi: Munshiram Manoharlal, 1980).

24. Śrī Gaṅga Śarmā, *Kamrup Kamakhya* (Guwahati: Bishnu Prakashan, 2002), 23. The period of impurity is also in every household of the temple complex, where widows typically fast on these three days while others "avoid digging of soil, cutting of nails, shaving, washing of daily clothes and physical contact with their spouses" (Mishra, *Kamakhya*, 52).

25. Śrī Gaṅga Śarmā, *Kāmarūpa Kāmākhyā: Itihāsa o Dharmmamūlaka* (Guwahati: Viṣṇu Prakāśa, 2003), 108. As multiple devotees told me during interviews in June 2017 and June 2022, the cloth is believed to be a powerful source of luck, good fortune, and well-being, as well as "a protection against all kinds of dangers" (interviews with author, Guwahati, Assam, June 15–22, 2022).

26. Patricia Dold, "The Mahavidyas at Kamarupa: Dynamics of Transformation in Hinduism," *Religious Studies and Theology* 23, no. 1 (2004): 89–122, at 101.

27. See Urban, *Power of Tantra*, ch. 2.

28. As Janet Chawla notes, the focus here is very much on flow, process, and becoming, in a kind of Deleuzian sense: "What is worshipped at Kamakhya during the mela (fair) is not an image of the goddess, but rather a process—and a female process at that—menstruation. It is believed that during the monsoon rains the creative and nurturing power of the 'menses' of Mother Earth becomes accessible to devotees at this site during Ambubachi" ("Celebrating the Divine Female Principle," *Boloji.com*, September 16, 2002, https://www.boloji.com/articles/6151/celebrating-the-divine-female-principle).

29. Interview with author, Guwahati, Assam, June 27, 2017. See also interviews with female devotees in *Shakti: The Performance of Gender at Kamakhya Assam*, directed by Tracy Wares (2001; Berkeley: Department of Anthropology, University of California, Berkeley): "This place is worshipped for its fecundity, its fertility, the spirit of regeneration. . . . She immediately comes and helps you if call . . . she symbolizes strength. If you worship her with your heart and soul you get a lot of strength. . . . She is your mother, anytime she will help you."

30. Interviews with author, Guwahati, Assam, June 23, 2022.

31. Mishra, *Kamakhya*, 53. See Apffel-Marglin and Jean, "Weaving," 260.

32. Interview in Wares, dir., *Shakti*. As a female *tāntrikā* who called herself Kālī put it in a conversation with me in Guwahati, Assam, on June 23, 2022, "Kāmākhyā is the mother of everything. She is the will and desire that is the source of everything. She flows through the whole universe. If you can tap into that power, she can give all protection, all desires."

33. Interview in Wares, dir., *Shakti*.

34. Interviews with author, Guwahati, Assam, June 21–24, 2017. The naked Nāga was able to support an adult male standing on a staff that was wrapped around his penis.

35. Nārāyaṇ Nāth, interview with author, Guwahati, Assam, June 21, 2017. The female *tāntrikā* Kālī cited above made very similar comments; interview with author, Guwahati, Assam, June 23, 2022.

36. Apffel-Marglin and Jean, "Weaving," 259.

37. On this point, see Hugh B. Urban, *Economics of Ecstasy: Tantra, Secrecy, and Power in Colonial Bengal* (New York: Oxford University Press, 2001), ch. 7.

38. Interviews with author, Guwahati, Assam, June 17, 2022.

39. Sanskrita Bharadwaj, "Snapshots from Guwahati's Ambubachi Mela," *Firstpost*, June 27, 2018, https://www.firstpost.com/living/snapshots-from-guwahatis-ambubachi-mela-a-yearly-festival-marking-the-goddess-kamakhyas-menstrual-cycle-4607531.html.

40. Majo Garigliano, "Brahmans," 200.

41. B. N. Shastri, ed., *Kālikā Purāṇa* (Delhi: Nag Publishers, 1991), 85.79–80; see Urban, "Womb of Tantra."

42. Mukunda Madhava Sharma, *Inscriptions of Ancient Assam* (Guwahati: Gauhati University Press, 1978), 164, 201, 206, 213, 226–27, 236.

43. Chandra Kanta Sarma, *An Early History of Kamarup Kamakhya* (Gauhati: Kalita Art Press, 1998), 16; Nirmal Kumar Bose, *Assam in the Ahom Age 1228–1826* (Calcutta: Sanskrit Pustak Bandhar, 1970), 64.

44. Ramos, *Pilgrimage and Politics*, 59. See Swarupa Gutpa, "Samaj, Jati, and Desh: Reflections on Nationhood in Late Colonial Bengal," *Studies in History* 23, no. 2 (2007): 198.

45. Halirām Phukkan, *Āsām Burañjī* (Guwahati: Mokṣadā Pustakālaya, 1962), 95. See Phukkan, *Kāmākhyā Yātra Paddhati*, British Museum Library, manuscript 14033b3; Jayeeta Sharma, *Empire's Garden: Assam and the Making of India* (Durham, NC: Duke University Press, 2011), 182.

46. Ramos, *Pilgrimage and Politics*, 60–61.

47. See Samkara, *The Monk as Man* (Delhi: Penguin Books, 2011), 79, 86; Debendranath Tagore, *The Autobiography of Maharshi Devendranath Tagore* (London: MacMillan, 1914), 180–83.

48. Nivedita, *The Web of Indian Life* (New York: Longman's, Green and Co., 1904), 241.

49. Nivedita, *The Web of Indian Life*, 237, 240.

50. Van der Veer, *Religious Nationalism*, xii.

51. Diana L. Eck, "India's 'Tīrthas': 'Crossings' in Sacred Geography," *History of Religions* 20, no. 4 (1981): 336.

52. PTI, "Narendra Modi Accuses Centre." See also Ramos, *Pilgrimage and Politics*, 106.

53. Gujarat Tourism, "Akhand Ambaji," *GujaratTourism.com*, accessed April 12, 2023, https://www.gujarattourism.com/content/dam/gujrattourism/images/ebroucher/ambaji_6.pdf.

54. Modi, "Shri Narendra Modi Highlights the Need to Develop Tourism."

55. Ramos, *Pilgrimage and Politics*, 105.

56. Mark Elmore, *Becoming Religious in a Secular Age* (Berkeley: University of California Press, 2016), 213–22; Parvis Ghassem-Fachandi, *Pogrom in Gujarat: Hindu Nationalism and Anti-Muslim Violence in India* (Princeton, NJ: Princeton University Press, 2012), 15–20.

57. Sarbananda Sonowal was chief minister of Assam from 2016 to 2021 and currently serves in Prime Minister Modi's cabinet. Himanta Biswa Sarma served in the Sonowal administration and was in charge of tourism; he is currently the chief minister of Assam.

58. Himanta Biswa Sarma, "Message," in Directorate of Tourism, *Ambubachi Mela*, 2.

59. PTI, "Religious Tourism Centre to Be Built."

60. PTI, "Religious Tourism Centre to Be Built."

61. Sumir Karmakar, "Nilachal Hill Sees Scores of Devotees," *Telegraph*, June 22, 2017, https://www.telegraphindia.com/north-east/nilachal-hill-sees-scores-of-devotees/cid/1434213.

62. PTI, "Religious Tourism Centre to Be Built."

63. "Assam CM Inaugurates Ambubachi Mela," *India Blooms*, June 22, 2016, https://www.indiablooms.com/news-details/N/21734/assam-cm-inaugurates-ambubachi-mela.html.

64. "Ambuvachi Festival 2017," *India.com*, June 22, 2017, https://www.india.com/viral/ambubachi-festival-2017-indian-television-stars-implore-fans-to-visit-nilachal-hill-assam-for-ambubachi-mela-2259007/.

65. "Ambuvachi Festival 2017."

66. Abdul Gani, "Assam Readies for Ambubachi Mela in Kamakhya Temple," *Times of India*, May 17, 2017, https://timesofindia.indiatimes.com/city/guwahati/assam-readies-for-ambubachi-mela-in-kamakhya-temple/articleshow/58713627.cms.

67. Samudra Gupta Kashyap, "Ambubachi Mela: 25 Lakh Visitors, 2000 Volunteers, No Procession by Naga Sanyasis," *Indian Express*, June 21, 2017, http://indianexpress.com/article/india/ambubachi-mela-25-lakh-visitors-2000-volunteers-no-procession-by-naga-sanyasis-4714348/.

68. Kangkan Kalita, "Golden Dome Unveiled at Kamakhya Temple in Guwahati," *Times of India*, November 19, 2020, https://timesofindia.indiatimes.com/city/guwahati/golden-dome-unveiled-at-kamakhya-temple-in-guwahati/articleshow/79310060.cms. See also Vinay Kumar Mishra, "Mukeś Ambānī kar rahe 19 kilo gold kā dān, jānie

kahāṅ lagegā," *Good Returns Hindi*, November 8, 2020, https://hindi.goodreturns.in/news/mukesh-ambani-donated-19-kg-of-gold-to-kamakhya-temple-017429.html.

69. Angana Chakrabarti, "Kamakhya Temple Still Shut, No Ambubachi: Assam Economy Is Hit 'in a Big Way,'" *Print*, June 21, 2020, https://theprint.in/india/kamakhya-temple-still-shut-no-ambubachi-mela-assam-economy-is-hit-in-a-big-big-way/444071/.

70. For a good discussion of the historical background of this dispute from British colonial times up to 2015, see Majo Garigliano, "Brahmans," 254–315. As Majo Garigliano recounts, "I started to sense the enmity between two groups of Kamakhyans regarding the management of the temple complex. . . . Their strongly emotional reactions . . . made it clear that the issue was of utmost relevance to them. . . . [M]any Kamakhyans were . . . personally engaged in supporting their party and therefore mobilized their resources (time, energy, money). . . . I realized that a seventeen-year-old dispute had been going on between the majority of Bardeuris, who made up the Kamakhya Bardeuri Samaj, and a second 'mixed' body, the Kamakhya Debutter Board, which brings together individuals of all castes including some influential Bardeuris" (254–55).

71. Interview with author, January 15, 2022. See Samudra Gupta Kashyap, "As SC Directs the Return of Old Order at Kamakhya, Looking Back, and Ahead," *Indian Express*, July 14, 2015, https://indianexpress.com/article/explained/as-sc-directs-the-return-of-old-order-at-kamakhya-looking-back-and-ahead/.

72. Majo Garigliano, "Brahmans," 341. On the rhetoric of "democracy" used by the Debutter Board, see Majo Garigliano, "Brahmans," 280.

73. Kashyap, "As SC Directs the Return of Old Order at Kamakhya." See also "Bordeuri Samaj Gets Hold of Kamakhya Temple Shrine," *Times of India*, August 7, 2015, https://timesofindia.indiatimes.com/city/guwahati/bordeuri-samaj-gets-hold-of-kamakhya-shrine-property/articleshow/48380912.cms; "Supreme Court Dissolves Kamakhya Debutter Board," *Sentinel*, July 8, 2015, https://www.sentinelassam.com/top-headlines/supreme-court-dissolves-kamakhya-debutter-board/.

74. This feeling was expressed to me by several members of the community in interviews from January 2022 and June 2022.

75. Large signboard inside the sacrificial area at Kāmākhyā Temple, dated December 22, 2021. Similar ads for corporate sponsors such as Star Cement and numerous others can be seen along the main roadway leading to the temple and elsewhere around the hill.

76. Various community members, interviews with author, Guwahati, Assam, January–March 2022 and June 2022.

77. Kalita, "Golden Dome Unveiled." See also Mishra, "Mukeś Ambānī kar rahe 19 kilo gold kā dān."

78. Interview with author, Guwahati, Assam, June 21, 2017.

79. EMI, interview with author, Guwahati, Assam, March 18, 2022.

80. Bandana Sarma, interviews with author, June 24, 2017 and June 22, 2022.

81. Likewise, the back cover of the tourist book for the event reads: "When there is both inner and outer cleanliness, it approaches godliness" (Directorate of Tourism, *Ambubachi Mela*).

82. Kabindra Sarma, interview, in Kangkan Kalita, "Assam: Ambubachi Mela Set to Return This Year," *Times of India*, May 19, 2022, https://timesofindia.indiatimes.com

/city/guwahati/assam-ambubachi-mela-set-to-return-this-year-priests-want-curbs-to-check-covid-return/articleshow/91672130.cms.

83. Interviews with author, various locations, January 2022.

84. Assam Tourism Development Corporation, *Celebrate the Fertility of Mother Nature*, 2.

85. Kashyap, "Ambubachi Mela: 25 Lakh Visitors."

86. Nandi Sarma and Paban Sarma, interviews with author, Guwahati, Assam, January 30–31, 2022.

87. Utpala Bora and others, interviews with author, Guwahati, Assam, January 2022.

88. Wendy Doniger, "God's Body, or the Lingam Made Flesh: Conflicts over the Representation of the Sexual Body of the Hindu God Shiva," *Social Research* 78, no. 2 (2011): 485–508, at 491–92.

89. Doniger, "God's Body," 505.

90. Chetan Bhatt, *Liberation and Purity: Race, Religious Movements, and the Ethics of Postmodernity* (New York: Routledge, 2016), 229.

91. Nitoo Das, *Cyborg Proverbs* (Mumbai: Paperwall Media, 2017).

92. Stausberg, *Religion and Tourism*, 222. See Hall and Tucker, *Tourism and Postcolonialism*; Magliocco, *Two Madonnas*, xiii.

93. On capitalism and desire, see Gilles Deleuze and Félix Guattari, *Anti-Oedipus: Capitalism and Schizophrenia* (Minneapolis: University of Minnesota Press, 1983); Eugene Holland, *Deleuze and Guattari's Anti-Oedipus: Introduction to Schizoanalysis* (New York: Routledge, 1999), 2. "Neoliberalism" has been defined in various ways. In this book, I use David Harvey's definition, which is that neoliberalism is essentially the "commodification of everything." It is an economic model and political ideology that grew out of twentieth-century forms of capitalism and became the dominant system in the US and UK in the 1980s, followed by most of the rest of the world in the 1990s and 2000s (*A Brief History of Neoliberalism* [New York: Oxford University Press, 2007]). On neoliberalism and religion, see Andrea R, Jain, *Peace, Love, Yoga: The Politics of Global Spirituality* (New York: Oxford University Press, 2020); Hugh B. Urban, *Zorba the Buddha: Sexuality, Spirituality, and Capitalism in the Global Osho Movement* (Berkeley: University of California Press, 2016); Jeremy Carrette and Richard King, *Selling Spirituality: The Silent Takeover of Religion* (New York: Routledge 2004).

94. Magliocco, *Two Madonnas*, 1–2.

95. Christophe Jaffrelot, *Hindu Nationalism, a Reader* (Princeton, NJ: Princeton University Press, 2007), 6: "Its motto, 'Hindu, Hindi, Hindustan,' echoed many European nationalisms based on religious identity, a common language, or even racial feeling. All the same, the essential characteristics of Hinduism scarcely lent themselves to such an 'ism' . . . Hinduism has often been described not as a religion but as a 'conglomeration of sects' . . . The development of Hindu nationalism is therefore a modern phenomenon that has developed on the basis of strategies of ideology-building and *despite* the original characteristics of a diverse set of practices clubbed under the rubric of Hinduism." See also Chettan Bhatt, *Hindu Nationalism: Origins, Ideologies, and Modern Mystics* (London: Bloomsbury Academic, 2001).

96. See Daniel Bell, *The Cultural Contradictions of Capitalism* (New York: Basic Books, 1996). The phrase "cultural contradictions of neoliberalism" has been used by others, including Ien Ang, "Beyond the Crisis: Transitioning to a Better World?," *Cultural Studies* 35, nos. 2–3 (2021): 598–615, https://doi.org/10.1080/09502386.2021.1898013.

97. See Harvey, *Brief History of Neoliberalism*; Urban, *Zorba the Buddha*; Jain, *Peace, Love, Yoga.*

CHAPTER SIX

1. Indira Goswami, *The Man from Chinnamasta* (Delhi: Katha, 2006), 182.

2. *Jādūgar,* directed by Prakash Mehra (1989; Mumbai: Eros Entertainment).

3. *Śaitān Tāntrik,* directed by Wajid Sheikh (1999; Mumbai: Gold Mines).

4. See the films *Indiana Jones and the Temple of Doom,* directed by Stephen Spielberg (1984; Hollywood, CA: Paramount Pictures); *Help!,* directed by Richard Lester (1965; London: Walter Shenson Films); *Gunga Din,* directed by George Stevens (1939; Los Angeles, CA: RKO Productions); as well as the following novels: F. E. F. Penny, *The Swami's Curse* (London: Heinemann, 1929); Elizabeth Sharpe, *Secrets of the Kaula Circle* (London: Luzac and Co., 1936).

5. David Gordon White, *Sinister Yogis* (Chicago: University of Chicago Press, 2009).

6. See Hugh B. Urban, *Tantra: Sex, Secrecy, Politics and Power in the Study of Religion* (Berkeley: University of California Press, 2003), and Hugh B. Urban, *The Power of Tantra: Religion, Sexuality, and the Politics of South Asian Studies* (London: I. B. Tauris and Palgrave MacMillan, 2010).

7. See Gowsami, *Man from Chinnamasta.* The *Bhūt-pret-tantra-mantra* series from Manoj Comics includes a number of horror stories, such as "Kabristān kī Ghaṛī" (The cemetery clock), "Post Mortem," and others. On Tantric black magic websites, see Hugh B. Urban, "Dark Webs: Tantra and Black Magic in Cyberspace," *International Journal of Hindu Studies* 26 (2022): 237–52.

8. *Kathānadī,* directed by Bhāskar Hāzarikā (2015; New Delhi: Metanormal Motion Pictures). While *Kathānadī* is not specifically about Tantra, it is filled with magical and supernatural themes drawn from four Assamese folktales that are skillfully woven together. One is the tale of a girl who is tormented and eventually killed by her evil, insane stepmother. A second tale follows a young bride who is married off to a giant snake in hope of receiving magical riches. A third story involves a magical child who emerges from an elephant-apple. And the last is the dark tale of a father who buries his newborn infants alive at the direction of his uncle and later discovers that the babies would each have grown up to kill him.

9. *Khūnī Tāntrik,* directed by Teerat Singh (2001; Shagufta Arts Productions); *Nāṉ Kaṭavuḷ,* directed by Bala (2009; Chennai: Pyramid Saimira Group); *Tantra (Black Magic),* directed by Rajesh Ranshinge (2018–2019; Mumbai: Swastik Productions). See Hugh B. Urban, "Horrifying and Sinister *Tāntriks,*" in *Bollywood Horrors: Religion, Violence and Cinematic Fears in India,* ed. Ellen Goldberg, Aditi Sen, and Brian Collins (New York: Bloomsbury Academic, 2020), 78–93.

10. Mehra, dir., *Jādūgar*; *Gahrāī,* directed by Aruna Desai and Vijay Tendulkar (1980; Bombay: Avikam); *Saṅghaṛṣ,* directed by Tanuja Chandra (1999; Mumbai: Vishesh Films);

Ammoru, directed by Kodi Ramakrishna (1995; New Delhi: MS Arts); *Tārānāth Tāntrik*, directed by Qaushik Mukherjee (2019; Kolkata: Oddjoint Art).

11. Julia Kristeva, *The Powers of Horror: An Essay in Abjection* (New York: Columbia University Press, 1982); Judith Butler, *Bodies That Matter: On the Discursive Limits of Sex* (New York: Routledge, 2011).

12. Vijay Mishra, *Bollywood Cinema: Temples of Desire* (New York: Routledge, 2001), 3–4: "As the major shaper of an emerging pan-Indian popular culture and subjectivity, Bombay Cinema sems to have transcended class and even linguistic difference by emphatically stressing the myths on which the Indian social order survives in spite of changes. The structure of the film is therefore designed to accommodate deep fantasies belonging to an extraordinarily varied group of people, from illiterate workers to sophisticated urbanites."

13. See Douglas Brooks, "Encountering the Hindu 'Other': Tantrism and the Brahmans of South India," *Journal of the American Academy of Religion* 60, no. 3 (1992): 405–36; Urban, *Tantra*, introduction.

14. Gwendolyn Layne, trans., *Kādambarī: A Classic Sanskrit Tale of Magical Transformation* (New York: Garland, 1991), 226.

15. See David Lorenzen, *The Kāpālikas and Kālamukhas: Two Lost Śaivite Sects* (Delhi: Motilal Banarsidass, 1991).

16. Sita Krishna Nambiar, trans., *Prabodhacandrodaya of Kṛṣṇa Miśra* (Delhi: Motilal Banarsidass, 1971), 3.12–13.

17. Wilhelm Halbfass, *India and Europe: An Essay in Understanding* (Albany, NY: SUNY Press, 1988), 339.

18. Bankimcandra Caṭṭopādhyāy, *Kapālakuṇḍalā* (Calcutta: Tipti Publishing, 1966), 87–88.

19. See Hugh B. Urban, "'My Life in a Love Cult': Tantra, Orientalism and Sex Magic in Early Twentieth Century Fiction," in *Fictional Practice: Magic, Narration, and the Power of Imagination*, ed. Bernd-Christian Otto and Dirk Johannsen (Leiden: Brill, 2021), 203–22.

20. Penny, *Swami's Curse*, 48.

21. Goswami, *Man from Chinnamasta*, 182.

22. See Urban, *Tantra*, chs. 2–4.

23. Frederick M. Smith, *The Self Possessed: Deity and Spirit Possession in South Asia* (New York: Columbia University Press, 2006), 363–90.

24. Desai and Tendulkar, dirs., *Gahrāī*.

25. Desai and Tendulkar, dirs., *Gahrāī*.

26. Mehra, dir., *Jādūgar*.

27. See Hugh B. Urban, *Zorba the Buddha: Sexuality, Spirituality, and Capitalism in the Global Osho Movement* (Berkeley: University of California Press, 2016); Tulasi Srinivas, *Winged Faith: Rethinking Globalization and Religious Pluralism through the Sathya Sai Movement* (New York: Columbia University Press, 2010).

28. Mehra, dir., *Jādūgar*.

29. Mehra, dir., *Jādūgar*.

30. William E. Ellison, Christian Lee Novetzke, and Andy Rotman, *Amar Akbar Anthony: Bollywood, Brotherhood and the Nation* (Boston, MA: Harvard University Press, 2016), 3; See also *Amar Akbar Anthony*, directed by Manmohan Desai (1977; Bombay: Manmohan Films); Mihir Bose, *Bollywood: A History* (London: Tempus Publishing Limited, 2006), 279; As Mishra notes, *Amar Akbar Anthony* portrays three brothers "who grow up in different religions but can come together as one in a secular India," while still not challenging the dominance of the Hindu majority: "The secular can be celebrated provided that (Hindu) dharma remains intact" (*Bollywood Cinema*, 176–77).

31. See Richard King, *Orientalism and Religion: Postcolonial Theory, India, and the Mystic East* (New York: Routledge, 1999), 118–42; Halbfass, *India and Europe*. As Halbfass summarizes this theme in Vivekānanda's version of Neo-Hinduism: "The idea and practice of toleration and brotherhood is India's gift to the world. . . . As Vivekānanda sees it, 'the world is waiting for this grand idea of universal toleration' and spirituality to be passed on by India" (231).

32. *The Silence of the Lambs*, directed by Jonathan Demme (1991; Los Angeles, CA: Orion Pictures).

33. See Urban, *Tantra*, ch. 1.

34. Chandra, dir., *Saṅgharṣ*.

35. Chandra, dir., *Saṅgharṣ*.

36. Chandra, dir., *Saṅgharṣ*.

37. Urban, *Power of Tantra*, 94–97.

38. B. N. Shastri, ed., *Yoginī Tantra* (Delhi: Bhāratīya Vidyā Prakāśana, 1982), 2.7.163–66. See also Urban, *Power of Tantra*, 215.

39. See Stevens, dir., *Gunga Din*; Lester, dir., *Help!*; Spielberg, dir., *Indiana Jones and the Temple of Doom*.

40. Ramakrishna, dir., *Ammoru*.

41. Tārādās Bandyopādhyāy, *Tārānāth Tāntrik* (Kolkata: Mitra o Ghoś, 2014).

42. Shamik Dasgupta, *Taranath Tantrik: City of Sorrows* (Kolkata: Speech Bubble, 2015).

43. *Tārānāth Tāntrik*, season 1, episode 1, directed by Qaushiq Mukherjee, January 18, 2019, Hoichoi TV, https://www.hoichoi.tv/films/title/taranath-tantrik.

44. Bandyopādhyāy, *Tārānāth Tāntrik*, 1–13; *Tārānāth Tāntrik*, season 1, episode 5, directed by Qaushiq Mukherjee, January 18, 2019, Hoichoi TV, https://www.hoichoi.tv/films/title/betal.

45. *Tārānāth Tāntrik*, season 1, episode 5.

46. Sumit Menāriyā, *Tāśrī* (Bhopal, India: Ekatra, 2021).

47. In his comments during the early development of the proposed series, Menāriyā himself cited *Westworld* and *Inception* as key influences (Sumit Menāriyā, "*Tashree*: Author's View and Response on Storyworld," unpublished PDF on file with author, 2020).

48. Consultancy agreement, Lore Works, Mumbai, India, June 13, 2020.

49. Menāriyā, *Tāśrī*, ch. 1. As Menāriyā commented on his representation of Tantra in the novel, "There is a reason why Tantra/Spiritual part was not introduced at initial level of the novel. 90% of readers do not have idea about these concepts. People consider these

concepts so complex that serving these at initial level would result in readers leaving the story. Tantra/Spirituality is not some sweet which can be displayed at show rack rather it is medicine which should be given carefully to readers" ("*Tashree*: Author's View").

50. Sameer Pitalwalla, "Tashree Original Series Bible," unpublished PDF on file with author, 2020.

51. Saurav Mahopatra and Aditya Bhattacharya, "Tashree: Bible for an Original Series," unpublished PDF on file with author , 2021.

52. Pitalwalla, "Tashree Original Series Bible."

53. Bharati used the phrase "pizza effect" to describe the complex feedback loop between Indian and Western ideas of yoga and Tantra; just as pizza began as a simple Italian dish, then was radically transformed by Americans, and was finally reimported to Italy, so too Hindu traditions have been exported to the United States, radically transformed and "Americanized," and then reimported to India: "Western things are not desirable in the Indian culture universe; but neither are the themes and the works of the tradition which is thought reactionary and obsolete. Yet, one and all, they gather momentum and respect through a process of re-enculturation. I have coined the facetious-sounding term 'pizza-effect' for this pervasive pattern" (Bharati, "The Hindu Renaissance and Its Apologetic Patterns," *Journal of Asian Studies* 29, no. 2 [1970]: 267–87; see also Urban, *Tantra*, 204).

54. Mahopatra and Bhattacharya, "Tashree: Bible for an Original Series."

55. Kristeva, *Powers of Horror*, 3; see Butler, *Bodies That Matter*.

56. Kristeva, *Powers of Horror*, 1.

57. Brooks, "Encountering the Hindu 'Other.'"

58. See Urban, *Tantra*; King, *Orientalism and Religion*.

59. See Halbfass, *India and Europe*; King, *Orientalism and Religion*.

60. See Urban, *Tantra*, chs. 1–3.

61. Vivekānanda, *The Complete Works of Swami Vivekananda* (Calcutta: Advaita Ashram, 1984), 6:226: "From central Asia the cruel barbarians came, having established their terrible practices in their own land; in order to attract the ignorant barbarians the true path took on the form of the Tantras and Mantras; and that is why, when they became misunderstood, weakened and corrupt . . . they resulted in the terrible abominations of Vamachara."

62. Vivekānanda, *Complete Works of Swami Vivekananda*, 7:174.

63. Vivekānanda, *Complete Works of Swami Vivekananda*, 3:340.

64. In the sense, the appearance of the "sinister *tāntrik*" is perhaps an example of what Vijay Mishra calls the sort of "regulated transgression" that is allowed in Indian film, which ultimately serves to uphold the *dharmik* order (Mishra, *Bollywood Cinema*, 33).

CONCLUSIONS

1. Kisori Mohan Ganguli, trans., *Mahābhārata, Volume 8: Śānti Parva, Part I* (Delhi: Munshiram Manoharlal, 1982), 368.

2. On the insider-outsider debate, see Russell T. McCutcheon, ed., *The Insider/Outsider Problem in the Study of Religion: A Reader* (New York: Continuum, 1999); George D.

Chryssides and Stephen E. Gregg, eds., *The Insider/Outsider Debate: New Perspectives* (London: Equinox, 2019).

3. On neoliberalism and religion, see Andrea R. Jain, *Peace, Love, Yoga: The Politics of Global Spirituality* (New York: Oxford University Press, 2020); Jeremy Carrette and Richard King, *Selling Spirituality: The Silent Takeover of Religion* (New York: Routledge 2004); Hugh B. Urban, *Zorba the Buddha: Sexuality, Spirituality, and Capitalism in the Global Osho Movement* (Berkeley: University of California Press, 2016). As mentioned in the introduction, I follow David Harvey by defining neoliberalism as a late capitalist economic system characterized by the "commodification of everything," including religious practices. See Harvey, *A Brief History of Neoliberalism* (New York: Oxford University Press, 2007).

On Tantra and globalization, see Urban, *Zorba the Buddha*; Hugh B. Urban, *Tantra: Sex, Secrecy, Politics and Power in the Study of Religion* (Berkeley: University of California Press, 2003); Julian Strube, *Global Tantra: Religion, Science and Nationalism in Colonial Modernity* (New York: Oxford University Press, 2022).

4. See Alexis Sanderson, "Purity and Power among the Brahmins of Kashmir," in *The Category of the Person: Anthropology, Philosophy, History*, ed. Michael Carrithers, Steven Collins, and Steven Lukes (Cambridge: Cambridge University Press, 1985), 190–216.

5. See Jain, *Peace, Love, Yoga*; Carrette and King, *Selling Spirituality*; Urban, *Zorba the Buddha.*

6. See Hugh B. Urban, "Dark Webs: Tantra and Black Magic in Cyberspace," *International Journal of Hindu Studies* 26 (2002): 237–52; Urban, "Horrifying and Sinister *Tāntriks*," in *Bollywood Horrors: Religion, Violence and Cinematic Fears in India*, ed. Ellen Goldberg, Aditi Sen, and Brian Collins (New York: Bloomsbury Academic, 2020), 78–93.

7. On Weber and the idea of disenchantment, see H. H. Gerth and C. Wright Mills, *From Max Weber: Essays in Sociology* (New York: Oxford University Press, 1958), 246–47; Jason Josephson-Storm, *The Myth of Disenchantment: Magic, Modernity, and the Birth of the Human Sciences* (Chicago: University of Chicago Press, 2017).

8. On this point, see Josephson-Storm, *Myth of Disenchantment*; Urban, *Zorba the Buddha*, conclusion. On the concept of "enchanted capitalism," see also Steve Penfold, *A Mile of Make-Believe: A History of the Eaton's Santa Claus Parade* (Toronto: University of Toronto Press, 2018), 181–88.

9. On the debates over American scholarship on South Asian religions, see Hugh B. Urban, *The Power of Tantra: Religion, Sexuality, and the Politics of South Asian Studies* (London: I. B. Tauris and Palgrave MacMillan, 2010), introduction. Many of these debates were triggered by Jeffrey J. Kripal's controversial book *Kālī's Child: The Mystical and the Erotic in the Life and Teachings of Ramakrishna* (Chicago: University of Chicago Press, 1995), and then by a critical piece by Rajiv Malhotra, "The Wendy's Child Syndrome" (first published independently online in 2002; later republished in digital book form, 2021), https://www.rajivmalhotra.com/books/academic-hinduphobia/table-of-contents. Many other American scholars such as Wendy Doniger, David Gordon White, Paul Courtright, and others were drawn into the debate, which led to calls to ban Doniger's book *The Hindus* in India. See Doniger, "Banned in Bangalore," *New York Times*, March 5, 2014, https://www.nytimes.com/2014/03/06/opinion/banned-in-bangalore.html.

10. Anna Tsing, *Mushroom at the End of the World: On the Possibility of Life in Capitalist Ruins* (Princeton, NJ: Princeton University Press, 2017), 28–29. Tsing offers the hope that this collaborative model might serve as an alternative to the highly privatized, commodified, competitive model that dominates most scholarship today: "What if we imagined intellectual life as a peasant woodland, a source of many useful products emerging in unintentional design? . . . To encourage the unknown potential of scholarly advances—like the unexpected bounty of a nest of mushrooms—requires sustaining the common work of the intellectual woodland" (*Mushroom at the End of the World*, 286).

11. See Bruce Lincoln, "Theses on Method," *Method and Theory in the Study of Religion* 8, no. 3 (1996): 225–27.

12. Saba Mahmood, *The Politics of Piety: The Islamic Revival and the Feminist Subject* (Princeton, NJ: Princeton University Press, 2011); see Saba Mahmood, "Feminist Theory, Embodiment, and the Docile Agent: Some Reflections on the Egyptian Islamic Revival," *Cultural Anthropology* 16, no. 2 (2001): 202–36, at 203. As she put it, the goal is to "make material speak back to normative liberal assumptions about freedom and agency."

13. Webb Keane, "Saba Mahmood and the Paradoxes of Self-Parochialization," *Critical Times* 2, no. 1 (2019): 3–4. See Mahmood, "Feminist Theory," 223: "A politically responsible practice . . . departs not from a position of certainty but one of risk, critical engagement, and a willingness to reevaluate one's views in light of the Others."

14. Gilles Deleuze and Félix Guattari briefly compare their notion of desire in its "destratified," nonhierarchical state of flow to the Chinese concept of Tao (*A Thousand Plateaus: Capitalism and Schizophrenia* [Minneapolis: University of Minnesota Press, 1987], 157). See also Jihai Gao, "Deleuze's Conception of Desire," *Deleuze and Guattari Studies* 7, no. 3 (2103): 406; Ronald Bogue, Hanping Chiu, and Yu-lin Lee, eds., *Deleuze and Asia* (Newcastle upon Tyne, UK: Cambridge Scholars Publishing, 2014).

15. See Hannah Stark, *Feminist Theory after Deleuze* (New York: Bloomsbury Academic, 2016), 4: "Instead of positioning desire as a lack, they theorize it as a prepersonal force that is everywhere and productive of connections between things. Desire is anarchic . . . causing ruptures in organized systems. Desire is what animates the connections between things." See also Philip Goodchild, *Deleuze and Guattari: An Introduction to the Politics of Desire* (London: Sage, 1996), 5: "Desire naturally seeks multiplicity and creation . . . social formations come about that prevent desire's auto-production."

16. See William Deal and Tim Beal, *Theory for Religious Studies* (New York: Routledge, 2004), 63.

17. On desire and capital in Deleuze's work, see Eugene Holland, *Deleuze and Guattari's Anti-Oedipus: Introduction to Schizoanalysis* (New York: Routledge, 1999), 2.

18. Rosi Braidotti, "Discontinuous Becomings: Deleuze on the Becoming-Woman of Philosophy," *Journal of the British Journal for Phenomenology* 24, no. 1 (1993): 44–55, at 48 and 52.

19. Braidotti, "Discontinuous Becomings," 48. For critiques of Deleuze's idea of "becoming Woman," see Stark, *Feminist Theory after Deleuze*, 3. As Janice Richardson argues, the notion of "becoming Woman" seems to imply a rather stereotypical view of "Woman" as the sex associated with change and disintegration (in contrast to a more

stable, bounded notion of "Man"): "In using the term 'woman' to signify a process of becoming deterritorialized, they fit too easily into a tradition which views women as subject to dissolution and disintegration, unable to defend the boundaries of our bodies or the state" ("'Woman' in the Work of Irigaray and Deleuze," *Law and Critique* 9, no. 1 [1998]: 109).

20. See Urban, *Power of Tantra*, chs. 2, 4, and 5; Loriliai Biernacki, *Renowned Goddess of Desire: Women, Sex, and Speech in Tantra* (New York: Oxford University Press, 2007).

21. On this point, see Hugh B. Urban, "Desire, Blood, and Power: Georges Bataille and the Study of Hindu Tantra in Northeast India," in *Negative Ecstasies: Georges Bataille and the Study of Religion*, ed. Jeremy Biles and Kent L. Brintnall (New York: Fordham University Press, 2015), 68–80.

22. See Urban, *Power of Tantra*, ch. 5. Some scholars have read these traditions through a more sympathetic feminist lens; see Biernacki, *Renowned Goddess*; Frédérique Apffel-Marglin and Julia A. Jean, "Weaving the Body and the Cosmos: Two Menstrual Festivals in Northeastern India," *Worldviews* 24, no. 3 (2020): 245–84.

23. See French feminist theorists such as Luce Irigarary, *Ce sexe qui n'est pas un* (Paris: Minuit, 1977) and *Speculum of the Other Woman* (Ithaca, NY: Cornell University Press, 1985). On the women's spirituality and goddess movements, see Carol Christ, *Rebirth of the Goddess: Finding Meaning in Feminist Spirituality* (New York: Routledge, 1998); Mary Daly, *Gynecology: The Metaethics of Radical Spirituality* (Boston, MA: Beacon, 1978); Starhawk, *The Spiral Dance: A Rebirth of the Ancient Goddess in the Twentieth Century* (New York: HarperOne, 1999); Jone Salomonsen, *Enchanted Feminism: The Reclaiming Witches of San Francisco* (New York: Routledge, 2002).

24. Apffel-Marglin and Jean, "Weaving," 279. See also Brenda Dobia, "Approaching the Hindu Goddess of Desire," *Feminist Theology* 16, no. 1 (2007): 61–78; Janet Chawla, "Celebrating the Divine Female Principle," *Boloji.com*, September 16, 2002, https://www.boloji.com/articles/6151/celebrating-the-divine-female-principle: "The Ambubachi worship . . . may reveal an important contribution to global cultural representation of the female body. Kamakhya seems to question both the dominant religious legacies of the pollution inherent in female bodily processes. . . . Ambubachi Mela provides a sacred space for empowering images of the female body—a space where the maternal and erotic aspects of women's lives are encoded and embraced as divine."

25. On this point, see ch. 1 above; E. Sundari Johansen Hurwitt, "The Voracious Virgin: The Concept and Worship of Kumārī in Kaula Tantrism" (PhD diss., California Institute of Integral Studies, 2019), 433–40; Urban, *Power of Tantra*, ch. 5.

26. See for example, Judith Butler, *Gender Trouble: Feminism and the Subversion of Identity* (New York: Routledge, 1990); Diana Fuss, *Essentially Speaking: Feminism, Nature, and Difference* (New York: Routledge, 1989)

27. On this point, see Urban, *Power of Tantra*, ch. 5. As Biernacki also points out, Tantric texts from northeast India often use the term *yoni* to refer to the female partner herself, thereby essentially identifying her with the sexual organ (*Renowned Goddess*, 230n2).

28. Keane, "Saba Mahmood," 3–4; my italics. See Mahmood, "Feminist Theory," 225: "In order for us to judge, in a morally and politically informed way, even those

practices we consider objectionable, it is important to take into consideration the desires, motivations, commitments, and aspirations of the people to whom these practices are important."

29. Jonathan Z. Smith, *Imagining Religion: From Babylon to Jonestown* (Chicago: University of Chicago Press, 1988), xi.

30. Leonard Primiano, "Vernacular Religion and the Search for Method in Religious Folklore," *Journal of Western Folklore* 54, no. 1 (1995): 44; Leonard Primiano, "Afterword," in *Vernacular Religion in Everyday Life*, ed. Marion Bowman and Ülo Valk (New York: Routledge, 2014), 382–94. See also Hugh B. Urban, "Talking to the Other Side: Spiritualism as 'Vernacular Religion' in Central Ohio," in *Living Folk Religions*, ed. Sravana Borkataky-Varma and Aaron Ullrey (New York: Routledge, forthcoming).

31. See Robert Orsi, *The Madonna of 115th Street: Faith and Community in Italian Harlem, 1880–1950* (New Haven, CT: Yale University Press, 2010); Robert Orsi, *Between Heaven and Earth: The Religious Worlds People Make and the Scholars Who Study Them* (Princeton, NJ: Princeton University Press, 2006); Sabina Magliocco, *The Two Madonnas: The Politics of Festival in a Sardinian Community* (Long Grove, IL: Waveland Press, 2005).

32. See, for example, Stanley Tambiah, *The Buddhist Saints of the Forest and the Cult of Amulets* (Cambridge: Cambridge University Press, 1984); John Strong, *The Legend and Cult of Upagupta* (Princeton, NJ: Princeton University Press, 2005); Jeff Wilson, *Mourning the Unborn Dead: A Buddhist Ritual Comes to America* (New York: Oxford University Press, 2009).

33. Smith, *Imagining Religion*, 18.

ACKNOWLEDGMENTS AND ENTANGLEMENTS

1. Anna Tsing, *The Mushroom at the End of the World: On the Possibility of Life in Capitalist Ruins* (Princeton, NJ: Princeton University Press, 2017), viii. On mycelial entanglements and nodes, see Hugh B. Urban, *Zorba the Buddha: Sex, Spirituality and Capitalism in the Global Osho Movement* (Berkeley, CA: University of California Press, 2016).

2. On the etymology of *tantra*, see Hugh B. Urban, *Tantra: Sex, Secrecy, Politics and Power in the Study of Religion* (Berkeley, CA: University of California Press, 2003), 1–43; André Padoux, *The Hindu Tantric World: An Overview* (Chicago: University of Chicago Press, 2017).

3. On this point, see Hugh B. Urban, *The Power of Tantra: Religion, Sexuality, and the Politics of South Asian Studies* (New York: Palgrave MacMillan, 2010).

Selected Bibliography

WORKS IN ASSAMESE, BANGLA, HINDI, AND SANSKRIT

Āgamavāgīśa, Kṛṣṇānanda. *Bṛhat-Tantrasāra*. Edited by Śrīrasikamohana Caṭṭopādhyāya. Calcutta: Navabhārata Publishers, 1996.

Bagchi, Prabodh Chandra, ed. *Kaulajñānanirṇaya and Some Minor Texts of the School of Matsyendranātha*. Calcutta: Metropolitan Printing and Publishing House, 1934.

Bandyopādhyāy, Tārādās. *Tārānāth Tāntrik*. Kolkata: Mitra o Ghoś, 2014.

Barua, B. K., and S. N. Sharma, eds. *Manasā Kāvya*. Gauhati, 1951.

Bhāgavatī, Śrī Rādhikmohan. "Yajña: Iyār Tātparya." In *Souvenir Viswa Shanti Devi Yajña*, edited by Sri Jadu Nath Sarma, Rajib Sarma, and Sri Naba Kanta Sarma, 21–45. Guwahati: Viswa Shanti Devi Yajña Committee, 2014.

Bhaṭṭācārya, Debendranāth. *Asamat Śaktipūjā*. Guwahati: Bāṇī Prakāśa, 1977.

Brahmānandagiri. *Śāktānandataraṅgiṇī*. Varanasi: Sampurnanand Sanskrit University, 1987.

Cakravartī, Śrīmaṇṭa. *Ādi o āsal Kāmākṣyā Tantrasār*. Calcutta: Sacdev Prakāśan, n.d.

Caṭṭopādhyāy, Bankimcandra. *Kapālakuṇḍalā*. Calcutta: Tipti Publishing, 1966.

Dās, Jyotirlāl, ed. *Kāmākhyātantram: mūla, ṭīkā o baṅgānubāda sameta*. Calcutta: Navabhārata Publishers, 1978.

———, ed. *The Kubjikātantram: Mūla Saṃskṛta o Bāṅgānuvāda Sameta*. Calcutta: Navabhārata Publishers, 1978.

Datta, Parimla Kumar, ed. *Kāmākhyātantra and the Mysterious History of Kāmarūpa*. Kolkata: Punthi Pustak 2017.

Deva Śarmā, Adhyapaka Śrī Umākānta. "Asame Tantrasādhanā." In *Souvenir Viswa Shanti Devi Yajña*, edited by Sri Jadu Nath Sarma, Rajib Sarma, and Sri Naba Kanta Sarma, 27–30. Guwahati: Viswa Shanti Devi Yajña Committee, 2014.

Dvija, Bhūṣaṇa. *Mahāpuruṣa Śaṅkaradeva*. Jorhat, India: Durgādhar Barkataki, 1925.

Eggeling, Julius, ed. *Śatapatha Brāhmaṇa*. Delhi: Motilal Banarsidass, 1963.

Goudriaan, Teun, and J. A. Schoterman, eds. *Kubjikāmatatantra: Kulālikāmnāya Version*. Leiden: Brill, 1988.

Kalam Mantra. Manuscript ACC no. MMAY/LOK/12. Mayong Central Museum, Mayong, Assam.

Kāmarūpīyanibandhatantra. Manuscript 1087 E 3700. British Library Indian Office Collection, London.

Kṣemarāja Śrī Kṛṣṇdāsa. *Devībhāgavatapurāṇam*. Delhi: Nag Publishers, 1986.

Lakṣmaṇadeśikendra. *Śāradātilakatantram*. Delhi: Caukhambā Saṃskṛta Pratiṣṭhāna, 2001.

Mankar and Durgābar. *Manasā-kāvya*. Edited by Kālirām Medhi. Guwahati: Dattabaruwa, 1964.

Mantra. Manuscript ACC no. MMAY/LOK/09. Mayong Central Museum, Mayong, Assam.

Menāriyā, Sumit. *Tāśrī*. Bhopal, India: Ekatra, 2021.

Miśra, Śrī Viveka Kumāra. "Vaidika Yajña." In *Souvenir Viswa Shanti Devi Yajña*, edited by Sri Jadu Nath Sarma, Rajib Sarma, and Sri Naba Kanta Sarma, 37–45. Guwahati: Viswa Shanti Devi Yajña Committee, 2014.

Mohinī. Manuscript ACC no. MMAY/LOK/14. Mayong Central Museum, Mayong, Assam.

Nārāyaṇadeva. *Padmapurāṇa: Manasā-Maṅgala*. Edited by Tamonash Chandra Das Gupta. Calcutta: University of Calcutta Press, 1947.

Nāth, Rameś Candra. "Māyaṅgar Bej āru Bejāli: Ji Dekhilo Ji Śunilo." In *Kālśilā: Smṛtigrantha*, edited by Utpal Nāth, 33–38. Jagirod, India: Abhinab Offset Printers, 2010.

Nāth, Utpal. "Māyaṅgar Jāduvidyār Sādhanā: Vijñān, Viśvās āru Andhviśvās." In *Kālśilā: Smṛtigrantha*, edited by Utpal Nāth, 120–26. Jagirod, India: Abhinab Offset Printers, 2010.

———, ed. *Māyār Rājya Māyaṅgar Kāhinī*. Mayong, India: Studio Nath Brothers, 2013.

———. *Mohanīya Māyaṅg*. Mayong, India: Office of the Range Officer, Pobitora Wildlife Sanctuary, 2011.

———, ed., *Tantram*. Rajamayong, India: Mayang Anchalik College, 2017.

Nigamānanda, Svāmī. *Tāntrik Guru, vā Tantra o Sādhana Padhati*. Calcutta: Sāradā Press, 1991 (1911).

Phukkan, Halirām. *Āsām Burañjī*. Guwahati: Mokṣadā Pustakālaya, 1962.

———. *Kāmākhyā Yātra Paddhati*. Manuscript 14033b3. British Library Indian Office Collection, London.

Puṇyānandanātha. *Kāmakalāvilāsa*. Edited and translated by Arthur Avalon. Madras: Ganesh and Co., 1961.

Rābhā, R. *Rābhā Jana Jāt*. Jorhat, India: Assam Sāhitya Sabhā, 1974.

Rāy, Pradīp Kumār, ed. *Muṇḍamālātantram*. Varanasi: Prācya Prakāśana, 2010.

Śaṅkaradeva, Śrīmanta. *Kīrtana Ghoṣā*. Nagaon, India: Śrīmanta Śaṅkaradeva Saṅgha, 2010.

Sarma, K. N., ed. *Kāmaratna Tantra*. Guwahati: Lawyer's Book Stall, 1998.

Śarmā, Muktināth. "Tantra." In *Souvenir Viswa Shanti Devi Yajña*, edited by Sri Jadu Nath Sarma, Rajib Sarma, and Sri Naba Kanta Sarma, 4–12. Guwahati: Viswa Shanti Devi Yajña Committee, 2014.

Śarmā, Puṇyaśīla, ed. *Gupta-sādhana Tantra*. Prayāga: Kalyāṇa Mandir, 1970.

Śarmā, Rājīv. *Śrī Śrī Kāmākhyā Devī Kāmarūpar Māhātmya: Saral Asamīyā Bhāvārthar Saite*. Guwahati: Assam Book Hive, 2011.

Śarmā, Śrī Gaṅga. *Kāmarūpa Kāmākhyā: Itihāsa o Dharmmamūlaka*. Guwahati: Viṣṇu Prakāśa, 2003.

Śarmādalai, Harināth. *Asamat Śakti-Sādhanā āru Śākta-Sāhitya*. Nalbari, India: Padmapriya Library, 1998.

Śāstrī, M. "Dharma āru darśan." In *Asamīya Jātir Itivṛtta*, edited by G. Sarma. Jorhat, India: Assam Sāhitya Sabhā, 1977.

Śāstrī, Tāntrikācārya Śrībhairava. *Kāmarūpī Tantrasāra*. Kolkata: Rajendra Library, n.d.

———. *Siddha Śābarar Tantra-Mantra*. Kolkata: Sajal Publishers, n.d.

Śāstrī, Viśvanārāyaṇa, ed. *Kāmākhyā Tantra*. Varanasi: Bhāratīya Vidyā Prakāśana, 1990.

Schoterman, J. A., ed. *Yoni Tantra*. Delhi: Manohar, 1980.

Shastri, B. N., ed. *Kālikā Purāṇa*. Delhi: Nag Publishers, 1991.

———, ed. *Yoginī Tantra*. Delhi: Bhāratīya Vidyā Prakāśana, 1982.

Snellgrove, David, ed. *The Hevajra Tantra: A Critical Study*. London: Oxford University Press, 1959.

Śrī Kṣudirām. *Kāmākṣā Tantra Sāra Ādi o Prācīn*. Kolkata: Sajal Pustakālay, 2008.

Śrībrahmānanda, Tāntrikācārya. *Sarvva Manaskāmanā Siddha Pustak*. Calcutta: Rajendra Library, n.d.

Śrīvasiṣṭha, ed. *Ādi o Āsal Kāmarūp Kāmākṣyā Tantramantra Sār*. Calcutta: Sajal Pustakālay, n.d.

Tantrajyotiṣaśāstrī, Ratneśvara, ed. *Kāmākṣyā Tantrasār*. Calcutta: Orient Library, n.d.

Tāntrik Bahal, Tantra Guru. *Kāmarūpa Kāmākhyā kā Tāntrik Rahasya*. Delhi: Rājā Pocket Books, 2017.

Upādhyāya, Śītalā Prasāda, ed. *Tripurārṇava Tantra*. Varanasi: Sampurnanand Sanskrit University, 1992.

Vidyāratna, Tārānātha, ed. *Kulārṇava Tantra*. Delhi: Motilal Banarsidass, 1975.

FILMS IN ASSAMESE, BANGLA, HINDI, AND TELEGU

Borpujari, Utpal, dir. *Mayong: Myth/Reality*. 2013; Guwahati: Darpan Cine Production.

B.R.A.N.D. Production. *Mayong*. 2016; Guwahati: B.R.A.N.D. Production.

Chandra, Tanuja, dir. *Sangharṣ*. 1999; Mumbai: Vishesh Films.

Desai, Aruna, and Vijay Tendulkar, dirs. *Gahrāī*. 1980; Bombay: Avikam.

Desai, Manmohan, dir. *Amar Akbar Anthony*. 1977; Bombay: Manmohan Films.

Hāzarikā, Bhāskar, dir. *Kathānadī*. 2015; New Delhi: Metanormal Motion Pictures.

Hāzarikā, Prabīn, dir. *Hāte mudrā mukhe pada mayer sadṛśa nāc*. 2012; Gauhati, India: Krisangi Creation.

Mehra, Prakash, dir. *Jādūgar*. 1989; Mumbai: Eros Entertainment.

Mukherjee, Qaushik, dir. *Tārānāth Tāntrik*. 2019; Kolkata: Oddjoint Art.

Ramakrishna, Kodi, dir. *Ammoru*. 1995; New Delhi: MS Arts.

Ranshinge, Rajesh, dir. *Tantra (Black Magic)*. 2018–2019; Mumbai: Swastik Productions.

Sheikh, Wajid, dir. *Śaitān Tāntrik*. 1999; Mumbai: Gold Mines.

Sikandar, dir. *Māyaṅgare Bej*. 2016; Guwahati.

TEXTS IN ENGLISH, FRENCH, GERMAN, AND ITALIAN

Acri, Andrea, and Paolo E. Rosati, eds. *Tantra, Magic and Vernacular Religions in Monsoon Asia: Texts, Practices, and Practitioners from the Margins*. London: Routledge, 2022.

Apffel-Marglin, Frédérique. "Female Sexuality in the Hindu World." In *Immaculate and Powerful: The Female in Sacred and Social Reality*, edited by Clarissa W. Atkinson, Constance H. Buchanan, and Margaret R. Miles, 39–60. Boston, MA: Beacon Press, 1985.

———. *Wives of the God-King: The Rituals of the Devadasis of Puri*. New York: Oxford University Press, 1985.

Apffel-Marglin, Frédérique, and Julia A. Jean. "Weaving the Body and the Cosmos: Two Menstrual Festivals in Northeastern India." *Worldviews* 24, no. 3 (2020): 245–84.

Appadurai, Arjun. *Modernity at Large: Cultural Dimensions of Globalization*. Minneapolis: University of Minnesota Press, 1996.

Avalon, Arthur, trans. *The Tantra of the Great Liberation (Mahānirvāṇa Tantra)*. New York: Dover, 1972.

Bagchi, Subhendugopal. *Eminent Indian Śākta Centres in Eastern India: An Interdisciplinary Study in the Background of the Pīṭhas of Kālīghāṭa, Vakreśvara and Kāmākhyā*. Calcutta: Punthi Pustak, 1980.

Banerji, S. C. *A Companion to Tantra*. New Delhi: Abhinav Publications, 2007.

Barthakuria, Apurba Chandra. *The Tantric Religion of India: An Insight into Assam's Tantra Literature*. Kolkata: Punthi Pustak, 2009.

Bataille, Georges. *The Accursed Share*. Vol. 2. New York: Zone Books, 1999.

———. "Attraction and Repulsion." In *The College of Sociology (1937–39)*, edited by Denis Hollier, 103–12. Minneapolis: University of Minnesota Press, 1988.

Bharati, Agehananda. "The Hindu Renaissance and Its Apologetic Patterns." *Journal of Asian Studies* 29, no. 2 (1970): 267–287.

———. *The Ochre Robe: An Autobiography*. New York: Ross-Erikson, 1980.

Bhatt, Chetan. *Liberation and Purity: Race, Religious Movements, and the Ethics of Postmodernity*. New York: Routledge, 2016.

Bhattacharjee, Kishore. "Constructing Community and Kinship through Epic Singing." *Indian Folklore Research Journal* 6 (2006): 1–12.

Biardeau, Madeleine. "Devi: The Goddess in India." In *Asian Mythologies*, edited by Yves Bonnefoy, 95–98. Chicago: University of Chicago Press, 1993.

———. *Hinduism: The Anthropology of a Civilization*. Paris: Flammarion, 1981.

Biardeau, Madeleine, and Charles Malamoud. *Le sacrifice dans l'Inde ancienne*. Paris: Presses universitaires de France, 1976.

Biernacki, Loriliai. *Renowned Goddess of Desire: Women, Sex, and Speech in Tantra*. New York: Oxford University Press, 2007.

Boaz, Danielle N. "The 'Abhorrent' Practice of Animal Sacrifice and Religious Discrimination in the Global South." *Religions* 10, no. 3 (2019): 1–20.

Borah, Lekha, and Madhushree Das. "Witch-Hunting in Assam: Myth or Reality?" *Space and Culture India* 7, no. 3 (2019): 99–114.

Borkataky-Varma, Sravana. "The Dead Speak: A Case Study from the Tiwa Tribe Highlighting the Hybrid World of Śākta Tantra in Assam." *Religions* 8, no. 221 (2017): 1–15.

———. "In the Tea Light of Tantra: An Ethnographic Study of *Kuṇḍalinī* Rising in Women's Bodies." PhD diss., Rice University, 2016. https://www.academia.edu/9047767/In_the_Tea_Light_of_Tantra_an_Ethnographic_Study_of_Ku%E1%B9%87%E1%B8%8Dalin%C4%AB_Rising_in_Women_s_Bodies.

———. "Red: An Ethnographic Study of Cross-Pollination between the Vedic and the Tantric." *International Journal of Hindu Studies* 23, no. 2 (2019): 179–94.

Bose, Samaresh. "The Tantrik Quest." *Sunday*, January 25, 1981. http://www.shrikaliashram.org/tantric-quest.

Bowman, Marion, and Ülo Valk, eds. *Vernacular Religion and Everyday Life: Expressions of Belief*. New York: Routledge, 2014.

Bronson, Miles. *A Dictionary in Assamese and English*. Sibsagar: American Baptist Mission, 1867.

Brooks, Douglas R. *The Secret of the Three Cities: An Introduction to Hindu Śākta Tantra.* Chicago: University of Chicago Press, 1990.

Brown, Karen McCarthy. *Mama Lola: A Vodou Priestess in Brooklyn.* Berkeley: University of California Press, 2011.

Brunner-Lachaux, Hélène, Gerhard Oberhammer, and André Padoux, eds. *Tāntrikābhidhānakośa: Dictionnaire des termes techniques de la littérature hindoue tantrique.* 3 vols. Wien: Verlag der Österreichischen Akademie der Wissenschaften, 2000–2013.

Buchanan, Ian, George Varghese K., and Manoj N. Y., eds. *Deleuze, Guattari, and India: Exploring a Postcolonial Multiplicity.* New York: Routledge, 2022.

Bühnemann, Gudrun. "The Six Rites of Magic." In *Tantra in Practice*, edited by David Gordon White, 447–62. Princeton, NJ: Princeton University Press, 2000.

Burley, Mikel. "Dance of the Deodhas: Divine Possession, Blood Sacrifice and the Grotesque Body in Assamese Worship." *Religions of South Asia* 12, no. 2 (2019): 207–33.

Butler, Judith. *Bodies That Matter: On the Discursive Limits of Sex.* New York: Routledge, 2011.

———. *Gender Trouble: Feminism and the Subversion of Identity.* New York: Routledge, 1990.

———. *Subjects of Desire: Hegelian Reflections in Twentieth Century France.* New York: Columbia University Press, 1987.

Chakraborty, Joya. "Witch Hunting in Assam: Strategising Alternative Media for Women Empowerment and Overcoming Superstition." *Journal of North East India Studies* 3, no. 2 (2013): 15–24.

Chatterjee, Partha. *The Nation and Its Fragments.* Princeton, NJ: Princeton University Press, 1993.

Courtright, Paul B. "The Iconographies of Sati." In *Sati: The Blessing and the Curse: The Burning of Wives in India,* edited by John Stratton Hawley, 27–48. New York: Oxford University Press, 1994.

Daimari, Anjali. "Witch-Hunting and Resistance to the Formation of Women's Community." In *Communities of Women in Assam: Being, Doing and Thinking Together,* edited by Nandana Dutta, 41–66. London: Routledge, 2015.

Daimari, Simashree. "Beliefs in Witchcraft among the Tribes of Goalpara District of Assam." PhD diss., Gauhati University, 2007.

Dasgupta, Shamik. *Taranath Tantrik: City of Sorrows.* Kolkata: Speech Bubble, 2015.

Davidson, Ronald M. *Indian Esoteric Buddhism: A Social History of the Tantric Movement.* New York: Columbia University Press, 2002.

De, Rohit. *A People's Constitution: The Everyday Life of Law in the Indian Republic.* Princeton, NJ: Princeton University Press, 2018.

Dehejia, Vidya. *Yoginī Cult and Temples: A Tantric Tradition.* Delhi: National Museum, 1986.

Deka, Pranav. *Nīlācala Kāmākhyā: Her History and Tantra.* Guwahati: Lawyer's Book Stall, 2004.

Deleuze, Gilles. "Désir et plaisir." *Magazine littéraire* 325 (October 1994): 59–65.

Deleuze, Gilles, and Félix Guattari, *Anti-Oedipus: Capitalism and Schizophrenia.* Minneapolis: University of Minnesota Press, 1983.

———. *A Thousand Plateaus: Capitalism and Schizophrenia.* Minneapolis: University of Minnesota Press, 1987.

Devi, Kulasundari. "Dancing with Devotion towards Liberation: Intersections and Theological Exploration of Society, Orthodoxy and the Shakta Tantric Ideal." In

Souvenir Viswa Shanti Devi Yajña, edited by Sri Jadu Nath Sarma, Rajib Sarma, and Sri Naba Kanta Sarma, 92–99. Guwahati: Viswa Shanti Devi Yajña Committee, 2014.

Dimock, Edward C., and A. K. Ramanujan. "The Goddess of Snakes in Medieval Bengali Literature, Part II." *History of Religions* 3, no. 2 (1964): 300–22.

Directorate of Tourism. *Ambubachi Mela*. Guwahati: Directorate of Tourism, 2017.

Dobia, Brenda. "Approaching the Hindu Goddess of Desire." *Feminist Theology* 16, no. 1 (2007): 61–78.

———. "Śakti Yātrā—Locating Power, Questioning Desire: A Women's Pilgrimage to the Temple of Kāmākhyā." PhD diss., University of Western Sydney, 2008. https://researchdirect.westernsydney.edu.au/islandora/object/uws:29498.

Dold, Patricia. "The Mahavidyas at Kamarupa: Dynamics of Transformation in Hinduism." *Religious Studies and Theology* 23, no. 1 (2004): 89–122.

———. "Pilgrimage to Kamakhya through Text and Lived Religion: Some Forms of the Goddess at an Assamese Temple Site." In *Studying Hinduism in Practice*, edited by Hillary P. Rodrigues, 46–61. New York: Routledge, 2011.

———. "Re-Imagining Religious History through Women's Song Performance at the Kamakhya Temple Site." In *Reimagining South Asian Religions: Essays in Honor of Professors Harold G. Coward and Ronald W. Neufeldt*, edited by Michael Hawley and Pashaura Singh, 133–54. Leiden: Brill, 2011.

Donaldson, Thomas E. *Kamadeva's Pleasure Garden: Orissa*. New Delhi: B. R. Publishing, 1987.

Doniger, Wendy. "God's Body, or the Lingam Made Flesh: Conflicts over the Representation of the Sexual Body of the Hindu God Shiva." *Social Research* 78, no. 2 (2011): 485–508.

———. *The Hindus: An Alternative History*. New York: Penguin, 2009.

Doniger, Wendy, and Sudhir Kakar, trans. *Vatsyayana, Kamasutra: A New Translation*. New York: Oxford University Press, 2009.

Dowdy, Sean. "*Goroka*: Cosmography and the Shared Account in Assam." PhD diss., University of Chicago, 2017. https://knowledge.uchicago.edu/record/1565?ln=en.

———. "Reflections on a Shared Name: Taboo and Destiny in Mayong (Assam)." *SAMAJ: South Asia Multidisciplinary Academic Journal* 12 (2015). https://journals.openedition.org/samaj/4027.

Dupuche, John R. *Abhinavagupta: The Kula Ritual, as Elaborated in Chapter 29 of the Tantrāloka*. Delhi: Motilal Banarsidass, 2003.

Dyczkowski, Mark S. G. *The Canon of the Śaivāgama and the Kubjikā Tantras of the Western Kaula Tradition*. Albany, NY: SUNY Press, 1989.

———. *A Journey into the World of the Tantras*. Varanasi: Indica Books, 2004.

Eliot, Charles. *Hinduism and Buddhism: An Historical Sketch*. London: Routledge and Kegan Paul, 1921.

Elmore, Mark. *Becoming Religious in a Secular Age*. Berkeley: University of California Press, 2016.

Endle, Sidney. *The Kacharis*. Delhi: Cosmo Publications, 1975.

Erzen, Tanya. *Straight to Jesus: Sexual and Christian Conversions in the Ex-Gay Movement*. Berkeley: University of California Press, 2006.

Flood, Gavin. *An Introduction to Hinduism*. New York: Cambridge University Press, 1996.

———. *The Tantric Body: The Secret Tradition of Hindu Religion*. London: I. B. Tauris, 2005.

Foucault, Michel. *The History of Sexuality, Volume I: An Introduction*. New York: Vintage, 1978.
Fremantle, Francesca, trans. *A Critical Study of the Guhyasamāja Tantra*. London: University of London, 1971.
Gait, Edward Albert. *A History of Assam*. Calcutta: Thacker, Spink, and Co., 1963.
———. "Human Sacrifice in Ancient Assam." *Journal of the Royal Asiatic Society of Bengal* 67 (1898): 56–65.
Ghassem-Fachandi, Parvis. *Pogrom in Gujarat: Hindu Nationalism and Anti-Muslim Violence in India*. Princeton, NJ: Princeton University Press, 2012.
Glucklich, Ariel. *The End of Magic*. New York: Oxford University Press, 1997.
Gnoli, Raniero, trans. *Luce delle sacre scritture (Tantrāloka) di Abhinavagupta*. Milano: Adelphi, 1999.
Goet, Prema. "Aghora Tantra in Kāmākhyā." Paper presented at the Oxford Center for Hindu Studies, Oxford, September 20, 2020.
———. *The Path of Śakti*. Oxford: Oxford Center for Hindu Studies, 2019.
Gohain, Bikash Chandra. *Human Sacrifice and Head-Hunting in Northeastern India*. Gauhati: Lawyer's Book Stall, 1977.
Goodall, Dominic, and Harunaga Isaacson. "Tantric Hinduism." In *Continuum Companion to Hindu Studies*, edited by Jessica Frazier. Leiden: Brill, 2011.
Goodchild, Philip. *Deleuze and Guattari: An Introduction to the Politics of Desire*. London: Sage, 1996.
Goswami, Indira. *The Man from Chinnamasta*. Delhi: Katha, 2006.
Goswami, Kali Prasad. *Kamakhya Temple: Past and Present*. New Delhi: A. P. H. Publishing Corporation, 1998.
Goswami, Madhurima. "Folk Dances of Assam: A Short Appraisal." *Indian Folklife* 31 (2008): 21–22.
Goswami, M. C. "An Annual Shamanistic Dance." *Journal of the University of Gauhati* 11, no. 2 (1960): 37–58.
Goto-Jones, Chris. *Conjuring Asia: Magic, Orientalism and the Making of the Modern World*. Cambridge: Cambridge University Press, 2016.
Goudriaan, Teun. *Māyā Divine and Human: A Study in Magic and Its Religious Foundations in Sanskrit Texts*. New Delhi: Motilal Banarsidass, 1978.
Grünwedel, Albert. *Der Weg nach Sambhala*. München: J. Roth, 1915.
Gupta, Sanjukta. *The Cosmic Play of Power: Goddess, Tantra, and Women*. Delhi: Motilal Banarsidass, 2013.
Gupta, Sanjukta, Teun Goudriaan, and Dirk Jan Hoens. *Hindu Tantrism*. Leiden: Brill, 1979.
Halbfass, Wilhelm. *India and Europe: An Essay in Understanding*. Albany, NY: SUNY Press, 1988.
Hansen, Thomas Blom. *The Saffron Wave: Democracy and Hindu Nationalism in Modern India*. Princeton, NJ: Princeton University Press, 1999.
Harper, Katherine Anne, and Robert L. Brown, eds. *The Roots of Tantra*. Albany, NY: SUNY Press, 2002.
Harvey, David. *A Brief History of Neoliberalism*. New York: Oxford University Press, 2007.
Hatley, Shaman. *The Brahmayāmalatantra or Picumata, Volume 1: Revelation, Ritual, and Material Culture in an Early Śaiva Tantra*. Pondicherry: Institut Français de Pondicherry, 2018.

———. "Tantra, Overview." In *Hinduism and Tribal Religions*, edited by Jeffery D. Long, Rita D. Sherma, Pankaj Jain, and Madhu Kanna. New York: Springer, 2022.

———. "Tantric Śaivism in Early Medieval India: Recent Research and Future Directions." *Religion Compass* 4, no. 10 (2010): 615–28.

Heesterman, J. C. *The Broken World of Sacrifice: An Essay in Ancient Indian Ritual*. Chicago: University of Chicago Press, 1993.

———. *The Inner Conflict of Tradition: Essays in Indian Ritual, Kingship, and Society*. Chicago: University of Chicago Press, 1985.

Holland, Eugene. *Deleuze and Guattari's Anti-Oedipus: Introduction to Schizoanalysis*. New York: Routledge, 1999.

Inden, Ronald. *Imagining India*. London: Blackwell, 1990.

Jacobsen, Knut A. *Pilgrimage in the Hindu Tradition: Salvific Space*. London: Routledge, 2012.

Jaffrelot, Christophe. *Hindu Nationalism, a Reader*. Princeton, NJ: Princeton University Press, 2007.

Jain, Andrea. *Peace, Love, Yoga: The Politics of Global Spirituality*. New York: Oxford University Press, 2020.

———. *Selling Yoga: From Counterculture to Pop Culture*. New York: Oxford University Press, 2014.

Johansen Hurwitt, E. Sundari. "The Inconvenience of History: The Politics of Myth and the Construction of Public Tantric Identity." Paper presented at the annual meeting of the American Academy of Religion, San Antonio, TX, November 21, 2021.

———. "The Voracious Virgin: The Concept and Worship of Kumārī in Kaula Tantrism." PhD diss., California Institute of Integral Studies, 2019.

Kakati, Banikanta, ed. *Aspects of Early Assamese Literature*. Guwahati: Gauhati University Press, 1959.

———. *The Mother Goddess Kamakhya*. Guwahati: Publication Board, Assam, 1989.

Kalita, Dilip Kumar. "A Study of the Magical Beliefs and Practices in Assam with Special Reference to Magical Lore of Mayong." PhD diss., Gauhati University, 1992.

Kent, Eliza. *Sacred Groves and Local Gods: Religion and Environmentalism in South India*. New York: Oxford University Press, 2013.

Khanna, Madhu. "The Goddess-Woman Equation in the Tantras." In *Gendering the Spirit: Women, Religion and the Post-Colonial Response*, edited by Durre S. Ahmed, 35–69. New York: Zed Books, 2002.

King, Richard. *Orientalism and Religion: Postcolonial Theory, India, and the Mystic East*. New York: Routledge, 1999.

Kristeva, Julia. *Powers of Horror: An Essay on Abjection*. New York: Columbia University Press, 1982.

Layne, Gwendolyn, trans. *Kādambarī: A Classic Sanskrit Tale of Magical Transformation*. New York: Garland, 1991.

Lidke, Jeffrey S. *The Goddess within and beyond the Three Cities: Śākta Tantra and the Paradox of Power in Nepāla Maṇḍala*. New Delhi: D. K. Printworld, 2017.

Lincoln, Bruce. *Death, War, and Sacrifice: Studies in Ideology and Practice*. Chicago: University of Chicago Press, 1991.

———. *Discourse and the Construction of Society: Comparative Studies in Myth, Ritual, and Classification*. New York: Oxford University Press, 2014.

———. "Theses on Method." *Method and Theory in the Study of Religion* 8, no. 3 (1996): 225–27.

Lokeswarananda, Swami, ed. *Studies on the Tantra.* Calcutta: Ramakrishna Mission Institute of Culture, 1989.

Lorenzen, David. *The Kāpālikas and Kālamukhas: Two Lost Śaivite Sects.* Delhi: Motilal Banarsidass, 1991.

Magliocco, Sabina. *The Two Madonnas: The Politics of Festival in a Sardinian Community.* Long Grove, IL: Waveland Press, 2005.

Mahanta, Khagen Chandra. "Shamanistic Dance and Treatment of Disease in Assam." In *Contemporary Tribal Studies,* edited by George Pfeffer and Deepak Kumar Behera, 309–19. New Delhi: Concept Publishing Company, 1997.

Mahmood, Saba. "Feminist Theory, Embodiment, and the Docile Agent: Some Reflections on the Egyptian Islamic Revival." *Cultural Anthropology* 16, no. 2 (2001): 202–36.

———. *The Politics of Piety: The Islamic Revival and the Feminist Subject.* Princeton, NJ: Princeton University Press, 2011.

Maity, Pradyot Kumar. *Historical Studies in the Cult of the Goddess Manasā: A Socio-Cultural Study.* Calcutta: Punthi Pustak, 1966.

Majo Garigliano, Irene. "The Brahmans of the Kāmākhyā Temple Complex: Customary Rights, Relations with Pilgrims, and Administrative Power." PhD diss., Istituto Italiano di Studi Orientali, 2015. https://iris.uniroma1.it/handle/11573/917777.

Malamoud, Charles. *Cooking the World: Ritual and Thought in Ancient India.* Delhi: Oxford University Press, 1996.

McClymond, Kathryn. *Beyond Sacred Violence: A Comparative Study of Sacrifice.* Baltimore, MD: Johns Hopkins University Press, 2008.

McDaniel, June. *Offering Flowers, Feeding Skulls: Popular Goddess Worship in West Bengal.* New York: Oxford University Press, 2004.

Mehra, Madhu, and Anuja Agrawal. "'Witch-Hunting in India': Do We Need Special Laws?" *Economic and Political Weekly,* March 26, 2016: 51–57.

Mishra, Nihar Ranjan. *Kamakhya: A Socio-Cultural Study.* New Delhi: D. K. Printworld, 2004.

Moodie, Deonnie. "Of Blood, Power, and Public Interest: Concealment of Sacrificial Rites under Indian Law." *Journal of Law and Religion* 34, no. 2 (2019): 165–82.

Muñoz, Adrián. "Matsyendra's 'Golden Legend': Yogi Tales and Nāth Ideology." In *Yogi Heroes and Poets: Histories and Legends of the Nāths,* edited by David Lorenzen, 109–27. Albany, NY: SUNY Press, 2012.

Nanda, G. C. "Mayong: The Heritage of Black Magic and Traditional Treatment." *International Journal of Research in Ayurveda and Pharmacy* 5, no. 2 (2014): 235–37.

Nath, Bhrigu, and Prasanta Bhattacharya. "Development of Eco-Tourism and Panorama of Rural Tourism in Pabitora-Mayong Area, Assam, India." *International Journal of Interdisciplinary Research in Science Society and Culture* 2, no. 1 (2016): 185–90.

Nath, Utpal. *Mayong, the Land of Black Magic and Pobitora Wild Life Sanctuary.* Mayong, India: Mayong Village Museum and Research Centre, 2008.

———. *Tourism in Mayong: Problems and Prospects.* Rajamayong, India: Mayong Anchalik College, 2019.

Neog, M. *Early History of the Vaiṣṇava Faith and Movement in Assam.* Delhi: Motilal Banarsidass, 1980.

O'Flaherty, Wendy Doniger. *The Origins of Evil in Hindu Mythology.* Berkeley, CA: University of California Press, 1976.

Orsi, Robert. *Between Heaven and Earth: The Religious Worlds People Make and the Scholars Who Study Them.* Princeton, NJ: Princeton University Press, 2006.

———. *The Madonna of 115th Street: Faith and Community in Italian Harlem, 1880–1950*. New Haven, CT: Yale University Press, 2010.
Padoux, André. *The Heart of the Yoginī: A Sanskrit Tantric Treatise*. New York: Oxford University Press, 2013.
———. *The Hindu Tantric World: An Overview*. Chicago: University of Chicago Press, 2017.
———. "Tantrism, an Overview." In *Encyclopedia of Religion*, vol. 14, edited by Mircea Eliade, 272–74. New York: MacMillan, 1986.
———. "Transe, possession ou absorption mystique? *L'āveśa* selon quelques textes tantriques cachemiriens." In *La possession en Asie du Sud: Parole, corps, territoire*, edited by J. Assayag and G. Tarabout, 133–47. Paris: École des Hautes Études en Sciences Sociales, 1999.
———. *Vāc: The Concept of the Word in Selected Hindu Tantras*. Albany, NY: SUNY Press, 1990.
———. "What Do We Mean by Tantrism?" In *The Roots of Tantra*, edited by Katherine Anne Harper and Robert L. Brown, 17–24. Albany, NY: SUNY Press, 2002.
Partners for Law Development. *Witch Hunting in Assam: Individual, Structural, and Legal Dimensions*. Guwahati: North East Network, 2015.
Pinney, Christopher. *Photos of the Gods: The Printed Image and Political Struggle in India*. London: Reaktion Books, 2004.
Primiano, Leonard. "Afterword." In *Vernacular Religion in Everyday Life*, edited by Marion Bowman and Ülo Valk, 382–94. New York: Routledge, 2014.
———. "Vernacular Religion and the Search for Method in Religious Folklore." *Journal of Western Folklore* 54, no. 1 (1995): 37–56.
———. *Vernacular Religion: Collected Essays of Leonard Norman Primiano*, edited by Deborah Dash Moore. New York: New York University Press, 2022.
Rajbangshi, Hrishita. *The After Effects of Witch-Hunting: Trauma, Struggle, and Revolution*. New Delhi: Zubaan, 2018.
Rajkhowa, Benudhar. *Assamese Popular Superstitions and Assamese Demonology*. Guwahati: Gauhati University Press, 1972.
Ramos, Imma. *Pilgrimage and Politics in Colonial Bengal: The Myth of the Goddess Sati*. London: Routledge, 2017.
———. *Tantra: Enlightenment to Revolution*. London: Thames and Hudson, 2020.
Rao, Mani. *Living Mantra: Mantra, Deity, and Visionary Experience Today*. New York: Palgrave MacMillan, 2018.
Rosati, Paulo E. "The Cross-Cultural Kingship in Early Medieval Kāmarūpa: Blood, Desire and Magic." *Religions* 8, no. 10 (2017). https://doi.org/10.3390/rel8100212.
———. "The Yoni Cult at Kāmākhyā: Its Cross-Cultural Roots." *Religions of South Asia* 10, no. 3 (2016): 278–99.
Saikia, Kaustuv. "Demystifying Black Magic: Mayong Village Museum and Research Centre." *Critical Collective*, 2020. https://criticalcollective.in/Museums.aspx?tid=28.
Saikia, Yasmin. *Fragmented Memories: Struggling to Be Tai-Ahom in India*. Durham, NC: Duke University Press, 2004.
Samuel, Geoffrey. *The Origins of Yoga and Tantra: Indic Religions to the Thirteenth Century*. Cambridge: Cambridge University Press, 2008.
Sanderson, Alexis. "Purity and Power among the Brahmins of Kashmir." In *The Cate-*

gory of the Person: Anthropology, Philosophy, History, edited by Michael Carrithers, Steven Collins, and Steven Lukes, 190–216. Cambridge: Cambridge University Press, 1985.

———. "Śaiva Texts." In *Brill's Encyclopedia of Hinduism*, vol. 6, edited by Knut A. Jacobsen, 10–42. Leiden: Brill, 2015.

———. "Śaivism and the Tantric Traditions." In *The World's Religions*, edited by Stewart Sutherland, Leslie Houlden, Peter Clarke, and Friedhelm Hardy, 660–704. New York: Routledge, 1988.

Saran, Prem. *Tantra: Hedonism in Indian Culture*. D. K. Printworld, 1998.

———. *Yoga, Bhoga and Ardhanariswara: Individuality, Wellbeing, and Gender in Tantra*. New York: Routledge, 2008.

Sarbadhikary, Sukanya. *The Place of Devotion: Siting and Experiencing Divinity in Bengal Vaishnavism*. Berkeley: University of California Press, 2015.

Sarma, Chandra Kanta. *An Early History of Kamarup Kamakhya*. Gauhati: Kalita Art Press, 1998.

Sarma, Rajib. "Kamakhya Temples' Complex: A Socio-Religious Perspective." Unpublished PDF on file with author, 2017.

Sharma, Jayeeta. *Empire's Garden: Assam and the Making of India*. Durham, NC: Duke University Press, 2011.

Sharma, Mukunda Madhava. *Inscriptions of Ancient Assam*. Guwahati: Gauhati University Press, 1978.

Sharma, Navamallika, and Madhushree Das. "Priests and Practices: Understanding the Socio-Religious Scenario of Kamakhya Temple." *Clarion: International Multidisciplinary Journal* 4, no. 1 (2015): 120–26.

Shin, Jae-Eun. *Change, Continuity, and Complexity: The Mahāvidyās in East Indian Śākta Traditions*. New Delhi: Manohar, 2018.

Silburn, Lilian. *Kuṇḍalinī: The Energy of the Depths*. Albany, NY: SUNY Press, 1988.

Sircar, D. C. *The Śākta Pīṭhas*. Delhi: Motilal Banarsidass, 1973.

Smith, Brian K. *Classifying the Universe: The Ancient Indian Varna System and the Origins of Caste*. New York: Oxford University Press, 1994.

Smith, Donald Eugene. *India as a Secular State*. Princeton, NJ: Princeton University Press, 1963.

Smith, Frederick M. *The Self Possessed: Deity and Spirit Possession in South Asia*. New York: Columbia University Press, 2006.

Smith, Jonathan Z. *Imagining Religion: From Babylon to Jonestown*. Chicago: University of Chicago Press, 1988.

Stark, Hannah. *Feminist Theory after Deleuze*. New York: Bloomsbury Academic, 2016.

Strube, Julian. *Global Tantra: Religion, Science and Nationalism in Colonial Modernity*. New York: Oxford University Press, 2022.

Tamta, Priyanka, and Sukanya Sharma. "Understanding the Pattern and Distribution of Sculptural and Architectural Remains in the Archeological Site of Kamakhya." *Archeological Research in Asia* 22, special issue no. 3 (June 2020). https://doi.org/10.1016/j.ara.2020.100193.

Tsing, Anna. *Friction: An Ethnography of Global Connection*. Princeton, NJ: Princeton University Press, 2005.

———. *The Mushroom at the End of the World: On the Possibility of Life in Capitalist Ruins*. Princeton, NJ: Princeton University Press, 2017.

Ullrey, Aaron Michael. "Grim Grimoires: Pragmatic Ritual in Magic Tantras." PhD diss., University of California, Santa Barbara, 2016. https://alexandria.ucsb.edu/lib/ark:/48907/f3t72hmp.

Urban, Hugh B. "Assam—Hinduism." *Oxford Bibliographies Online*, last modified January 12, 2022. https://www.oxfordbibliographies.com/display/document/obo-9780195399318/obo-9780195399318-0245.xml.

———. "The Conservative Character of Tantra: Secrecy, Sacrifice, and This-Worldly Power in Bengali Śākta Tantra." *International Journal of Tantric Studies* 6, no. 2 (2002). http://asiatica.org/ijts/vol6_no1/conservative-character-tantra-secrecy-sacrifice-and-worldly-power-bengali-kta-tantra/.

———. "The Cradle of Tantra: Modern Transformations of a Tantric Center in Northeast India, from Nationalist Symbol to Tourist Destination." *South Asia* 49, no. 2 (2019): 256–77.

———. "Dancing for the Snake: Possession, Gender, and Identity in the Worship of Manasā in Assam." *Journal of Hindu Studies* 11, no. 3 (2018): 304–27.

———. "Dark Webs: Tantra, Black Magic, and Cyberspace." *International Journal of Hindu Studies* 26 (2022): 237–52.

———. "Death, Nationalism, and Sacrifice: Ritual, Violence, Politics, and Tourism in Northeast India." In *Irreverence and the Sacred: Critical Studies in the History of Religions*, edited by Hugh B. Urban and Greg Johnson, 156–84. New York: Oxford University Press, 2018.

———. "Desire, Blood and Power: Georges Bataille and the Study of Hindu Tantra in Northeast India." In *Negative Ecstasies: Georges Bataille and the Study of Religion*, edited by Kent Brintnall and Jeremy Biles, 68–80. New York: Fordham University Press, 2015.

———. *The Economics of Ecstasy: Tantra, Secrecy, and Power in Colonial Bengal.* New York: Oxford University Press, 2001.

———. "Esotericism Socialized: Esoteric Communities." In *Secret Religion: Gnosticism, Esotericism, and Mysticism*, edited by April DeConick, 199–213. New York: MacMillan, 2016.

———. "Hinduism in Assam and the Northeast States." In *Brill's Encyclopedia of Hinduism*, vol. 1, edited by Knut Jacobson, 11–21. Leiden: Brill, 2009.

———. "Horrifying and Sinister *Tāntriks*." In *Bollywood Horrors: Religion, Violence and Cinematic Fears in India*, edited by Ellen Goldberg, Aditi Sen, and Brian Collins, 78–93. London: Bloomsbury Academic, 2020.

———. "The Left-Hand Path: From Hindu Tantra to Modern Satanism." In *Occult South Asia*, edited by Karl Baier and Mriganka Mukhopadhyay. Leiden: Brill, forthcoming.

———. "Matrix of Power: Blood, Kingship and Sacrifice in the Worship of Mother Goddess Kamakhya." *South Asia* 31, no. 3 (2008): 500–34.

———. "Modernity and Neo-Tantra." *Oxford Handbook of Tantric Studies*, edited by Glen A. Hayes and Richard Payne. New York: Oxford University Press, 2022. https://doi.org/10.1093/oxfordhb/9780197549889.013.12.

———. "'My Life in a Love Cult': Tantra, Orientalism and Sex Magic in Early Twentieth Century Fiction." In *Fictional Practice: Magic, Narration, and the Power of Imagination*, edited by Bernd-Christian Otto and Dirk Johannsen, 203–22. Leiden: Brill, 2021.

———. "The Path of Power: Impurity, Kingship and Sacrifice in Assamese Tantra." *Journal of the American Academy of Religion* 69, no. 4 (2001): 597–637.

———. *The Power of Tantra: Religion, Sexuality, and the Politics of South Asian Studies.* London: I. B. Tauris and Palgrave MacMillan, 2010.

———. "The Power of the Impure: Transgression, Violence and Secrecy in Bengali Tantra and Modern Western Magic." *Numen* 50 (2003): 269–308.

———. "Purity." In *The Handbook for the Study of Religion*, edited by Steven Engler, 609–22. New York: Oxford University Press, 2016.

———. "Śaṅkaradeva and Mādhavadeva." In *Brill's Encyclopedia of Hinduism*, vol. 4, edited by Knut Jacobson, 397–404. Leiden: Brill, 2012.

———. *Secrecy: Silence, Power, and Religion.* Chicago: University of Chicago Press, 2021.

———. "Tantra (in South Asia)." In *Oxford Research Encyclopedia of Asian History*, edited by David Ludden. New York: Oxford University Press, forthcoming.

———. *Tantra: Sex, Secrecy, Politics and Power in the Study of Religion.* Berkeley: University of California Press, 2003.

———. "The Torment of Secrecy: Ethical and Epistemological Problems in the Study of Esoteric Traditions." *History of Religions* 37, no. 3 (1998): 209–48.

———. "The Womb of Tantra: Goddesses, Tribals, and Kings in Assam." *Journal of Hindu Studies* 4 (2011): 231–47.

———. *Zorba the Buddha: Sexuality, Spirituality, and Capitalism in the Global Osho Movement.* Berkeley: University of California Press, 2016.

Urban, Hugh B., and Paul Christopher Johnson, eds. *The Routledge Handbook of Religion and Secrecy.* New York: Routledge, 2022.

Valk, Ülo. "Conceiving the Supernatural through Variation in Experience Stories: Assistant Spirits and Were-Tigers in the Belief Narratives of Assam." *Shaman* 23, nos. 1–2 (2015): 141–64.

———. "Shrines, Stones, and Memories: The Entangled Storyworld of a Goddess Temple in Assam." *South Asian History and Culture* 8 (2017): 1–15.

Valk, Ülo, and Neelakshi Goswami. "Generic Resources and Social Boundaries of Magic in Assam: Fieldwork Notes from Assam." *Journal of Folkloristics* 1 (2013): 5–13.

van Buitenen, J. A. B., trans. *The Mahābhārata, Volume 2, Book 2: The Book of the Assembly, Book 3: The Book of the Forest.* Chicago: University of Chicago Press, 1975.

van der Veer, Peter. *Religious Nationalism: Hindus and Muslims in India.* Berkeley: University of California Press, 1994.

van Kooij, K. R. *Worship of the Goddess According to the Kālikā Purāṇa.* Leiden: E. J. Brill, 1979.

Wedemeyer, Christian. *Making Sense of Tantric Buddhism: History, Semiology, and Transgression in the Indian Traditions.* New York: Columbia University Press, 2012.

White, David Gordon. *Kiss of the Yoginī: "Tantric Sex" in Its South Asian Contexts.* Chicago: University of Chicago Press, 2003.

———. *Sinister Yogis.* Chicago: University of Chicago Press, 2009.

———, ed. *Tantra in Practice.* Princeton, NJ: Princeton University Press, 2000.

———. "Tantrism: An Overview." In *Encyclopedia of Religion*, edited by Lindsay Jones, 8984–87. New York: MacMillan, 2005.

Woodroffe, John. *Shakti and Shākta.* New York: Dover, 1978.

———. *The World as Power.* Madras: Ganesh and Co., 1974.

Zimmer, Heinrich. "On the Significance of the Tantric Yoga." In *Spiritual Disciplines: Papers from the Eranos Yearbooks*, edited by Joseph Campbell, 3–58. New York: Pantheon, 1960.

FILMS IN ENGLISH

Cartosio, Alessandro, and Irene Majo Garigliano, dirs. *Ghora: Waiting for the Goddess.* 2013; Rome: Sapienza University of Rome.

Demme, Jonathan, dir. *The Silence of the Lambs.* 1991; Los Angeles, CA: Orion Pictures.

Lester, Richard, dir. *Help!* 1965; London: Walter Shenson Films.

Sharma, Aparna, dir. *Kamakhya: Through Prayerful Eyes.* 2012; Berkeley, CA: Berkeley Media.

Spielberg, Stephen, dir. *Indiana Jones and the Temple of Doom.* 1984; Hollywood, CA: Paramount Pictures.

Stevens, George, dir. *Gunga Din.* 1939; Los Angeles, CA: RKO Productions.

Wares, Tracy, dir. *Shakti: The Performance of Gender Roles at Kamakhya Assam.* 2001; Berkeley, CA: Department of Anthropology, University of California, Berkeley.

Index

abhicāra (black magic or sorcery), 26, 63. *See also* magic
Abhinavagupta, 33, 203n58, 209n24, 212n61
abjection, 27, 163, 180–82
Aghorīs, 3, 8, 22, 30–31, 39, 51–56, 138, 143, 156, 164, 173–74, 178, 199n24, 215nn107–8
ahiṃsā (nonviolence), 91–92, 106–7, 226nn19–20
Ahoms, 36, 97, 134, 145, 235n34
alchemy, 30, 43, 164, 191, 208n8
alcohol, 3, 30–31, 38, 41–43, 45–46, 48, 51, 55–56, 138, 208n16, 213n64, 213n67. See also *madya* (alcohol); wine
Ambuvācī Melā, 1–5, 8, 27, 52, 77, 126, 135–59, 185, 192, 197n5, 212n57, 228n56, 238n3, 239n16, 240n28, 251n24
Ammoru (film), 27, 163, 173–74, 181–82
Ardhanārīśvara, 15–16, 44
Assam, 1–2, 6, 12, 16–18, 29, 32–33, 36, 59–61, 64, 68, 71–72, 75, 87, 96, 104, 107, 110–11, 117, 119–20, 134–59, 183, 185–86, 210n32, 217n7, 225n16, 233n2, 242n57; as heartland of Tantra, 16–18, 29, 36, 135–36, 158; as land of magic, 59–61, 67–68, 72, 85, 217n7
Atharva Veda, 79
Avalon, Arthur. *See* Woodroffe, John (pseud. Arthur Avalon)
āveśa (possession), 27, 116, 123. *See also* possession
Ayodhya, 91–92
Bagalā, 124, 152
bali-dān (animal sacrifice), 26, 87, 90, 99, 106, 108–9, 123, 142. *See also* sacrifice
bali-kaṭās (temple functionaries responsible for animal sacrifices), 37, 99–100, 230n72
Bānabhaṭṭa, 12, 164
bardeurīs, 37, 150
Bardeurī Samāj, 150, 158, 243n70
Bataille, Georges, 29, 55
Bāuls, 3, 8, 23, 44, 143
Beatles, 161, 172
bej (folk healer), 12, 23, 26, 59–60, 68–69, 76, 79, 83, 86, 221n65
Bengal (Bangla), 8–9, 12, 36, 44, 48, 50, 90–91, 96, 104, 107, 117, 145–46, 186, 214n88, 216n114
Bhagavad Gītā, 88
Bhairava, 29, 33–34, 164
Bhairavī, 33, 124–25, 135
bhakti, 48, 56, 88
Bharati, Agehananda, 17, 56, 179
Bharatiya Janata Party (BJP), 5, 95, 107–8, 138, 147, 153, 155, 159, 231n94
Bhārat Mātā, 90–91, 147–48. *See also* Mother India
Bhaṭṭācārya, Kṛṣṇarāma, 36, 38
bhoga (cooked offerings; sensual enjoyment), 7, 9
Bhūtnāth, 3, 8, 23, 31, 52–54
Biardeau, Madeleine, 1, 6, 9, 87–89
BJP. *See* Bharatiya Janata Party (BJP)
blood, 26, 44, 87–88, 90, 98–99, 102, 104–6, 111, 122–23, 126, 139–42, 156–57, 164–65, 172, 181, 230n72

Bollywood, 5, 8, 27, 67, 162, 170, 180, 246n12
Brāhmaṇas, 89, 96–97, 102, 134, 140, 226n21
brāhmaṇs, 18, 30, 37, 45, 57, 90, 99, 108–9, 116–17, 119–20, 139, 145, 150, 164, 184, 192, 210n45, 233n4
Bṛhat Tantrasāra, 63, 212n60, 213n68, 216n114
Brown, Karen McCarthy, 24, 84, 134, 234n16
Buddhism, 31, 63, 68, 90, 192, 209n24, 212n57
buffaloes, 97–99, 101–2, 104, 106–7, 138, 142, 225n12, 227n44, 229n66
Butler, Judith, 13, 133–34, 163, 188, 237n84

Caitanya, 48, 104
cakrānuṣṭhāna (practice of the circle), 41, 47–48
cakrapūjā (circle worship), 47
cakras, 32, 42, 44, 178
Cāmuṇḍā, 33, 35, 124
Caṇḍī, 33, 174
capitalism, 5, 28, 157–59, 183–87, 189, 244n93, 249n8, 250n17
Caṭṭopādhyāy, Bankimcandra, 164–65
Chinnamastā, 124, 126
Christianity, 17, 30, 48–49, 56, 104, 154
colonialism, 20–21, 24, 30, 48–49, 56, 93, 104, 128, 146, 154, 162, 187–88, 192, 195
comic books, 25, 162
cows, 93–94, 104, 106–7, 227n38, 227n40, 231n94

ḍāinī (witches), 62, 68, 71–72, 81, 220n46. *See also* witchcraft
ḍākinī (witch), 68
dakṣiṇācāra (right-hand), 29, 51, 119, 207n6. *See also* right-hand path
Deleuze, Gilles, 1, 13, 30, 110, 142, 189–90, 201nn42–43, 202n46, 202n49, 208n8, 240n28, 244n93, 250n14
deodhāis (male temple dancers), 18, 27, 113–34, 184, 232n2, 233n6, 236n48
deodhanīs (female temple dancers), 113, 127–34, 184, 233n2, 233n6, 235n34, 237n68, 238n69

desire, 1, 6, 9, 12–14, 25, 28, 30, 43, 55, 62, 67, 69, 89, 98–99, 113, 132, 139, 142, 145, 148, 162, 182–83, 187–91, 201n37, 201nn43–45, 208n7, 219n40, 225n17, 230n72, 242n32, 244n93, 250n15. See also *kāma*
Devī Bhāgavata Purāṇa, 138, 140, 234n21, 239n16
Dharmapāla, King, 36
Doniger, Wendy, 19, 117, 200n30, 204n70, 226n19, 226n21, 249n9
Durgā, 88, 91, 98, 102, 120, 129, 174, 182, 238n69
Durgābar, 113, 118

"eco-magico-tourism," 77, 85, 158
ecotourism, 77
exorcism, 60, 75, 116, 163, 166, 192, 221n65

feminism, 14, 40–41, 190–91, 212n59, 251nn22–23
festivals, 76–77
film, 25, 27–28
fish, 38, 43, 46, 55, 213n70. See also *matsya* (fish)
five Ms, 41–51, 213n70. See also *pañca-makāra* (five Ms)
"folk" Tantra, 12, 192–93
Foucault, Michel, 13, 56, 185, 188
Freud, Sigmund, 13, 189

Gahrāī (film), 8, 27, 163, 166–68, 170, 180
Gaṇeśa, 97, 124, 166–68, 182
gender, 13–14, 16, 20, 113, 117, 126–27, 189–91, 202n46
Ghose, Aurobindo, 90
globalization, 5, 24, 28, 158–59, 163, 183–84, 186–89, 249n3
Goswami, Indira, 105–6, 161, 165–66
Guhyasamāja Tantra, 9, 63
Gunga Din (film), 161, 172
gurus, 21–22, 36, 38, 40, 163, 168–70, 184, 191, 205n75, 211n53

Hāzarikā, Tilak, 62, 77–80, 85–86
healing, 23, 59, 62–64, 70, 72, 75–76, 80, 85, 116, 125–26, 132, 143, 186
Hevajra Tantra, 16, 197n4

hijṛā (eunuch), 53, 216n110. See also *kinnara* (transgender women)
Hindutva, 28, 108, 110–11, 156, 159, 244n95

impurity, 8, 28, 29–30, 41, 98, 102, 142, 159, 164, 180, 207n6
Indiana Jones and the Temple of Doom (film), 161, 170–72, 180
initiation, 21, 23–24, 38, 47–48, 205n75, 206n88, 210n45, 213n72
Islam, 26, 107–8, 155

jādu (magic), 60, 71, 79. *See also* magic
Jādūgar (film), 161, 163, 167–70, 180, 182

Kādambarī, 12, 164
Kālī, 32, 38, 45, 49–50, 68, 88, 90, 98, 123–26, 131, 161, 165, 167, 171–74
Kālikā Purāṇa, 1, 11, 29, 33–34, 36, 87, 97–98, 102, 105, 139, 172, 239n16
Kālīkula, 37, 38, 210n37
kāma, 1, 6, 9–11, 13–14, 182, 185, 189, 200n30, 200n35, 208n7. *See also* desire
Kāmadeva, 11, 14, 34
Kāmakalā Vilāsa, 10
Kāmākhyā, 1–2, 7, 14, 17, 19, 21, 25–27, 30, 32, 36–37, 39, 52, 56–57, 67, 77, 83, 86–89, 97–100, 104–5, 109–11, 116, 120, 124–26, 131, 135–39, 142–45, 149, 152–54, 165, 174, 183–86, 189, 203n56, 210n45, 238n3, 239n16, 240n28, 242n32, 243n70, 243n75, 251n24
Kāmākhyā Debutter Board, 150–51, 158, 243n70, 243n72
Kāmākhyā Tantra, 11, 21, 205n82, 212n61, 215n101
Kāmākhyā Yātra Paddhati, 146
Kāmaratna Tantra, 61–67, 74, 212n61
Kāmaru, 16, 17, 202n54, 209n24
Kāmarūpa, 1, 16, 22, 29, 32–33, 67, 96, 197n4, 200n35, 202n54, 209n24
Kāma Sūtra, 9
Kāmeśvara, 10, 14, 145
Kāmeśvarī, 10–11, 145, 190, 200n35
Kannauj, 36, 209n32
Kāpālika, 7, 164–65, 176
Kartābhajā, 50
Kashmir Śaivism, 5, 116, 185
Kathānadī (film), 163, 183
Kaula, 7, 29–36, 40, 200n28, 203n58, 207n3, 208n16, 209n24
Kaulajñāna Nirṇaya, 29, 36, 209n22, 225n12
kingship, 145
kinnara (transgender women), 53, 55
Krama, 7
Kristeva, Julia, 27, 163, 180
Kṛṣṇa, 44, 48, 83, 97, 104–5, 124
Kubjikā, 32
Kubjikā Tantra, 141, 239n16
kula (family or clan), 29, 36, 39, 41, 190, 205n76, 207n3, 207n6, 211n54
Kulācāra, 7, 22, 29–36, 40, 55–56, 73, 86, 142, 183, 210n45
Kulārṇava Tantra, 32, 37, 200n28, 205n77, 212n61
kula-yāga (clan sacrifice), 88, 225n12
kuṇḍagolaka (sexual fluids), 31
kuṇḍalinī (divine energy within human body), 14, 32, 41–43, 46, 179, 202n51, 213n70
kuṇḍalinī yoga, 41–42, 46, 178–79

Lajjā Gaurī, 139–40, 154–56, 159
Lalit Ojā, 129–31, 235n23
left-hand path, 25–26, 29–57, 119, 181. See also *vāmācāra* (left-hand); *vāma-mārga* (left-hand path)
Lincoln, Bruce, 88, 110, 188
liṅgam (phallus), 13, 16, 44, 65, 143–44, 154–55, 190

Madana, 11
madya (alcohol), 41–42, 46. *See also* alcohol; wine
magic, 5–6, 8, 12, 17, 25–26, 59–86, 110, 144, 164, 168–69, 188, 192, 205n79, 206n88, 213n72, 217n12, 218n17, 219n37; black, 5, 8, 17, 26, 51, 59, 60–61, 63, 75, 79, 80–81, 85–86, 144, 162, 165, 167, 174, 183, 186. See also *abhicāra* (black magic or sorcery); *jādu* (magic); *māyā* (divine magic or illusion)
Mahābhārata, 16, 72, 96, 109–10, 173, 183, 202n55

Mahāmāyā, 135, 141
Mahānirvāṇa Tantra, 30, 50, 215nn102–3
Mahiṣāsuramardinī, 101–2
Mahmood, Saba, 188, 201n40, 250n12
maithuna (sexual union), 41, 43–51, 53–55, 205n79, 213n70, 213n72, 215nn101–2
māṃsa (meat), 41, 46, 213n70
Manasā, 20, 27, 113–14, 118–21, 123, 125, 129, 131, 133, 184, 233n4, 233nn6–7, 238n69
Manasā-kāvya, 113, 117–18
Manasā Pūjā, 20, 27, 98, 113–34, 184, 192, 233n7
mantra, 7, 12, 60, 65, 73–74, 77, 80–81, 83, 99, 164, 166–67, 171, 173, 206n88, 211n53, 230n76, 248n61
māntrik, 166–67
matsya (fish), 41, 46, 213n70
Matsyendranātha, 16, 29, 32–33, 203n58, 209n24
māyā (divine magic or illusion), 63, 72
Mayong, 12, 17, 26, 59–86, 114, 144, 183, 186, 217n7, 221n63, 221n65, 222n79, 222n84
meat, 29–33, 38, 41, 45, 55–56, 126, 138, 230n72, 232n101. See also *māṃsa* (meat)
menstrual blood, 44, 53, 135, 140–42
menstruation, 1, 17, 21, 27, 44, 50, 52–53, 65, 135, 140–41, 144, 159, 190, 205n82, 215n101
Modi, Narendra, 4–5, 92, 135–38, 147–49, 159
Mother India, 27, 88, 90–92, 111, 147, 156. *See also* Bhārat Mātā
mudrā (parched grain), 41, 212n60, 213n70
mūlādhāra (root *cakra*), 46
Muṇḍamāla Tantra, 172

Nāgas, 3, 143, 154, 156
Naraka, 53, 119, 202n55
Nāth, Lalit Candra, 129–30
Nāth, Phaṇīdhar, 59–62, 77, 80–81, 85–86
Nātha Siddhas, 7, 23, 199n26
nationalism, 4, 26–28, 77, 87–89, 91–92, 94, 110–11, 134–38, 145–48, 156–59, 163, 176, 184, 186, 225n13, 244n95. *See also* Hindutva
neoliberalism, 28, 157, 159, 183–85, 207n96, 244n93, 245n96, 249n3
Neo-Tantra, 5, 56, 198n9
Nepal, 14, 45, 87, 201n37
Nietzsche, Friedrich, 13, 201n45
Nīlācala, 37, 97, 139, 150–51

ojhā (folk healer), 12, 23, 26, 60, 68–71, 74, 76, 80, 83–84, 86, 220n46
Orientalism, 17, 21, 30, 48–49, 75, 86, 104–5, 128, 154, 157, 162, 170, 181, 187–88, 218n16, 222n79; auto-Orientalism, 75, 85, 157, 218n16, 222n79
Orsi, Robert, 18, 204n66

Padoux, André, 6, 9, 21, 63
pañcamakāra (five Ms), 26, 41–51, 212n61, 213n70
Pāñcarātra, 7, 209n32
Pāśupata, 7
Phukkan, Halirām, 146
pilgrimage, 141–50, 157–58
possession, 27, 31, 53, 113, 116, 122, 128, 132–34, 166, 183, 208n16, 234n11, 234n16, 236n48, 237n81, 238n88
power, 8, 11, 13, 30, 33, 36, 39, 41, 57, 59, 67, 73, 75, 79, 81, 86, 113, 126, 137, 139–41, 162, 166, 169, 176, 180, 182, 185–86, 189–90, 201n37, 201n45, 208n17, 216n114, 220n46, 234n11, 242n32. *See also* Śakti
Prāgjyotiṣa, 16, 96, 202n55
Primiano, Leonard, 18–19, 28, 192
purity, 29, 31, 57, 138, 142, 185–86, 207n6, 227n43

Rābhā, Birubālā, 70–71, 86
Rāma, 92
religion, 28, 169, 192–93, 204n66, 232n99, 249n3
Ṛg Veda, 9, 79, 109
right-hand path, 29, 34, 46, 48, 50–51, 55, 119. See also *dakṣiṇācāra* (right-hand)

Roy, Rāmmohun, 49
Rudra Siṅgha, 36, 119, 145

sacrifice, 4, 17, 26–27, 31, 49, 53, 87–111, 123–24, 126, 129, 138, 142, 158–59, 163, 165, 171–72, 224n7, 225nn12–14, 226n20, 228n47, 228n53, 228n56, 229n60, 232n101. See also *bali-dān* (animal sacrifice); *yajña* (animal sacrifice)
sādhanā, 8, 79, 213n67
Sahajiyā, 7, 44, 50
sahasrāra, 42, 46
Śaikīyā, Prabīn, 62, 77, 81–83, 85–86
Śaitān Tāntrik (film), 8, 161–63, 170
Śākta, 7, 12, 27, 40, 48, 68, 104, 110, 119, 132, 133, 140, 145, 158, 190, 201n37, 203n58, 209n24, 211n48
śākta pīṭha (seat of power), 1, 16, 72, 96–97, 111, 120, 137–39, 145–51, 153, 156, 197n4
Śakti, 10–11, 16, 39–40, 42, 46, 77–79, 102, 105, 120, 124–27, 141, 143, 148, 199n19, 211n52, 213n70
Saṅgharṣ (film), 8, 27, 163, 170–72, 181
Śaṅkaradeva, 48–49, 104–5
Śāradātilaka, 63
Sarma, Himanta Biswa, 148, 150, 242n57
Satī, 139, 229n57
ṣaṭ-karman (six acts), 62–64
śava sādhanā (corpse worship), 53–55, 67, 138, 165, 216n114
secrecy, 20–25, 29–31, 45, 56, 60, 73, 83, 99, 154, 182, 204–5n75, 205n77, 206n88, 206n90, 222n69
semen, 21, 44–46, 53
sex, 9, 12–13, 17, 21, 24, 27, 30–31, 33, 40, 43–51, 56–57, 65, 74, 138, 153, 159, 162, 165, 170, 183–84, 187, 189–90, 199n20, 205n79, 213n72. See also *maithuna* (sexual union)
sexual fluids, 3, 14, 21, 30–31, 44, 53, 65, 213n72
siddhas (male adepts), 31
Silence of the Lambs, The (film), 170–72, 180
Śiva, 10, 14, 16, 29, 32–33, 45–46, 64, 96–98, 104, 116, 124, 126–27, 129, 139, 152–54, 164, 199n19, 209n32, 213n70, 238n69
Śiva Siṅgha, 36, 145
Smith, Jonathan Z., 192–93
Sonowal, Sarbananda, 135, 148–49, 159, 242n57
Śrīkula, 37–38, 210n37
Śrīvidyā, 7, 12, 39
Śrī Yantra, 44

Tagore, Rabindranath, 91, 146
Tantra, 1–18, 25–28, 29–31, 48, 55–57, 59–64, 77, 81, 89, 104–5, 110, 119, 123, 132, 135–38, 145, 152–53, 158–59, 161–93, 195, 199n20, 200n27, 210n46, 213n67, 221n63, 247n49, 248n53, 249n3, 252n2; definitions of, 7–12, 77, 185, 193, 195, 199n20, 200n27, 219n39; living, 5–7, 183–93; as "path of desire," 1, 4, 6, 9, 28, 31, 162; sanitized, 47–49, 152–58, 214n88
tantra-mantra, 7, 12, 23, 26, 60–61, 67–68, 71–73, 75, 77–79, 81, 83–85, 110, 144, 183–84, 186, 221n65, 222n84. *See also* magic
Tantrasadbhāva Tantra, 16, 197n4
tantricity, 31, 33, 56–57, 208n15
Tārā, 124, 172, 174
Tārānāth Tāntrik (web series), 163, 174–76
Tāśrī (web series), 28, 163, 176–80
tourism, 4–5, 18, 27–28, 59, 62, 72, 74–77, 81, 95, 135–59, 183–86, 222n84
transgression, 3, 8, 25–27, 29–30, 32, 41, 48, 51–52, 55, 57, 69, 134, 142, 159, 164, 166, 207n6, 248n64
tribal traditions, 19, 26, 33, 68–69, 96, 98, 106, 108, 111, 113, 116–17, 119–20, 128–29, 133, 202n55, 213n64
Trika, 7, 12
Tripura, 95, 107
Tsing, Anna, 24–25, 187–88, 195, 250n10
Turner, Victor, 84

Ugratārā, 33
Upaniṣads, 88, 90, 226n21

Vaiṣṇava, 143
Vajrayāna, 7
vāmācāra (left-hand), 29, 47–49, 51, 105, 119, 181, 207n6, 248n61. *See also* left-hand path
vāma-mārga (left-hand path), 26. *See also* left-hand path
Vasiṣṭha, 33
Vedas, 29, 33, 39, 48, 54, 57, 64, 86, 88–90, 97, 108–9, 123, 181, 205n77, 207n6, 232n101
vernacular religion, 18–20, 28, 192–93
violence, 89
Viṣṇu, 53, 124, 140, 209n32
Vivekānanda, Swāmī, 49, 146, 181, 247n31, 248n61

Weber, Max, 187
wine, 29–30, 32–33, 38, 40, 42, 140. *See also* alcohol; *madya* (alcohol)
witchcraft, 12, 17, 26, 62, 67–71, 79, 85–86, 220n46
women, 14, 17–18, 20–21, 26, 32, 39–41, 47–50, 68–71, 127–34, 142–43, 189–90, 202n49, 205n77, 211n48, 211nn52–54, 212n58, 250n19, 251n27
Woodroffe, John (pseud. Arthur Avalon), 10, 51, 179, 213n70

yajña (animal sacrifice), 26, 88–92, 109, 142
Yama, 33
yoga, 7–8, 41–42, 46, 178–79, 185, 190
yoginī (divine female beings), 14, 17, 29, 31–32
Yoginī Tantra, 41, 43, 46, 97, 212n60, 225n12, 239n16
yoni (womb or sexual organ), 1, 11, 14, 16, 32, 39, 44, 99, 137, 139, 141, 143, 153–56, 180, 190, 205n82, 212n60, 251n27
Yoni Tantra, 39, 53, 172, 225n12
YouTube, 71, 74, 77, 85, 186, 221n60

www.ingramcontent.com/pod-product-compliance
Lightning Source LLC
Chambersburg PA
CBHW022042290426
44109CB00014B/955
9780226831121